D0884546

Mammals of
MADAGASCAR

Mammals of
MADAGASCAR

NICK GARBUTT

YALE UNIVERSITY PRESS
NEW HAVEN AND LONDON

Published 1999 in the United Kingdom by Pica Press (an imprint of Helm Information Ltd)
and in the United States by Yale University Press.

ISBN 1-300-07751-3

Library of Congress Cataloging in Publication Number 98-86267

Printed in Hong Kong.

A catalogue record for this book is available from the British Library.

The paper for this book meets the guidelines for permanence and durability of the Committee on
Production Guidelines for Book Longevity of the Council on Library Resources.

10 9 8 7 6 5 4 3 2 1

CONTENTS

PREFACE

My fascination with Madagascar began as a child. Entries in the books I read were always brief, the word 'unknown' appearing with frustrating regularity. My animal encyclopaedias told tales of bizarre creatures living in the depths of unexplored forests. Yet these scant passages also conveyed a great fragility. Words such as rare, endangered and extinct were sprinkled liberally in the text. It was clear that if I was going to see it for myself, it had to be sooner rather than later.

It was 1991 when the chance finally came. I had been based on the tiny island of Mauritius some 600 km further east into the Indian Ocean, working on a project endeavouring to save the island's critically endangered birds. Absorbing as the bird conservation work was, I could not help thinking of the 'Great Red Island' lying to the west. Long nights were spent plotting various options and eventually I scraped the necessary resources together and jumped on a aeroplane bound for Antananarivo.

Two days after my arrival in Madagascar I sat at the side of a dirt road in Fianarantsoa, a large highland town in the south-east. It was 4.30am and people were just beginning to stir. The *taxi-brousse* (bush taxi) finally arrived and I clambered in. It was heading for Ranomafana, a small village nestling in the eastern rainforest some 60 kilometres away. There in the recently created eponymous national park I hoped to see some of the wildlife that I had read so much about. Pinned in by baskets of fruit and an assortment of livestock, I sat hunched and crumpled in a corner. The *taxi-brousse* limped over hopelessly pot-holed roads and everyone and everything inside bounced around like corks on a rough sea. I loved every minute of it. After five bone-numbing hours we arrived. I fell out onto the track and tried to stand on legs of jelly. But eagerness and impatience are instant remedies and I soon set off into the park with a guide, along steep slippery trails and followed by a cloud of mosquitoes.

Walking into a rainforest in Madagascar is an unforgettable experience. It is like entering a cathedral. The air is filled with sounds that engulf. A myriad of creatures lend voice to the choir – insects chirrup, frogs croak, geckos squeak, birds sing and lemurs chunter and grunt. Yet at other times there is an eerie silence that prompts a sense of unease. It is broken only by the occasional groan from an aged tree or the odd call from an animal, seemingly out of sync with everything else. How can the world's most diverse habitat seem so lifeless? Yet this is one of the qualities that makes rainforests so alluring.

We walked for about half an hour, up towards a campsite at the top of the hill. My guide suggested a short stop to catch breath. Who was I to disagree? We sat and listened. What had seemed lifeless forest, drowned out by my panting and pounding heart, came to life. There was a rustling of branches in the canopy above, an unfamiliar shape sat in the dappled light and peculiar grunts percolated down through the canopy. Binoculars arrived at my eyes in trembling hands and I looked up spellbound. It was a group of Red-bellied Lemurs. Aching limbs and numb feet were at once cured.

There were only three animals in the group: probably a male and female with their dependent off-spring. They did not appear perturbed by our presence and carried on their daily foraging routine, pulling down branches for inspection, then choosing only the most suitable leaves or fruit. The characteristics they shared with other primates were immediately evident: dextrous grasping hands, forward-facing eyes and perfect balance in their tree-top environment. Yet there were equally obvious differences: prominent ears, fox-like features and long snouts betraying the importance of smell in their lives.

As the tropical dusk descended the lemurs began to bed down and we carried on up the hill to pitch camp. There was little twilight and soon it was dark. I peered into the enveloping inky blackness. A twig cracked and something scurried along a branch. My torchbeam criss-crossed the foliage searching for the creature responsible. The movement stopped and startled eyes glowed fiery orange. It was a tiny Brown Mouse Lemur, twitching with nervous energy. Rest is only brief for these pygmies of the primate world and it soon scampered off along one of its aerial highways. Within minutes, rustling leaves on the forest floor betrayed a foraging Fanaloka, one of the island's unusual carnivores. I only managed to catch a glimpse of this shy creature, which if anything increased the thrill. At every turn I found something new and unfamiliar.

Such experiences linger in the memory, and each time I return to Madagascar they have been enhanced. Many lifetimes' work have still to be done before the full extent of the island's natural riches can be fully appreciated. What is clear is that each new discovery will raise an eyebrow and further enhance Madagascar's utterly unique reputation.

Nick Garbutt
Bristol

To my parents, Lynne and Mike, and sister Jody,
for their steadfast support and encouragement.
I love them dearly and owe them so much.

ACKNOWLEDGEMENTS

This volume is a review of the current literature and state of knowledge relating to Madagascar's mammalian fauna. As such, much of the information presented here has been drawn from research papers and articles published in scientific journals or similar technical works. This has been supplemented where appropriate by my personal observations from many hours in the field. I owe a great debt to the many biologists and researchers whose original reference papers and publications appear in this volume's bibliography. To them I extend my grateful thanks: without their skill and dedication our knowledge of the mammals of Madagascar would be but a fraction of its current extent.

I would also like to thank the many people who have helped me more specifically. Without their assistance, this project would have never come to fruition. I began the groundwork for this book when I first visited Madagascar seven years ago and during numerous visits since have relied upon the cooperation of biologists who have welcomed me into their research camps and helped me find the species I sought to observe and photograph.

I thank Joyce Powzyk (Duke University Primate Center), not only for the hospitality at her field site in Mantadia National Park and her sacrifice of valuable research time to help me track down Diademed Sifakas and Indris, but also for later very kindly commenting on the profiles I had written for those species. In doing so she has graciously chosen to set aside a severe error of judgement on my part, when I inadvertently failed to give her appropriate credit in a previous publication – something I now realise had unfortunate repercussions and caused considerable distress. My appreciation of her understanding in this matter cannot be overstated.

In a similar regard I am grateful to: Jörg Ganzhorn, Peter Kappeler, Jutta Schmid, Joanna Fietz, Clare Hawkins and Greg Corbin (Kirindy), Alison Jolly and Helen Crowley (Berenty), Andrea Katz and Charlie Welch (Parc Ivoloina), Don Reid and Germain Rakotobearison (Ampijoroa), Patricia Wright, Benjamin Andriamihaja and Sukie Zeeve (Ranomafana) and Alison Richards (Beza Mahafaly) for their guidance in the field.

I am indebted to Ken Glander and all the staff at Duke University Primate Center for their friendly welcome and assistance during my visit in April/May 1996. Equally, my thanks extend to Stephanie Stovall (and family) and Carey Cornette, who took me under their wing as a virtual stranger, provided a comfortable sofa to sleep on and extended the most wonderful North Carolina hospitality. We soon became good friends and I look forward eagerly to my next visit. Likewise, my thanks are due to Albert Randrianjafy, Gilbert Rakotoarisoa and Gabe Sigerson at Parc Tsimbazaza in Antananarivo for their permission and help in photographing some species in their care.

During my excursions into the field, I have benefited enormously from the local knowledge and help of a great many Malagasy guides – all of whom know the forests as their back gardens and whose ability to find and spot wildlife is, at times, beyond belief. Here my gratitude extends to: Loret Rasobo, Emile Rajeriarison, Jean Emilien Rafidison, Jean Chry Rafidison and Roland Rakotozafy (Ranomafana National Park), Maurice Besoa Ratsisakanana, Patrice Rabcarisoa, Ndriana Kotonirina and Honoré Randrianasolo (Analamazaotra Special Reserve and Mantadia National Park); Olivier Rahanitriniaina (Berenty); Jackie, Romain and Charles (Ampijoroa Forestry Station); Olivier Rabetsimialona (Mitsinjo) and the many other guides who have helped me and whose names I am afraid I do not know. Special thanks too to my good friend Serge Harizo, who has co-led so many tours with me in Madagascar and who constantly assists in solving the multitude of problems that arise when I'm travelling around the island.

The text for this book has undergone numerous revisions. These have largely been prompted by authorities introducing me to important references I had overlooked, magnanimously making available their unpublished data and/or commenting on, correcting and consequently improving the sections relating to their areas of expertise. They are far more qualified than I to write about Madagascar's mammals and have shared freely both their knowledge and time. To one and all (in no particular order) I cannot express sufficient thanks:

Josephine Andrews (Black Lemur Forest Project), Alison Jolly (Princeton University), Elizabeth Balko (State University of New York at Syracuse), Joyce Powzyk and Ken Glander (Duke University Primate Center), Joanna Durbin, Anna Feistner, Don Reid and Richard Lewis (Jersey Wildlife Preservation Trust), Frank Hawkins (BirdLife International, Madagascar), Hilary Simons Morland, Clare Kremen and Matthew Hatchwell (Wildlife Conservation Society), Steve Goodman, Olivier Langrand, Dominique Halleux, Peter Schachenmann and Giselle Ramaroson (WWF, Madagascar), Jutta Schmid, Jörg Ganzhorn and Peter Kappeler (German Primate Centre), Clare Hawkins, Emma Long and Paul Racey (University of Aberdeen), Joanna Fietz and Simone Sommer (University of Tübingen), Elke Zimmermann (Institute of Zoology, Hannover), Eleanor Sterling, Ian Tattersall, Rob de Salle, George Amato and Karl Koopman (American Museum of Natural History), Ian Colquhoun (University of Western Ontario), Christine Egar and Lorelie Mitchell (Royal Ontario Museum, Toronto), Ruth Warren and Laura Harste (University of Liverpool), Paulina Jenkins (The Natural History Museum, London), Lee Ann Nash (Arizona State University), Thomas Mutschler, Pie Müller and Urs Thalmann (Anthropology Institute and Museum, University of Zurich), Bernhard Meier and Helga Schulze (Ruhr University, Bochum), Deborah Curtis (Institute of Zoology, London), Martin Göpfert and Professor L.T. Wasserthal (Institute of Zoology, Erlangen), James Hutcheon (University of Wisconsin), Chris Wozencraft (Lewis-Clark State College, Idaho), Patricia Wright (Institute of the Conservation of Tropical Environments, State University of New York at Stony Brook), Martin Nicoll (WWF, Ethiopia), Peter J. Stevenson (WWF, Tanzania), Rob McCall (Oxford University), Tony Hutson (The Bat Trust), Yves Rumpler (University Louis Pasteur, Strasbourg), Henke Bentje and David Du Puy (Royal Botanical Gardens, Kew), Caroline Harcourt and Roger Safford.

Paulina Jenkins and other members of staff in the Mammal Section of The Natural History Museum (London) have been most supportive and helpful and allowed me access to specimens in the Museum's valuable collection. Similarly, the staff in the General and Zoology Library have patiently endured my endless requests for references and information during the long stints of research.

Despite considerable endeavour in the field, the task of taking photographs of all Madagascar's mammal species proved too great for me alone. I have, therefore, relied on the help and generosity of the following photographers who have kindly supplied some crucial images of important species: Chris Wozencraft, Peter Schachenmann, Bernhard Meier, Yves Rumpler, Peter Stephenson, Roland Seitre, Olivier Langrand, Martin Nicoll, Dominique Halleux, Thomas Mutschler, Don Reid, Colin Taylor, Roger Safford, Frank Hawkins, Pete Morris, David Haring, Gavin and Val Thomson, Professor Lutz T. Wasserthal and the Field Museum of Natural History, Chicago.

My friends and Madagascar stalwarts, Hilary Bradt and Derek Schuurman, have provided useful snippets on so many things Malagasy: their enthusiasm for the country is infectious. Tricia Handley and colleagues at Air Madagascar UK (Aviareps) have always done their best to help with my transportation requests, and Seraphine Tierney at the Malagasy Consulate in London is ever-efficient in issuing my visas, even when I make my typical eleventh-hour requests.

From typing the first word to publication this book has taken four years. During this time I have been utterly indebted to Eileen Nedelev and Sîan Waters for helping provide a roof over my head and somewhere to plug in my computer. I would not have kept my head above water without their generosity. At numerous times in between I have also been similarly indebted to Andy Sparks, who above all else is a terrific life-long friend. He also solves my computing and other technical ills, periodically offers his home as a bolt hole and provides wonderful companionship on the riverbank, when we are both bored with work and in pursuit of wild brown trout with fly rod and line.

A final thought for JLH and friends for making all the right sounds when my midnight oil burned.

Photo Credits

Nick Garbutt (Indri Images/Planet Earth Pictures/BBC Natural History Unit Picture Library)

1a, 1b, 3, 4, 5, 6, 7, 9, 10, 11, 12, 13, 14, 15, 16, 17, 18, 19, 20, 26, 27, 36, 38, 50, 51, 53,55, 62, 63, 64, 67, 68, 71, 74, 75, 76, 77, 78, 82, 83, 84, 85, 86, 87, 92, 93, 94, 95, 96, 99, 101, 102, 103, 104, 105, 106, 107, 108, 112, 113, 114, 115, 117, 118, 119, 120, 121, 122, 123, 124, 125, 126, 127, 128, 129, 130, 131, 132, 133, 134, 135, 136, 137, 140, 141, 142, 143, 144, 145, 146, 148, 149, 150, 151, 152, 153, 154, 155, 156, 157, 158, 159, 161, 162, 163, 164, 165, 166, 167, 168, 169, 170, 172, 173, 174, 175, 176, 177, 178, 179, 181, 182.

Dominique Halleux (BIOS)	60
David Haring	147
Frank Hawkins	160
Olivier Langrand (BIOS)	40, 45, 61, 100
Bernard Meier	90, 91
Pete Morris	35, 37, 111
Thomas Mutschler	109, 110
Martin Nicholl (BIOS)	25, 34, 39, 43, 44, 57, 59
Don Reid	28
Yves Rumpler	138, 139
Roger Safford	8
Peter Schachenmann	79
Roland Seitre	23, 46, 69, 88, 98, 171, 180
Simone Sommer	54
Peter J. Stephenson	41, 47, 48, 49
Colin Taylor	31, 32
Gavin and Val Thomson	72
Lutz T. Wasserthal	29
Chris Wozencraft	80
The Field Museum, Chicago	81 (Neg# 77043)

Illustration Credits

Where possible, my own photographs have been used for inspiration, but I have also used photographs taken by others when necessary. Here I thank Roland Albignac, Quentin Bloxam, Wolfgang Dreier, Bernard Meier and Russel Mittermeier.

Other illustrations have been adapted and re-drawn from the following works: bat heads and faces from Peterson, Eger and Mitchell (1995), Aquatic Tenrec and Lowland Streaked Tenrec from Macdonald (1989) and Tuft-tailed Rat tail studies from Carleton (1994).

INTRODUCTION

Charles Darwin's theories about evolution were triggered by his observations in the Galapagos archipelago. Many of the creatures he found there were basically similar to those he had seen in mainland South America. But there were important differences. The iguanas on the mainland climbed trees and ate fruit and leaves, while in the Galapagos they clambered over shoreline's surf-beaten rocks and grazed on seaweed. On the mainland, he had seen cormorants patrolling rainforest rivers, yet those he saw in the Galapagos had stunted wings and had lost the ability to fly. Instead they flapped their wings underwater like penguins, then hopped out onto the rocks to dry. There were also tortoises that were basically similar to those on the mainland, but much larger; furthermore there was variation between tortoises from the different islands within the archipelago.

His suspicions grew; perhaps species were not fixed and unchanging for ever. Perhaps they could, over many thousands of years, gradually alter to best suit the places they lived and the changing environments they inhabited. It was many years after leaving the Galapagos that Darwin was finally able to clarify his ideas on evolution. His theory of natural selection revolutionised the thinking of the day. With new discoveries and scientific advancement this theory has been refined and built upon, but it remains the key to, and the driving force behind, our understanding of life and the natural world.

Had Darwin's ship, the HMS *Beagle*, reached Madagascar instead of the Galapagos, his thoughts on evolution would probably have been provoked in much the same way. He would have noted the absence of many of the familiar creatures from mainland Africa: no antelope or zebra grazing, no big cats lurking in ambush and no monkeys leaping through the trees. Instead, he would have seen strange and unfamiliar creatures, some showing a basic resemblance to the African forms, but nevertheless very different. There would have been no large animals browsing the vegetation (although in the past creatures like giant lemurs and huge birds performed this function, but by Darwin's time they had already become extinct). Instead of big cats there were other predators like the Fosa – cat-like in appearance but a relative of the civets. And instead of monkeys there were lemurs – variations on the primate theme that lived in ways far more diverse than their mainland relatives.

Although Darwin found in the Galapagos the stimulus for his theories, it is clear Madagascar would have been an equally good source. Well before Darwin's time travellers were returning from Madagascar to their native lands with tales of rich forests inhabited by bizarre creatures. In the mid-seventeenth century Etienne de Flacourt compiled some of the first detailed accounts of the fauna and flora which were to remain the standard for nearly two centuries. Then around a century later, in 1771, a French doctor, Joseph-Philibert Commerson, made his now famous statement in a letter to his former tutor in Paris.

> Of Madagascar I can announce to naturalists that this is truly their promised land. Here Nature seems to have created a special sanctuary whither she seems to have withdrawn to experiment with designs different from any she has created elsewhere. At every step, one meets more remarkable and marvellous forms of life.

Yet despite these tantalising early accounts, in the following two and a half centuries only a handful of explorers and scientists managed to gain an insight into the island's riches, and much of Madagascar's natural history remained shrouded in mystery. Early collecting expeditions by François Pollen, J. C. van Dam, Josef-Peter Audebert, Alfred Crossley and I. Geoffroy Saint-Hilaire sent a stream of intriguing specimens back to the museums of Europe. Then the French explorers Alfred Grandidier and A. Milne-Edwards made the first systematic attempts to bring order to these findings and document the discoveries. Their efforts culminated in the publication of the immaculately illustrated 32-volume *Histoire Physique, Naturelle, et Politique de Madagascar*, between 1875 and 1921. Several other notable collections were made towards the end of the nineteenth century, by J. M. Hildebrandt, W. Abbott and C. I. Forsyth Major amongst others, that further supplemented this knowledge.

However, it was not until the late 1950s that behavioural and ecological data began to be collected – at first concentrating on the island's unique primate fauna. Jean-Jacques Petter's initial studies were soon followed by those of Alison Jolly. This research broke new ground and laid the foundations for the plethora of work that has subsequently been undertaken and is ongoing.

To some extent, similar detailed work relating to the behaviour and ecology of other mammal groups on the island has lagged behind. Although a number of pioneering studies of the carnivores (R. Albignac), rodents (F. Petter, S. M. Goodman, J. M. Ryan, S. Sommer), tenrecs (J. F. Eisenberg, E. Gould, M. E. Nicoll, P. J. Stephenson, S. M. Goodman) and bats (R. L. Peterson, M. C. Göpfert) have taken place, by and large our knowledge of these groups remains somewhat limited. So much so that the distributions of many taxa remain far from clear, and new species and even genera are still being discovered on a fairly regular basis.

Naturally, these discrepancies are reflected in the published literature: there is relatively little information concerning carnivores, rodents, tenrecs and bats, but a wealth of material covering all aspects of lemur evolution, classification, behaviour and ecology.

One major academic work has attempted to synthesise contemporary knowledge of Madagascar's fauna – published by the Natural History Museum in Paris, *Faune de Madagascar* now runs to over 80 volumes. However, the vast majority of these are concerned with invertebrates and only three volumes relate to the mammals – Albignac, R. (1973) Mammifères: Carnivores, Vol. 36; Petter, J.-J., Albignac, R. and Rumpler, Y. (1977) Mammifères: Lémuriens, Vol. 44; and Peterson, R. L., Eger, J. L. and Mitchell, L. (1995) Chiroptères, Vol. 84 – and much of the information presented in these is now well out of date. There have also been several further detailed volumes dealing specifically with the lemurs, most notably Tattersall, I. (1982) *The Primates of Madagascar*; Harcourt, C. and Thornback, J. (1990) *Lemurs of Madagascar and the Comoros*; and Mittermeier, R. A., Tattersall, I., Konstant, W. R., Meyers, D. and Mast, R. B. (1994) *Lemurs of Madagascar*.

Accepting that available information is far from complete, it is hoped that by presenting a concise, well-illustrated synopsis of contemporary knowledge relating to the mammals of Madagascar this book will, at least in part, fill a gap in the literature and prove a useful tool for those wishing to discover more about one of the most fascinating mammalian assemblages on earth. If nothing else, it will highlight how much we still have to learn.

STYLE AND LAYOUT

The aims of this volume are two-fold. Firstly, to provide a thorough and up-to-date review of current knowledge relating to Madagascar's mammals. There has been no previous single detailed treatise dealing with this unusual fauna that has been directed both to the amateur natural historian and biologist alike. In attempting to bridge this gap, information has been drawn from a considerable number and wide variety of disparate sources, the majority of which are generally only accessible to specialists and the scientific community. This information has been enhanced in many instances by the addition of unpublished data generously provided by a large number of eminent field biologists (see Acknowledgements), together with my own personal observations.

Little is known about a substantial number of Madagascar's less glamorous mammal species and there is often only fleeting reference to them in existing texts. Hence, the depth and detail of the individual species profiles vary considerably. Nonetheless, this volume should provide a first step for those wishing to learn about the species concerned, and also a window to access more detailed information (via the extensive Bibliography) for those who would like to delve further and develop a greater breadth of knowledge.

The second aim is to provide a practical synopsis for visitors to the island, not only for the mammals themselves, but also the best places to go and see them. As interest in Madagascar and its wildlife grows, so does the number of people wishing to see it firsthand. To this end, each of the species accounts has been arranged (as far as the available data allow) to provide clear, concise information relating to the important morphological, behavioural and ecological aspects of the animal under discussion. Similarly, the profiles of the major mammal-watching sites are divided by subheadings into appropriate categories.

Introductory Chapters

The introductory chapters discuss the creation of the island of Madagascar and the influences its long isolation has had on the evolution of its fauna and flora in general, and its mammal communities in particular. This is followed by a brief review of the main biogeographic regions and domains that have been identified on the island and the major habitat types these areas support.

Species Accounts

The bulk of this book comprises the species accounts for each of the five mammalian orders that naturally occur on Madagascar. The individual species and subspecies accounts are subdivided into the following categories to ease information access: measurements, description, identification, habitat, distribution, behaviour, population, threats and viewing. This arrangement applies in its complete form principally to the lemur accounts. The available data are generally less detailed for the other major taxonomic groupings and so do not permit all the divisions to be dealt with. In these instances only the major categories – measurements, description, distribution, behaviour and viewing – are presented.

Measurements

The basic body measurements of importance to field recognition are quoted in metric units. If there are notable differences between the sexes or significant seasonal variation, these too are outlined. The majority of these figures are based on published information or data provided by field researchers. In some instances, however, no direct information is available and estimates have been made using measurements from museum specimens and knowledge from closely related forms. Estimated measurements are indicated by an asterisk (*).

Description

The descriptions concentrate on external features that are of use in field identification. These include pelage characteristics and coloration and notable morphological traits. Where differences between the sexes or between adult and immature individuals are apparent, they are also highlighted. Variations between populations, some of which may be regarded as subspecific, are outlined where appropriate. In some instances more detailed information is given on a feature which may not be obvious in the field, but which is a significant factor that helps differentiate the form from similar taxa.

Identification

A concise summary of the main features used in identifying a species, for instance, approximate size and body posture, is followed by comparisons with taxa that may potentially cause confusion and misidentification. The main external characteristics on which to concentrate are outlined and the differences between similar taxa are highlighted. Armed with this information, the reader ought to be able systematically to check through the relevant features, relate them to the species under consideration and then make a correct identification.

Habitat

The majority of Madagascar's terrestrial mammals are essentially native forest dwellers. There are a number of quite distinct forest and habitat types on Madagascar which broadly correspond to the biogeographic regions and domains the island has been divided into. The preferred habitat type of the species is documented: in some instances, species with extensive distributions have developed wider tolerances and may be found in more than one forest type and perhaps also in some human-altered habitats and cultivated areas.

Distribution

This section outlines in as much detail as is available each species' range and also suggests altitudinal preferences and limits where they are known. In the section dealing with bats (order Chiroptera) this is expanded, where appropriate, to include broader global distributions of the species or genus.

Where subspecies are known, distinction is made between the ranges of each race. In most cases, this is fairly straightforward as subspecies are allopatric, their respective ranges being separated by an obvious geographical barrier like a mountain range or major river. However, in some instances this is not the case and the boundaries between subspecific populations are unclear. Here morphological clines may exist at the boundaries as one taxon gradually changes into another.

Maps illustrate the known ranges of all taxa, again with appropriate divisions to show the distributions of individual subspecies. Where a taxon is known to have a very localised distribution, further expanded maps provide a more detailed outline of the range within this locality.

Unlike the majority of previous accounts relating to Madagascar's mammals (and the Lemuriformes in particular), an attempt has been made, where possible, to outline the approximate *actual* range of a species or subspecies, by relating distributional information to remaining native forest cover. This approach undoubtedly has its pitfalls and will be erroneous in places. Even within the shaded areas, forests are not continuous and neither are the species' populations. Further, there may also be isolated fragments of forest lying outside the shaded areas in which small remnant populations of the species survive. However, as perhaps less than 20% of original forests remains intact, this approach should provide a far more realistic impression of each taxon's present distribution. In many instances, this serves to highlight the severely fragmented nature of populations and the inherent threat to their viability and long-term survival.

A number of species are documented from only a single or handful of localities. In these instances the localities are pinpointed and the probable range that extends between them suggested. Again, this is to be treated as an approximate guide, rather than a definitive statement of the species' distribution.

Behaviour

Information relating to the behaviour and ecology of each taxon is discussed. This may include information on daily and seasonal activity patterns, social interaction, group composition and structure, range size, foraging preferences, diet, breeding habits, development and predation. However, a proportion of the species under discussion have not been studied to any extent or even at all. Therefore, in such instances information relating to the majority of these subjects is not available and in some cases only very scant data can be presented.

Population

It is generally only possible to quote a total population figure where the species or subspecies under consideration has a restricted range that makes estimating an overall population feasible. For taxa with broad or as yet unclear distributions it was not considered appropriate to give an estimate, even between two orders of magnitude, as these would undoubtedly be inaccurate and potentially misleading.

However, in many instances it is possible to quote population density estimates relating to either specific localities or habitat types. It is interesting to note that species with broad ranges and/or habitat tolerances have often been estimated to occur at quite different densities at different localities. Furthermore, field researchers working at the same locality at different times have often arrived at varying population density estimates. Both of these factors serve to highlight the dangers of extrapolating total population figures from density estimates relating to specific localities or habitats.

Threats

Virtually all of Madagascar's native species of mammal (and other faunal groups for that matter) face a very uncertain future. The island's forests are in a beleaguered state which has serious long-term implications for the species they support. In this section the specific threats to each species or subspecies are highlighted. In all instances the major issue is habitat destruction and degradation, but some taxa are also threatened more directly in other ways that are outlined. Where possible an estimate of the number of protected areas (national parks and reserves – see Appendix II) in which the species occurs is given.

Viewing

As mentioned above, one of the two major aims of this volume is to provide a practical guide for the visiting mammal enthusiast. There is no substitute for seeing a wild animal where it should be – in the wild. Madagascar is fortunate in having forests that are safe to wander around on foot. There is also an increasing number of accessible protected areas aiming to cater for visitors' needs. In combination, these make Madagascar an exceptional place to watch wildlife.

In some instances species have already been studied at great length in certain parks and reserves and are now habituated to human presence. This often makes tracking down and seeing these animals relatively easy. However, the majority of species have not been studied, are only found in remote areas or have secretive habits. This of course makes observation difficult, unlikely and generally fleeting.

This section recommends the best localities to try to see the species under consideration. If the species is known to have a seasonally variable lifestyle, some times of the year are better than others and these too are highlighted. Where possible, alternative localities in different parts of the species' range are also suggested to offer variety. Nonetheless, it needs to be stressed that there are no guarantees at any of the recommended sites and considerable patience may be required to catch sight of the species in question.

Conservation and Protected Areas

To complement the species accounts, this section begins with an outline of the conservation concerns facing Madagascar and its natural heritage, and discusses some of the proposed solutions currently being pursued. There is also a brief explanation of the structure of the protected areas network and the obligations of visitors wishing to make use of it.

TOP MAMMAL-WATCHING SITES

The bulk of this chapter is devoted to the recommended mammal-watching sites around the island. These have been selected on the basis of quality of potential viewing and accessibility, and to provide a complete cross-section of habitat types and, therefore, cover an extensive array of mammal species. Each profile is divided by the following subheadings.

Permits

Information on where to obtain the necessary permits to visit the area in question. Also the availability of local guides is given.

Location and Access

Where the site is located, including grid references, and the best ways to reach it.

Elevation

The minimum and maximum heights above sea level that the site covers.

Habitat and Terrain

What type of habitats are covered at the site and their characteristics, the extent of the site, the terrain that is typical and the seasonal variation in conditions that it experiences.

Key Species

A list arranged by major taxonomic groupings of the main species to be found at the site. A species highlighted in **bold type** indicates that observations can be particularly rewarding and corresponds to the recommended sites suggested in the 'Viewing' section of the individual species accounts.

To reinforce the cautious approach adopted in the 'Viewing' sections of the species accounts, it needs to be stressed here that there are no guarantees of seeing the species included in these lists. However, given normal conditions, there should be a reasonable chance of seeing some of them.

Season

Seasonal variation in the climate, particularly rainfall, is highlighted and recommendations are made as to the best time of the year to visit the site.

Facilities

At present only a handful of parks and reserves have even the most basic visitor facilities in place. This situation seems sure to improve in the future. This section briefly describes the current facilities and includes the nearest hotels and lodges, where appropriate, camping recommendations for those sites where no permanent accommodation is available, and an assessment of the path and trail network.

Visiting

Here recommendations are made as to the best way to visit the park or reserve in order to maximise mammal-watching opportunities and enjoy the experience as a whole. To enhance this the hiring of a local guide is generally suggested.

BIOGEOGRAPHY AND
BIOGEOGRAPHIC REGIONS OF MADAGASCAR

That Madagascar is home to one of the most unusual mammalian assemblages on earth is not disputed. How and why this should be so, however, is the subject of considerable debate and speculation and one of the fundamental questions biologists working in the region seek to answer. To state that Madagascar is an island, and that its biota is different because it has evolved in isolation, is a dramatic over-simplification that reveals little of the many subtleties that have been brought to bear in the composition and development of the island's wildlife.

In seeking solutions to these questions of origin, evidence of Madagascar's geological past must be examined. Until around 160 million years ago (Jurassic period), Madagascar was part of an enormous southern super-continent known as Gondwanaland. This comprised the present-day continents of South America, Africa, Antarctica and Australia joined together along with the Indian sub-continent and Madagascar. Within this land mass, geological evidence indicates that Madagascar nestled against the west coast of Africa in the region of present-day Somalia and the Indian sub-continent butted against the east coast of Madagascar. Between 150 and 160 million years ago, colossal forces acting on the earth's crust, wrenched Madagascar and the Indian sub-continent away from the mainland and they began a slow south eastward drift until Madagascar reached its present position around 120 million years ago. Some 40 million years later (80 million years ago), India parted company with Madagascar (breaking along a vast fault line that today forms much of Madagascar's remarkably straight east coast) and began a north-eastward journey until it collided with southern Asia approximately 45 million years ago and consequently formed the Himalayas.

The Jurassic (195-136 million years ago) was dominated by the dinosaurs, only a few very primitive early mammals having evolved towards the end of this period. Therefore, it is highly unlikely that any of the precursors of Madagascar's present-day mammal fauna were on the landmass when it first became an island (c. 150mya). Dinosaurs certainly were present, as the many fossil deposits discovered on Madagascar signify, until their mass extinction in the later stages of the Cretaceous period (c. 70mya). Therefore, the only conclusion that can be drawn is that mammals colonised Madagascar at some point after it had broken away from the mainland and reached its current position in the Indian Ocean.

Figure 1. The obvious outward similarities between the Lesser Galago, Galago senegalensis, (1a, above left) from west and east Africa and the Brown Mouse Lemur, Microcebus rufus, (1b, above right) from Madagascar betray their close common ancestry. It now seems highly probable that the precursors of both contemporary prosimians evolved in Africa and strongly resembled these present-day species. Perhaps around 50 million years ago some of these small early prosimians were washed out into the Mozambique Channel clinging to mats of vegetation and similar debris floating down rivers after heavy rain. A handful may have made it all the way across to Madagascar, providing the founding stock for the subsequent evolution of the lemurs, while those left on mainland Africa changed little, forced to remain in the shadows and become exclusively nocturnal when more intelligent and competitive primates – monkeys and apes – evolved to dominate the forests by day.

However, this provides only half a solution to the conundrum. How did the early mammals colonise an island separated from the mainland by more than 400km of open ocean? And why did only a small number of major taxonomic groups successfully complete the voyage?

One possibility is that at some stage during the early colonisations a land bridge or chain of islands existed between Madagascar and the mainland that acted as convenient ports of call for the pioneer mammals. Then not long after, this bridge or series of stepping stones disappeared, preventing later-evolving mammals making a similar journey. There is some geological evidence to support this. It is known that Madagascar made its southward journey from Africa along a fault line that extends from the Somali coast into the Mozambique Channel (known as the Davie Fracture Zone). Examination of the earth's crust and marine sediments along this zone suggests that this part of the Mozambique Channel at least may have been dry up until around 45 millions years ago. On the face of it, this seems to be the basis of a plausible explanation: Madagascar's first mammalian colonists arrived on foot, then, before more advanced mammals came along, the land bridge became submerged, isolating those which had already made the journey, but preventing further invasions from later-evolving forms.

However, there is one major objection to this theory. The demise of the dinosaur dynasty heralded the dawn of the Age of Mammals. By the beginning of the Eocene epoch 54 million years ago, this group of hitherto small and rather insignificant creatures had diversified and speciated dramatically. The continent of Africa was undoubtedly at the heart of this massive radiation. Why then, if a land bridge existed between Africa and Madagascar, did a tide of early carnivores and ungulates not flood onto the island? Subfossil evidence indicates that at least five species of ungulate (three dwarf hippopotamuses and two false aardvarks) have existed on Madagascar in the past (see Appendix I) – but these species are suspected to be relatively recent arrivals and probably managed to reach the island long after any possible land bridge had submerged.

Perhaps the second theory will provide a more complete solution. Despite the obvious difficulties, it has long been suggested that many animals reach isolated islands by rafting on matted clumps of floating vegetation that are regularly washed out to sea from large river estuaries on continental mainlands. On the face of it this seems a highly improbable method for any land-based animal to reach distant shores. However, if the immensity of geological time is fully appreciated the explanation becomes highly plausible – after all, any event that is not absolutely impossible becomes probable if enough time elapses – it has been calculated that if the chances of a species crossing an expanse of open ocean in any one year are one in a million, then in a million years the probability is 63% and in 10 million years it is 99.995%!

Certainly, the crossing the Mozambique Channel by rafting (sweepstake dispersal) appears to be a prime candidate for explaining the arrival of Madagascar's first mammals. However, this explanation alone is not detailed enough to answer all the necessary questions. For instance, if the forebears of Madagascar's mammal communities could make the crossing, why have other groups that proliferate on Africa not done so subsequently? After all, we know Madagascar has been in its current position for approximately 120 million years, so reaching it on floating vegetation ought to be as easy today as it was when the early colonists made the journey millions of years ago.

Consequently, we need to consider possible reasons that may have made the pioneer mammals better mariners (in terms of their ability to survive a long sea-crossing) than mainland species that came along later in evolutionary history. It is obvious that a small body size would be an advantage in being able to stay afloat on a makeshift raft. And although relatively large species have existed, and continue to exist, on Madagascar, evidence suggests these evolved at a later date and that original colonising stock consisted only of small species. But why then are there many small mammals on Africa which are absent from Madagascar? Furthermore, small body size usually correlates to a high metabolism and the need to eat regularly. Clearly this trait would appear to place small mammals at a severe disadvantage in the sea-crossing stakes. The results of recent research may provide the missing elements that are needed to solve this riddle. It is now known that many of Madagascar's smaller mammals have the capacity to lower their metabolism and become dormant during periods of low food availability. In conjunction, they can also build up fat reserves during times of plenty to sustain themselves through such leaner periods. This ability has been demonstrated both in mouse and dwarf lemurs (family Cheirogaleidae), which are probably very similar to Madagascar's early primate colonists, and in tenrecs (family Tenrecidae), which have apparently changed little since they arrived on the island. It is also known that some of the island's endemic civet-like carnivores (family Viverridae) are able to lay down fat reserves in their tails to help see them through times of food deprivation.

Here then may be the solution. Madagascar was colonised from Africa by small mammal species rafting on natural debris, and the only species to survive the journey were those with the ability to lower their metabolism, become dormant and/or live without food for long periods on previously built-up reserves. As it turned out, the successful species represented only five main mammalian groupings: Lemuriformes, Viverridae, Herpestidae, Tenrecidae and Rodentia. To complete the picture we may assume that the one remaining mammalian group present on Madagascar – the bats (order Chiroptera) – reached the island by flying.

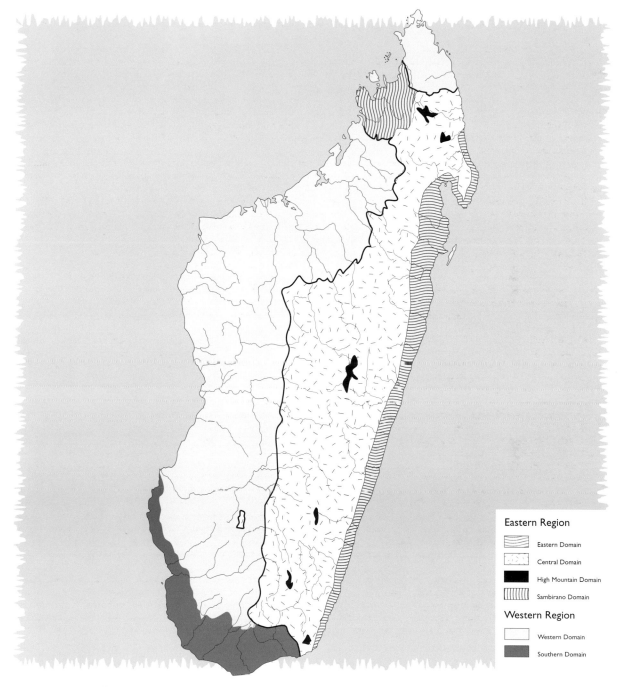

Figure 2. Biogeographic regions of Madagascar.

One of Madagascar's most remarkable features is its diversity of habitats. The island covers an area of about 590,000km^2 – it is the world's fourth largest island after Greenland, New Guinea and Borneo – yet the diversity of ecological environments it contains rivals that of an entire continent: there are rainforests in the east, deciduous forests in the north and west, dense bush and xerophytic forests in the south and high mountain forests in the island's interior. It is not surprising that such variety has fostered the evolution of a faunal assemblage so unusual as to rival that of any comparable area on earth.

This habitat variety is the result of quite dramatic climatic variability, which in turn is a consequence of Madagascar's geographic position and its topography.

Figure 3. Lowland rainforest, Masoala Peninsula.

Figure 4. Dawn mist over lowland rainforest, Masoala Peninsula.

Figure 5. Namorona River, mid-altitude montane rainforest, Ranomafana.

Madagascar lies virtually totally within the tropics and has an entirely tropical climate. From north to south spans some 1,600km, between 11° 57'S and 25° 32'S. There is considerable variation in basic sea-level temperatures: at the island's northern tip the annual mean is 81°C, while at the southern extremity the annual mean drops to 71°C.

The island consists of a backbone of Precambrian crystalline rocks running from north to south down the length of the island. This forms the high plateau. To the east there is an abrupt escarpment, while in the west the highlands slope more gently down to the Mozambique Channel. The highest mountains are in the north and rise to 2,876m (Tsaratanana Massif), and there are other scattered massifs and peaks on the high plateau, some of which reach over 1,800m. The eastern coastal plain between the escarpment and the Indian Ocean is generally narrow, while the coastal plain to the west is far broader.

The prevailing weather comes from the Indian Ocean brought by the trade winds which are forced to rise over the escarpment. Consequently, the majority of rain falls on the eastern side of the island. The western regions lie in a permanent rainshadow. Hence, conditions gradually become hotter and drier towards the west coast.

However, during the austral summer these western regions are subject to a monsoon regime which originates in the north and whose influence dwindles towards the south. Hence, there is a double rainfall gradient over the island: declining from east to west on the one hand, and north to south on the other. As a result the north-east of Madagascar is the wettest part of the island and the south-west regions are the driest.

The combined effect of these rainfall regimes and Madagascar's varied relief is a profusion of localised climatic conditions, which consequently result in the variety of biomes and habitat types found on the island.

Two major biogeographic regions are recognised in Madagascar: the Eastern Malagasy Region and the Western Malagasy Region. These are further divided into domains which broadly correspond to the major habitat types found across the island. The extent of these native habitats has been dramatically compromised by humans in most areas: the ranges that are broadly outlined here refer to the natural limits of the climax formations, rather than to their current extent, which is now much reduced.

Figure 6. The aftermath of slash-and-burn ('tavy') cultivation: Betsimisaraka woman planting manioc.

Eastern Malagasy Region

This region is divided into four naturally occurring domains and one anthropogenic zone that has largely replaced the original vegetation in many areas. The region encompasses just under half of the island and extends from the east coast westward to cover the central highlands and an enclave of moist forest in the north-west known as the Sambirano. At the generic level around 22% of plant species are endemic and at the species level this rises to about 82%. On pristine Madagascar, this region would probably have been almost completely forested.

Eastern Domain (Lowland Rainforest)

This zone of lowland rainforest grows at elevations from sea-level up to around 800m and extends along the east coast from just south of Vohemar in the north to the Tolagnaro region in the south. It corresponds to the areas of highest rainfall, receiving at least 2,400mm per year with some areas in the north-east, for instance, the Masoala Peninsula (figs. 3 & 4) receiving in excess of 3,500mm per annum. There is no clearly defined dry season, although the months of December to March are consistently wetter than at other times.

There is enormous species richness and diversity within lowland rainforest coupled with very high levels of endemism, for instance over 85% in the case of flowering plants. The largest trees have huge buttress roots and the canopy averages 30-35m, but there are generally none of the emergent trees that often characterise lowland rainforests in other parts of the world. The understorey is dominated by small trees, but there is little herbaceous growth beneath. Epiphytic plants such as orchids are abundant.

This is one of the most threatened vegetation zones on Madagascar: vast areas have already been cleared, particularly on the coastal plain, and only a fraction of the original forest cover remains.

Mammal diversity

Very high. All the major taxonomic groups are represented in this domain.

Chiroptera:	Five families, including 13 of the 17 genera (76%).
Tenrecidae:	Two subfamilies, including five of the eight genera (62%).
Rodentia:	Single subfamily, including four of the eight endemic genera (50%).
Viverridae:	Both subfamilies, including all three endemic genera (100%).
Herpestidae:	Single subfamily, including three of the four endemic genera (75%).
Lemuriformes:	All five families, including 12 of the 14 genera (85%).

Examples: Masoala Peninsula, Mananara, Nosy Mangabe.

Central Domain (Mid-Altitude Montane Rainforest)

Montane rainforest occurs mainly between 800m and 1,300m (fig. 5), although there are localised patches which approach 2,000m. This zone is found to the west of the lowland rainforest belt and extends parallel to the east coast from the region north of Sambava in the north to the vicinity of Tolagnaro in the south. Annual rainfall exceeds 1,500mm and there is no discernible dry season, although again the wettest period corresponds to the austral summer.

These forests are highly diverse and species-rich, with levels of endemism equivalent to those in the lowland rainforest belt. The canopy averages 20-25m and occasionally reaches 30m, and the understorey and herbaceous layers are better developed than in lowland forests. Epiphytes like tree-ferns abound and many trees are festooned with mosses and lichens.

The majority of these forests have already been destroyed. The remaining areas of montane rainforest are highly threatened by slash-and-burn (*tavy*) agriculture (figs. 6 & 7), felling for building timber and the collection of firewood.

Mammal diversity

Very high. All the major taxonomic groups are represented. Both the Tenrecidae and Nesomyinae reach their highest levels of species richness in this domain.

Chiroptera:	Five families, including 13 of the 17 genera (76%).
Tenrecidae:	Two subfamilies, including six of the eight genera (75%).
Rodentia:	Single subfamily, including five of the eight endemic genera (62%).
Viverridae:	Both subfamilies, including all three endemic genera (100%).
Herpestidae:	Single subfamily, including three of the four endemic genera (75%).
Lemuriformes:	All five families, including 12 of the 14 genera (85%).

Examples: Analamazaotra, Mantadia, Ranomafana, Montagne d'Ambre.

Figure 7. Slash-and-burn 'tavy' cultivation, Anjanaharibe-Sud.

Figure 8. High-altitude montane and sclerophyllous forest, Marojejy Massif.

Figure 9. Eastern anthropogenic grasslands and Traveller's Trees Ravenala madagascariensis.

Figure 10. Anthropogenic grasslands, eastern central highlands.

High Mountain Domain (High-Altitude Montane Forest)

High-altitude montane forest is generally restricted to elevations between 2,000m and 2,876m (Madagascar's highest peak Maromokotro, in the Tsaratanana Massif), but does occur locally below 2,000m. It occurs in a broken belt inland from the montane rainforest zone: the northerly limit is the Sambava area (Marojejy Massif) (fig. 8) and the southerly extreme is to the north of Tolagnaro (Andohahela Massif). Annual precipitation is high, much of it occurring as dense mists and low cloud. There are also considerable daily and seasonal temperature variations: during the austral winter night-time temperatures sometimes fall below freezing and snow has been known on occasion (Andringitra Massif).

The species diversity in these forests is far lower than in montane or lowland rainforests, although the levels of endemism remain high. Canopy height is between 10m and 15m at lower elevations and declines gradually with altitude to become sclerophyllous forest. Distinguishing canopy layers from the understorey is often difficult: the forest appears to be a dense single stratum. The leaves on most trees are much smaller than in lower-altitude rainforests and have a tough leathery cuticle to counter the desiccating effect of the wind. Most of the trees are encrusted with mosses and lichens, and mosses often form a dense carpet on the forest floor. The very highest areas in this domain are above the treeline and consist of alpine meadow type formations.

Fire is the major threat to this habitat type. These may be started deliberately to clear forest, spread accidentally from already cultivated areas, or even ignite naturally as a result of lightning. Given the extremely restricted natural range of this vegetation type the overall level of threat is very acute.

Mammal diversity

Moderately high. Most major taxonomic groups are represented, but species diversity within these is reduced in comparison with rainforest at lower elevations.

Chiroptera:	Three* families, including six* of the 17 genera (35%*).
Tenrecidae:	Two subfamilies, including five of the eight genera (62%).
Rodentia:	Single subfamily, including five of the eight endemic genera (62%).
Viverridae:	Both subfamilies, including two of the three endemic genera (66%).
Herpestidae:	Single subfamily, including two of the four endemic genera (50%).
Lemuriformes:	Four families, including seven of the 14 genera (50%).
	* estimated figures.

Examples: Tsaratanana, Marojejy, Andringitra.

Figure 11. Ankazafotsy village on the edge of Andohahela.

Sambirano Domain (Seasonal Humid Forest)

The Sambirano is an enclave of humid rainforest that is restricted to north-west Madagascar and lies approximately between the Nosy Faly Peninsula to the north and the Andranomalaza river to the south. This enclave represents an extension of the north-eastern rainforest zones, through the Tsaratanana Massif to the west coast. The average yearly rainfall is above 2,000mm, but at lower elevations there is a drier season between July and September.

The Sambirano represents a transition between the floral communities of the east and the west: it shares many features with the eastern and central domains, but also with the western domain. There is high species diversity and high levels of endemism. The forest structure is similar to eastern domain forests: canopy height reaches 30m and at lower elevations some trees emerge to around 35m. The understorey and shrub layers are substantial, with epiphytes, vines and creepers abundant.

Forest clearing for rice and, to a lesser extent, coffee cultivation constitutes the major threat to this zone. The domain's very limited extent intensifies this: the Sambirano is one of the most highly threatened habitat types.

Mammal diversity

Moderate. Most major taxonomic groups are represented, with some notable exceptions, for instance *Propithecus* spp. Both the tenrec and rodent faunas appear impoverished in comparison with other humid forest areas, but this may be a consequence of an incomplete inventory as few detailed small mammal surveys have taken place in this domain.

Chiroptera:	Six families, including 13* of the 17 genera (76%).
Tenrecidae:	Two subfamilies, including three of the eight genera (37%).
Rodentia:	Single subfamily, including two of the eight genera (25%).
Viverridae:	Both subfamilies, including all three endemic genera (100%).
Herpestidae:	Single subfamily, including one of the four endemic genera (25%).
Lemuriformes:	All five families, including nine of the 14 genera (64%).
	* estimated figure.

Example: Manongarivo.

Eastern Anthropogenic Grasslands

Where climax formations have been removed, they are largely replaced by a mosaic of secondary vegetation that is created and maintained by human activity. The composition and structure of these habitats, which are dominated by grasses, vary with altitude. At lower elevations coastal grassland savanna predominates, often interspersed with extensive stands of *Ravenala madagascariensis* (fig. 9). Grassland savanna also dominates higher elevations (figs. 10 & 11) including those on western slopes of the high plateau where the Eastern and Western regions meet. Highland savanna is also found on some mountain ridges.

In all areas the levels of species diversity and endemism are very low. At low and middle altitudes the grasses reach a height of around 50cm in higher montane areas they rarely exceed 25cm in height and are often shorter.

These zones are maintained and extended by deliberate fires that are started several times per year, to promote new growth for cattle grazing. These fires further reduce what little species diversity there is. Severe overgrazing further undermines the habitat resulting in large-scale erosion in many areas, particularly those of highest rainfall.

Mammal diversity

Very low. Virtually all of these regions are devoid of native terrestrial mammal species: in some marginal areas endemic tenrec and rodent species have occasionally been found. A higher proportion of indigenous bat species are able to utilise these habitats in areas when trees are present. However, bat diversity is still very low when compared with native forest areas. The only mammals that have colonised these areas are introduced rodent and insectivore species, for instance *Rattus rattus*, *Mus musculus* and *Suncus murinus*, which live as human commensals.

Figure 12 (above). Western deciduous forest and Lac Ravelobe, Ampijoroa.

Figure 13 (left). Limestone karst ('tsingy'), Lac Vert and deciduous forest, Ankarana.

Figure 14 (right). Grandidier's Baobab Adansonia grandidieri in western deciduous forest, near Morondava.

Western Malagasy Region

The Western Malagasy Region is further divided into two natural domains and one anthropogenic zone. This region extends from the flat west coast plains eastwards to elevations around 800m, and includes the southern areas of the island. Within this region the levels of generic and specific endemism are very high – 38% and 89% respectively.

Western Domain (Dry Deciduous Forest)

This area of dry deciduous forest (figs. 12 & 13) extends at altitudes from sea-level to 800m from the area of Antsiranana in the north to the vicinity of Morombe in the south-west, excluding the Montagne d'Ambre Massif and the Sambirano domain (which are classified as part of the Eastern Malagasy Region). Annual rainfall ranges from around 2,000mm in the north to only 500mm in the south: the majority of this falls between December and March, the rest of the year being mainly dry.

Figure 15. Charcoal produced from southern spiny forests, near Amboasary-Sud.

Species diversity in western dry deciduous forests is very high, although it is lower than in those of the Eastern Region. However, the levels of species endemism are higher – often around 90%. The canopy averages around 12m to 15m but in some areas reaches 20m to 25m. The understorey and shrub layers, including lianas, are well developed, but herbaceous and epiphytic growth is rare. Most of the trees lose their leaves during the dry season (May to October) and the forest floor is permanently carpeted in dead leaves.

In some areas where sandy soils predominate these forests may be dominated by baobabs (*Adansonia* spp.), which have huge swollen water-storage trunks. Excellent examples of the largest species, Grandidier's Baobab *A. grandidieri* can be seen near Morondava (fig. 14).

Most dry deciduous forests on the island have already been cleared and those that remain are under considerable pressure. Slash-and-burn agriculture poses a continuing and persistent threat to this habitat type. Forest clearing for timber is also a major threat and intentional but uncontrolled pasture fires often spread to damage forest at the margins.

Mammal diversity

High. Most major taxonomic groups are represented, but species diversity is reduced in comparison with the rainforest areas of the east.

Chiroptera:	Six families, including 16* of the 17 genera (94%).
Tenrecidae:	Two subfamilies, including five of the eight genera (62%).
Rodentia:	Single subfamily, including four of the eight endemic genera (50%).
Viverridae:	Both subfamilies, including two of the three endemic genera (66%).
Herpestidae:	Single subfamily, including three of the four endemic genera (75%).
Lemuriformes:	All five families, including 10 of the 14 genera (71%).
	* estimated figure.

Examples: Ankarafantsika, Kirindy, Ankarana, Analamera.

Southern Domain (Subarid Thorn Scrub)

Subarid thorn scrub is often referred to as xerophytic spiny forest (figs. 16 & 17) and extends southwards along the coastal plain from Morombe, it includes the whole of the southern area around to a point approximately 40km to the west of Tolagnaro, and is restricted to elevations below 400m. In the region of Morombe annual rainfall reaches around 500mm; this declines further to the south, the driest areas receiving on average only 300mm per year. The dry season is very marked and long, extending for up to ten months of the year (March to December). However, this is highly variable and 18-month dry periods have been recorded in some areas.

Despite the harsh conditions, species diversity is high and levels of endemism are extremely high. The height and density of the formations vary with climatic and soil conditions: in some areas trees reach 8m to 10m, but in other areas only around 2m. All plant species are adapted for the harsh xerophytic conditions, most having abundant sharp thorns and small waxy leathery leaves that are short-lived. Growth is very dense and often impenetrable. This region is dominated and characterised by plants belonging to the endemic family Didiereaceae and members of the Euphorbiaceae.

Along major watercourses in the region, spiny forest gives way to narrow bands of riparian habitat known as gallery forest (fig. 18). In general appearance these areas closely resemble the dry deciduous forests of the western domain. The canopy is of a similar height (up to 15m) and there is often an extensive understorey and herbaceous layer. These forests are characterised and often dominated by the tamarind tree *Tamarindus indica*.

Direct forest clearing for firewood and the production of charcoal (fig. 15) constitutes the major threat to this region. In marginal areas grazing and browsing by cattle and goats also has a detrimental effect.

Mammal diversity

Moderate. A number of major taxonomic groups are notable absentees from this domain, for instance, *Eulemur* spp. (they have been introduced to one area) and the viverrid subfamilies Fossinae and Euplerinae. Small mammal species diversity is dramatically reduced: only two rodent species are represented (*Eliurus myoxinus* and *Macrotarsomys bastardi*) and the prolific tenrec genus *Microgale* is probably absent.

Chiroptera:	Five families, including 12* of the 17 genera (70*%).
Tenrecidae:	Two subfamilies, including four of the eight genera (50%).
Rodentia:	Single subfamily, including two of the eight endemic genera (25%).
Viverridae:	A single subfamily including one of the three endemic genera (33%).
Herpestidae:	Single subfamily, including two of the four endemic genera (50%).
Lemuriformes:	Four families, including 5 of the 14 genera (35%).
	* estimated figure.

Examples: Ifaty, Tsimanampetsotsa, Beza Mahafaly (spiny and gallery forest), Hazafotsy, Berenty (gallery forest).

Figure 16. Xerophytic spiny forest dominated by Alluadia procera, *near Amboasary-Sud.*

Figure 17. Octopus Trees, Didierea trolli: *spiny forest, south-western Madagascar.*

Figure 18. Gallery forest on the banks of the Mandrare River, Berenty.

Figure 19. Fire-resistant palms, Borassus madagascariensis, *near Isalo.*

Figure 20. Western anthropogenic grassland and palms, Bismarckia *and* Hyphaene *spp., near Katsepy.*

Western Anthropogenic Grasslands and Palm Savanna

The vast majority of original forest formations in the Western Region have now been replaced by anthropogenic grassland and palm savannas (fig. 20) that cover around 80% of the area. There are very low levels of species diversity and endemism. Coarse grasses dominate throughout but in some areas these are broken by locally scattered stands of fire-resistant palms such as *Bismarckia nobilis*, *Hyphaene coriacea* and *Borassus madagascariensis* (fig. 19).

These areas are further impoverished and extended by deliberate fires started several times per year, to encourage new shoots for cattle. Overgrazing is also commonplace and locally severe.

Mammal diversity

Very low. In the majority of these areas, native terrestrial mammal species are totally absent: the one exception appears to be the endemic mouse *Macrotarsomys bastardi*, which is known to occur locally. Some bat species are able to utilise these habitats in the areas where palms are present. As with similar regions in the east, the only mammals that have colonised western grasslands are the introduced human commensals, *Rattus rattus*, *Mus musculus* and *Suncus murinus*.

THE
MAMMALS
OF
MADAGASCAR

Figure 21. Indri.

The mammal fauna of Madagascar is perhaps as remarkable for the major taxonomic groupings that are absent as it is for the suite of unusual species that are present. Given the island's proximity to mainland Africa, it would be easy to assume Madagascar contains simply an impoverished version of the vast diversity of mammals living on the continent. This could not be further from the truth. For instance, there are none of the large herbivores that so dominate the plains of Africa; carnivores, such as wild cats, wild dogs and members of the weasel family are conspicuous by their absence, as are monkeys and apes and a host of other smaller forms like lagomorphs (rabbits and hares).

In fact, only six major mammal groups are found on Madagascar today (seven if a probable introduced species, the Bush Pig, is included): the bats (order Chiroptera), tenrecs (order Insectivora; family Tenrecidae), rats and mice (order Rodentia; family Muridae), civet-like carnivores (order Carnivora; family Viverridae), mongooses (order Carnivora; family Herpestidae) and the lemurs (order Primates; infraorder Lemuriformes). In total there are approximately 117 native species, yet no less than 90% of these are endemic, that is they occur naturally nowhere else. What is more, if bats are excluded and only native terrestrial mammals considered, this level of endemicity rises to a staggering 100%.

In essence, the reasons for this are simple, Madagascar has been an island for a very long time, which has allowed the mammals present to evolve along totally different lines to anywhere else. However, the likely sequence of events, consequences and requirements that combined to produce such a powerful biological filter are far from fully understood.

It is now suspected that all terrestrial mammals reached Madagascar by rafting on natural debris across the Mozambique Channel. Although it is difficult to pinpoint when the first mammalian colonists arrived, evidence suggests that they probably resembled the present-day tenrecs (family Tenrecidae) in many ways. However, the lottery and rigours of crossing the Mozambique Channel severely restricted further mammalian invasions and only a handful of other forms proved capable of achieving this. Once on Madagascar, however, these early colonists largely had the island to themselves (as the dinosaurs had long since died out) and were able to diversify spectacularly, evolving into species exploiting niches occupied elsewhere by other groups of mammals and even birds. Ring-tailed Lemurs live in a similar manner to some baboons, the Giant Jumping Rat shows remarkable similarities in body form and lifestyle to rabbits and hares, the Fosa is a member of the civet family but in appearance and behaviour resembles a cat, while the bizarre Aye-aye extracts insect grubs from tree bark much as woodpeckers, a family unrepresented on the island, would do.

Even within the limited number of major taxa that reached the island it may be that only one of two founder forms arrived. Consequently, despite today exhibiting large degrees of ecological and morphological diversity, members within some of these taxonomic groupings probably share a common ancestry. For instance, the lemurs, whose diversity in size and lifestyle is unmatched amongst lower primates (suborder Strepsirhini) elsewhere, evidently owe their origins to a single small ancestral primate. Likewise, the Malagasy civet-like carnivores and Malagasy mongooses are each probably monophyletic. Amongst the terrestrial mammals, only the tenrecs and perhaps rodents seemingly evolved from more than one founder species: the tenrecs are likely to be derived from two ancestral forms which gave rise to the contemporary subfamilies Tenrecinae and Oryzorictinae, while the present-day endemic rodents (subfamily Nesomyinae) may be a consequence of several independent waves of colonisation.

There are, however, some anomalies in the mammal fauna that warrant explanation. Subfossil evidence indicates that in the recent past three species of dwarf hippopotamus (*Hexaprotodon madagascariensis*, *Hippopotamus lemerlei* and *H. laloumena*) and two 'false' aardvarks (*Plesiorycteropus madagascariensis* and *P. germainepetterae*) were present on Madagascar (see Appendix I). These were probably later arrivals (late Quaternary) on the island than any of the original mammalian founder species. It is likely they made the crossing from Africa during the mid to late Cenozoic (38 to 7 million years before present), but how is not known. Being semi-aquatic the hippopotamuses, at least, could perhaps have made their own way across the Mozambique Channel under freak circumstances. It is suspected that all five species became extinct around 1,000 years ago as a consequence of adverse human persecution. Furthermore, an ungulate, the Bush Pig *Potamochoerus larvatus*, still survives on the island to this day. However, it is suspected this animal is either a comparatively recent natural arrival or more likely was introduced by early human colonists.

Classification

There is currently no single reference that offers an up-to-date classification of Madagascar's mammals. The results of recent and ongoing research have shed further light on evolutionary relationships which have prompted various systematic revisions within each of the five mammalian orders that naturally occur on the island. Given that much of this research is still in its infancy and that new genetic techniques are constantly being refined to elucidate taxonomic relationships, it seems reasonable to presume that further revisions will be proposed in the future; this applies particularly to the small mammal communities (tenrecs, rodents and micro-bats), where the current inventories are almost certainly incomplete. Therefore, the classification followed in this volume is a synthesis based on a number of previously proposed taxonomies relating to each of the mammalian orders, but with departures due to the invalidation of some species and addition of others resulting from recent taxonomic work.

The classification of the Lemuriformes mirrors that of Mittermeier *et al*. (1994), except that the bamboo lemurs (*Hapalemur* spp.) are recognised as a separate subfamily, Hapalemurinae, within the family Lemuridae. There is also the addition of the newly described Golden-brown Mouse Lemur *Microcebus ravelobensis* (Zimmermann *et al*. 1998).

The arrangement of the carnivores follows Wozencraft (1993), whereby the civet-like carnivores are placed in the family Viverridae, and rather than being incorporated into this family the mongooses are given their own family (Herpestidae) with the Malagasy mongooses aligned as the subfamily Galidiinae within this. The alternative view, which is now considered out of date, is to include the mongooses in the broadly defined family Viverridae, and to divide the Malagasy representatives between three or four subfamilies.

Within the Tenrecidae, two subfamilies are recognised from Madagascar: Tenrecinae and Oryzorictinae. The taxonomy of the latter remains confused, particularly with respect to the shrew tenrecs (genus *Microgale*). New species are regularly being described and existing forms often amalgamated as synonyms. Here the sequence follows that proposed by Stephenson (1995), with additions and amendments by Goodman *et al*. (1997 and in press) and Jenkins *et al*. (1997).

The studies by Carleton and colleagues (1990, 1996 and 1997, and in press) have provided the basis for the arrangement of the rodents, the endemic subfamily Nesomyinae being placed within the broad Old World family Muridae. There have been several recent additions to the inventory including a new genus, *Monticolomys* (Carleton and Goodman 1996), while further new genera and species are currently under description (Carleton and Goodman in press).

Bats, particularly within the suborder Microchiroptera, perhaps present the greatest challenge to the mammalian taxonomist in Madagascar (and probably throughout the world as a whole). Such is their diversity and number of species that several systematic lists have been proposed, often radically differing from one another. That new species will be described and existing taxa lumped together in the future seems without doubt. However, for the purposes of this volume, the latest review specifically relating to the Malagasy bat fauna (Peterson *et al*. 1995) has been followed.

With all the above under consideration, the following sequence should provide a sound basis for the classification of Madagascar's mammals within the context of this book. However, it is abundantly clear that many taxonomic questions still need to be addressed and answered; hence this list can only be treated as provisional.

Order Chiroptera
Suborder Megachiroptera

Family **Pteropopidae** (Old World Fruit Bats)

Madagascar Flying Fox	*Pteropus rufus*
Madagascar Straw-coloured Fruit Bat	*Eidolon dupreanum*
Madagascar Rousette	*Rousettus madagascariensis*

Suborder Microchiroptera

Family **Emballonuridae** (Sheath-tailed Bats)

Madagascar Sheath-tailed Bat	*Emballonura atrata*
Mauritian Tomb Bat	*Taphozous mauritianus*

Family **Nycteridae** (Slit-faced Bats)

Madagascar Slit-faced Bat	*Nycteris madagascariensis*

Family **Hipposideridae** (Old World Leaf-nosed Bats)

Commerson's Leaf-nosed Bat	*Hipposideros commersoni*
Trouessart's Trident Bat	*Triaenops furculus*
Rufous Trident Bat	*Triaenops rufus*

Family **Myzopodidae** (Sucker-footed Bat)

Sucker-footed Bat	*Myzopoda aurita*

Family **Vespertilionidae** (Vespertilionid Bats)
    Subfamily **Vespertilioninae**

Malagasy Mouse-eared Bat	*Myotis goudoti*
Madagascar pipistrelles	*Pipistrellus* spp.
Madagascar Serotine	*Eptesicus matroka*
Somali Serotine	*Eptesicus somalicus*
	Scotophilus robustus
	Scotophilus borbonicus

    Subfamily **Miniopterinae**

	Miniopterus majori
	Miniopterus manavi
Lesser Long-fingered Bat	*Miniopterus fraterculus*
	Miniopterus gleni

Family **Molossidae** (Free-tailed Bats)

Peters's Goblin Bat	*Mormopterus jugularis*
Natal Goblin Bat	*Mormopterus acetabulosus*
Large Free-tailed Bat	*Tadarida fulminans*
	Tadarida (Chaerephon) leucogaster
Little Free-tailed Bat	*Tadarida (Chaerephon) pumila*
Midas Free-tailed Bat	*Tadarida (Mops) midas*
	Tadarida (Mops) leucostigma
Madagascar Free-tailed Bat	*Otomops madagascariensis*

Order Insectivora

Family **Tenrecidae** (Tenrecs and Otter-Shrews)
    Subfamily **Tenrecinae** (Spiny Tenrecs)

Common Tenrec	*Tenrec ecaudatus*
Greater Hedgehog Tenrec	*Setifer setosus*
Lesser Hedgehog Tenrec	*Echinops telfairi*
Lowland Streaked Tenrec	*Hemicentetes semispinosus*
Highland Streaked Tenrec	*Hemicentetes nigriceps*

    Subfamily **Oryzorictinae** (Furred Tenrecs)

Aquatic Tenrec	*Limnogale mergulus*
Large-eared Tenrec	*Geogale aurita*
	Oryzorictes hova
	Oryzorictes talpoides
	Oryzorictes tetradactylus
Lesser Long-tailed Shrew Tenrec	*Microgale longicaudata*
Greater Long-tailed Shrew Tenrec	*Microgale principula*
Talazac's Shrew Tenrec	*Microgale talazaci*
Long-nosed Shrew Tenrec	*Microgale longirostris*
Thomas's Shrew Tenrec	*Microgale thomasi*
Gracile Shrew Tenrec	*Microgale gracilis*
Dobson's Shrew Tenrec	*Microgale dobsoni*
Cowan's Shrew Tenrec	*Microgale cowani*
Pygmy Shrew Tenrec	*Microgale parvula*
Short-tailed Shrew Tenrec	*Microgale brevicaudata*
Lesser Shrew Tenrec	*Microgale pusilla*
Taiva Shrew Tenrec	*Microgale taiva*
Striped Shrew Tenrec	*Microgale drouhardi*
Naked-nosed Shrew Tenrec	*Microgale gymnorhyncha*
Pale-footed Shrew Tenrec	*Microgale fotsifotsy*
	Microgale dryas
	Microgale soricoides

Introduced Species

Family **Soricidae** (Shrews)

Musk Shrew	*Suncus murinus*
Pygmy Musk Shrew	*Suncus etruscus*

Order Rodentia

Family **Muridae** (Old World Rats and Mice)
    Subfamily **Nesomyinae** (Malagasy Rodents)

Giant Jumping Rat	*Hypogeomys antimena*
Eastern Red Forest Rat	*Nesomys rufus*
Lowland Red Forest Rat	*Nesomys audeberti*
Western Red Forest Rat	*Nesomys lambertoni*
Western Tuft-tailed Rat	*Eliurus myoxinus*
	Eliurus majori
	Eliurus penicillatus
	Eliurus tanala
	Eliurus minor
	Eliurus webbi
	Eliurus ellermani
	Eliurus petteri
Voalavoanala	*Gymnuromys roberti*
White-tailed Tree Rat	*Brachytarsomys albicauda*
	Brachytarsomys villosa
	Brachyuromys ramirohitra
	Brachyuromys betsileoensis
Malagasy Mountain Mouse	*Monticolomys koopmani*
Western Forest Mouse	*Macrotarsomys bastardi*
	Macrotarsomys ingens

Introduced Species

Subfamily **Murinae** (Old World Rats and Mice)

Black Rat	*Rattus rattus*
Brown Rat	*Rattus norvegicus*
House Mouse	*Mus musculus*

Order Carnivora

Family **Viverridae** (Civets and their allies)
    Subfamily **Euplerinae** (Malagasy Civets)

Fanaloka	*Fossa fossana*
Falanouc	*Eupleres goudotii*

Subfamily **Cryptoproctinae** (Fosa)

Fosa	*Cryptoprocta ferox*

Introduced Species

Subfamily **Viverrinae** (Civets)

Small Indian Civet	*Viverricula indica*

Family **Herpestidae** (Mongooses)
    Subfamily **Galidiinae** (Malagasy Mongooses)

Ring-tailed Mongoose	*Galidia elegans*
Narrow-striped Mongoose	*Mungotictis decemlineata*
Broad-striped Mongoose	*Galidictis fasciata*
Grandidier's Mongoose	*Galidictis grandidieri*
Brown-tailed Mongoose	*Salanoia concolor*

Order Artiodactyla
Introduced Species

Family **Suidae** (Old World Pigs)

Bush Pig	*Potamochoerus larvatus*

Order Primates
Infraorder Lemuriformes

Family **Cheirogaleidae** (Mouse and Dwarf Lemurs)

Grey Mouse Lemur	*Microcebus murinus*
Brown Mouse Lemur	*Microcebus rufus*
Pygmy Mouse Lemur	*Microcebus myoxinus*
Golden-brown Mouse Lemur	*Microcebus ravelobensis*
Hairy-eared Dwarf Lemur	*Allocebus trichotis*
Greater Dwarf Lemur	*Cheirogaleus major*
Fat-tailed Dwarf Lemur	*Cheirogaleus medius*
Coquerel's Dwarf Lemur	*Mirza coquereli*
Fork-marked Lemur	*Phaner furcifer*
Eastern Fork-marked Lemur	*Phaner furcifer furcifer*
Pale Fork-marked Lemur	*Phaner furcifer pallescens*
Pariente's Fork-marked Lemur	*Phaner furcifer parienti*
Amber Mountain Fork-marked Lemur	*Phaner furcifer electromontis*

Family **Megaladapidae** (Sportive Lemurs)
    Subfamily **Lepilemurinae**

Weasel Sportive Lemur	*Lepilemur mustelinus*
Small-toothed Sportive Lemur	*Lepilemur microdon*
Northern Sportive Lemur	*Lepilemur septentrionalis*
Grey-backed Sportive Lemur	*Lepilemur dorsalis*
Milne-Edwards's Sportive Lemur	*Lepilemur edwardsi*
Red-tailed Sportive Lemur	*Lepilemur ruficaudatus*
White-footed Sportive Lemur	*Lepilemur leucopus*

Family **Lemuridae** ('True' Lemurs)
    Subfamily **Hapalemurinae** (Bamboo or Gentle Lemurs)

Grey Bamboo Lemur	*Hapalemur griseus*
Eastern Grey Bamboo Lemur	*Hapalemur griseus griseus*
Western Grey Bamboo Lemur	*Hapalemur griseus occidentalis*
Alaotra Reed Lemur	*Hapalemur griseus alaotrensis*
Golden Bamboo Lemur	*Hapalemur aureus*
Greater Bamboo Lemur	*Hapalemur simus*

    Subfamily **Lemurinae** ('True' Lemurs)

Ring-tailed Lemur	*Lemur catta*
Mongoose Lemur	*Eulemur mongoz*
Crowned Lemur	*Eulemur coronatus*
Red-bellied Lemur	*Eulemur rubriventer*
Brown Lemur	*Eulemur fulvus*
Common Brown Lemur	*Eulemur fulvus fulvus*
Sanford's Brown Lemur	*Eulemur fulvus sanfordi*
White-fronted Brown Lemur	*Eulemur fulvus albifrons*
Red-fronted Brown Lemur	*Eulemur fulvus rufus*
White-collared Brown Lemur	*Eulemur fulvus albocollaris*
Collared Brown Lemur	*Eulemur fulvus collaris*
Black Lemur	*Eulemur macaco*
Black Lemur	*Eulemur macaco macaco*
Blue-eyed Black Lemur	*Eulemur macaco flavifrons*
Ruffed Lemur	*Varecia variegata*
Black-and-white Ruffed Lemur	*Varecia variegata variegata*
Red Ruffed Lemur	*Varecia variegata rubra*

Family **Indriidae** (Avahis, Sifakas and Indri)

Eastern Avahi	*Avahi laniger*
Western Avahi	*Avahi occidentalis*
Diademed Sifaka	*Propithecus diadema*
Diademed Sifaka	*Propithecus diadema diadema*
Milne-Edwards's Sifaka	*Propithecus diadema edwardsi*
Perrier's Sifaka	*Propithecus diadema perrieri*
Silky Sifaka	*Propithecus diadema candidus*
Verreaux's Sifaka	*Propithecus verreauxi*
Verreaux's Sifaka	*Propithecus verreauxi verreauxi*
Coquerel's Sifaka	*Propithecus verreauxi coquereli*
Decken's Sifaka	*Propithecus verreauxi deckeni*
Crowned Sifaka	*Propithecus verreauxi coronatus*
Golden-crowned Sifaka	*Propithecus tattersalli*
Indri	*Indri indri*

Family **Daubentoniidae** (Aye-aye)

Aye-aye	*Daubentonia madagascariensis*

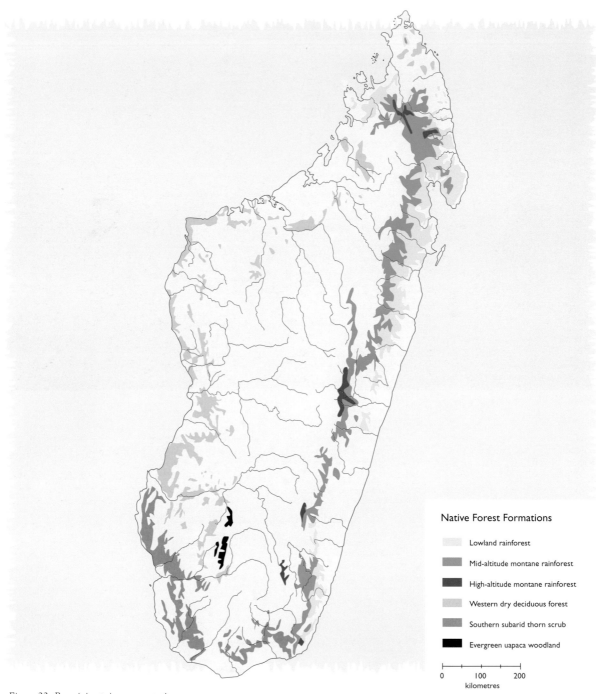

Figure 22. Remaining primary vegetation

Native Forest Formations

Lowland rainforest

Mid-altitude montane rainforest

High-altitude montane rainforest

Western dry deciduous forest

Southern subarid thorn scrub

Evergreen uapaca woodland

0   100   200
kilometres

BATS
ORDER CHIROPTERA

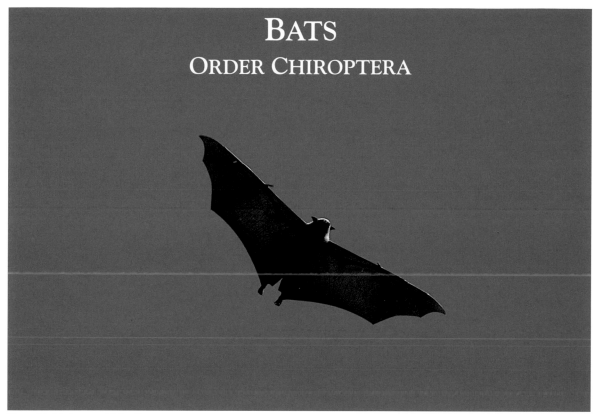

Figure 23. Madagascar Flying Fox.

Bats are amongst the most diverse and geographically dispersed of mammalian orders. They form the largest known aggregations of mammals and may possibly be the most abundant in terms of total number of individuals. Within the class Mammalia, only the order Rodentia contains a greater number of species.

The order Chiroptera is divided into two major suborders: the Megachiroptera, containing a single family Pteropodidae, and the Microchiroptera, which encompasses the other 16 families. These terms can be misleading as some members of the Megachiroptera are smaller than the larger members of the Microchiroptera (Megachiroptera approximately 15 –1,600g; Microchiroptera approximately 2–200g).

Bats are the only mammals with the true capability of powered flight (all other mammals that may be referred to as 'flying', e.g. flying squirrels, are only capable of gliding). This capacity has obviously been a major factor in their wide distribution. They are known to occur on all continents with the exception of Antarctica and are absent only from the polar regions and a handful of very isolated oceanic islands.

Their ability to migrate over large expanses of water has resulted in reduced levels of endemism in the bats of Madagascar when compared to the other mammalian orders present on the island. Approximately 60% of Madagascar's bats are thought to be endemic, whereas 100% of Madagascar's native non-bat mammal species are endemic. Nonetheless, this is a very high degree of endemism when compared to chiropteran assemblages on similar-sized landmasses elsewhere in the world and is testament to Madagascar's relative isolation.

As would be expected from its current geographic position, the majority of chiropteran taxa present on Madagascar, whether endemic or not, owe their origins to founder populations from mainland Africa. However, evidence suggests that the closest affinities of at least six species lie in Asia (*Pteropus rufus*, *Rousettus madagascariensis*, *Emballonura atrata*, *Mormopterus jugularis*, *Scotophilis robustus* and *Otomops madagascariensis*).

Some taxonomic arrangements within the Chiroptera (particularly in the Microchiroptera) are confused: there is much debate among authorities as to the correct classification of various families, genera and species. In many cases taxa have been described under several different names, both at the generic and specific level, while other distinct and isolated taxa have variously been regarded as synonymous.

This has been particularly true of a number of species present on Madagascar, a state of affairs that is hardly surprising as bats are the least studied of the island's mammalian groups. In a great many cases the information available is meagre at best. It seems certain that this situation will clarify as more research is conducted into their distribution and natural history.

There are around 29 currently accepted bat species from Madagascar: 15 of these are endemic at the specific level and a further five at the subspecific level. At higher taxonomic levels only one out of the seven families represented on Madagascar is endemic to the island (Myzopodidae).

SUBORDER MEGACHIROPTERA

Old World Fruit Bats
Family Pteropodidae

The suborder Megachiroptera encompasses a single family, Pteropodidae, restricted to the Old World. This family of exclusively fruit- and nectar-feeding bats contains around 44 genera and more than 166 species. There is considerable size variation within the family: total lengths ranging from around 50mm to over 400mm and weights from 15g to 1,600g. In almost all species the tail is short or rudimentary. In general they lack the complex ultrasonic echolocation systems possessed by some of the Microchiroptera and instead have large eyes and good vision, together with well-developed olfactory senses used for locating food (ripe fruits and flowers). Three species, divided among three genera, are known from Madagascar.

FLYING FOXES genus *Pteropus* Erxleben, 1777

Fruit bats belonging to the genus *Pteropus* are often known as flying foxes and include the largest of all bats. Around 59 species are currently known; some attain wingspreads up to 1.7m and none of them possesses a tail. They originate in South-East Asia, Australasia and islands in the western Pacific and have spread west across to western Indian Ocean islands, although they have not yet reached the African mainland.

Islands in the western Indian Ocean are remarkable for the radiation of this oriental fruit bat genus. Several species occur (or did so until recently) on a variety of islands within the region: Madagascar, *P. rufus*; Mauritius, *P. niger*, *P. subniger*, *P. rodricensis*; Réunion, *P. niger*, *P. subniger*; Rodrigues, *P. rodricensis*; Aldabra, *P. aldabrensis*; Seychelles, *P. seychellensis seychellensis*; Comoros, *P. seychellensis comorensis*; Anjouan and Moheli islands (Comoros), *P. livingstonii*; Mafia Island (off Tanzania), *P. seychellenis comorensis*; and Pemba Island (off Tanzania), *P. voeltzkowi*.

By day they roost in trees, often in large colonies that may contain several hundred individuals. These colonies may use the same roost sites year after year and are sometimes responsible for defoliating their roost trees. During the day the colonies are generally very noisy as individuals jostle for prime roosting places. They are easily disturbed and will often take to the air *en masse* for brief periods if threatened.

Around dusk they leave their roosts in search of fruit trees in which to feed. They are strong fliers and can cover large distances during foraging trips, sometimes flying for more than two hours in one direction (20-30km or more). Flying foxes are almost entirely frugivorous, feeding mainly on fruit pulp and fruit juices, although some also feed on flowers and occasionally leaves. They eat, rest and digest their food at the feeding site before returning to the roost site by dawn.

MADAGASCAR FLYING FOX *Pteropus rufus* Tiedemann, 1808

Malagasy: Fanihy

MEASUREMENTS Total length: 235-270mm. Forearm: 155-175mm. Wingspan: 1,000-1,250mm. Weight: 500-750g.

DESCRIPTION The basic body colour is brown, with the back and anal region being darker. The upper chest and shoulders are much lighter and vary between rufous-brown and yellow-golden brown. The face, crown and nape are also lighter and more yellowish in colour. A pronounced muzzle gives the face a 'fox-like' appearance. The eyes are large and the ears pointed, prominent and widely separated. The wings are slate-grey to black and there is a claw on the second digit in addition to the thumb. This is the largest bat in Madagascar and one of the world's largest species.

DISTRIBUTION The Madagascar Flying Fox is found primarily in eastern rainforest regions, but also in western dry forest regions and some areas in the south. It is absent from the high plateau. It appears to be most common in the humid forests of the east and dry forests of the west, and like many congeners shows a preference for coastal or near-coastal roosting sites, including offshore islands.

In the past two subspecies have been proposed: *P. r. rufus* from eastern, central and northern regions and *P. r. princeps* from the south; but this distinction is no longer considered valid.

BEHAVIOUR During the day, *P. rufus* rests in large colonies, sometimes numbering several thousand, in the canopy of favoured roost trees in primary and secondary forests and occasionally plantations. Many major roosts are located within 100km of the coast.

There is almost constant activity at roost sites: this species is very noisy and colonies are generally heard before they are seen. Their manic cackling chatter intensifies considerably if they are disturbed. The presence of potential predators like the Fossa *Cryptoprocta ferox* may cause the whole colony to take to the air. Large raptors circling above roosts also cause considerable distress, with individuals emitting alarm calls and some taking to the wing. Other than resting, bats often fly to different localities within the roost. When they land, there are generally noisy and mildly agonistic exchanges occur between the incoming individual and those bats already at the site.

During the early hours of the day the bats often hang with their wings outstretched to absorb heat. Later in the day, when ambient temperatures are much higher, they lick the inner and outer wing membranes whilst hanging with them outstretched, so as to reduce their body temperature by evaporation. Further, they may also 'fan' their wings to keep cool: this behaviour is especially common in mothers with suckling or roosting young (E. Long pers. comm.).

Around dusk these bats begin to leave the roost and fly off to foraging sites which may be many kilometres away. In such instances, several 'scouts' fly ahead of the main group to locate suitable fruiting trees. *En route* they may stop to drink. Bats roosting on offshore islands fly to neighbouring islands or back to the mainland to find fruiting trees. They do not navigate by echolocation, but instead have excellent vision.

probable range

Madagascar Flying Fox

The diet of *P. rufus* is dominated by fruit juices: this is obtained by squeezing pieces of fruit pulp in their mouths, swallowing the juice and rejecting the remaining pulp fibres. Very soft fruit pulps may be swallowed, along with some seeds. A wide variety of native fruits are taken; *Ficus* spp. (Moraceae) appear to be particularly relished, although cultivated crops like papayas, lychees and guava are also important. At times of the year when fruit is scarce, pollen and leaf matter, which contain important proteins that an entirely fruit-based diet lacks, are also eaten. Some flowers, for instance *Ceiba* spp. (Bombacaceae), are chewed to obtain juices, nectar and pollen. Flying foxes are important agents of both seed dispersal and pollination in Malagasy forests.

These bats normally invert their bodies to defecate and urinate so as to avoid soiling themselves. However, sexually active males urinate onto their chest and neck and then rub it into the fur with their feet and forearms. Such males will often pursue females by crawling along branches with their thumbs and feet. It is thought that the main birth season is around October: single young are the norm, with twins only produced occasionally.

The Madagascar Flying Fox is widely hunted for food but there is no indication at present that this is causing the overall population to decline. However, continued forest destruction will obviously reduce the number of roost sites and increase the distances between foraging patches, which may begin to have a detrimental affect both locally and *in toto*.

VIEWING *P. rufus* colonies may be encountered in many forest regions in the east and west. However, the most accessible colony is at Berenty Reserve, some two hours drive from Tolagnaro in the south. Here between 800 and 1,800 Madagascar Flying Foxes roost in the small parcel of gallery forest (the numbers varying seasonally). Alternatively, there are colonies on Nosy Ravina just to the south of Nosy Mangabe in the Bay of Antongil and on Nosy Tanikely off Nosy Be in the north-west. There are also numerous colonies on the Masoala Peninsula, but these tend to be rather more difficult to reach.

Colonies should never be approached too closely (less than 100m), as this causes considerable distress to the bats and can be particularly detrimental when females are pregnant or lactating.

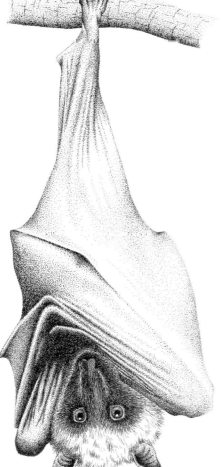

Figure 24. Madagascar Flying Fox roosting.

Figure 25. Madagascar Flying Foxes at roost, Berenty.

STRAW-COLOURED FRUIT BATS genus *Eidolon* Rafinesque, 1815

This genus was once considered to be monotypic, the single recognised species being *Eidolon helvum* which is Africa's most widely distributed fruit bat and is found on the Arabian Peninsula and throughout sub-Saharan Africa. The form represented on Madagascar was regarded as a subspecies, *E. h. dupreanum*. However, this has now been elevated to full species status. Hence the genus now contains two species, *E. helvum* and *E. dupreanum*.

Straw-coloured fruit bats are gregarious and roost by day in colonies in large trees and also some buildings and caves. On mainland Africa some of these colonies are known to attain huge proportions and may contain several hundred thousand bats.

Eidolon has a more pointed head than other fruit bats, and has very long narrow wings adapted for flying long distances during seasonal migrations. The wings are also used for climbing around in branches at roost sites.

MADAGASCAR STRAW-COLOURED FRUIT BAT *Eidolon dupreanum* (Schlegel, 1867)

Malagasy: Fanihy

MEASUREMENTS Total length: 190-215mm. Forearm: 115-130mm. Wingspan: 750-950mm. Weight: 250-340g. Males around 10% larger than females.

DESCRIPTION Sexes similar.

The pelage is short and covers the head, dorsum and venter. On the neck it is slightly longer and more woolly than over the rest of the body. The face in front of and below the eyes is bare. The overall colour of the head and body appears medium grey-brown but the upperparts may be slightly more yellowish while the underparts are often tawny-olive. There are reddish-cinnamon patches forming a collar around the neck; these are more conspicuous in males, but otherwise the sexes are alike. The wings are dark blackish-brown. *E. dupreanum* is larger than its mainland Africa cousin *E. helvum*, and is the second largest bat on Madagascar.

DISTRIBUTION *E. dupreanum* has been recorded in all regions of Madagascar and is the only fruit bat known to occur on the high plateau.

BEHAVIOUR This species spends the day at roost sites around rocky crags and caves or in tall trees. On Madagascar colonies do not appear to reach the enormous sizes of some on the mainland. When roosting these bats tend to be very restless and noisy and spend time regularly moving from place to place. They leave the roost around dusk and set off in search of fruiting trees.

It seems likely that they are quite wide-ranging in their search. Large roosts are rarely close to one another, and are often more than 60km apart, which suggests the bats forage up to 30km away from the roost site. The diet consists primarily of fruit juice which is squeezed out of fruit pulp, together with nectar and the blossoms themselves and some young shoots. The tip of the long tongue is quite 'brush-like' (papillaceous) and obviously helps extract nectar and pollen from deep flowers. The pulp of the *Borassus* palm fruit also seems to be important and soft wood is sometimes chewed to obtain moisture.

It is possible this species has delayed implantation. From mating to birth (i.e. the apparent gestation period) is about nine months but the actual period of embryonic development is only four months. Births generally occur in December and January, the single infant weighing approximately 50g. At this time large numbers of females may gather together to form 'nursery' colonies. *E. dupreanum* is thought to live over 20 years.

VIEWING The Madagascar Straw-coloured Fruit Bat can be encountered at its roost sites in many native forest areas around the island, e.g. in rainforest areas, Ranomafana National Park and Mananara-Nord Biosphere Reserve and Ankarana Special Reserve in deciduous forest areas.

probable range

Madagascar
Straw-coloured Fruit Bat

ROUSETTE FRUIT BATS genus *Rousettus* Gray, 1821

This genus contains nine species which are widely distributed from the Middle East to South-East Asia and as far as New Guinea, Sulawesi and the Solomon Islands. In Africa the genus extends south as far as South Africa including the Comoros and Madagascar where a single species is present.

Some members of *Rousettus* are known to produce very high-pitched sounds using tongue click, and these form the basis of a rudimentary echolocation system. However, unlike members of the suborder Microchiroptera, this is only used for orientation; vision and olfaction remain the primary senses for food detection.

MADAGASCAR ROUSETTE *Rousettus madagascariensis* G. Grandidier, 1928

MEASUREMENTS Total length: 115-145mm. Forearm: 65-75mm. Wingspan: 425-520mm. Weight: 50-80g.

DESCRIPTION The pelage is longish and dense, although less so on the neck, throat and shoulders. The upperparts are greyish-brown with some reddish-brown hues, while the underparts are paler grey-brown. The muzzle is rather pointed and the ears relatively short (see Figure 24). The wings are proportionately broad. *R. madagascariensis* is a small-sized delicate fruit bat and is the smallest representative of its genus in the African region.

Although most authorities now accept *R. madagascariensis* as a valid species, some degree of taxonomic confusion still persists. At times this taxon is referred to as a subspecies of the larger mainland African form *R. lanosus*, thus becoming *R. lanosus madagascariensis*. Furthermore, the closely related congener from the Comoros, *R. obliviosus*, may be referred to as a subspecies of *R. madagascariensis*. However, majority opinion regards all three of these taxa as valid species.

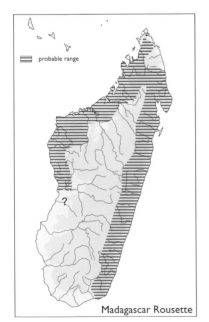

probable range

Madagascar Rousette

DISTRIBUTION This species is endemic to Madagascar and is known to occur throughout the eastern rainforest region from Tolagnaro in the south to the Sambava area in the north. It is also found in deciduous forest areas from the Tsingy de Bemaraha region of the west to the Ankarana Massif in the far north.

BEHAVIOUR Although the Madagascar Rousette is known to roost in large trees and tree holes it prefers caves as roosting sites. Indeed, it may be that the species is restricted to areas where caves are present. Some of the larger colonies, containing 300 to 500 bats, are known from the limestone karst formations at Bemaraha, Namoroka and Ankarana as well as rock outcrops and cave systems in the eastern rainforest belt. During the daytime roost sites are always noisy and the bats restless. There is continuous jockeying for position and fights are not uncommon. That this species seems inextricably associated with cave roost sites suggests it has the rudimentary echolocation capabilities that congeners are known to possess, although this is not known for certain.

R. madagascariensis feeds primarily on fruit juices, soft fruit pulp and nectar. They are known to fly considerable distances each night to find sufficient food.

Single young are most common, but twins are born occasionally after a gestation period of around four months.

VIEWING The cave systems of the Ankarana Massif in northern Madagascar are probably the best and most accessible locality to try to see this species. In the larger caves, colonies of several hundred may gather. It is always best to seek the assistance of a renowned local guide if wishing to do this.

It is also worth investigating any large caves within the eastern rainforest region for this species. There are some near the village of Andasibe where *R. madagascariensis* and several other bat species are known to roost.

SUBORDER MICROCHIROPTERA

The suborder Microchiroptera is far more ecologically diverse than Megachiroptera. It contains 16 families, around 135 genera and over 760 species that are distributed worldwide. Their greatest diversity occurs in tropical regions – species richness decreases with increasing latitude. Six families from this suborder are represented on Madagascar but only one of these, Myzopodidae, is endemic.

All members of this suborder possess an echolocation system which is used for both orientation and prey capture. The degree of use and importance is highly variable from species to species. Most echolocation calls are ultrasonic, that is, beyond the range of 'normal' human hearing. These sounds are produced by contractions of the muscles in the larynx and are emitted by most bats from the mouth. The calls are characterised by their frequency or pitch, duration and intensity or loudness.

Sheath-tailed Bats
Family Emballonuridae

This family contains around 50 species arranged in 13 recent genera that are widely distributed in tropical and subtropical regions. There are just two representatives known from Madagascar. Sheath-tailed bats are characterised by a shortish tail which extends freely beyond the interfemoral membrane, but is retracted into a sheath in the membrane during flight. The males of a number of species have small glandular wing sacs, while others have pungent throat glands: it is assumed secretions from these are used to attract females.

OLD WORLD SHEATH-TAILED BATS genus *Emballonura* Temminck, 1838

A genus of South-East Asian origin containing ten species, only one of which occurs on Madagascar. This is the only genus within the family with two pairs of upper incisors. Wing sacs are absent.

MADAGASCAR SHEATH-TAILED BAT *Emballonura atrata* Peters, 1874

Other name: Peters's Sheath-tailed Bat.

MEASUREMENTS Total length: c. 55-60mm. Forearm: c. 37-40mm. Wingspan: 268mm*. Weight: 4-5g.
* based on a single specimen

possible range

Madagascar
Sheath-tailed Bat

DESCRIPTION A small bat that is uniformly dark slate-grey to black in coloration but generally slightly paler underneath. Nasal appendages are poorly developed and the snout is quite pointed. The ears are prominent, broad and rounded, with a distinct 'notch' near their tip.

DISTRIBUTION This species is endemic to Madagascar. It has been recorded in central-eastern and north-eastern rainforest regions, the Sambirano region in the north-west and in areas between Toliara and Tolagnaro in the extreme south.

BEHAVIOUR The Madagascar Sheath-tailed Bat is known to roost in caves, although invariably quite close to the entrance in the twilight zone. It has also been known to roost in buildings and is often associated with *Triaenops* and *Miniopterus* species. The diet consists principally of insects.

Figure 26. Madagascar Rousettes, near Andasibe.

TOMB BATS genus *Taphozous* E. Geoffroy, 1818

Tomb bats have a wide distribution across Africa, Asia and Australasia. A total of 13 species are currently recognised including a single species from Madagascar. This group was given its vernacular name by scientists accompanying Napoleon on his campaigns to Egypt, who first discovered the animals in the burial chambers of the pyramids.

A wing pocket or pouch is present in all species and most also have a glandular sac in the lower neck, which is more apparent in males than females and is sometimes completely absent in the latter. They are found in a variety of habitats from rainforest to open country and get their name from their habit of roosting in tombs, although they will also utilise buildings, rocky crevices and shallow caverns. They are often highly colonial.

MAURITIAN TOMB BAT *Taphozous mauritianus* E. Geoffroy, 1818

MEASUREMENTS Total length: 80-90mm*. Forearm: 60-65mm. Wingspan: not measured. Weight: 20-30g*.
  * estimated measurement

DESCRIPTION A small to medium-sized bat with pale brownish-grey upperparts and head. The underparts are much paler grey and sometimes creamy-white. Juveniles are generally a darker grey-brown than the adults. The head is quite flattish and triangular, and the face bare below and in front of the eyes. The ears are broad and moderately rounded.

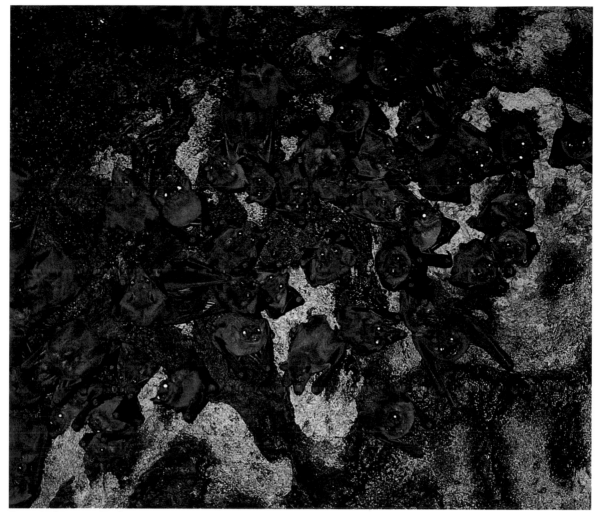

Figure 27. Mauritian Tomb Bats roosting in caves, Ankarana.

DISTRIBUTION As its specific name suggests, this species was originally described from the island of Mauritius. It is now known to occur throughout sub-Saharan Africa south to the Cape, as well as Mauritius, Réunion, Assumption Island, Aldabra and Madagascar. On Madagascar, *T. mauritianus* is distributed throughout all regions, including the central highlands.

BEHAVIOUR During the day this species rests on a variety of vertical surfaces including tree trunks (particularly palms), rock faces and the walls of buildings. Preferred sites give overhead shelter from the sun and rain. When disturbed this species moves quickly sideways in a crab-like manner or will fly off to a neighbouring site.

The Mauritian Tomb Bat hunts mainly after dark, often hawking for insects around lights in urban areas, but will also take insects that may pass within easy reach while it is resting. It is not clear whether echolocation is well developed but eyesight seems to play an important role as the species roosts in broad daylight. Some tomb bats are highly colonial at roost; however, *T. mauritianus* is most likely to be encountered in single pairs or a number of pairs, but occasionally also in groups of up to 30 individuals (fig. 27).

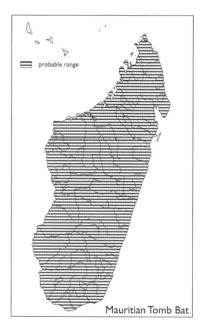

probable range

Mauritian Tomb Bat

49

Slit-faced Bats
Family Nycteridae

Nycteridae is a monogeneric family, the single genus being *Nycteris* which is found throughout Africa, the eastern Mediterranean and across Asia as far as Indonesia. Slit-faced bats (sometimes called hollow-faced bats) are also characterised by obvious folds of skin flanking a groove containing the nostrils and a deep pit between the eyes. The ears are typically large. These bats are unique amongst mammals in having a T-shaped tail.

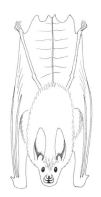

SLIT-FACED BATS genus *Nycteris* G. Cuvier and E. Geoffroy, 1795

This single genus contains 14 species including one endemic species from Madagascar. All are insectivorous/carnivorous, the larger taxa being capable of taking arthropods like spiders and scorpions. They roost either singly or in small groups and probably give birth twice per year.

MADAGASCAR SLIT-FACED BAT *Nycteris madagascariensis* G. Grandidier, 1937

possible range

Madagascar
Slit-faced Bat

MEASUREMENTS Total length: around 115mm. Forearm: 50-52mm. Wingspan: not measured. Weight: 15-20g*.
*estimated measurement

DESCRIPTION A small to medium-sized bat with longish pelage. The upperparts are reddish-brown, while the underparts are predominantly grey. This species is recognisable by its very large ears and distinctive slit in the muzzle with folds of skin either side.

DISTRIBUTION In the past, this species has variously been regarded as synonymous with Egyptian Slit-faced Bat *N. thebaica* from mainland Africa, Arabia and the Middle East or Dobson's Slit-faced Bat *N. macrotis* from sub-Saharan Africa south to Angola. However, it is now accepted by most authorities to be a valid species which is endemic. Within Madagascar the distribution of *N. madagascariensis* appears to be very localised and it may be restricted to the northern part of the island. The type specimen was probably collected from the Irodo region ('Valley of Rodo') north of Analamera and the species is also known to occur in the nearby Ankarana Massif.

BEHAVIOUR Very little is known of the behaviour and ecology of this species. Its preferred roost sites include caves and large hollow trees. It is insectivorous.

Old World Leaf-nosed Bats
Family Hipposideridae

A widely distributed family that occurs throughout the Old World tropics from Africa, through Asia, South-East Asia and into Australasia. There are at least 77 species arranged between nine genera. These bats are easily recognisable by their well-defined and elaborate nose-leaf and large pointed ears. They are closely related to the horseshoe bats (family Rhinolophidae) but lack the well-defined lancet on the nose-leaf and have a different ear and foot structure. Both families are unusual in that they emit ultrasounds from their nostrils, where the basal portion of the nose-leaf acts like a megaphone.

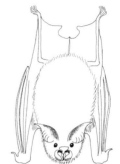

OLD WORLD LEAF-NOSED BATS genus *Hipposideros* Gray, 1831

This is by far the largest genus in the family Hipposideridae and contains 55 species, only one of which occurs on Madagascar. Their diet is dominated by large insects and other arthropods, although very large individuals are also capable of tackling vertebrate prey. They roost mainly in caves, but will also use other similar shelters including buildings. A few species are known to roost singly, but most are colonial.

COMMERSON'S LEAF-NOSED BAT *Hipposideros commersoni* (E. Geoffroy, 1813)

MEASUREMENTS Total length: 110-145mm. Forearm: 85-95mm. Wingspan: 540-560mm. Weight: 40-80g.

probable range

Commerson's
Leaf-nosed Bat

DESCRIPTION The upperparts and head are pale grey-brown to reddish-brown, while the underparts are pale tawny. The ears are very large, falcate and rounded at the tips. The nose-leaf is large, elaborate and prominent. *H. commersoni* is larger than the other leaf-nosed bats on Madagascar and one of the largest species in the suborder Microchiroptera. Five subspecies have been proposed (see below), the representative from Madagascar, *H.c.commersoni*, being one of the smallest. Males are generally slightly larger than females.

DISTRIBUTION This species is divided into five subspecies by some authorities: the nominate race, *H. c. commersoni*, is endemic to Madagascar; *H. c. thomensis* is restricted to São Tomé Island and Principe Island on the Equator off the coast of Gabon; *H. c. marungensis* occurs throughout East Africa and south to South Africa and Namibia; *H. c. gigas* is found throughout equatorial West Africa and *H. c. niangarae* is restricted to the Niangara region of the Congo.

In Madagascar, *H. c. commersoni* is known to occur throughout northern, eastern, western and southern regions, although it appears less common on the high plateau.

BEHAVIOUR The preferred roosts of this subspecies include caves and hollow trees, although it will also utilise the open roofs of rural buildings (fig. 28). On mainland Africa *H. commersoni* has been found in colonies numbering several hundred, but it is not known whether such large aggregations occur on Madagascar where most colonies contain fewer than 20 individuals. Each bat usually roosts slightly apart – at wing-tip distance – from it neighbour, rather than forming a tight cluster.

Commerson's Leaf-nosed Bat generally hunts in the lower levels of the forest, often hawking along trails and in similar open areas for insects such as beetles, cicadas, cockroaches and termites. Some larvae from the inside of wild fruits may also be taken. This bat will often return to its roost to consume larger prey items, the site being within an established feeding territory that it regularly patrols.

VIEWING This bat may be encountered around the campsites and buildings in the Kirindy Forest and at Ampijoroa Forestry Station.

Figure 28. Commerson's Leaf-nosed Bat.

TRIDENT OR TRIPLE LEAF-NOSED BATS genus *Triaenops* Dobson, 1871

This genus resembles *Hipposideros*, but differs in the features of the nose-leaf: in *Triaenops* there is a trident-shaped membranous process which is absent in *Hipposideros*. The genus is distributed throughout East Africa, north into Ethiopia, Somalia, around the coast of the Arabian Peninsula and up into Iran and southern Pakistan. How many species the genus contains is a matter of conjecture; depending on the authority consulted, between two and five species are recognised.

TROUESSART'S TRIDENT BAT *Triaenops furculus* Trouessart, 1906

MEASUREMENTS Total length: 60-75mm. Forearm: 42-45mm. Wingspan: 265-280mm. Weight: 4-7g.

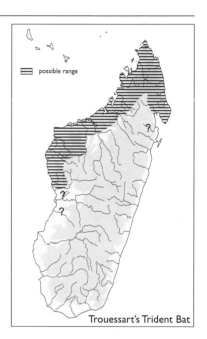

possible range

Trouessart's Trident Bat

DESCRIPTION This is a relatively small trident bat. The basic colour is drab brown to grey, although some individuals have russet tinges. The ears are moderately large, broad at their bases, slightly falcate and quite pointed at their tips.

The taxon *T. aurita* has been proposed as a distinct species, although it is only known from the type specimen collected in Madagascar. Most authorities regard *T. aurita* as synonymous with *T. furculus*.

DISTRIBUTION Endemic to the Madagascar region. On Madagascar it appears to be restricted to western and northern regions. The type specimen comes from Namoroka south of Mahajanga in the west. Also known to occur on Picard, Aldabra and Cosmoledo Islands.

BEHAVIOUR Trouessart's Trident Bat roost in caves, often in large mixed-species colonies that include *Miniopterus*, *Myotis* and *Otomops* species. They often emerge before total darkness and may hunt close to the ground. The diet consists mainly of insects but may include other small arthropods.

RUFOUS TRIDENT BAT *Triaenops rufus* Milne-Edwards, 1881

MEASUREMENTS Total length: 85-90mm. Forearm: 50-55mm. Wingspan: not measured. Weight: 8-10g*. *estimated measurement.

possible range

Rufous Trident Bat

DESCRIPTION The taxonomy of this particular bat is rather confused. Specimens from eastern Madagascar are pale grey to reddish-brown and were originally described as *T. rufus* and *T. humbloti* (these two taxa later being regarded as synonymous). More drab grey-brown specimens from mainland Africa and elsewhere have been described as the Persian Trident Bat (*T. persicus*). It has since been suggested that *T. rufus* should be regarded as a subspecies of *T. persicus*.

DISTRIBUTION In Madagascar *T. rufus* is found in both eastern and western regions: in the east it is found from Tolagnaro in the south to the Maroantsetra area in the north, while in the west it has been recorded from the Morondava region to Ankarana in the far north. *T. persicus* is far more widespread and is found from southern Pakistan, through Oman and Yemen, into Egypt and East Africa from Ethiopia to Mozambique.

BEHAVIOUR Little is known about this species's behaviour and ecology. It roosts in caves or equivalent sites offering similar protection, often in mixed colonies which may number several hundred. Its diet is mainly insect-based, but also includes other small arthropods.

Figure 29. Sucker-footed Bat.

Sucker-footed Bat
Family Myzopodidae

This family consists of a single species. The common name is derived from peculiar suction discs that are present on the wrists and ankles. However, unlike the convergent adaptations found on disc-winged bats (family Thyropteridae) from South America, the suckers of this bat are not on stalks and may be less efficient at supporting the bat's weight.

SUCKER-FOOTED BAT genus *Myzopoda* Milne-Edwards and A. Grandidier, 1878

This genus contains a single species that is now restricted to Madagascar. Fossil evidence indicates that *Myzopoda* once occurred on the African mainland, although it is not clear when it died out there.

SUCKER-FOOTED BAT *Myzopoda aurita* Milne-Edwards and A. Grandidier, 1878

Other name: Golden Bat.

MEASUREMENTS Total length: 105-125mm. Forearm: 45-50mm. Wingspan: not measured. Weight: 8-10g.

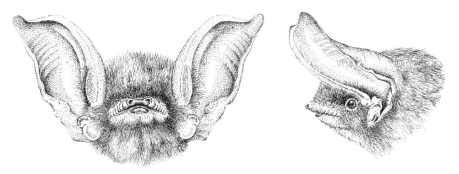

DESCRIPTION The pelage is moderately dense and mid-brown to golden-brown, with some weak russet tinges. The most conspicuous features of M. *aurita* are the suction pads on the thumbs and soles (see illustration on p.58). The thumb also has a small vestigial claw. The ears are very large (30-35mm in length) with a tragus, and have a unique small mushroom-shaped process at their base, the function of which is not clear. The upper lip extends significantly beyond the lower.

DISTRIBUTION This species is endemic to Madagascar, where it seems to be restricted to eastern rainforest regions. There have probably been fewer than 20 records from localities in the east – Marojejy Massif, Maroantsetra, Mananara, Mahambo, Toamasina, Mananjary and north of Tolagnaro. There is also a single record from western Madagascar near Mahajanga. It would appear to be rare throughout its range.

BEHAVIOUR The suction pads possessed by this species allow it to cling to smooth vertical surfaces. These peculiar organs also contain glands that secrete directly onto the surface of the suction pads and presumably help adhesion, such that its entire body weight can be supported. It has been suggested that the Sucker-footed Bat roosts exclusively in the leaves of the Traveller's Tree *Ravenala madagascariensis* but this belief is based on a single observation. It seems highly likely that a variety of other palm species and similar types of vegetation are also used (fig. 29). M. *aurita* roosts with its head uppermost and uses its stiff projecting tail as a prop.

This species possesses a complex echolocation system and produces remarkably long calls. These are used to hunt insects, in particular small moths (Microlepidoptera).

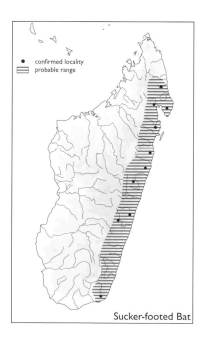

confirmed locality
probable range

Sucker-footed Bat

Vespertilionid Bats
Family Vespertilionidae

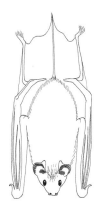

This is the most abundant and widespread family of bats and contains 42 genera and at least 355 species. They are found throughout the world with the exception of the polar regions and some very remote islands, and have colonised all habitats from arid deserts to rainforests and to elevations at the limits of tree growth. Vespertilionid bats are characterised by a tail which is completely, or almost completely, contained within the tail membrane (interfemoral).

On Madagascar the family is represented by five genera arranged between two subfamilies: *Myotis*, *Pipistrellus*, *Eptesicus* and *Scotophilus* all belong to the subfamily Vespertilioninae, while *Miniopterus* is included in its own subfamily Miniopterinae.

Subfamily Vespertilioninae

MOUSE-EARED BATS genus *Myotis* Kaup, 1829

The genus *Myotis* is divided among at least four subgenera that between them contain some 83 known species: *Myotis* is probably the most widely distributed mammalian genus other than our own, *Homo*. Most members of the genus are insectivorous, but at least one species (*M. vivesi*) and possibly two others feed on fish. In Madagascar this genus is represented by a single endemic species.

MALAGASY MOUSE-EARED BAT *Myotis goudoti* A. Smith, 1834

MEASUREMENTS Total length: 90-100mm. Forearm: 37-40mm. Wingspan: not measured. Weight: 5-6g.

possible range

Malagasy Mouse-eared Bat

DESCRIPTION The upperparts are sombre brown, while the underparts are paler. The head appears somewhat flattened and the muzzle is short. The ears are large and rounded and the tragus is erect and tapering.

DISTRIBUTION Two subspecies are generally recognised: M. *goudoti goudoti*, which is endemic to Madagascar and distributed in the east, west and south-west, and M. *goudoti anjouanensis*, which is restricted to Anjouan Island in the Comoros.

BEHAVIOUR This species roosts in small colonies, sometimes with other species, for instance *Miniopterus manavi*. It feeds primarily on insects. No other aspects of its behaviour and ecology are known.

PIPISTRELLE BATS genus *Pipistrellus* Kaup, 1829

Pipistrellus is large genus that is divided into seven subgenera containing at least 60 species. Which species occur on Madagascar has yet to be accurately determined. In the past, pipistrelles on the island have been identified as a subpopulation of the Banana Bat (*Pipistrellus nanus*) which is found throughout sub-Saharan Africa.

However, it is now suspected that at least two, and probably three, different *Pipistrellus* species are represented on Madagascar. One species is certainly closely related to *P. nanus*, but differs in its dentition and stucture of the penial bone (M. Göpfert pers. comm.). The second species appears to exhibit close links to the 'kuhlii-group' of pipistrelles – its skull and bacular morphology are very similar to that of *P. kuhlii* from South Africa.

The third taxon probably represents an undescribed species. On the basis of dentition and bacular morphology, it shows some resemblance to the 'pipistrellus-group' of the genus and but appears to have its closest links with species in the oriental region. Indeed this taxon may be sufficiently distinct from *Pipistrellus* to warrant the creation of its own monotypic genus (M. Göpfert pers. comm.).

It is obvious that further research is necessary before the specific identity of pipistrelles in Madagascar can be accurately determined.

probable range

Pipistrelle Bats

SEROTINES OR BROWN BATS genus *Eptesicus* Rafinesque, 1820

This genus is similar to *Pipistrellus*, some authorities maintaining that differentiation is only warranted at the subgeneric level. It is divided into two subgenera that contain a total of at least 18 species.

MADAGASCAR SEROTINE *Eptesicus matroka* Thomas and Schwann, 1905

MEASUREMENTS Total length: 75-90mm. Forearm: 30-35mm. Wingspan: 220-255mm. Weight: 4-9g.

probable range

Madagascar Serotine

DESCRIPTION This species shows considerable variation in both size and colour. Females are generally slightly larger than males. The upperparts are shades of yellowish-brown, while the underparts are paler yellowish-white. In the past *Eptesicus* specimens from Madagascar have been documented under various specific names – *pusillus*, *humbloti* and *capensis* – all of which are now considered to be *E. matroka*.

DISTRIBUTION This species is endemic to Madagascar and is widely distributed throughout the island.

BEHAVIOUR The Madagascar Serotine roosts in small numbers under the bark of trees or the eaves of buildings. It generally flies at a height of 10-15m and often follows the same route around the tree canopy. It is entirely insectivorous. Females usually give birth to one, two or exceptionally three young.

SOMALI SEROTINE *Eptesicus somalicus* (Thomas, 1901)

Somali Serotine

Malagasy race *Eptesicus somalicus malagasyensis* Peterson *et al.* 1995

MEASUREMENTS Total length: c. 85mm. Forearm: c. 30mm. Wingspan: c. 225mm. Weight: c. 9g.

DESCRIPTION This is a recently described subspecies that is slightly larger than the nominate race, *E. s. somalicus*. The nominate race tends to be sombre brown in colour, whereas *E. s. malagasyensis* has some reddish-brown hues.

DISTRIBUTION The nominate race is found from East Africa south to Mozambique and Namibia. The endemic Malagasy race *malagasyensis* is known only from the Sakaraha region to the north-east of Toliara in south-west Madagascar. It is the only *Eptesicus* species known from the subarid southern region of the island.

BEHAVIOUR The type specimen was collected in palm savanna and it is assumed this subspecies is generally associated with this habitat. It is suspected to feed on insects, as other serotines do. No other aspects of the behaviour and ecology of this bat are currently known.

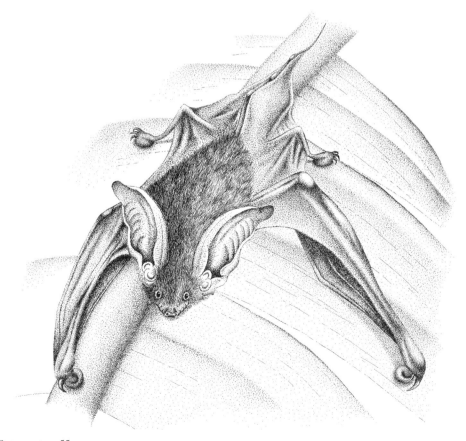

Sucker-footed Bat – see page 55.

HOUSE OR YELLOW BATS genus *Scotophilus* Leach, 1821

A genus containing some 10 species that are widely distributed throughout Africa, Asia and South-East Asia. Their name is derived from the common habit of roosting in buildings and house attics, although natural cavities in trees and palms are also used. Most species roost in small colonies of 20 or less.

There is considerable controversy regarding the systematics of this genus, especially as to whether several mainland African taxa are conspecific with *S. borbonicus* from the Mascarene Islands and Madagascar. Two members of this genus have been recorded in Madagascar.

Scotophilus robustus Milne-Edwards 1881

MEASUREMENTS Total length: 135-170mm. Forearm: 60-65mm. Wingspan: not measured. Weight: not measured.

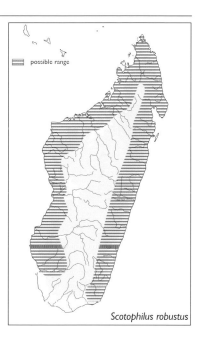

possible range

Scotophilus robustus

DESCRIPTION A largish, heavy- bodied species with a robust head. It is mid-brown to yellowish-brown in colour, the underparts generally being paler. The jaws and teeth are powerful. In the past this species has been regarded as a subspecies of the African Yellow House Bat *S. dinganii* but is now considered to be distinct.

DISTRIBUTION *S. robustus* is endemic to Madagascar. It has been recorded in the deciduous forests of Zombitse in the south and the rainforest regions between Andasibe and Toamasina, but no further information on its distribution is available.

BEHAVIOUR In common with congeners this species is known to roost in and around human habitation, although natural sites are also used. Leaves its roosting sites around dusk and is a strong flier. Hunting flights occur between three and 12 meters above the ground. Insects, including, beetles, moths and termites are the mainstay of the diet. No other behavioural or ecological information is available.

Scotophilus borbonicus (E. Geoffroy, 1803)

MEASUREMENTS Total length: not measured. Forearm: 45.5mm*. Wingspan: not measured. Weight: not measured.
*from single specimen

DESCRIPTION The upperparts are light brown or beige, while the underparts are much paler and often appear whitish.

DISTRIBUTION This species was originally described from Réunion and is now thought to be extinct on that island. There are also records from the neighbouring Mascarene island of Mauritius, but these are now known to be erroneous. It is possible that this species is now restricted to Madagascar where it has been caught in both eastern and western regions, but it appears to be rare.

BEHAVIOUR The behaviour and ecology of this species are unknown.

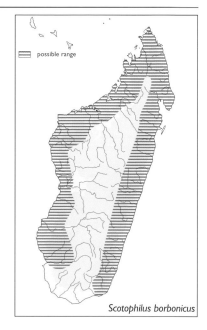

possible range

Scotophilus borbonicus

Subfamily Miniopterinae

LONG-FINGERED AND BENT-WINGED BATS genus *Miniopterus* Bonaparte, 1837

This genus has one of the broadest distributions of any in the Old World. It occurs widely across Europe, Africa, Asia, South-East Asia and Australasia. The second finger bone of the longest finger (third finger) is around three times the length of the first finger bone. This feature gives the genus one of its vernacular names. At rest these bats hang by their hind feet and the third finger is folded back.

All members of the genus are superficially very similar, often the only apparent differences being in size. As a result, the taxonomy of *Miniopterus* is highly confused, the number of species described varying between 12 and 23 depending on the authority consulted. One major reason for these discrepancies is the treatment given to the species *M. schreibersi*: some describe all populations from southern Europe to Africa to Japan and South-East Asia as a single species, whereas others differentiate a number of populations as full species. Only further taxonomic investigation will clarify this situation.

Miniopterus majori Thomas, 1906

MEASUREMENTS Total length: 89-100mm*. Forearm: 42-47mm. Wingspan: not measured. Weight: 8-10g.
*estimated measurement

Miniopterus majori

DESCRIPTION Originally described as an endemic taxon, this species was later regarded as a subspecies of *M. schreibersi* but is now once again accepted as a good species. The pelage is greyish-brown and generally slightly paler on the ventral side. The head is rounded and the muzzle short. The ears are moderately large and squarish in shape; the tragus is kidney-shaped and prominent.

DISTRIBUTION This species is endemic to Madagascar and its neighbouring islands. In Madagascar it is distributed throughout the eastern region and is also found at many localities on the high plateau (for example Antsirabe, Ambositra, Betsileo area). There are also records south of Toliara in the south-west.

BEHAVIOUR This is mainly a cave-dwelling species. It is gregarious and often roosts in mixed colonies with congeners such as *M. fraterculus* and *M. manavi*. Caves are an essential habitat requirement, *M. majori* preferring to hang from the ceiling in tightly packed groups. On occasions this bat has also been recorded in tree holes. It is a very rapid flier and tends to fly high and swoops in the air when hunting. Insects like small beetles and moths are its main prey.

Miniopterus manavi Thomas, 1906

MEASUREMENTS Total length: 90-110mm. Forearm: 35-40mm. Wingspan: not measured. Weight: 6-8g*.
*estimated measurement

possible range

Miniopterus manavi

DESCRIPTION This species was originally described as M. *manavi* from Madagascar, but was subsequently regarded as a subspecies of M. *minor* from mainland Africa. More recent research has deemed that the two taxa do indeed warrant separation as full species.

The pelage is variously greyish-brown to reddish-brown. The ears are angular and the tragus prominent. This is the smallest *Miniopterus* species in Madagascar and one of the smallest members of the genus as a whole.

DISTRIBUTION M.*manavi* is restricted to Madagascar and Grand Comoro: in Madagascar it is widely distributed throughout the island including the high plateau.

BEHAVIOUR This species is known to roost in caves and similar environs, often in mixed-species colonies, especially with congeners. It has been reported as the most common and widespread bat in the caves of Ankarana, where it roosts in groups of up to 10 individuals. It feeds on small insects like moths and beetles. The reproductive season may be highly synchronised, the majority of births taking place in October and November. It has been suggested that this species has delayed embryonic development, as do several congeners. All other aspects of its behaviour and ecology remain unknown.

LESSER LONG-FINGERED BAT *Miniopterus fraterculus* Thomas and Schwann, 1906

MEASUREMENTS Total length: 100-115mm. Forearm: 40-45mm. Wingspan: 305-330mm. Weight: 8-12g.

DESCRIPTION The pelage is greyish to greyish-brown.

DISTRIBUTION This species is principally distributed on the African mainland, from South Africa north to Malawi and Zambia and possibly as far as Kenya. On Madagascar it has been recorded in the south, east, north-east and central regions, including Antananarivo.

BEHAVIOUR Aspects of the behaviour and ecology of this species in Madagascar remain unknown.

possible range

Lesser Long-fingered Bat

Miniopterus gleni Peterson *et al.* 1995

possible range

Miniopterus gleni

MEASUREMENTS Total length: 95-100mm*. Forearm: 47-50mm. Wingspan: not measured. Weight: 8-10g*.
*estimated measurement

DESCRIPTION This is one of the larger members of the genus. The pelage is long, soft and sombre brown-grey in colour.

DISTRIBUTION M. *gleni* is a recently described species that is thought to be endemic to Madagascar. It has been recorded in northern, eastern, central and south-western regions of the island.

BEHAVIOUR This species is known to roost together with *Miniopterus majori*, *M. manavi*, *Myotis goudoti*, *Triaenops furculus* and *Otomops madagascariensis*. All other aspects of this species's behaviour and ecology are unknown.

Free-tailed Bats
Family Molossidae

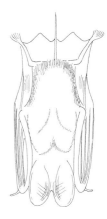

Free-tailed bats are widely distributed in warm and tropical areas around the world. Most are robust and small to medium-sized. A large proportion of their thick tail projects beyond the tail (interfemoral) membrane, a feature which gives rise to their common name. The membranes are leathery and the wings long and narrow for fast flying. The ears have a tragus and are usually joined across the forehead and directed forward.

The taxonomy of this family is the subject of much conjecture, different authorities proposing alternative arrangements of subfamilies and subgenera: at least 80 species are currently recognised. Following the most recent revision, the free-tailed bats are represented on Madagascar by eight species divided between three genera, *Mormopterus*, *Tadarida* and *Otomops*, with the genus *Tadarida* being further divided into three subgenera, *Tadarida*, *Chaerephon* and *Mops*.

LITTLE GOBLIN BATS genus *Mormopterus* Peters, 1865

This genus contains ten species with a peculiar global distribution: most species occur in Australasia, but there are other representatives in South America, the Caribbean and on south-west Indian Ocean islands, including at least one species on Madagascar. *Mormopterus* is occasionally treated as a subgenus of *Tadarida*, but majority opinion regards the two as independent. *Mormopterus* is itself further divided into two subgenera, *Mormopterus* and *Micronomus*: only the former is represented on Madagascar. There has been very little study of this genus and what limited information is available principally concerns Australian species.

PETER'S GOBLIN BAT *Mormopterus jugularis* (Peters, 1865)

MEASUREMENTS Total length: 90-95mm. Forearm: 37-40mm. Wingspan: 260-280mm. Weight: c. 10-12g.

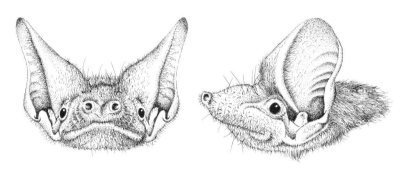

possible range

Peters's Goblin Bat

DESCRIPTION The pelage is soft and dense. Upperparts are greyish-brown to charcoal, while underparts are paler. The muzzle is blunt and slightly upturned, and the ears are large, prominent and broad at their base.

DISTRIBUTION This species is probably endemic to Madagascar. It has been recorded in the east, south-east, south and south-west and has also been found in attics in Antananarivo.

BEHAVIOUR The behaviour and ecology of this species are not known.

[NATAL GOBLIN BAT *Mormopterus acetabulosus* (Herman, 1804)

MEASUREMENTS Total length: 90-95mm. Forearm: 37-40mm. Wingspan: not measured. Weight: c. 10-12g.

DESCRIPTION This species is very similar in size to M. *jugularis*, but is clearly distinct on the basis of ear shape – in M. *acetabulosus* they are triangular while in M. *jugularis* they are rounded. There are also noticeable cranial differences between the two species.

DISTRIBUTION This bat is known only from records in South Africa and Ethiopia on the African mainland and from the Mascarene Islands (Mauritius and Réunion). There have been records of this species on Madagascar but their validity is regarded as questionable.

BEHAVIOUR This species roosts in large aggregations (over 1,000 have been recorded on Réunion) in caves and sometimes buildings. It appears to have the ability to enter torpor and hibernate in response to low temperatures and is able to survive prolonged periods at less than 4°C. This potentially allows it to live at higher elevations than many other species of bat. No further information is available on the behaviour and ecology of this species.]

FREE-TAILED BATS genus *Tadarida* Rafinesque, 1814

The systematics of this genus are the subject of considerable debate. The subgeneric divisions used here, *Chaerephon* and *Mops*, are sometimes regarded as full genera (along with a further subgeneric division, *Nyctinomops*, which is not represented on Madagascar) and the genus *Mormopterus* (see above) is occasionally included as a subgenus within *Tadarida*.

FREE-TAILED BATS subgenus *Tadarida* Rafinesque, 1814

Tadarida is characterised by wrinkled lips, relatively thin jaws and large ears that may be joined by a band of skin across the crown. Some members of the genus form the largest colonies of any warm-blooded vertebrate – large nursery colonies of some species are estimated to contain several million bats.

LARGE FREE-TAILED BAT *Tadarida fulminans* (Thomas, 1903)

• type locality

Large Free-tailed Bat

MEASUREMENTS Total length: 120-130mm*. Forearm: 57-60mm. Wingspan: not measured. Weight: 25-30g*.
*estimated measurement

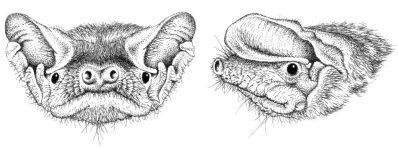

DESCRIPTION The body is dark chestnut-brown dorsally and pale grey to whitish on the chest and belly. The wings are noticeably paler than the body. The head is small and relatively narrow, and the tail is up to 50mm in length.

DISTRIBUTION The type locality of the endemic nominate race, *T. fulminans fulminans*, is near Fianarantsoa in southern-central Madagascar. No other distributional information from Madagascar is available. Elsewhere, another subspecies of *T. fulminans* is found in Central and East Africa as far south as the Transvaal.

BEHAVIOUR A gregarious species that is seldom seen in colonies of more than 20. Rock crevices and small caves are the usual daytime roost sites. This species is a fast and direct flier.

LESSER MASTIFF BATS subgenus *Chaerephon* Dobson, 1874

Chaerephon is sometimes regarded as a distinct genus. The ears are joined by a band of skin across the forehead, which often sports a crest of tufted long straight glandular hairs, which are particularly prevalent in males.

Tadarida (Chaerephon) leucogaster A. Grandidier, 1869

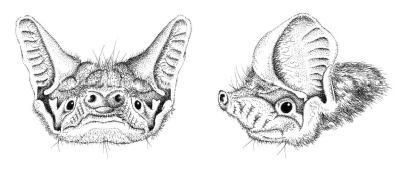

MEASUREMENTS Total length: 75-85mm*. Forearm: 33-38mm. Wingspan: 260-280mm. Weight: 10-15g*. *estimated measurement

possible range

Tadarida (Chaerephon) leucogaster

DESCRIPTION The dorsal and ventral pelage are mid-brown, although the abdominal regions are generally pale greyish-white. The wings are similar in colour to the body. This is the smallest Malagasy representative of this taxonomic group. It is sometimes considered to be a subspecies of *T. pumila*.

DISTRIBUTION This species has been recorded in the Sambirano, western and south-western regions of Madagascar. It is often associated with more open habitat.

BEHAVIOUR The behaviour and ecology of this species remain unknown.

LITTLE FREE-TAILED BAT *Tadarida (Chaerephon) pumila* (Cretzschmar, 1830)

MEASUREMENTS Total length: 85-95mm*. Forearm: 38-41mm. Wingspan: 290-300mm. Weight: 15-20g*. *estimated measurement

DESCRIPTION The pelage of this species is rather variable in colour. In Madagascar, the upperparts are dark brown, with white underparts and a brown throat. In southern Africa the fur ranges from deep blackish-brown upperparts with a paler underside to more brownish upperparts with a broad whitish band extending from the chest down to the anus.

DISTRIBUTION This species occurs from the south-west Arabian Peninsula, through most of sub-Saharan Africa and also on Madagascar and the island of Aldabra. In Madagascar it is found only in the eastern rainforest region and eastern band of the high plateau at elevations between 500m and 1,100m. Records from some deciduous forest areas in the west and south are probably the result of confusion with *Tadarida (Mops) leucostigma*.

BEHAVIOUR *T. pumila* has not been studied on Madagascar. However, research on mainland Africa has revealed that it often roosts singly, but may also form large colonies numbering several hundred in favourable habitats. Roost sites include cracks in trees, rock crevices and roofs of buildings. In some areas, clusters of over 20 females and their single offspring have been found, these 'harems' being attended by a single male.

Various small insects are the primary component of their diet. They generally fly at heights up to 12m and often swoop down suddenly to three or four metres above ground level. The flight is fast and erratic.

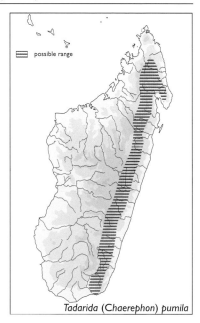

possible range

Tadarida (Chaerephon) pumila

GREATER MASTIFF BATS subgenus *Mops* Lesson, 1842

Mops is regarded as a full genus by some authors. This taxon is characterised by a band of skin joining the ears across the crown, very wrinkled lips, a robust skull and heavy jaw. Cranial and dental morphology distinguishes *Mops* from the subgenera *Tadarida* and *Chaerephon*.

MIDAS FREE-TAILED BAT *Tadarida (Mops) midas* (Sundevall, 1843)

MEASUREMENTS Total length: 150-170mm*. Forearm: 62-63mm. Wingspan: not measured. Weight: 55-60g*. *estimated measurement

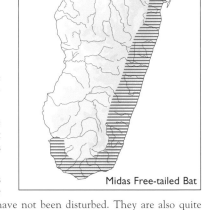

possible range

Midas Free-tailed Bat

DESCRIPTION The upperparts are brown to greyish-brown, while the underparts are slightly paler and more tawny; however, the overall appearance is of fairly uniform coloration. Reddish and orange-red colour phases have also been described.

DISTRIBUTION Two subspecies are recognised on the basis of distribution: the nominate form, *T. midas midas*, occurs from the south-west Arabian Peninsula south through most of the savanna regions of sub-Saharan Africa; *T. midas miarensis* is an endemic subspecies that has been recorded in eastern, southern and south-western regions of Madagascar.

BEHAVIOUR On mainland Africa this species usually prefers roost sites in total darkness such as deep caves, secure tree holes and old attics. Colonies are often large, tightly packed and very noisy. Constant chatter is always audible even when the animals have not been disturbed. They are also quite aggressive and fly swiftly, often at heights of 30-40m. The breeding season appears to be well defined, births occurring between January and February. A single offspring appears to be the norm.

Tadarida (Mops) leucostigma Allen, 1918

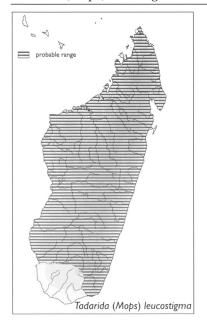

probable range

Tadarida (Mops) leucostigma

MEASUREMENTS Total length: 110-120mm*. Forearm: 41-47mm. Wingspan: 330-360mm. Weight: 30-35g*. *estimated measurement

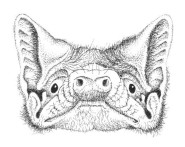

DESCRIPTION The upperparts are brown, while the underparts are almost completely white. This species was originally described as *Mops leucostigma*, then later regarded as a subspecies of the mainland African taxon *T. (M.) condylurus*. It is now recognised by some authorities as a valid species which is endemic.

DISTRIBUTION *T. leucostigma* has been recorded in all regions of the island with the exception of the extreme south.

BEHAVIOUR The behaviour and ecology of this species remain unknown.

LARGE-EARED FREE-TAILED BATS genus *Otomops* Thomas, 1913

This genus contains seven widely distributed species: two from Papua New Guinea, one in the Lesser Sunda islands, one from Java, one from southern India, one from mainland Africa and one from Madagascar. All are medium-large bats with very large ears that are forward-facing and have a series of small dermal projections along their leading edge. There have been few studies of these species and little is known of the genus as a whole.

MADAGASCAR FREE-TAILED BAT *Otomops madagascariensis* Dorst, 1953

MEASUREMENTS Total length: 130-140mm*. Forearm: 60-65mm. Wingspan: 420-450mm. Weight: 20-30g.
*estimated measurement

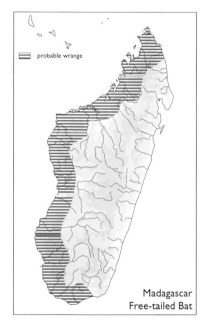

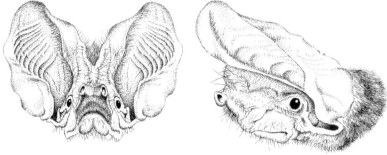

DESCRIPTION A largish bat (males are slightly larger than females) most notable for its peculiarly shaped flattened head and large ears. The upperparts vary from dark brown to reddish-brown, with the underparts generally a slightly paler brown. There may also be a greyish area on the nape and upper dorsal region. The ears are 30-35mm in length and are directed forward at a very oblique angle which makes them highly distinctive.

In the past, *O. madagascariensis* has been regarded by some authorities as a subspecies of Martienssen's Free-tailed Bat *O. martiensseni* of mainland Africa.

DISTRIBUTION This species is endemic to Madagascar, where it appears to be restricted to the north west and south west of the island.

BEHAVIOUR This species is both solitary and gregarious and can occur in large colonies. It roosts in caves, hollow trees and some human made structures. In marine caves to the south of Toliara it has been recorded roosting together with *Triaenops furculus*, *Myotis goudoti*, *Miniopterus manavi*, *Miniopterus majori* and *Miniopterus gleni*. No other aspects of the behaviour and ecology of this species are available.

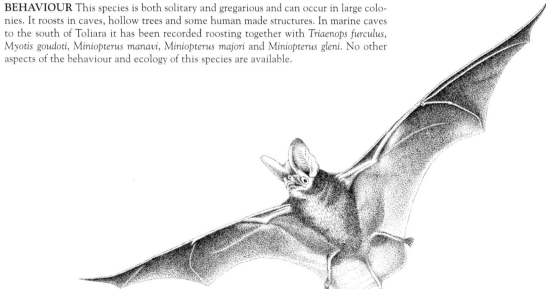

Figure 30. Madagascar Free-tailed Bat.

67

Figure 31. Common Tenrec.

Figure 32. Common Tenrec with young.

INSECTIVORES
ORDER INSECTIVORA

Figure 33. Lowland Streaked Tenrec.

Tenrecs
Family Tenrecidae

The family Tenrecidae comprises 10 genera, divided between three subfamilies – the otter-shrews (Potamogalinae) from west and central Africa, the spiny tenrecs (Tenrecinae) and furred tenrecs (Oryzorictinae) that are endemic to Madagascar. In Madagascar, the Tenrecidae have undergone an extensive adaptive radiation: from two probable founder forms they have diversified to fill insectivore niches occupied elsewhere by several families.

They are also considered to be amongst the most primitive of placental mammals, retaining several basic characteristics that have been lost in more advanced forms. General characteristics include: largely nocturnal activity patterns, variable body temperature (according to ambient temperature), a cloaca (common opening for the anal and uro-genital tracts), a relatively long gestation period, altricial young and undescended testes in males. They were probably the first mammals to arrive on Madagascar and are, therefore, the oldest surviving mammalian lineage on the island.

In general insectivore diversity varies with altitude: different species having different elevational preferences. Mid-altitude levels (1200-1500m) in rainforest areas support the greatest diversity of species.

The taxonomy of the Tenrecidae has become very confused, particularly within the subfamily Oryzorictinae. In the past some species have been described under several different names, while others that are evidently distinct have been lumped together. As more field research takes place this situation should begin to clarify. Furthermore, thorough surveying of the more remote and hitherto unstudied forests in Madagascar is likely to reveal as yet undescribed species.

Spiny Tenrecs
Subfamily Tenrecinae

The spiny tenrecs are all more or less hedgehog-like in appearance, although they have considerably shorter tails than true hedgehogs (Erinaceidae). The subfamily contains five species, arranged in four genera. They range in size from around 80g to 2kg and are widely distributed throughout the various forest types of the island. They are primarily terrestrial, although one species – the Lesser Hedgehog Tenrec *Echinops telfairi* does exhibit semi-arboreal characteristics. Except for *Hemicentetes* species they are mainly solitary although they do sometimes aestivate in small groups.

COMMON TENREC genus *Tenrec* Lacépède, 1799

This genus, which gave its name to the entire family, contains just a single endemic species. The genus *Centetes* is synonymous with *Tenrec*.

COMMON TENREC *Tenrec ecaudatus* (Schreber, 1777)

Other name: Tailless Tenrec
Malagasy: Tandraka, Kelora

MEASUREMENTS Total length: 285-400mm. Head/body length: 265-390mm. Tail length: 10-15mm. Weight: 1-2kg. Males larger than females.

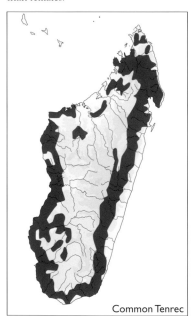

Common Tenrec

DESCRIPTION Adults are rotund with shortish limbs (fig. 31), the hind limbs being longer than the forelimbs. The snout is long and pointed with conspicuous long dark vibrissae. The basic colour is grey-brown, with reddish-brown areas. Some individuals are darker brown on the back and rump. The face and venter are light tan. The pelage is sparse and consists of a mixture of coarse hairs and spine-like hairs, the latter being more apparent on the crown and nape. There are also longer dark guard hairs on the dorsum. The young are much darker, sometimes almost black with the paler cream spines arranged in longitudinal rows, giving an overall streaked appearance (fig. 32). This is the largest tenrec and one of the largest extant insectivores. The specific name implies no tail, although a very short one is actually present. In appearance this species resembles the Moon Rat *Echinosorex gymnurus* from the Malay Peninsula, Sumatra and Borneo.

DISTRIBUTION This species is endemic to Madagascar and common in all areas (except the arid south-west), from sea level to around 900m. It is found in a wide range of habitat types from rainforests to deciduous forests, preferring areas with brush/undergrowth and a source of free-standing water. The Common Tenrec has also been introduced to the Comoros, Seychelles and Mascarene Islands.

BEHAVIOUR Common Tenrecs are mainly nocturnal, activity normally peaking at 18:00–21:00 and at 01:00–05:00 hours. The day is spent in an excavated burrow under tree roots or in a hollow log. They forage in leaf-litter and the very top layers of soil, often vigorously 'rooting' around with their long and powerful snout to break up soil fragments. They are omnivorous, feeding primarily on insects, especially beetle larvae, but also other invertebrates, some fruits and even small vertebrates on occasion. The prey is detected by a combination of smell, sound and touch, the latter from very long, highly sensitive vibrissae that are swept from side to side. This species has better eyesight than other tenrecs but for the most part still relies on its well-developed tactile and olfactory senses. When alarmed or angry Common Tenrecs erect a mane on their upper back, which has longer, coarser hairs than the rest of the body; simultaneously they may emit a low hissing sound in conjunction with various squeaks and squeals.

Common Tenrecs aestivate during the austral winter (dry season, May to October) in response to unfavourable climatic conditions and decreased food availability, although in rainforest areas, where food and temperature fluctuations are less marked, the torpid period is reduced. Aestivation takes place in a long (1-2m) narrow burrow, which is plugged with soil before the tenrec becomes torpid. The breathing rate of torpid individuals drops to 30 breaths per minute, while body temperature fluctuates with ambient temperature and has been known to fall as low as 11°C. Sleep is continuous, the animal being totally reliant on fat reserves during this period.

T. ecaudatus is solitary for most of the year: associations between the sexes are generally brief and occur during the austral spring (October–November). Most births occur during the warm wet season (December–January) after a gestation period of 56 to 64 days, when the invertebrate food base is at its peak.

Reproduction in Common Tenrecs is quite remarkable. They are one of the most prolific eutherian mammals. No less than 32 embryos have been recorded and in captivity 31 young have been successfully reared. In the wild a litter size of 12 to 16 is more normal. These are fed by the mother from 12 pairs of nipples, the most recorded in any mammal. The young are altricial and do not begin to open their eyes until nine days and this is not completed until 14 days. At around 20 to 25 days the young start to take solid food and begin foraging with their mother on the forest floor.

The demand for milk from such litters is clearly very high, so the mother is regularly forced to extend foraging bouts beyond the hours of darkness. Such behaviour undoubtedly has its risks and it may be that the striped coloration of the young increases camouflage and so helps reduce predation. Adult females with young are also darker than males, presumably for the same reason. Nonetheless, infant mortality is high and it is rare to see a female with more than 10 well-developed offspring. The young continue to forage with their mother for three to six weeks and remain together briefly after separation from the mother. The moult to adult coloration begins around 36 days and is accompanied by a shift to a more nocturnal activity pattern. The juvenile streaks completely disappear by 60 days. Between three and four months they become fully grown.

The Common Tenrec is regularly preyed upon by the Fosa *Cryptoprocta ferox* and the large boid snakes belonging to the genera *Sanzinia* and *Acrantophis*.

VIEWING It is possible to encounter this species at night in almost any forest reserve in the west or east, during the warmer, wetter months of the year (November to April). The guides at Analamazaotra Special Reserve, Ranomafana National Park, Montagne d'Ambre National Park, Kirindy Forest and Ampijoroa Forestry Station are adept at locating these animals.

GREATER HEDGEHOG TENREC genus *Setifer* Froriep, 1806

This genus also contains just a single species. As its common name implies, this species closely resembles the Eurasian Hedgehog *Erinaceus europaeus*, although it is appreciably smaller. The genera *Ericulus* and *Dasogale* are synonyms of *Setifer*.

GREATER HEDGEHOG TENREC *Setifer setosus* (Schreber, 1777)

Malagasy: Sokina, Sora, Soky

MEASUREMENTS Total length: 160-225mm. Head/body length: 160-210mm. Tail length: 15mm. Weight: 180-270g.

DESCRIPTION The body is rounded with short legs. Other than the face and underparts, which are covered in sparse hair, the body is completely covered in stiff non-detachable spines. Overall, the colour appears grey-brown (fig. 34). The spines are creamy-white at their base, gradually changing to dark grey-brown towards the tip, with a fine white point. Much darker melanistic forms have also been reported. The snout is moderately long and pointed with many vibrissae up to 75mm in length.

DISTRIBUTION This species is found throughout the island, although it is only sparsely distributed in the extreme south-west. It is probably more common in the rainforest regions of the east than the drier areas in the west. The Greater Hedgehog Tenrec has even colonised some urban areas, including Antananarivo, and is occasionally encountered where there is rubbish.

BEHAVIOUR The Greater Hedgehog Tenrec is nocturnal and omnivorous, taking a wide range of insects, grubs, other invertebrates and fruits as well as scavenging. The majority of foraging takes place at ground level, although this tenrec has been known to climb. Its anti-predator response is the same as a hedgehog's, curling into a tight ball with spines outermost.

The Greater Hedgehog Tenrec excavates short tunnels underneath fallen logs or tangles of tree roots. These end in a leaf-lined nest chamber where the animal sleeps tightly curled with its head tucked underneath its body. There is a specific latrine site close to the burrow entrance. Although generally active throughout the year, individuals

Greater Hedgehog Tenrec

in more seasonal areas, for instance the west and higher elevations in the east, do have the ability to reduce their levels of activity and become torpid for short periods.

Adults appear to be solitary, with temporary associations between the sexes only occurring during the breeding season. Individuals communicate through series of grunts, squeaks and chirps. Mating takes place between late September and mid-October. A week or so prior to birth the female increases her nest-building activities. A litter of one to four (average three) is born after a gestation period which may vary according to ambient conditions: higher temperatures possibly result in a shorter gestation period. Reported gestation periods are between 51 and 69 days. The mother closely tends the young for the first two weeks; their eyes begin to open at nine days and are fully open at 14 days. At this time they begin to take solid food and accompany their mother outside the burrow on short foraging excursions.

This species is eaten by large snakes, for instance the Madagascar Tree Boa *Sanzinia madagascariensis* (fig. 35) and Madagascar Ground Boa *Acrantophis madagascariensis*, and by the island's largest mammalian carnivore, the Fosa *Cryptoprocta ferox*.

VIEWING This species can be seen on night walks in many of the popular reserves, for example: Montagne d'Ambre National Park, Nosy Mangabe Special Reserve, Analamazaotra Special Reserve, Ranomafana National Park, Berenty Reserve, Ankarana Special Reserve, Ampijoroa Forestry Station and Kirindy Forest.

Figure 34. Greater Hedgehog Tenrec.

Figure 35. Greater Hedgehog Tenrec predated by Malagasy Tree Boa, Sanzinia madagascariensis.

Figure 36. Lesser Hedgehog Tenrec.

Figure 37. Lesser Hedgehog Tenrec, climbing in spiny forest, Ifaty

LESSER HEDGEHOG TENREC genus *Echinops* Martin, 1838

The montypic genus *Echinops* is morphologically similar to *Setifer*, but internally there are dental differences. *Echinops* has the most reduced dentition within the Tenrecidae.

LESSER HEDGEHOG TENREC *Echinops telfairi* Martin, 1838

Malagasy: Tambotriky, Tanibodrika

MEASUREMENTS Total length: 140-180mm. Head/body length: 140-180mm. Tail length: around 10mm. Weight: 110-230g.

Lesser Hedgehog Tenrec

DESCRIPTION The coloration is variable, ranging from very pale grey to deep slate-grey. The face and underparts are generally paler, sometimes almost white (fig. 36). The species is outwardly very similar in appearance to the Greater Hedgehog Tenrec *Setifer setosus*, but smaller and with a slightly less pointed snout. The Lesser Hedgehog Tenrec has only two molars in each jaw (total number of teeth 32), while the Greater Hedgehog Tenrec has three molars in each jaw (total number of teeth 36).

DISTRIBUTION *E. telfairi* is confined to the dry deciduous forest areas of western Madagascar and the xerophytic spiny forest and gallery forest regions of south-west Madagascar.

BEHAVIOUR The Lesser Hedgehog Tenrec is nocturnal and semi-arboreal. Surprisingly perhaps for an animal of rotund shape and seemingly ponderous gait, it is quite agile and capable of climbing along quite thin branches (fig. 37), when the short tail is often used as a brace. It forages alone in dense shrubbery, both on the ground and in branches, and feeds on insects and fruits.

South-west Madagascar regularly experiences long periods of drought. During such dry seasons, when food is scarce, the Lesser Hedgehog Tenrec becomes torpid for between three and five months (May to September). This usually takes place in a hollow log or tree hole several metres off the ground: the nest is lined with grasses and leaves that are carried in the mouth and arranged to form a neat cup. The Lesser Hedgehog Tenrec aestivates either individually or in small groups of two or three. The animals sleep in a tightly curled ball. The anti-predator response is similar to the Greater Hedgehog Tenrec although this species rolls into a tighter ball and also emits hisses and grinds its teeth.

Males may be very aggressive towards one another, but males and females are more tolerant when together. Mating begins in October, shortly after emergence from torpor. Females begin building the natal nest about a week before birth and continue to add to the nest even after the young have been born. The gestation period is 60 to 68 days, with the litter size varying between one and ten, seven being average. The young weigh less than 10g at birth and are naked. They open their eyes between seven and nine days and at ten days will follow the mother to the nest entrance. The female will retrieve any offspring that fall from the nest. They begin to take solid food at 14 days, are weaned at 18 days and become fully independent in just over a month. Sexual maturity is reached after their first period of aestivation.

VIEWING Beza Mahafaly Special Reserve and the spiny forest areas around Ifaty, north of Toliara, are probably the best places to try to see this tenrec.

STREAKED TENRECS genus *Hemicentetes* Mivart, 1871

This genus contains two small but highly distinctive tenrecs that are broadly similar in appearance. They are immediately recognisable by their characteristic colour and body markings: blackish-brown with either yellowish or creamy-white longitudinal stripes.

If threatened, streaked tenrecs produce an audible rattling sound from a specialised patch of quills on the middle of the back behind the neck. This is called the stridulating organ and is capable of producing sounds varying widely in frequency.

Hemicentetes has been reported as being the only diurnal member of the family Tenrecidae. However, although day-time activity does sometimes occur, these species are principally nocturnal. Both species of streaked tenrec are preyed on by the Fosa *Cryptoprocta ferox*, Fanaloka *Fossa fossana*, Ring-tailed Mongoose *Galidia elegans* and large snakes.

LOWLAND STREAKED TENREC *Hemicentetes semispinosus* (G. Cuvier, 1798)

Malagasy: Sora, Tsora

MEASUREMENTS Total length: 130-190mm. Head/body length: 130-190mm. Tail length: none. Weight: 90-220g.

DESCRIPTION This is a medium-small, fairly slender tenrec with a very pronounced pointed snout. The basic colour is blackish-brown, with longitudinal yellowish stripes and a yellowish crown. There is a narrowing yellowish band extending from the crown down the forehead and nose to near the tip of the snout (fig. 38). The quills are barbed and detachable and are particularly prominent around the crown (the nuchal crest). The underparts are chestnut-brown. This species is similar in appearance to juvenile Common Tenrecs *Tenrec ecaudatus*, but more spiny.

DISTRIBUTION *H. semispinosus* is endemic to Madagascar and restricted to lowland and mid altitude rainforests of the eastern region.

BEHAVIOUR The resemblance of both species of streaked tenrec to immature Common Tenrecs is no coincidence, as these species are partially active during daylight hours, when their coloration and pattern provides a degree of crypsis. They forage amongst leaf-litter on the forest floor and actively seek out earthworms and other soft-bodied invertebrates: this is a more specialised diet than other tenrecs and one correlated with a substantially reduced dentition.

Lowland Streaked Tenrec

Lowland Streaked Tenrecs excavate burrows often near a stream or body of water. These are up to 150cm in length, descend to a depth of 15cm and contain a nest chamber. The entrance is generally plugged with leaves and there is a latrine site close by.

This species lives in multi-generational family groups which form the most complex social systems of any insectivore. Young are born during the wet season after a gestation period of 45 to 55 days: the litter size varies between five and eight in the wild (average six). The young develop with exceptional speed, reaching sexual maturity after only 30 to 35 days, and so are able to reproduce in the same season as their birth. Thus a family group may produce several litters in a season and attain a size in excess of 20 individuals consisting of three related generations. They forage together, in subgroups or singly (fig. 39). When together they communicate by vibrating quills in the stridulating organ. This produces low-frequency ultrasonic sounds (similar to dry grass being rubbed together) which the tenrecs can detect at distances in excess of four metres. This is important in keeping a mother and her offspring in contact as they forage in undergrowth.

During the cooler winter months (May–October) these animals are able to lower their body temperature to within 2°C of ambient to conserve energy, but still remain active. If temperature, day length and food supply decrease sufficiently, they may become torpid, only emerging when more favourable environmental conditions prevail. Therefore, there is considerable variation in this behaviour across this species's range.

Despite their small size, these tenrecs have an effective deterrent when threatened. They erect a crest of spines (nuchal crest) and buck their heads violently, attempting to embed the detachable barbed quills into the snout of the would-be predator.

VIEWING The Lowland Streaked Tenrec is more readily seen during the warmer wetter months (November to April) and is often encountered at places like Ranomafana National Park and Analamazaotra Special Reserve. It also seems to be common in gardens around Maroantsetra in the north-east.

Figure 38. Lowland Streaked Tenrec.

Figure 39. Lowland Streaked Tenrec with young, Analamazaotra.

Figure 40. Highland Streaked Tenrec.

Figure 41. Aquatic Tenrec.

HIGHLAND STREAKED TENREC *Hemicentetes nigriceps* Günther, 1875

Highland Streaked Tenrec

Malagasy: Sora, Tsora

MEASUREMENTS Total length: 120-160mm. Head/body length: 120-160mm. Tail length: none. Weight: 70-160g.

DESCRIPTION This species is very similar in size, shape and coloration to the Lowland Streaked Tenrec. The pelage is less spiny and the streaks are more whitish than yellowish. There is no median stripe on the crown. The underparts are creamy-white, while the forehead and crown are black (fig. 40). The underfur is more developed in this species than in *H. semispinosus*, giving it a more woolly appearance.

DISTRIBUTION The Highland Streaked Tenrec is endemic to Madagascar and found at higher altitudes on the eastern escarpment and some areas of the central plateau, particularly in the region of Fianarantsoa and the Andringitra Massif.

BEHAVIOUR The Highland Streaked Tenrec is strictly nocturnal, although the peak activity period is normally the first three or four hours of darkness. Aestivation is more marked than in the lowland streaked tenrec and occurs between May and October. This is presumably because the prevailing conditions at higher altitudes become too harsh during the austral winter to allow them to remain active. The onset of torpor is stimulated by reductions in ambient temperature, day length and food supply, but is also influenced by endogenous rhythms.

In common with *H. semispinosus*, females become sexually mature after only 30 to 35 days. The litter size is one to five, with three or four average. All other known aspects of the behaviour and ecology are similar to the Lowland Streaked Tenrec.

VIEWING The Andringitra Massif, south-west of Fianarantsoa, is probably the best place to try to see this species.

Furred Tenrecs
Subfamily Oryzorictinae

This subfamily consists of four highly diversified endemic genera, some of which have radiated spectacularly, most notably the shrew tenrecs (genus *Microgale*). A large number of species in this subfamily are very good examples of convergent evolution as they demonstrate very similar morphological and ecological traits to those found in other insectivore families. Different Oryzorictinae species exploit niches filled elsewhere by shrews, moles and desmans. They are found mainly in the eastern rainforest regions.

AQUATIC TENREC genus *Limnogale* Major, 1896

The genus Limnogale contains just a single, highly specialised species. The behaviour and ecology of this species show close parallels to the otter-shrews (Potamogalinae) of West and Central Africa and the desmans (Talpidae) of Europe.

AQUATIC TENREC *Limnogale mergulus* Major, 1896

Other names: Web-footed Tenrec
Malagasy: Voalavondrano

MEASUREMENTS Total length: 240-330mm. Head/body length: 120-170mm. Tail length: 120-160mm. Weight: 60-90g.

DESCRIPTION This is the largest member of the subfamily Oryzorictinae. The pelage is close, dense and soft. The head and upperparts are brownish with reddish and blackish guard hairs. The underparts are a paler yellowish-grey. The head is broad, short and flattened (fig. 41). The eyes are small as are the ears, which are flattened and hidden beneath the fur. The fore-feet are fringed and the toes webbed. The tail is powerful and squarish, becoming increasingly laterally compressed towards the tip. All these features are obvious adaptations to an aquatic mode of life.

DISTRIBUTION This tenrec is limited to some faster-flowing streams in the central highlands, at altitudes between 600m and 2,000m. Localities where this species is known to occur at relatively high densities include: north-east of the Andringitra Massif; approximately 35km south of Antsirabe; close to Ranomafana; and Antsampandrano near Antsirabe.

BEHAVIOUR The Aquatic Tenrec is nocturnal and carnivorous, foraging at night almost entirely in water for frogs, small fish, crustaceans and aquatic insect larvae. The webbed and fringed hind feet and flattened tail are the primary means of propulsion under water in pursuit of this prey (fig. 42).

Their chosen habitat may sometimes be associated with the aquatic lace plant (*Aponogeton*), the bases and stems of which harbour an abundant supply of aquatic invertebrates. However, this relationship is by no means exclusive and the tenrec does frequent streams where the lace plant does not grow. Burrows are often excavated close to the water's edge, with breeding taking place between December and January. The average litter size appears to be three.

VIEWING This is a very difficult species to see. Ranomafana National Park offers the only realistic opportunity, although a considerable amount of effort will be needed to ensure success. Here individuals have been seen in the stream that runs by the village of Ambatolahy, around one kilometre down the hill from the park entrance.

probable range

Aquatic Tenrec

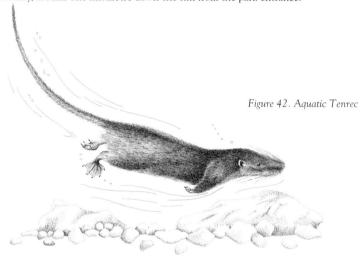

Figure 42. Aquatic Tenrec

LARGE-EARED TENREC genus *Geogale* Milne-Edwards and A. Grandidier, 1872

Geogale is another monotypic genus within the subfamily Oryzorictinae. Some authorities have chosen to place the genus *Geogale* in its own subfamily Geogalinae.

LARGE-EARED TENREC *Geogale aurita* Milne-Edwards and A. Grandidier, 1872

MEASUREMENTS Total length: 90-105mm. Head/body length: 60-75mm. Tail length: about 30mm. Weight: average 6-8g.

DESCRIPTION A small tenrec with large ears, a triangular head and a pointed snout (fig. 43). Its general appearance is intermediate between that of a shrew and a field mouse. The pelage is soft and dense. Upperparts are pale grey and underparts creamy-white. The tail is scaly and covered in fine hairs. The ears are large, rounded and clearly visible. The dentition of this species is also unusual: it has only 34 teeth.

DISTRIBUTION *Geogale* is widely distributed in the dry deciduous forests of the west, south of the Tsiribihina River and the spiny forest areas of the south and south-west, together with gallery forest areas of this region. It has also been recorded in the rainforest areas at Andohahela in the extreme south-east.

BEHAVIOUR This species is nocturnal. During the day it rests inside fallen logs. A wide variety of invertebrate prey is taken, but there is a marked preference for small insects like ants and termites.

After a variable gestation period ranging from 54 to 69 days, females give birth to a litter of one to five young (average three or four), between November and February. The young are highly altricial: they are born naked with their eyes closed and weigh less than one gram. At birth the young from larger litters weigh less than those from smaller litters. The eyes of the young open at between 21 and 33 days and they are weaned and become independent from their mothers after around 35 days.

The Large-eared Tenrec is unique within the Tenrecidae in that females are able to conceive a second litter while still suckling their first (called post-partum oestrous).

Large-eared Tenrec

This enables them to produce up to 10 offspring per year (average six to seven). Large-eared Tenrecs inhabit an unpredictable environment – rainfall in western and southern Madagascar is highly irregular from year to year and within individual years – and this breeding strategy allows the tenrecs to maximise their reproductive output when favourable breeding conditions prevail.

VIEWING The best places to try to find this species are: Beza Mahafaly Special Reserve, where it appears to be particularly abundant; Kirindy Forest; and Zombitse Forest.

Figure 43. Large-eared Tenrec

RICE TENRECS genus *Oryzorictes* A. Grandidier, 1870

Malagasy: Voalavonarabo, Antsangy

This rather specialised genus contains three species which outwardly resemble moles Talpidae. They are adapted to a fossorial lifestyle, their morphological modifications including enlarged forelimbs and reduced eyes and ears. They are generally associated with primary forests and marshy areas in eastern Madagascar.

They measure between 115 and 160mm (head/body length: 85-120mm; tail length: 30-50mm). Their upperparts are dark grey-brown giving a generally black appearance, while their upperparts are paler grey or buffy-brown. The pelage is soft, dense and velvety, the tail is bicoloured like the body, the forelimbs are enlarged with strong digging claws, and the eyes and ears are reduced. Their bodies are far more robust than the other furred tenrecs (figs. 44 & 45), particularly when compared with the shrew tenrecs (genus *Microgale*).

The *Oryzorictes* species prefer eastern rainforests and associated marshy areas. *O. talpoides* has also been recorded in gardens and river flood plains. On the strength of this it has been suggested that deforestation and the cultivation of rice paddies may create habitats suitable for the genus. However, the evidence that they prefer native rainforest habitats seems more compelling. Rice tenrecs eat insects and other invertebrates, particularly worms. They are fossorial (or semi-fossorial) and are thought to forage underground or in leaf-litter and humus on the rainforest floor. They appear to be mainly nocturnal although they may be active at all times of the day in their extensive burrow systems. Because of their lifestyle these species are rarely encountered. Most known specimens have been caught in forest floor pit-fall traps at night. Information on their general behaviour has been pieced together from observations made after their release.

Figure 44. Rice tenrec Oryzorictes
talpoides.

Figure 45. Rice tenrec Oryzorictes
tetradactylus.

Oryzorictes hova A. Grandidier, 1870

Oryzorictes hova

MEASUREMENTS Total length: c. 120-160mm. Head/body length: c. 90-110mm. Tail length: c. 40-50mm. Weight: c. 30-40g.

DESCRIPTION The pelage is dense and velvety. Upperparts are dark grey-brown to black, while the underparts are more greyish or buffy-brown. The tail is short (around 50% head/body length) and bicoloured like the body. There are five digits on the forefeet.

DISTRIBUTION The distributional limits of *O. hova* remain unclear. Evidence suggests it is found in rainforest areas in central-eastern and north-eastern Madagascar. Specimens have been captured at Anandrivola on the Masoala Peninsula and in Analamazaotra Special Reserve in central-eastern Madagascar. Both localities consisted of relatively undisturbed forest with a generous covering of leaf-litter on the forest floor.

BEHAVIOUR This species has been observed foraging at ground level using its muzzle to probe beneath the leaf-litter and humus. The period of observation lasted in excess of ten minutes. In captivity this species has been observed dragging earthworms underneath the soil surface before consuming them. No other behavioural information is available for this species.

Oryzorictes talpoides G. Grandidier and Petit, 1930

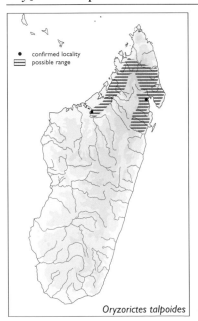

Oryzorictes talpoides

MEASUREMENTS Total length: c. 120-160mm. Head/body length: c. 90-110mm. Tail length: c. 40-50mm. Weight: c. 30-40g.

DESCRIPTION This species is very similar in appearance to *O. hova* and distinguishing the two is highly problematic. The differences are slight, mainly in the size of the thumb, which in *O. talpoides* is larger, and in the dentition: *O. talpoides* has a third lower and upper incisor which *O. hova* lacks. Such is their similarity that some authorities regard *O. talpoides* as a subspecies of *O. hova*, but sympatry between the two has been recorded.

DISTRIBUTION The distribution of *O. talpoides* is poorly known. It appears to be restricted to north-west and north-east Madagascar and seems particularly common around Maroantsetra in the north-east. *O. talpoides* appears to have wide environmental tolerances and has been recorded in gardens and river plains as well as undisturbed rainforests.

BEHAVIOUR The behaviour and ecology of this species are unknown.

Oryzorictes tetradactylus Milne-Edwards and A. Grandidier, 1882

confirmed locality
possible range

Oryzorictes tetradactylus

MEASUREMENTS Total length: c. 115-140mm. Head/body length: c. 85-100mm. Tail length: c. 30-40mm. Weight: c. 25-40g.

DESCRIPTION *O. tetradactylus* is very similar to the other two species of rice tenrec, except that the fur tends to be much coarser in texture. The forefeet have only four digits, rather than the usual five.

DISTRIBUTION This species appears to be restricted to the southern-central highlands of Madagascar. In the Andringitra Massif it has only been recorded above the forest zone at elevations between 2,000 and 2,500m.

BEHAVIOUR The behaviour and ecology of this species remain unknown.

SHREW TENRECS genus *Microgale* Thomas, 1882

Malagasy: Forimenjy

The genus *Microgale* is often considered the most primitive in the family Tenrecidae and contains more species than any other in this family. However, considerable debate surrounds the taxonomy of this group. Early identification was often based on relative body proportions (head/body: tail: hind foot: ear length) and this can still give a reasonable idea of the species under consideration. However, it now appears that some of these original descriptions are not valid. The number of species currently recognised varies between 10 and over 20 depending on the authority consulted. Furthermore, systematic changes are still taking place on a regular basis and the number of species seems sure to increase as further research takes place (at least two new species are currently awaiting description). Here 17 species are listed, following the latest taxonomic revisions and the addition of new species recently described.

Shrew tenrecs are the most problematic Malagasy mammals to identify to species level. Size, relative tail length and to a lesser extent pelage colour are the only external characters which are of use, and even here considerable overlap exists between species. The only accurate method of identification is detailed morphological examination including dentition.

There follows a general review of the characteristics of *Microgale*. If there is variation from this, or more detailed information is available, it is included under each species' description.

General Description The pelage is soft and velvety. The head and upperparts can vary from buffy to olive-brown, dark russet-brown or slate grey-black. The ears are prominent and tend to project well above the fur. The forelimbs are not as well developed as in *Oryzorictes* species and all limbs have five digits. As their common name implies, *Microgale* species are very shrew-like in appearance and occupy similar habitats and niches to those of the true shrews (Soricidae) on mainland Africa.

Distribution and Habitat *Microgale* prefer primary habitats and are generally associated with dense vegetation. The centres of *Microgale* species richness lie within the eastern rainforests, although some specimens have been recorded from dry and arid regions in the west and south-west. In rainforest regions there appears to be a mid-elevational peak in species richness between 1,200m and 1,500m. Very few species occur right across the altitude zones from lowland forests below 800m to high-altitude forest above 1,650m. Instead, most species show a preference for particular elevations and are replaced by others at different altitudes. Irrespective of altitude, shrew tenrecs appear to prefer valley bottoms, rather than valley sides or ridgetops. This is probably a reflection of the greater density and diversity of the invertebrate food prey in valley bottoms. Distributional data of shrew tenrec species are very scant: in some instances only single or a few locations have been recorded.

Behaviour Shrew tenrecs are both diurnal and nocturnal (i.e. cathemeral). Most species are terrestrial, but some are known to be scansorial and arboreal, and spend time climbing in vegetation. Births appear to coincide with the onset of the rainy season (November-December), so that juveniles can take advantage of the seasonal increase in invertebrate populations. Many immature *Microgale* species are able to achieve a large body size whilst still maintaining their deciduous dentition and in fact these teeth may be retained into full adulthood.

Diet This is very varied and includes invertebrates, especially insects, but also small vertebrates such as reptiles and amphibians.

Viewing *Microgale* species may be found in any native humid forest area. However, because of their small size and secretive lifestyle, they are rarely observed. Searching hollow logs and similar areas at night may prove successful. Most specimens are caught in traps on the forest floor.

Figure 46. Lesser Long-tailed Shrew Tenrec.

LESSER LONG-TAILED SHREW TENREC *Microgale longicaudata* Thomas, 1882

MEASUREMENTS Total length: 170-230mm. Head/body length: 60-75mm. Tail length: 110-160mm. Weight: 5-12g.

DESCRIPTION The dorsal pelage is dark brown with a reddish-brown wash, while the underparts are grey with a reddish-buff wash. The tail is grey-brown above which contrasts sharply with the reddish-buff underside. Along with the Greater Long-tailed Shrew Tenrec *M. principula*, this is probably the most easily recognisable *Microgale* species on account of the extreme body proportions. The actual body size is small, but the tail extremely long, sometimes more than twice the head/body length (fig. 46). The end of the tail is prehensile: evidence for this is a conspicuous naked area (up to 15mm long) on the tail's underside at the tip. There is also an elongated fifth digit on the hindfoot.

DISTRIBUTION *M. longicaudata* occurs in lowland and mid-altitude eastern rainforest from Montagne d'Ambre near Antsiranana in the extreme north as far south as the Andringitra Massif. There is an unconfirmed record from Kirindy Forest in western Madagascar. This species appears to be equally common on ridgetops, slopes or in valley bottoms: this is probably linked to its semi-arboreal way of life.

This species appears to have one of the widest altitudinal tolerances of any *Microgale*: at Montagne d'Ambre it occurs between 650m and 1,250m, and in the Andringitra Massif it has been recorded from 720m to 1,625m.

Anjanaharibe-Sud Special Reserve in north-eastern Madagascar is the only locality where *M. longicaudata* and *M. principula* are known to occur sympatrically (i.e. live within the same forest block). However, they appear to be allopatric in terms of their elevational distribution, *M. longicaudata* only being found at higher elevations up to 1,550m and *M. principula* being restricted to elevations below 875m.

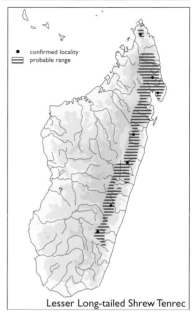

confirmed locality
probable range

Lesser Long-tailed Shrew Tenrec

BEHAVIOUR A number of morphological features (prehensile tail, elongate digit) indicate that this species is at least scansorial if not totally arboreal. It actively climbs and forages in vegetation and is able to jump amongst the branches.

GREATER LONG-TAILED SHREW TENREC *Microgale principula* Thomas, 1926

MEASUREMENTS Total length: 200-250mm. Head/body length: 65-80mm. Tail length: 135-170mm. Weight: 8-11g.

DESCRIPTION A medium-sized *Microgale* with a tail up to twice the head/body length. The upperparts are reddish-brown, while the lower parts are grey with a buff wash. The distal portion of the tail is naked and transversely wrinkled on the upper surface. The fifth digit on the hindfoot is elongate.

DISTRIBUTION This species has been recorded from disparate lowland and mid-altitude rainforest localities in the extreme south-east (Grotte d'Andrahomana), central-east (Mantadia, Ambatovaky) and north-east (Anjanaharibe-Sud). At Anjanaharibe-Sud there seems to be a preference for slopes rather than valley bottoms. (See *M. longicaudata* for altitudinal separation).

BEHAVIOUR As for *M. longicaudata*, several morphological features, including the long prehensile tail and elongate hind digit, indicate that this species is at least partially arboreal. It is known to climb and forage in vegetation above ground level and is able to jump amongst the branches.

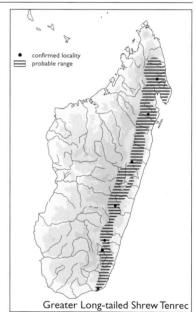

confirmed locality
probable range

Greater Long-tailed Shrew Tenrec

TALAZAC'S SHREW TENREC *Microgale talazaci* Major, 1896

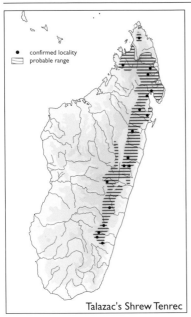

Talazac's Shrew Tenrec

confirmed locality
probable range

MEASUREMENTS Total length: 220-280mm. Head/body length: 100-130mm. Tail length: 120-150mm. Weight: 30-45g.

DESCRIPTION A very large *Microgale* with a tail longer than the head/body length. The head is large and robust. The dorsal pelage is mid-brown, while the venter is grey with a reddish-buff wash. Overall this species is similar to Dobson's Shrew Tenrec M. *dobsoni*, but on average slightly larger, although overlap in size does occur. The pelage of M. *talazaci* is darker brown than that of M. *dobsoni* and lacks rufous tinges.

DISTRIBUTION This is one of the most widely distributed *Microgale* species and has been recorded throughout the eastern rainforest region from the vicinity of Vondrozo in the south to Montagne d'Ambre in the north and including the humid forests of the Sambirano region. This species seems to prefer primary forests and has a very broad altitudinal tolerance: it has been recorded at elevations from 100-2,300m. In areas where M. *talazaci* is sympatric with its close relative, M. *dobsoni*, it appears to favour higher altitudes.

BEHAVIOUR The species forages on the ground and in the lower branches of undergrowth, and it may dig some burrow systems. It does not lay down any fat reserves and shows no tendency towards seasonal inactivity. This is probably a reflection on the more stable nature of its rainforest habitat, where seasonal variations in climate and food availability are less marked. Males and females may be together throughout the year and breed in the austral spring/summer. The young are born after a gestation period of 58-63 days; litter size varies from one to three (average two).

LONG-NOSED SHREW TENREC *Microgale longirostris* Major, 1896

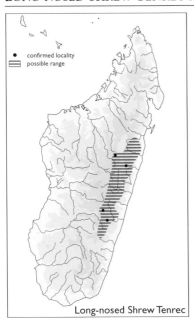

Long-nosed Shrew Tenrec

confirmed locality
possible range

MEASUREMENTS Total length: 135-175mm. Head/body length: 80-100mm. Tail length: 55-75mm. Weight: c. 25g.

DESCRIPTION The dorsal and ventral pelage is brown to dark brown in colour. The snout is particularly elongate. The validity of this species is questioned by some authorities who regard it as synonymous with M. *cowani*. However, M. *longirostris* is larger and there are also significant behavioural differences between the two species.

DISTRIBUTION Specimens have been collected from central-eastern and south-eastern rainforest localities.

BEHAVIOUR The highly elongate muzzle of this shrew tenrec is used to forage under leaf-litter to a greater extent than in most other *Microgale* species. The Long-nosed Shrew Tenrec also frequently emits high-pitched squeaks – something that has not been heard in any congener.

THOMAS'S SHREW TENREC *Microgale thomasi* Major, 1896

MEASUREMENTS Total length: 135-180mm. Head/body length: 75-95mm. Tail length: 60-85mm. Weight: 12-16g.

DESCRIPTION Very similar to Cowan's Shrew Tenrec, but slightly larger in size. The pelage is dark russet-brown.

DISTRIBUTION A species that appears to have a restricted range and to be rather rare. It is only known from localities in the southern part of the eastern rainforest.

BEHAVIOUR This species is known to forage on the ground. No other behavioural information is available.

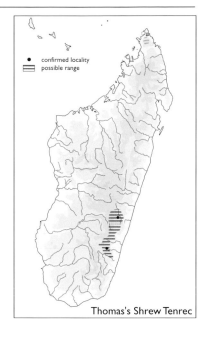

confirmed locality
possible range

Thomas's Shrew Tenrec

GRACILE SHREW TENREC *Microgale gracilis* (Major, 1896)

MEASUREMENTS Total length: 165-190mm. Head/body length: 90-105mm. Tail length: 75-85mm. Weight: 20-25g.

DESCRIPTION This is a largish *Microgale* species, with a tail shorter than the head/body length. The head is elongate and gracile and the muzzle is very long. The eyes and ears are very small and partially obscured by the pelage. The upperparts are dark brown with buff speckles, while the underparts are dark grey with a buff wash. The tail is bicoloured, dark brown dorsally and light brown ventrally. Juveniles appear to be less speckled than adults, particularly around the rump. The dentition is much reduced; both incisors and canines are very slender.

DISTRIBUTION This species is known only from the type locality – Ambohinitombo forest, 40km south-east of Ambositra – and by specimens caught in the nearby Andringitra Massif. In Andringitra it shows a marked preference for higher-altitude montane forests, 1,200m to 2,100m, and appears to be quite common at these elevations.

BEHAVIOUR A number of morphological features, for example elongate muzzle, reduced eyes and ears and broadened feet with large claws, suggest this species's habits are semi-fossorial.

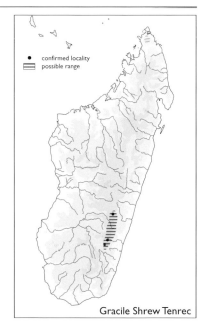

confirmed locality
possible range

Gracile Shrew Tenrec

DOBSON'S SHREW TENREC *Microgale dobsoni* Thomas, 1884

Dobson's Shrew Tenrec

MEASUREMENTS Total length: 170-240mm. Head/body length: 80-110mm. Tail length: 90-130mm. Weight: 25-45g.

DESCRIPTION The body size is large with the tail length roughly equal to or slightly longer than the head/body length. The pelage is quite long and dorsally brown with a buff wash and sometimes more reddish areas around the throat (fig. 47). The venter is mainly grey with a buff or reddish wash. The tail is grey above and buff below.

DISTRIBUTION This is a widespread species recorded in eastern rainforest regions and in eastern areas of the central highlands. Its northerly limit appears to be the Anjanaharibe-Sud area, while its southern limit extends to the Andringitra Massif and the vicinity of Antampona. It may show a preference for medium-altitude montane forest areas (1,100-1,300m) and is often found on slopes rather than in valley bottoms. In areas where M. *dobsoni* and its close relative M. *talazaci*, are sympatric, for example Anjanaharibe-Sud in the north-east, M. *dobsoni* appears to prefer slightly lower elevations, but trapping evidence indicates that individuals of this species and M. *talazaci* may at times have overlapping home ranges. M. *dobsoni* has also been recorded from non-forested areas and agricultural zones in the central highlands.

BEHAVIOUR Dobson's Shrew Tenrec forages on the ground amongst leaf-litter, detecting its prey by sound. There is some evidence also that it possesses a basic echolocation system that aids movement through the undergrowth and in the dark.

Like the majority of tenrecs, this is a solitary species, which shows some territorial behaviour – individuals are normally spread out and evenly distributed and are highly antagonistic towards one another if they meet. Fights are not uncommon. Males and females may establish a stable relationship during the breeding season which takes place in the austral spring/summer. After a gestation period of 62-64 days a litter of one to five young is produced.

This is the only *Microgale* species that is known to accumulate fat reserves in the body and tail prior to the austral winter: body weight may increase to over 80g. However, it does not enter full torpor with the onset of winter, but does become inactive, constructing a nest and sleeping for much of the time, eating less and lowering its body temperature. This is probably an adaptation to higher elevations where there may be marked seasonal climatic variation.

COWAN'S SHREW TENREC *Microgale cowani* Thomas, 1882

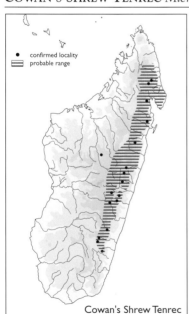

Cowan's Shrew Tenrec

MEASUREMENTS Total length: 130-165mm. Head/body length: 70-95mm. Tail length: 60-80mm. Weight: 10-16g.

DESCRIPTION A medium-sized *Microgale* species, with a moderately short tail – shorter than or equal to the head/body length. The dorsal pelage is dark brown to rufous-brown with some paler russet flecking (fig. 48), except on the rump where this is reduced. Overall the upperparts appear speckled brown. There may also be a faint, slightly darker dorsal stripe. The underparts are grey with a reddish-brown wash. The tail is bicoloured: the dark brown dorsal surface is sharply demarcated from the reddish-buff ventral surface.

DISTRIBUTION This animal was once considered to be a common species with a wide distribution throughout the central-eastern and north-eastern rainforests. However, recent evidence suggests that its range is more limited: the southern limit may be the Andringitra Massif and Ankafina areas, while the northern limit is probably Anjanaharibe-Sud and the Marojejy Massif. Cowan's Shrew Tenrec probably prefers valley bottoms in montane rainforest, although in Andringitra it has been recorded at elevations between 810m and 1,625m. Cowan's Shrew Tenrec has also been recorded in non-forested areas, anthropogenic grassland and agricultural zones in the central highlands.

In the Andringitra Massif M. *cowani* occurs sympatrically with M. *drouhardi* and M. *taiva*, while at Anjanaharibe-Sud this species is sympatric with M. *longicaudata*, M. *principula*, M. *parvula*, M. *dobsoni*, M. *talazaci*, M. *soricoides* and M. *gymnorhyncha*.

BEHAVIOUR Cowan's Shrew Tenrec forages in leaf-litter, where its tends to move in a very cryptic fashion. Evidence suggests that females are able to become sexually mature while still dentally immature.

Figure 47. Dobson's Shrew Tenrec.

Figure 48. Cowan's Shrew Tenrec.

PYGMY SHREW TENREC *Microgale parvula* G. Grandidier, 1934

confirmed locality
probable range

Pygmy Shrew Tenrec

MEASUREMENTS Total length: 95-130mm. Head/body length: 50-65mm. Tail length: 45-65mm. Weight: 3-4g.

DESCRIPTION A very small *Microgale* species with a tail less than or equal to the head/body length. The head is very small, delicate and elongate. The dorsal pelage is dark brown and appears almost black in places, while ventrally it is dark grey-brown. The tail and feet are uniform dark grey-brown.

This species was first described from a single juvenile specimen. A later description referring to an adult specimen was given the name M. *pulla*, but it is now known these two descriptions refer to the same species, M. *parvula* taking precedence.

Because of its very small size the Pygmy Shrew Tenrec can only be confused with M. *pusilla*. However, M. *parvula* is dark grey-brown above and only slightly paler below, while M. *pusilla* is reddish buffy-brown dorsally with an abrupt transition to grey-brown venter.

DISTRIBUTION The original specimen was collected at Montagne d'Ambre in northern Madagascar and this species has since been recorded at the same locality at an elevation between 1,125-1,225m. However, the Pygmy Shrew Tenrec is now known to be very widespread and has also been recorded at Manongarivo, Marojejy, near Maroantsetra, Zahamana, Ambohitantely, Mantadia, the Andringitra Massif and as far south as the Vohimena Mountains near Tolagnaro. M. *parvula* also appears to have a wide elevational tolerance, having been recorded at altitudes from around 100m up to 1,625m.

BEHAVIOUR The habits and behaviour of this species are unknown.

SHORT-TAILED SHREW TENREC *Microgale brevicaudata* G. Grandidier, 1899

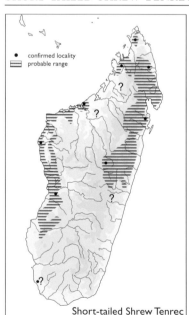

confirmed locality
probable range

Short-tailed Shrew Tenrec

MEASUREMENTS Total length: c. 100mm. Head/body length: c. 65mm. Tail length: c. 35mm. Weight: 8-10g.

DESCRIPTION A very small *Microgale* species with a relatively short tail. The pelage is very similar to M. *pusilla*, with noticeable reddish highlights on the dorsal surface and a grizzled appearance. However, the significantly shorter tail of M. *brevicaudata* should prevent confusion. Internally, M. *brevicaudata* is characterised by a robust skull and a short rostrum.

The type of M. *occidentalis* G. Grandidier and Petit, 1931 is now considered to be an immature specimen of M. *brevicaudata*.

DISTRIBUTION The type specimen of M. *brevicaudata* was collected near Mananara in north-east Madagascar. However, it has since been recorded in other eastern rainforest and humid forest localities, for instance Montagne d'Ambre (340m-670m) and Manongarivo in the Sambirano region, as well as some western dry forest areas, including the Kirindy Forest. The Short-tailed Shrew Tenrec has also been recorded from non-forested areas and agricultural zones in the highlands.

BEHAVIOUR This species is probably semi-fossorial. Litter sizes of 1 to 8 have been recorded.

LESSER SHREW TENREC *Microgale pusilla* Major, 1896

MEASUREMENTS Total length: 110-145mm. Head/body length: 50-60mm. Tail length: 60-85mm. Weight: 2.5-4g.

DESCRIPTION This species is recognisable by its very small size and relatively long tail. The dorsal pelage is reddish buffy-brown and grizzled while the ventral surface is grey-brown, the transition between the two being abrupt and noticeable. The tail is dark grey-brown with the underside slightly paler. This species is similar in size to the Pygmy Shrew Tenrec, but lighter in colour.

DISTRIBUTION *M. pusilla* is known from a variety of localities within the eastern rainforest belt and on the central plateau, and is encountered in a wide variety of habitats including non-forested areas, agricultural zones and sedge marshes. Its remains have been found in Barn Owl *Tyto alba* pellets close to Antananarivo, where it lives in highly modified habitats including anthropogenic grasslands. Records also exist from forest remnants on the Mahafaly plateau in south-west Madagascar.

BEHAVIOUR The Lesser Shrew Tenrec forages on the ground and in the lower branches of undergrowth. No other information is available.

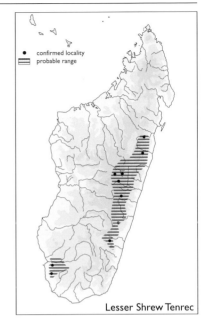

confirmed locality
probable range

Lesser Shrew Tenrec

TAIVA SHREW TENREC *Microgale taiva* Major, 1896

MEASUREMENTS Total length: 160-180mm. Head/body length: 70-90mm. Tail length: 80-95mm. Weight: 10-25g.

DESCRIPTION A medium-sized shrew tenrec, with a moderately long tail – equal to or slightly longer than head/body length. The dorsal pelage is dark russet-brown with buffy-brown speckling, while ventrally it is grey-brown. The tail is not bicoloured, but is dark grey above and a slightly paler grey below.

DISTRIBUTION The type specimen of this species was probably collected south-east of Ambositra in south-eastern Madagascar, and it has also been recorded nearby in the Andringitra Massif in both lowland and montane rainforests between 720m and 1,625m. There is a possible further record of this species from the central-eastern region at Analamazaotra Special Reserve near Andasibe.

BEHAVIOUR Males may become sexually mature before they attain other adult characteristics such as permanent dentition. No other aspects of behaviour and ecology are known.

confirmed locality
possible range

Taiva Shrew Tenrec

Figure 49. Striped Shrew Tenrec.

STRIPED SHREW TENREC *Microgale drouhardi*, G. Grandidier, 1934

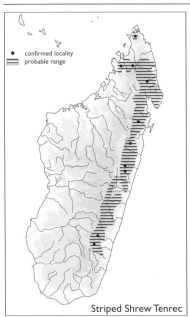

- confirmed locality
- probable range

Striped Shrew Tenrec

MEASUREMENTS Total length: 115-160mm. Head/body length: 60-80mm. Tail length: 55-80mm. Weight: c. 11g.

DESCRIPTION A medium-sized shrew tenrec with a tail generally slightly shorter than head/body length. The upperparts are dark grey-brown to dark rufous-brown with some yellowish speckles, while the underparts are silver-grey with a buff or reddish-buff wash. The transition from dorsal to ventral coloration is moderately distinct. This species takes its name from the dark brown mid-dorsal stripe (fig. 49) which extends from the head between the ears to the base of the tail. The tail is bicoloured: dark grey dorsally and buff ventrally.

There appears to be a considerable degree of size variation between populations, those from central-eastern regions (Ambatovaky and Zahamena) generally being appreciably smaller than specimens from other localities. The overall appearance of M. *drouhardi* is similar to Cowan's Shrew Tenrec M. *cowani* and the Taiva Shrew Tenrec M. *taiva*, but differs principally in being paler and having the distinctive dorsal stripe.

In the past, this species has also been described as M. *melanorrhachis*, which is now considered a synonym.

DISTRIBUTION Recorded from rainforest localities in the north (Montagne d'Ambre), north-west (Manongarivo, Tsaratanana), north-east and central-east (Anjanaharibe-Sud, Ambatovaky, Zahamena, Andasibe, Mantadia) and south-east (Andringitra, Ambalavao) of Madagascar.

This species of *Microgale* has the largest known elevational range in the genus (300-2,350m). It has been recorded in lowland, mid-altitude and high-altitude forests and a high proportion of specimens have been collected in valley bottoms: Montagne d'Ambre, 1,000-1,350m; Manongarivo, 1,150m: Tsaratanana, 2,350m; Ambatovaky, 300-600m; Zahamena, 420-920m; Andasibe, 920m; Mantadia, 1,100m; Andringitra, 720-810m; Pic d'Ivohibe, 1,525m.

BEHAVIOUR The Striped Shrew Tenrec conceals itself under leaves and vegetation on the forest floor. However, it is also a very active species and can move rapidly beneath this layer. No other aspects of this species's behaviour and ecology are known.

NAKED-NOSED SHREW TENREC *Microgale gymnorhyncha* Jenkins *et al.*, 1996

MEASUREMENTS Total length: 145-175mm. Head/body length: 85-105mm. Tail length: 60-70mm. Weight: 12-20g.

DESCRIPTION A moderately large *Microgale* with a tail noticeably shorter than the head/body length. The dorsal pelage is dark grey-brown, soft and lustrous, with dark brown guard hairs, while the ventral pelage is dark grey. The tail is dark grey above grading to light grey below. The head is long and gracile and the muzzle very long, forming a proboscis which extends well beyond the mouth. The eyes are very small, as are the ears which are virtually concealed in the pelage. The forefeet are broad and have enlarged claws. The dentition is reduced.

This recently described species differs from all congeners, except M. *gracilis*, in having an elongate head, long muzzle, small ears concealed within the pelage and broad forefeet with large claws. M. *gymnorhyncha* differs from M. *gracilis* in being slightly smaller and less gracile with a relatively shorter tail.

DISTRIBUTION The Naked-nosed Shrew Tenrec is known from only three rainforest localities: the Andringitra Massif in south-east Madagascar, Fanovana near Andasibe in the central-eastern rainforest, and Anjanaharibe-Sud in the north-east. The specimen from Fanovana was collected at an estimated elevation of 600m-800m; however, those at Andringitra and Anjanaharibe-Sud seem to prefer montane and upper montane rainforests: all specimens have been collected between 1,210m and 1,625m. At all these localities valley bottoms appear to be preferred.

BEHAVIOUR M. *gymnorhyncha* shares a number of significant adaptive features with M. *gracilis* – an elongate proboscis-like muzzle, small eyes, reduced ears and broadened forefeet with large claws – all of which suggest this species is also semi-fossorial.

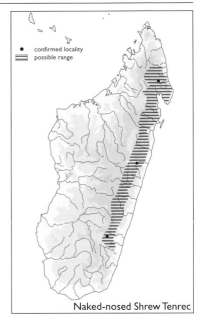

confirmed locality
possible range

Naked-nosed Shrew Tenrec

PALE-FOOTED SHREW TENREC *Microgale fotsifotsy* Jenkins *et al.*, 1997

MEASUREMENTS Total length: 135-175mm. Head/body length: 65-80mm. Tail length: 70-95mm. Weight: c. 15g.

DESCRIPTION A small to medium-sized shrew tenrec, with the tail slightly longer than the head/body length. The pelage is soft and silky in texture; upperparts are grizzled yellowish grey-brown with noticeable dark guard hairs, while the underparts are pale grey with a buff or reddish wash. The ears are prominent and pale in colour. The tail is more or less bicoloured, being grey-brown above and light grey-buff below, ending in a thin pencil of fine white hairs. The fore- and hindfeet are light brown with conspicuous, very pale digits that give rise to the species's name: *fotsifotsy* is Malagasy for pale or whitish. This species is probably most closely related to M. *soricoides*, but the combination of light body coloration, large ears and conspicuous pale feet and tail tip are unique to this shrew tenrec and help differentiate it from all other *Microgale* species.

There appears to be some variation between specimens from different localities; for instance individuals from Montagne d'Ambre are generally paler than those from other sites further to the south. Also specimens caught in Zahamena and the Andringitra Massif seem slightly larger than those from other localities.

DISTRIBUTION This species is known from several widely separate localities in northern-central and south-eastern rainforest regions: Montagne d'Ambre in the far north, Zahamena and Ambatovaky in the central-east, Ranomafana National Park and the Andringitra Massif in the south-east, and Marosohy in the far south. Mid-altitude rainforest appears to be favoured, the elevational range of M. *fotsifotsy* being 600-1,400m.

BEHAVIOUR The majority of specimens have been caught on the forest floor, suggesting that this species is largely terrestrial. However, some adaptations to a scansorial way of life have also been noted, although they are not as extreme as those of M. *longicaudata*.

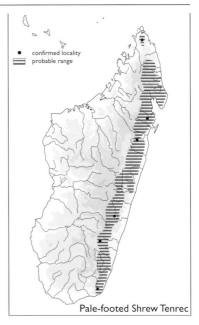

confirmed locality
probable range

Pale-footed Shrew Tenrec

Microgale dryas Jenkins, 1992

Microgale dryas

MEASUREMENTS Total length: 170-180mm. Head/body length: 105-110mm. Tail length: 65-70mm. Weight: c. 40g.

DESCRIPTION The upperparts are dark reddish-brown or grey-brown with a grizzled appearance and very long dark guard hairs. This gradually merges to grey underparts. The tail is uniformly grey. This recently described species is intermediate in size between the smaller M. *thomasi* and M. *gracilis* and the larger M. *dobsoni* and M. *talazaci*. It is distinguished from all other *Microgale* species by an unusual dorsal pelage, in which the long guard hairs are flattened and broadened in their mid-region. It also has a very much shorter tail than other larger species of shrew tenrec.

DISTRIBUTION This species is only known from Ambatovaky Special Reserve in the north-eastern rainforest. Here it occurs sympatrically with M. *cowani*, M. *principula* and M. *talazaci*.

BEHAVIOUR The behaviour and ecology of this species remain unknown.

Microgale soricoides Jenkins, 1993

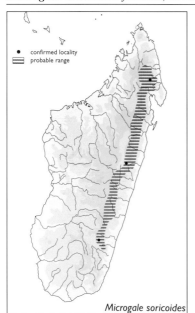

Microgale soricoides

MEASUREMENTS Total length: 155-200mm. Head/body length: 75-105mm. Tail length: 80-105mm. Weight: 16-22g.

DESCRIPTION A medium-large robust shrew tenrec with a tail equal to or longer than the head/body length. The upperparts are light grey-brown and slightly grizzled with longer black guard hairs. This gradually fades into the paler grey-brown underparts, which have a reddish-buff wash. The tail is grey-brown above and paler buffy-brown underneath and the tip may be white. This recently described species resembles M. *dobsoni* and M. *taiva*: it is differentiated by several unusual dental traits, including very distinct incisor morphology.

DISTRIBUTION This species probably prefers higher-altitude montane rainforest areas. The type specimen was collected from Mantadia National Park between 1,100m and 1,150m in the central eastern rainforest. M. *soricoides* has subsequently been recorded in the Andringitra Massif between 1,210m and 1,625m and Anjanaharibe-Sud Special Reserve to the south-east of the Marojejy Massif at similar elevations.

BEHAVIOUR This species is probably semi-scansorial: it has been collected on tree limbs and tangles of vines around 2m above the ground.

INTRODUCED SPECIES

Two species of insectivore have been introduced to Madagascar. Both are shrews (Soricidae) belonging to the genus *Suncus*, the musk or pygmy shrews. When these introductions actually occurred is unclear. One species, *Suncus murinus*, is of Asian origin, so may well have initially arrived with the first human colonists. However, more recently this species has been accidentally introduced to other parts of the world via freight in ships, etc., so several subsequent waves of introduction to Madagascar have probably also occurred.

The second species, *Suncus etruscus*, is more problematic and contentious. Some authorities regard it as a subspecies of the Pygmy Musk Shrew *Suncus etruscus*, whose natural range is North Africa, Europe and Asia. If so its arrival on Madagascar must have taken place many centuries ago. However, others regard the Malagasy population as sufficiently distinct to be treated as a valid species, *Suncus madagascariensis*. It is treated here as a race of *S. etruscus*.

Shrews
Family Soricidae

This is one of the largest insectivore families, containing around 290 species divided between 22 genera. Soricidae includes the world's smallest terrestrial mammal species – the Pygmy Musk Shrew *Suncus etruscus*. Their distribution is extensive, being found on all major landmasses with the exception of Arctic islands, Greenland, Iceland, the West Indies, New Guinea, Australia, New Zealand and some other Pacific islands. In the New World, they have spread down only as far as the northernmost part of South America. Shrews are all small, short-legged insectivores, with elongate pointed snouts. Their pelage is short and dense. The upperparts are generally grey to grey-brown, becoming paler underneath. The eyes are very small and often almost hidden, the vibrissae are long and prominent, while the ears are small.

MUSK SHREWS genus *Suncus* Ehrenberg, 1832

The resemblance of musk shrews *Suncus* to members of the native genus *Microgale* (the shrew tenrecs) is quite striking; so much so that differentiating them can be problematic without detailed examination. The dentition of true shrews is reduced (not more than 32 teeth) in comparison with the shrew tenrecs. Also, they do not possess a cloaca which *Microgale* does, although the urogenital and anal apertures do open into a common tract.

MUSK SHREW *Suncus murinus* (Linnaeus, 1766)

Other name: House Shrew
Malagasy: Voalavo fotsy, Voalavon'arabo

MEASUREMENTS Total length: 170-200mm. Head/body length: 120-135mm. Tail length: 50-65mm. Weight: across entire range: 30-100g. In Madagascar: females 30-35g; males 45-50g.

DESCRIPTION This is one of the largest species of shrew and has a very strong and distinct odour. The pelage is short, soft and velvety in texture. Two colour morphs are recognised: one with pale grey upperparts, slightly paler underparts and a whitish tail; the other with dark greyish-brown upperparts, paler grey underparts and a dark grey tail (fig. 50). Both morphs occur on Madagascar, although the pale form appears to be more common. In both morphs males are generally larger than females.

There are many introduced populations on different islands around the world, and a number of these subpopulations have now apparently diverged considerably in morphology, physiology and size, so that some authorities consider subspecific differentiation to be warranted. Individuals from Madagascar appear to be at the smaller end of the species's size range.

DISTRIBUTION *S. murinus* originates in Asia where it is widespread: its natural distribution extends from Japan in the east to Pakistan in the west. All records further to the west are probably the result of casual and intentional introductions by humans. This species is now widely distributed in Arabia, East Africa, the Comoros, the Mascarenes and Madagascar.

Evidence suggests that the Malagasy population is derived from several separate colonisations involving different founder stock localities within the species's natural range: some probably came from the Arabian Peninsula via East Africa and the island of Zanzibar, while others arrived directly from South-East Asia. The first official record of *S. murinus* on Madagascar was in 1858. Since then numerous specimens have been recorded over the entire island and it is now considered common. However, the highest densities are generally associated with eastern rainforest regions where it is known to penetrate primary forest. It appears to be less common in the extreme south.

probable range

Musk Shrew

BEHAVIOUR The Musk Shrew now lives as a human commensal throughout most of its range. It is generally found in human-made habitats, cultivated areas and around human habitation. The Musk Shrew is nocturnal and solitary, being quite intolerant of conspecifics. Their extensive vocal repertoire of high-pitched chirrups, clicks and buzzes is normally associated with aggressive behaviour. The day is spent in burrows or inside buildings.

These animals are voracious little hunters, their diet consisting mainly of insects, but also other invertebrates, even small vertebrates and whatever edible human refuse can be scavenged.

It is possible this species breeds throughout the year in Madagascar, with a peak occurring between October and December. The gestation period is 30 days and the litter size ranges from two to six, although three is average. Weaning usually takes place between 17 and 20 days and apparent sexual maturity is reached after just 36 days.

Because of its adaptability this species could spread and represent serious competition for the native shrew tenrecs (*Microgale* spp.).

VIEWING May be encountered at night in most areas of human settlement.

Figure 50. Musk Shrew on forest floor, Berenty.

PYGMY MUSK SHREW *Suncus etruscus* (Savi, 1822)

Other name: Pygmy White-toothed Shrew

Malagasy: Voalavo fotsy

MEASUREMENTS Total length: 80-90mm. Head/body length: 50-55mm. Tail length: 30-35mm. Weight: 3-4g.

DESCRIPTION The pelage is greyish-brown, short and soft in texture. This species is the smallest of the shrews and indeed the smallest of terrestrial mammals.

The form on Madagascar is sometimes treated as a full species, endemic to Madagascar and the Comoros: *S. madagascariensis* (Coquerel, 1848).

DISTRIBUTION The Pygmy Musk Shrew appears to be widely distributed throughout Madagascar including both eastern and western regions, although the full extent of its range is uncertain.

BEHAVIOUR Probably solitary and nocturnal. The diet consists primarily of small insects, which may include species like grasshoppers that are slightly larger than the shrew itself. No other aspects of behaviour and ecology are known.

Figure 51. Giant Jumping Rat, Kirindy.

Rats and Mice
Family Muridae

Such is the remarkable diversity in body form displayed by so few genera of rodents on Madagascar that their evolutionary affinities and taxonomy remain a contentious and unresolved issue: on the face of it their only common feature appears to be the cohabitation of Madagascar.

The conventional view has been that the Malagasy rodents represent a classic example of adaptive radiation from a single ancestral species. As such they have been assumed to be a closely interrelated group of common origin. Indeed some recent genetic studies have lent support to this theory, concluding that a number of endemic genera are far more closely related to one another than they are to apparently similar forms found in continental Africa.

In view of this, the Malagasy rodents have been placed in their own endemic subfamily Nesomyinae within the broadly defined family Muridae, although in the past Nesomyinae has variously been placed within the family Cricetidae (the hamsters) or in its own family Nesomyidae (which also included the African swamp rats: Otomyinae).

Other authorities have suggested that the Malagasy rodents are the result of several independent colonisations of the island, and concluded that some present-day Malagasy species are more closely related to continental African forms than their fellows on Madagascar; accordingly the Malagasy rodents have been divided between four subfamilies – Cricetinae, Gymnuromyinae, Tachyoryctinae and Microtinae – within the family Muridae.

More recent and ongoing field research into Madagascar's endemic rodent communities has re-opened this debate, and it has once again been suggested that rodents arrived on Madagascar in several waves of colonisation and, therefore, the contemporary endemic assemblage does not share an immediate common ancestry. It is clear that this question will only been answered conclusively after further investigation, and the taxonomy presented here will almost certainly be subject to subsequent amendment.

Three rodents have also been introduced to Madagascar by man: the Black Rat *Rattus rattus*, Brown Rat *Rattus norvegicus* and House Mouse *Mus musculus*. As in most other parts of the world, these species now live as human commensals.

97

Subfamily Nesomyinae

The endemic subfamily Nesomyinae contains only eight genera, although at least one new genus containing two new species is currently awaiting formal description. There are great differences between these genera, but very close relationships within them. Equally remarkable, the eight genera (nine if the undescribed genus is included) comprise only 20 species, a very small total for an island the size of Madagascar. Following accepted patterns relating to the colonisation of islands, one would expect around 50 indigenous rodent species on a land mass the size of Madagascar. There are two possible explanations for this apparent paucity. Either the rodent fauna of Madagascar is unusually impoverished, or the inventory is incomplete. Given the other peculiar features of Madagascar's fauna, the former is certainly possible. However, few comprehensive small mammal surveys have yet taken place, so the latter may also be true. Indeed, recent surveys (undertaken during the 1990s) have discovered no less than two new genera and seven new species of rodent, the majority of which still await formal description, and it seems probable that further new species will come to light as more surveys take place.

The apparent unremarkable speciation shown by the Malagasy rodents has been accompanied by impressive morphological and ecological divergence between them. There are great differences in body size, form and behaviour within the subfamily Nesomyinae. This striking variety is underlined by the comparisons that have been drawn to their outward appearance, the various genera being likened to gerbils (*Macrotarsomys*), voles (*Brachyuromys*), Old World murines (*Gymnuromys*), arboreal dormice (*Eliurus*), generalised cricetines (*Nesomys*) and even rabbits (*Hypogeomys*). Nevertheless, they do share certain features: all are native habitat dwellers and the majority appear to be predominately nocturnal.

As mirrored by the Tenrecidae, species abundance and diversity amongst Malagasy rodents appears to increase with altitude, reaching a peak at montane and upper montane elevations, at approximately 1,200m to 1,600m.

Figure 52. Giant Jumping Rat.

GIANT JUMPING RAT genus *Hypogeomys* A. Grandidier, 1869

This genus contains a single extant species. A second species of jumping rat has been described from subfossil remains dating back 4,400 years, found in caves 40km west of Tolagnaro in south-east Madagascar. On the basis of jawbone measurements, the now extinct *Hypogeomys australis* was distinctly larger than *H. antimena*.

GIANT JUMPING RAT *Hypogeomys antimena* A. Grandidier, 1869

Malagasy: Votsotsa, Votsotse, Vositse

MEASUREMENTS Total length: 540-585mm. Head/body length: 305-345mm. Tail length: 215-240mm. Weight: 1.1-1.3kg.

DESCRIPTION A rotund rabbit-like rodent with conspicuous large ears: this is the largest rodent on Madagascar (figs. 51 & 53). The fur is short, dense and quite coarse. The upperparts vary from medium/dark brown to light brown-grey, and there are even reddish tinges on some individuals. The head is usually the darkest area. The underparts are much paler, generally creamy-grey or off-white. There may also be a darker V-shaped area on top of the nose. The snout is blunt, the ears long (50-65mm) and protruding from the top of the head. The tail is muscular, dark in colour and covered in short stiff hairs. Juveniles have noticeably greyer upperparts and paler underparts.

DISTRIBUTION The Giant Jumping Rat is restricted to the narrow coastal zone of dry deciduous forest, north of the Andranomena River and south of the Tsiribihina River, in western Madagascar. This area is characterised by sandy soils and forest floor permanently covered in dry leaf-litter. The total range of the species may not exceed 1,000km². Within the best areas of habitat, population densities reach around 50 individuals/km².

Subfossil evidence indicates that this species was once much more widely distributed. Giant Jumping Rat remains from the Holocene (estimated to be around 1,400 years old) have been unearthed at two localities on the Mahafaly Plateau, south of Lac Tsimanampetsotsa in south-west Madagascar, more than 450km south of the current range. Further subfossil evidence also indicates that the range of *antimena* extended northward to at least the Antsirabe region in central Madagascar.

BEHAVIOUR The Giant Jumping Rat is strictly nocturnal and lives in monogamous social units comprising a pair with their offspring from each year. Pairbonds between adult males and females last more than one breeding season and persist outside the reproductive period, normally until one mate is predated. The predation rate is high, mainly from the Fosa *Cryptoprocta ferox* and Madagascar Ground Boa *Acrantophis madagascariensis*. If one of the pair is killed, the remaining mate normally develops a new pairbond within a few days or weeks.

The Giant Jumping Rat moves on all fours (fig. 54) or in a 'kangaroo-like' hop on its hind legs. This species forages, alone or in pairs, on the forest floor for fallen fruit and seeds, and is also known to strip bark from saplings. The food is held in the forepaws and manipulated in the mouth while the rat sits semi-upright (rather like a rabbit).

Births begin at the onset of the hot rainy season (late November) and this corresponds to a reduction in the parents' home range size. A litter of one to two is produced, the young remaining within the burrow for the first three to four weeks; when they first venture out they stay very close to the entrance. Female offspring remain with their parents for between two and three years, then leave to begin breeding themselves; males normally leave when around one year old, and are sometimes able to establish a territory and mate within a short period. More normally, however, they are unable to do this until at least two years of age.

Giant Jumping Rat

The family unit occupies a territory of between three and four hectares (it is larger in the dry season when food is more scarce), dotted around which are specific latrine sites where scent from both urine and faeces is important in demarcating territorial boundaries.

The home ranges of neighbouring pairs are mutually exclusive. Within the territory, usually on a slightly elevated area of bare soil, is the family burrow. This complex of tunnels (around 45cm diameter) may be up to 5m across and have 1-6 entrance holes, although only 1-3 of these are in use at any one time, the others being blocked by soil and leaves. Even the entrances in use are 'plugged' with a barrier of soil at a depth of around 50cm and must be excavated by the animals to allow passage in and out. These burrows provide protection for both young and adults against the elements (the heat is intense during the austral summer and the animals also return to the burrow during heavy rain at night) and against the Fosa and Madagascar Ground Boa. There are many unoccupied burrows within a territory which may be used as temporary refuges from predators during bouts of nightly activity or by young males who have recently vacated their parental burrow.

VIEWING The best place to see the Giant Jumping Rat is Kirindy Forest, about 60km north-east of Morondava in western Madagascar. It is perhaps more active on moonless nights and can be readily encountered in some areas of the main trail network.

Figure 53. Giant Jumping Rat.

Figure 54. *Giant Jumping Rat foraging, Kirindy.*

Figure 55. *Eastern Red Forest Rat, Ranomafana.*

RED FOREST RATS genus *Nesomys* Peters, 1870

This genus was previously thought to contain a single species, *Nesomys rufus*, divided into three subspecies. After recent research and review these subspecies have been elevated to full species status. However, the data on *Nesomys* remains scant and it seems likely that this genus will undergo further revision as more information becomes available. All three of the species currently recognised are forest-dwelling rats, with chestnut-reddish fur.

In the past they have generally been reported as being strictly nocturnal, but this is not the case. In fact they are primarily diurnal and crepuscular and are often encountered along rainforest tracks during daylight hours. In general, diurnal murid rodents are rare in tropical forests: diurnalism may be possible in *Nesomys* because of the reduced predator pressure in Malagasy forests compared to tropical forests elsewhere; it may also reduce competition with other Malagasy rodent species that are nocturnal.

EASTERN RED FOREST RAT *Nesomys rufus* Peters, 1870

Eastern
Red Forest Rat

MEASUREMENTS Total length: 310-410mm. Head/body length: 150-200mm. Tail length: 160-200mm. Weight: 125-200g; female average 150g; male average 175g.

DESCRIPTION A medium-sized, robust forest rat, similar in appearance to the Brown Rat *Rattus norvegicus*, but appreciably smaller. The pelage is longish, soft and smooth. Upperparts are reddish-brown, sometimes flecked with darker brown, and there are also darker guard hairs. Around the cheeks, flanks and rump there may be a hint of more reddish-chestnut coloration (fig. 55). The underparts are generally slightly paler rufous-brown. The chin and throat may be whitish. The ears are rounded and prominent (20-25mm), while the whiskers are fine and black. The tail is medium-long (similar to the head/body length), narrow, moderately covered in hair and occasionally white at the tip, but there is no suggestion of a terminal tuft.

DISTRIBUTION *N. rufus* occurs throughout the middle- and high-altitude (900-2,300m) rainforest regions of central eastern and north-eastern Madagascar from Tsaratanana and Sambava in the north to the Andringitra Massif in the south. Populations of *Nesomys* are also known from west of the Tsaratanana Massif in the moist forests of the Sambirano region; these are here provisionally assumed to be *N. rufus*.

BEHAVIOUR The Eastern Red Forest Rat is strictly terrestrial and diurnal. Both males and females occupy home ranges of between 0.4ha and 0.6ha, and which appear to be constant from year to year. Home ranges are non-exclusive and may be shared with several other individuals. There is considerable overlap between the ranges of males and females and between neighbouring individuals of the same sex.

A home range will contain a number of widely dispersed burrows or dens that are all in regular use, although there is often a preferred site. Burrows are generally located under fallen logs and brush piles, and each has several entrances. They are multi-chambered: upper chambers are lined with freshly clipped grass and may be used as food storage caches, while the deeper chambers are lined with deep beds of shredded palm fronds or similar vegetation and are used for sleeping. Occasionally males and females will share a den.

Activity usually begins just before sunrise, males often becoming active before females. Foraging bouts are more intense in the early morning and towards late afternoon and to a lesser extent around midday. Individuals rarely travel more than 500m in a day. Foraging efforts are concentrated in leaf-litter, around dead logs and in dense tangles of herbaceous vegetation. The diet consists mainly of seeds and fallen fruits, for example *Cryptocarya* (Lauraceae), *Canarium* (Burseraceae), *Artabotrys mabifolius* (Annonaceae) and *Sloanea rhodanta* (Elaeocarpaceae). *N. rufus* is also adept at scavenging around rainforest research camps and associated rubbish pits.

Adult males and females from the Andringitra Massif examined in November and December were found to be in reproductive condition, which suggests breeding occurs around this time. Litter sizes of one or two are implied.

In most rainforest areas the Eastern Red Forest Rat is sympatric with several other native rodents, for instance White-tailed Tree Rat *Brachytarsomys albicauda*, *Eliurus* species and Voalavoanala *Gymnuromys roberti*. *Nesomys rufus* appears to be the most abundant representative in such mixed communities.

VIEWING The Eastern Red Forest Rat can be encountered in many eastern rainforest parks and reserves. It is often seen in Ranomafana National Park in the vicinity of Belle Vue and around the research cabin near the main trail, particularly in late April and early May when fallen Chinese guava fruit are plentiful on the forest floor. Mantadia National Park and Analamazaotra Special Reserve are also good places to see this species.

LOWLAND RED FOREST RAT *Nesomys audeberti* Jentink, 1879

MEASUREMENTS Total length: 330-430mm. Head/body length: 160-210mm. Tail length: 170-220mm. Weight: 190-230g: females average 200g, males average 225g.

DESCRIPTION This species is very similar to *N. rufus*, but generally larger. The upper pelage is reddish-brown flecked with darker guard hairs. The underparts are much paler, often light brownish-grey to off-white. The tail has a white tuft at its tip.

DISTRIBUTION *N. audeberti* appears to prefer elevations below 800m in eastern lowland rainforests and is found from the Masoala Peninsula in the north to around Manantenina in the south. The Lowland Red Forest Rat has been recorded at elevations up to 1,000m and is probably sympatric at many localities with its congener *N. rufus* at altitudes between 800m and 1,000m (for instance Ranomafana). This zone corresponds to the transition from lowland to montane rainforest.

BEHAVIOUR The Lowland Red Forest Rat is terrestrial and forages on the forest floor for seeds and fallen fruits, but is also capable of climbing amongst fallen logs. The night is spent in a multi-chambered burrow, generally located under a tangle of roots, a fallen log or similar secluded spot. These burrows are similar to those of *N. rufus*: they are multi-chambered with several entrances, and the deeper chambers are used for sleeping.

Activity begins around sunrise and continues throughout most of the morning. It then begins to decline after midday and the rats return to their burrow before dark. Males occupy home ranges of up to 1.4ha and appear to be more active than females, whose home ranges are smaller, around 0.5ha. In common with *N. rufus*, these home ranges are non-exclusive. Animals generally travel no more than 400-500m in the day.

Being diurnal and terrestrial, *Nesomys* is able to avoid competition with other sympatric native rodents: *Brachytarsomys* and *Eliurus* species are nocturnal and arboreal, while *Gymnuromys* is terrestrial but nocturnal.

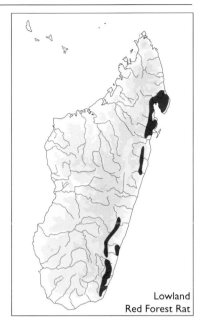

Lowland Red Forest Rat

VIEWING The forests in the vicinity of Ambanizana on the Masoala Peninsula are perhaps the most likely places to see this species. It can also be encountered at Ranomafana National Park, where it is sympatric with *N. rufus*.

WESTERN RED FOREST RAT *Nesomys lambertoni* G. Grandidier, 1928

MEASUREMENTS Total length: 310-410mm. Head/body length: 150-200mm. Tail length: 160-200mm. Weight: c. 140-170*g. *estimated measurement

DESCRIPTION This species is known from only a handful of specimens. Overall, it is very similar in appearance to *N. rufus*. The dorsal pelage is reddish-brown, while the underparts are paler, with a more orange wash. The tail is long and conspicuously hairy.

DISTRIBUTION The Western Red Forest Rat is known only from the type locality, near Maintirano on the west coast of Madagascar, and from a recently captured (1991) specimen in the Tsingy de Bemaraha National Park to the south of Antsalova. These remain the only records for *Nesomys* in western Madagascar.

BEHAVIOUR The behaviour and ecology of this species are unknown.

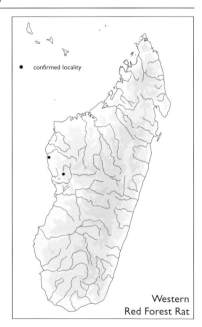

confirmed locality

Western Red Forest Rat

TUFT-TAILED RATS genus *Eliurus* Milne-Edwards, 1885

Members of the genus *Eliurus* are all small to medium in body size and have various distinctive body features associated with a scansorial way of life, the most noticeable being broad hindfeet with elongate fifth digits and a long tail; in all species the tail length exceeds the head/body length (115-120%). The tail itself is densely haired and ends in a conspicuous terminal tuft or pencil. Because of this latter feature, *Eliurus* are referred to as tuft-tailed rats.

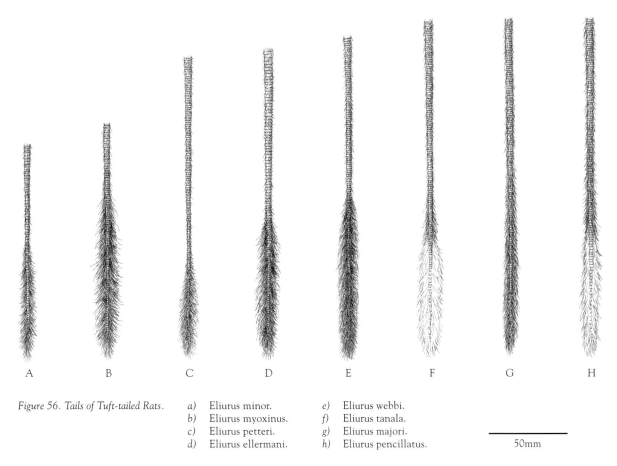

A   B   C   D   E   F   G   H

Figure 56. Tails of Tuft-tailed Rats.

a) Eliurus minor.	*e)* Eliurus webbi.
b) Eliurus myoxinus.	*f)* Eliurus tanala.
c) Eliurus petteri.	*g)* Eliurus majori.
d) Eliurus ellermani.	*h)* Eliurus pencillatus.

50mm

At present eight species are recognised (although four new species are currently under description): seven species from eastern rainforest regions and one (*E. myoxinus*) from the dry forests and scrub of the west and south. External differences between species are principally in size, relative tail length, colour and texture of the fur, and the colour, extent and characteristics of the tail tuft. Internally there are also cranial and dental differences between the species.

All are small to medium-sized rats, with long tails. The pelage is soft and fine, consisting of a thick coat of cover hairs, interspersed with longer, darker, coarse guard hairs. The dorsal pelage is usually longer and denser than the ventral pelage. Overall the upperparts appear a shade of brown to brownish-grey, while the underparts are generally creamy-grey to buff, the transition between the two being quite abrupt. In two species (*E. majori* and *E. pencillatus*), however, this is not the case, dorsal and ventral fur being similar shades with no pronounced lateral line.

Dark hairs around the eye often give the impression of an eyering, and facial vibrissae are well developed. The hindfeet are relatively short, broad and pale in colour. All the digits have claws. The tail is relatively long (110-135% head/body length) and ends in a brush-like tuft (pencillate) that covers the distal 1/2 to 1/4 of the tail. The sexes are similar in size.

The largely arboreal habits of the tuft-tailed rats make them a difficult group to observe in the wild. The majority of records are from species caught in traps placed in the lower branches of the forest understorey.

Figure 57. Western Tuft-tailed Rat, Ampijoroa.

WESTERN TUFT-TAILED RAT *Eliurus myoxinus* Milne-Edwards, 1885

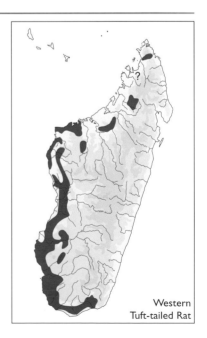

MEASUREMENTS Total length: 265-280mm. Head/body length: 125-135mm. Tail length: 140-145mm. Weight: 40-100g.

DESCRIPTION The upperparts are light sandy-brown, while the underparts, including the throat, are pale grey to creamy-grey. The tail is relatively short compared with congeners (105-110% head/body length). The proximal 1/3 is scaled, while the distal 2/3 are covered in brown hair (12-15mm long) which forms a thick dark brush. The head is quite stocky and squarish and the upper incisors a distinctive deep orange. Other than *E. minor*, this is the smallest member of the genus. It is the only member of the genus within its range and so should not be confused with any other species.

DISTRIBUTION This species is found in the western deciduous forests and south-western and southern spiny forests, from the Ankarana Massif in the north to Cape Sainte Marie in the south and around to east of the Mandrare River close to Tolagnaro. In the north-west it may also be present in the more humid forests of the Sambirano region. It is more common in deciduous forests than spiny forests and has not been recorded above 245m in altitude.

BEHAVIOUR *E. myoxinus* is totally arboreal, rarely, if ever, descending to ground level (fig. 57). It nests in tree holes. A gestation period of 24 days has been reported.

Western
Tuft-tailed Rat

Eliurus majori Thomas, 1895

confirmed locality
possible range

Eliurus majori

MEASUREMENTS Total length: 315-375mm. Head/body length: 145-170mm. Tail length: 170-205mm. Weight: 75-125g.

DESCRIPTION Together with *E. tanala* this is probably the largest-bodied member of the genus. The pelage is very soft, dense and woolly in texture. Both the upperparts and underparts are a sombre slate-grey to blackish-brown and there is generally little or no contrast between them. Occasionally, the underparts are slightly paler and creamier in colour. There is a dark eyering which is fairly distinct. The tail is relatively short (approximately 115% head/body length) and although it is well furred and noticeably pencillate, the tuft is less developed than in congeners – there is simply a gradual increase in the length and density of the dark hairs towards the tail tip. The scutellation at the tail base is very fine.

The dark coat, uniform coloration and less developed tail tuft of *E. majori* should prevent confusion with all congeners, except perhaps *E. penicillatus*. The pelage colour and morphology of *E. majori* and *E. penicillatus* are remarkably similar but the latter species has a characteristic white tip to its tail which should serve to differentiate the two.

DISTRIBUTION This species is known from just three widely separated rainforest localities, where it shows a preference for middle to high elevations: Montagne d'Ambre in the far north, at elevations above 1,150m; Ambohimitambo, the type locality, at 1,200m in the central-eastern highlands; and the Andringitra Massif in the south-eastern highlands. The records from Andringitra are at elevations between 1,250m (mid-altitude montane forest) and 2,000m (upper montane or sclerophyllous forest).

At Montagne d'Ambre this species is sympatric with *E. webbi*. In the Andringitra Massif, *E. majori* is known to be sympatric with *E. minor* and *E. tanala*.

BEHAVIOUR Trapping evidence from the Andringitra Massif suggests that *E. majori* is principally arboreal, making occasional forays to ground level. At middle elevations (1,210m) all specimens were caught in vines, lianas or the tangled lower branches of trees. At higher altitudes (1,625m) the majority of individuals were still captured above the ground, but some were also caught in the leaf-litter on the forest floor.

Breeding and births probably occur in November and December: in the Andringitra Massif at this time males with descended testes and females with enlarged mammae have been recorded. A litter size of up to four has been suggested.

Eliurus penicillatus Thomas, 1908

confirmed locality

Eliurus penicillatus

MEASUREMENTS Total length: c. 325mm. Head/body length: c. 150mm. Tail length: c. 175mm. Weight: c. 100g.

DESCRIPTION This species's size, proportions and coloration are very similar to *E. majori*. However, the dorsal pelage is often more brownish than greyish. The tail tuft is slightly more developed and has a conspicuous white tip covering the final 1/3 of the tuft.

DISTRIBUTION *E. penicillatus* is known only from the type locality – montane rainforest in the vicinity of Ambositra (Ampitambe forest). This specimen was collected at an elevation of 900m. It is sympatric with *E. minor*.

BEHAVIOUR The behaviour and ecology of this species are unknown.

Eliurus tanala Major, 1896

MEASUREMENTS Total length: 290-385mm. Head/body length: 125-175mm. Tail length: 165-210mm. Weight: 65-115g.

DESCRIPTION This is a distinctive species of *Eliurus* which, along with *E. majori*, is probably the largest member of the genus. The upperparts are dark greyish-brown, with the flanks a slightly paler tone than the back. In some individuals the back is noticeably darker. The underparts are a light buffy-grey, approaching creamy-grey in some individuals. The feet are also white or very pale grey. The tail is relatively long (120-130% head/body length) and the pencil is thin and relatively short, covering only the final 1/3 of the tail. The terminal tuft is bushy, white and very conspicuous. It is this feature which differentiates this species from *E. majori* and *E. webbi*, which are broadly similar in size.

DISTRIBUTION This species occurs in central-eastern and south-eastern rainforests at lower, middle and high altitudes (455-1,625m), although it appears to be more common at the higher elevations. Its range extends from just south-east of Lac Alaotra, southward to the Andringitra Massif south-east of Fianarantsoa.

BEHAVIOUR This species appears to utilise a variety of microhabitats including grassy glades, lush herbaceous growth, tangles of vines along watercourses, stands of tree ferns and bamboo thickets. It has been collected in lower branches, lianas and vines, so is at least partially scansorial, but also at ground level, particularly at higher elevations.

Adults in breeding condition have been noted in November and December. At Ranomafana National Park a litter size of two has been recorded and at Andringitra a pregnant female containing three embryos was collected. No other aspects of behaviour or ecology are known.

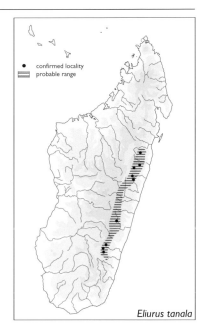

confirmed locality
probable range

Eliurus tanala

Eliurus minor Major, 1896

MEASUREMENTS Total length: 200-265mm. Head/body length: 90-125mm. Tail length: 110-140mm. Weight: 25-50g.

DESCRIPTION The upperparts are light greyish-brown to rich cinnamon-brown, with darker guard hairs. Underparts vary between grey and darkish grey, but are noticeably paler than the upperparts. The transition between the two is abrupt. The tail tuft is dark brown to blackish and well developed, covering around 60% of the tail length. It increases in density towards the tip. This species should not be confused with any congener and is easily recognisable by its small size (it is the smallest member of the genus), longish tail (120% head/body length) and well developed dark tail tuft.

Amongst the Malagasy rodents only the recently described Mountain Mouse (*Monticolomys koopmani*) approaches *E. minor* in overall size and general appearance: *E. minor* can be distinguished by its heavier build, shorter tail and conspicuous tail tuft.

It is possible *E. minor* could be differentiated further, into subspecies or even new species, as so much variation exists within the taxon. For instance, specimens from lowland forest areas around the Bay of Antongil in the north-east are larger and more russet-coloured than apparent conspecifics from other localities. More extensive research is certainly needed to clarify the situation.

DISTRIBUTION This species has a wide range within the eastern rainforests, from the eastern slopes of Tsarantanana in the north to the Vondrozo area in the south-east. It is known to have the greatest altitude tolerance of any nesomyine rodent and has been recorded from sea-level to around 1,800m, although middle elevations may be preferred. It also occurs sympatrically with several other congeners (*E. penicillatus*, *E. tanala* and *E. webbi*), and quite possibly all of them (with the exception of *E. myoxinus* which is restricted to western and southern areas).

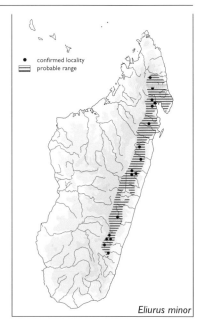

confirmed locality
probable range

Eliurus minor

BEHAVIOUR In lowland and mid-altitude rainforests, *E. minor* utilises a wide variety of terrestrial and arboreal microhabitats. It is known to forage both at ground level and amongst vines and lianas in the understorey, and has been observed climbing to a height of several metres. In the Andringitra Massif males and females have been recorded in breeding condition in December.

Eliurus webbi Ellerman, 1949

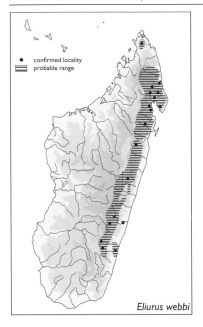

Eliurus webbi

MEASUREMENTS Total length: 260-355mm. Head/body length: 105-160mm. Tail length: 155-195mm. Weight: 55-95g.

DESCRIPTION A moderately large species of *Eliurus* that is lighter in build than its other large congeners, *E. majori* and *E. tanala*. The pelage has a soft texture and is quite long, particularly over the dorsal region and flanks. The upperparts are buffy-brown to grey-brown, while the underparts are dull yellowish-grey; the transition between the two is abrupt. Some slight regional variation in ventral pelage colour has been noted. The tail is relatively long (120-130% head body length), the tuft is entirely dark brown to blackish-brown and well-developed (hairs 10-12mm long) cover the distal 2/5 of the tail (fig. 58).

DISTRIBUTION This species has the most extensive known range of any rainforest dwelling *Eliurus*. It is found in undisturbed lowland and mid-altitude rainforests (up to around 1,500m) from Montagne d'Ambre in the north to the region of Vondrozo and Farafangana (the type locality) on the south-east coast and including the Andringitra Massif. At lower elevations in the Andringitra Massif (720-810m) this species is sympatric with *E. tanala*.

BEHAVIOUR *E. webbi* is at least partially scansorial. It has been observed and collected at ground level and in lianas and the lower branches of trees. There is evidence to suggest that *E. webbi* lives in monogamous pairs that occupy ground burrows up to a metre in depth. The rodents inhabit a chamber at the rear of the burrow which is also used to store seeds (*Cryptocarya* [Lauraceae] have been recorded). When leaving the burrow, *E. webbi* has been seen to clog the entrance with soil and leaf-litter. It seems likely that this species at least nests and forages at completely different levels in the forest.

Figure 58. Tuft-tailed rat, Eliurus webbi.

There is also a record of a pair of *E. webbi* occupying and sharing the same burrow system as a nesting Scaly Ground-roller *Brachypteracias squamiger*, a ground-dwelling rainforest bird belonging to the endemic family Brachypteraciidae. In this instance the ground-roller nest was located in the principal tunnel of the burrow system, while the rodents' food cache was located at the rear so that the rodents would have to climb over the ground-rollers' nest when entering and exiting the burrow.

It has been suggested that breeding probably takes place between July and September. In November and December in the Andringitra Massif very few individuals examined showed signs of reproductive activity: this contrasts sharply with specimens of *E. tanala* examined at the same locations at the same time. No other aspects of this species' sbehaviour and ecology are known.

Eliurus ellermani Carleton, 1994

MEASUREMENTS Total length: around 330mm**. Head/body length: 152mm**. Tail length: 177mm**. Weight: c. 100g*.
*estimated measurement, **measurements taken from a single specimen.

DESCRIPTION A moderately large *Eliurus*. The upperparts are drab dark grey-brown, while the underparts are dull creamy-buff. The pelage is longish and relatively coarse. There is a noticeably dark eyering and the upper incisors are bright orange. The tail is moderately long (115% head/body length) and the tail tuft extends over the final 1/3. The tuft is well developed (hairs 9-11mm long) and is dark all the way to the tip. The scutellation over the first 2/3 of the tail is very well developed and quite coarsely defined. Overall this species resembles a more robust version of *E. tanala*, except that the tail of *E. ellermani* is completely dark to the tip.

DISTRIBUTION This species is known from only two widely separate localities, which suggests that it occurs in lowland and mid-altitude rainforest in the north-east. The type specimen was collected around 40km north-west of Maroantsetra, while the other record came from the vicinity of Lohariandava in central-eastern Madagascar at an elevation of around 400m. This species is probably sympatric with *E. minor* and *E. webbi*.

BEHAVIOUR The behaviour and ecology of *E. ellermani* remain unknown.

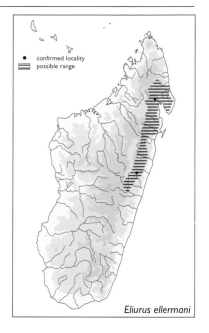

confirmed locality
possible range

Eliurus ellermani

Eliurus petteri Carleton, 1994

MEASUREMENTS Total length: 305-340mm. Head/body length: 130-135mm. Tail length: 175-205mm. Weight: c. 75g.

DESCRIPTION This is a moderately sized *Eliurus* with a very long tail. The pelage is longish and soft in texture, producing a noticeably sleek appearance. The upperparts are generally dark grey-brown, but may vary from charcoal-grey to paler grey-brown. The underparts are conspicuous bright white, something that sets this species apart from congeners. There is a very distinct line between the dorsal and ventral coloration. The tail tuft is weakly developed and covers only the final 1/4 of the tail. The tuft hairs are light brown or greyish-brown and relatively short (8-10mm). The tail itself is relatively the longest in the genus – around 135% head/body length.

DISTRIBUTION The three known specimens originate from neighbouring localities in the central-eastern rainforest – Fanovana, Andasibe and Rogez – at elevations between 400m and 1,000m. This suggests that the species has a rather restricted distribution, but the lack of information means its full extent cannot be accurately determined. *E. petteri* is probably sympatric with *E. minor*, *E. tanala* and *E. webbi*.

BEHAVIOUR The behaviour and ecology of this species are unknown.

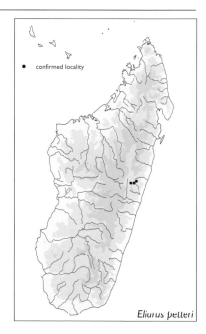

confirmed locality

Eliurus petteri

VOALAVOANALA genus *Gymnuromys* Major, 1896

This genus contains just a single species. Ellerman (1941) created a new subfamily Gymnuromyinae in recognition of the distinctive features of this species, which he believed to be derived from a *Nesomys*-like ancestor.

VOALAVOANALA *Gymnuromys roberti* Major, 1896

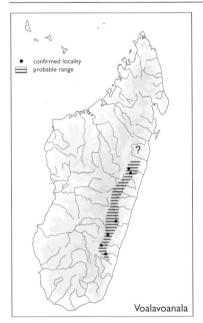

confirmed locality
probable range

Voalavoanala

MEASUREMENTS Total length: 275-355mm. Head/body length: 125-170mm. Tail length: 150-175mm. Weight: c. 70-125g.

DESCRIPTION A medium-sized typically rat-like rodent with a stout body and relatively short tail. The pelage is short and sleek: upperparts are blackish-grey to slaty-grey, while the underparts are grey-white to yellowish-white with a silvery sheen. The ears protrude and are rounded. The vibrissae are dark and long (50-60mm) (fig. 59). The scantily haired scaly tail appears naked to the unaided eye and is bicoloured, being dark grey on top and pale grey to white underneath: the final 25-30% of the tail is often completely white. The tail is around 105-110% of the head/body length and does not end in a terminal tuft.

In coloration this species superficially resembles young Black Rats *Rattus rattus* or some tuft-tailed rats *Eliurus* sp., particularly *E. majori*. However, in comparison *Rattus* has a uniformly dark and very much longer tail, while the coat of *E. majori* is more woolly and its tail considerably longer ending in a visible terminal tuft.

DISTRIBUTION This species occurs in central-eastern and south-eastern lowland and mid-altitude rainforest, from the vicinity of Andasibe in the north, south to the Vondrozo area and including the Andringitra Massif. *G. roberti* appears to have a very wide altitudinal tolerance and has been reported at elevations from 500m to 1,800m.

On the Andringitra Massif *G. roberti* has been recorded at all altitudes between 720m and 1,625m: at this locality the only other rodents to have such a broad elevational range are *Eliurus minor* and *Nesomys rufus*.

BEHAVIOUR Evidence suggests that the Voalavoanala is exclusively terrestrial and nocturnal, and probably forages for fallen seeds and fruits in leaf-litter and amongst roots, trunks and fallen logs. It lives in ground burrows up to a metre deep, often located under fallen logs. The burrow tunnel tends to be relatively straight and ends in a small chamber which is used for food storage: one chamber examined contained 22 fruits of *Canarium madagascariense* (Burseraceae), 21 of which were gnawed open and the cotyledons eaten.

It is possible this species is suffering increasing competition from the introduced Black Rat and Brown Rat *Rattus norvegicus*.

VIEWING Its nocturnal habits make this is a difficult species to observe in the wild. It can occasionally be seen at Analamazaotra Special Reserve, Mantadia National Park and Ranomafana National Park.

WHITE-TAILED TREE RATS genus *Brachytarsomys* Günther, 1875

This genus contains two species of large arboreal rat which exhibit a number of traits betraying their scansorial habits – most notably a prehensile, predominately white tail, giving rise to their specific and vernacular names. Some authorities consider *B. villosa* to be a subspecies of *B. albicauda*, and the taxonomy of the genus remains questionable.

WHITE-TAILED TREE RAT *Brachytarsomys albicauda* Günther, 1875

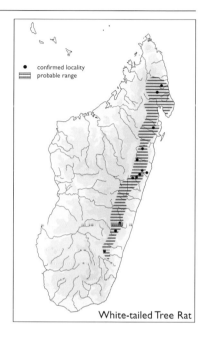

confirmed locality
probable range

White-tailed Tree Rat

MEASUREMENTS Total length: 385-480mm. Head/body length: 200-250mm. Tail length: 185-230mm. Weight: c. 200g*.
*estimated measurement

DESCRIPTION The pelage is soft, dense and quite 'woolly' in texture: the upperparts are greyish-brown, becoming more rufous on the flanks, while the underparts and feet are off-white. The head is more reddish-brown and the nose and mouth area are blackish. The prehensile tail is dark towards its base but white over most of its length and is sparsely haired. The snout is quite short, giving the head a rather blunt appearance, and there are five rows of longish dark whiskers (fig. 60). The eyes are largish, sometimes bulbous, and the ears are small. On the feet the claws are prominent and the hindfoot has an extra-long fifth digit. Overall this species has a typical 'rat-like' appearance, rather similar to *Nesomys*, although the hind feet are much shorter and broader in *Brachytarsomys* and there are considerable differences in cranial structure between the two.

DISTRIBUTION This species is found in eastern rainforest areas at low to middle elevations (450-1,300m), from the Marojejy and Anjanaharibe-Sud Massifs south to the vicinity of the Andringitra Massif.

BEHAVIOUR *B. albicauda* is nocturnal and probably totally arboreal, making its nest in tree holes. If disturbed during the day individuals may appear at their hole entrance and chatter. The diet consists mainly of various canopy fruits and seeds.

VIEWING This species can sometimes be seen at Analamazaotra Special Reserve, the nearby forests of Moromizaha, Mantadia National Park and Ranomafana National Park. If a likely-looking tree hole is located, a sharp thump on the trunk with a solid object will sometimes bring the occupant chattering to the entrance.

Brachytarsomys villosa Petter, 1962

MEASUREMENTS Total length: 450-500mm. Head/body length: 230-250mm. Tail length: 230-250mm. Weight: c. 220g*.
*estimated measurement

DESCRIPTION In overall appearance this species is very similar to its congener, *B. albicauda*. On the basis of generally larger size and longer tail hairs (10-14mm versus 2-4mm), *B. villosa* has been given full species status.

DISTRIBUTION *B. villosa* is known only from a single specimen, the collecting locality of which was not described. A distribution within the eastern rainforest belt is suspected.

BEHAVIOUR The behaviour and ecology of this species are unknown.

Figure 59. Voalavoanala.

Figure 60. White-tailed Tree Rat.

Figure 61. Vole rat, Brachyuromys ramirohitra.

VOLE RATS genus *Brachyuromys* Major, 1896

As noted by the discoverers of the two known species of *Brachyuromys*, these rodents show remarkable resemblance in body form and ecology to some Holarctic voles (Microtinae). For this reason they are often referred to as vole rats.

The head is broad with small rounded ears, and the torso is compact. The legs are short with relatively narrow hindfeet. The tail is conspicuously shorter than the head/body length – around 50-60%. The pelage is fine, but dense and soft in texture. Dorsally, *Brachyuromys* species are rich brown to reddish-brown; the venter is similarly coloured with no obvious transition. The uniformly dark tail is covered in short hairs.

These species live in native rainforests, sclerophyllous forests and moist meadows especially in areas of dense vegetation, tangles of roots, matted grasses and reeds. Beneath such vegetation they construct networks of runways, the vegetation above often being so dense that no sunlight penetrates. Within these 'tunnel' systems, they appear to be active at all hours, both day and night, feeding predominantly on grass. *Brachyuromys* may also live in the same areas as *Microgale*, *Eliurus* and introduced *Rattus* species.

The essentially fossorial nature of these species make observations difficult. In order to see them it is generally necessary to set traps.

Brachyuromys ramirohitra Major, 1896

Brachyuromys ramirohitra

MEASUREMENTS Total length: 225-275mm. Head/body length: 140-165mm. Tail length: 85-110mm. Weight: 65-115g.

DESCRIPTION The pelage is thick and soft. Upperparts are overall brown, with reddish and blackish tinges. The underparts tend to be more reddish although there is no obvious distinction between the two. The snout is blunt and the head broad and rounded. The tail is short, dark and hairy. These features should prevent confusion with all other native nesomyine species (fig. 61). This is the larger of the two *Brachyuromys* species.

DISTRIBUTION This vole rat is known only from three localities in the south-eastern highlands: Ampitambe (the type locality) at 900m; Amboasary at 1,300m; and the Andringitra Massif up to 1,625m. This indicates the species prefers higher altitudes, but the limits of its range are essentially unknown.

In all localities this species occurs in very close proximity to *B. betsileoensis*, if not in actual sympatry. Evidence from the Andringitra Massif suggests *B. ramirohitra* prefers slightly lower elevations than its congener: it has been recorded in primary montane forest at 1,210m and sclerophyllous forest at 1,625m.

BEHAVIOUR In the Andringitra Massif specimens have been caught on the ground close to extensive natural tunnel networks associated with tangled roots.

Brachyuromys betsileoensis (Bartlett, 1880)

Brachyuromys betsileoensis

MEASUREMENTS Total length: 190-240mm. Head/body length: 125-160mm. Tail length: 65-80mm. Weight: 85-100g.

DESCRIPTION The overall appearance of this species is very similar to *B. ramirohitra*, although it is noticeably smaller. The dorsal and ventral pelage is plain brown and lacks the rich reddish tones of its congener. The pelage is also shorter and less luxuriant than *B. ramirohitra*.

DISTRIBUTION This species is found in heathland, lush native meadows and wetland areas in the eastern-central highlands at higher elevations up to around 2,100m. The northern limits of its range appear to be south-east of Lac Alaotra, with the southern limit being the Andringitra Massif. At Andringitra, *B. betsileoensis* has been recorded in the upper portions of montane and sclerophyllous forests between 1,700m and 1,900m and heathland areas above the treeline at 2,000m to 2,100m.

BEHAVIOUR This species is known to be predated by the Fosa *Cryptoprocta ferox*: at Andringitra skeletal remains have been found in scats in heathland areas at elevations of 2,000-2,100m. No other aspects of the behaviour and ecology of this species are known.

In the map legends:
- confirmed locality
- probable range

MOUNTAIN MOUSE genus *Monticolomys* Carleton and Goodman, 1996

This is a recently described monotypic genus characterised by its small size, dense pelage, rounded ears and relatively long tail. Within the Nesomyinae only the allopatric genus *Macrotarsomys* is smaller. *Monticolomys* is also probably more closely related to *Macrotarsomys* than the other Nesomyine rodents.

MALAGASY MOUNTAIN MOUSE *Monticolomys koopmani* Carleton and Goodman, 1996

confirmed locality

Malagasy
Mountain Mouse

MEASUREMENTS Total length: 205-240mm. Head/body length: 90-100mm. Tail length: 115-140mm. Weight: c. 25g.

DESCRIPTION The pelage is fine and soft, yet relatively thick. The upperparts are sombre dark brown with black guard hairs, while the underparts, including the chin and throat, are dark grey. There is no sharp demarcation between the dorsal and ventral coloration. The ears are short, rounded and densely furred both inside and out. The tail is uniform grey, very long (about 140% of the head/body length) and covered in fine brown hairs. There is no noticeable terminal tuft.

The small size and general mouse-like appearance of M. *koopmani* should serve to distinguish it from most other sympatric rodents. Only *Eliurus minor* is similarly diminutive, but in comparison M. *koopmani* is lighter in build and has a longer tail which lacks a terminal tuft.

DISTRIBUTION This species is currently known from only two isolated localities in the central highlands: the Ankaratra Massif (1,800-2,000m) where the type specimen was collected, and the Andringitra Massif (1,625m). M. *koopmani* inhabits upper montane/sclerophyllous forest that is regularly covered in cloud and mist: these forests are often dominated by dense stands of bamboo and species from the families Podocarpaceae, Cunoniaceae and Pandanaceae, all of which are encrusted with mosses, lichens and epiphytes.

At Ankaratra M. *koopmani* may be sympatric with *Brachyuromys betsileoensis*, although the record of the latter at this locality is questionable. In the Andringitra Massif, M. *koopmani* is sympatric with six other endemic rodents (*Brachyuromys ramirohitra, Eliurus majori, E. minor, E. tanala, Gymnuromys roberti* and *Nesomys rufus*) and one introduced species (*Rattus rattus*).

BEHAVIOUR M. *koopmani* is an adept climber and has been caught on narrow lianas around 2m above the ground. Certainly the very long tail and enlarged hindfeet and claws suggest a scansorial way of life. However, it has also been recorded at ground level. No other aspects of the behaviour and ecology of this species are known.

Figure 62. Western Forest Mouse, Ampijoroa.

FOREST MICE genus *Macrotarsomys* Milne-Edwards and G. Grandidier, 1898

This genus contains two species of small forest mice that are clearly differentiated by their dimensions. They are nocturnal and superficially resemble some African gerbil species (Gerbillinae). *Macrotarsomys* appears to be restricted to the dry deciduous forest areas of western Madagascar and can be quite common and readily observed in some areas.

WESTERN FOREST MOUSE *Macrotarsomys bastardi* Milne-Edwards and G. Grandidier, 1898

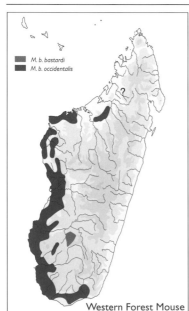

M. b. bastardi
M. b. occidentalis

Western Forest Mouse

Malagasy: Kelibotra, Voalavo

MEASUREMENTS Total length: 180-240mm. Head/body length: 80-100mm. Tail length: 100-140mm. Weight: 20-30g.

DESCRIPTION A small gerbil-like mouse with large ears and a very long tail (fig. 62). This is the smallest member of the subfamily Nesomyinae. The upperparts are light brown-fawn, with a slightly more greyish underfur showing through, while the underparts and legs are paler, often creamy or yellowish-white. The ears are oval in shape and relatively large (20-25mm). The eye is also relatively large, betraying the species's nocturnal habits. The tail is very long indeed (up to 140% of the head/body length), quite stiff and ends in a whitish terminal tuft.

DISTRIBUTION M. *bastardi* is widely distributed in the dry deciduous forests and some grasslands of the south and west. The nominate race, M. *b. bastardi*, is known from the open savanna and bush areas (750-915m altitude) of the central south-west in the vicinity of Ihosy; the second subspecies, M. *b. occidentalis*, has a much wider distribution from southern spiny forest areas close to Tolagnaro in the extreme south, right around to the deciduous forests south-east of Mahajanga in the north-west. Within this band it is found at elevations from sea-level to 245m. The species appears to be restricted by the 20°C isotherm.

BEHAVIOUR The Western Forest Mouse is strictly nocturnal and terrestrial. It moves around the forest floor in a typical hopping motion when covering larger areas of bare ground. The diet consists of seeds, fruits, berries, roots and some plant stems.

Pairs spend the day in long burrows (up to 1.5m) that are excavated under large rocks or tree stumps. These are rarely very deep and have closed concealed outlets. Reproductive activity peaks in April and May (but probably occurs throughout the year) and a litter of two or three individuals is born after a gestation period of around 24 days.

VIEWING This species is readily seen in the Kirindy Forest near Morondava and at Ampijoroa Forestry Station, part of the Ankarafantsika Nature Reserve, south-east of Mahajanga.

Macrotarsomys ingens Petter, 1959

Macrotarsomys ingens

• confirmed locality

MEASUREMENTS Total length: 305-390mm. Head/body length: 115-150mm. Tail length: 190-240mm. Weight: 50-60g.

DESCRIPTION M. *ingens* is very similar in appearance to M. *bastardi*, but appreciably larger in size and with relatively smaller ears. The dorsal pelage is light brown to fawn, while the ventral pelage is paler and creamy-white. The ears are rounded and the tail is very long (up to 170% of the head/body length).

DISTRIBUTION This species is known only from the dry deciduous forests of Ankarafantsika in north-west Madagascar, where the type specimen was collected, and possibly a recently discovered subfossil site south of Toliara in the south-west.

BEHAVIOUR M. *ingens* is known to be nocturnal and almost totally arboreal. The burrows it digs are recognisable by the small piles of soil thrown up outside the entrance. As with M. *bastardi*, however, the entrance is always kept closed.

INTRODUCED SPECIES

To date, three rodent species have been introduced to Madagascar. The Black Rat *Rattus rattus*, Brown Rat *R. norvegicus* and House Mouse *Mus musculus* have been introduced to virtually all parts of the planet and, with the exception of humans, must be the most widely distributed and prolific of all mammal species. Although it is not known exactly when the introductions to Madagascar occurred, it seems probable that these exotic rodents first reached the island around 1,000 years ago. Since then, other waves of introduction may have taken place and the frequency of these has probably increased in recent times.

It is known that there is considerable overlap in the diets of the endemic nesomyine rodents and introduced species, especially *Rattus*. A growing body of evidence indicates that these introduced species are displacing the endemic taxa from native forest habitats through competition and also direct predation. Furthermore, an increasing *Rattus* population may also have a devastating effect on endemic birds, particularly ground dwellers and nesters such as mesites (Mesitornithidae) and ground rollers (Brachypteraciidae).

Old World Rats and Mice
Subfamily Murinae

Due to their ability to survive and adapt to change, capacity to reproduce quickly and history of spectacular diversification, this large subfamily might well be considered one of the most successful groups of mammals on earth: the subfamily Murinae is naturally distributed throughout the Old World south of the Arctic Circle (although not Madagascar) and contains more than 410 species divided between at least 112 genera.

OLD WORLD RATS genus *Rattus* G. Fischer, 1803

Rattus is one of the largest mammalian genera, containing over 50 species that are found throughout the Old World. The two species mentioned here are certainly the most familiar because of their constant association with humans. However, they are certainly not representative of the genus as a whole: most species are more specialised, prefer natural forests, have restricted ranges and often avoid human habitation. All *Rattus* species are omnivorous and eat a wide variety of animal and plant matter. Seeds, grains, nuts, fruits and vegetables are preferred by most species.

BLACK RAT *Rattus rattus* (Linnaeus, 1758)

Other names: Ship Rat, Roof Rat, House Rat
Malagasy: Voalavo

Black Rat

MEASUREMENTS Total length: 310-480mm. Head/body length: 150-230mm. Tail length: 160-250mm. Weight: 85-280g.

DESCRIPTION The upperparts vary from dark slate-grey (almost black) to dark brown, while the underparts and throat are usually paler. The pelage appears quite coarse and shaggy due to the long dark guard hairs. The ears are relatively long, pinkish and hairless and the dark eye is prominent. The tail is also long (up to 115% head/body length), but thin and lacks hairs.

This species is larger than all native nesomyine rodents except the Giant Jumping Rat *Hypogeomys antimena*. Only immature Black Rats could be confused with any endemic species – possibly *Nesomys* or the larger members of *Eliurus*. Other native forms tend to be much smaller and at least partially arboreal. This species is distinguished from the Brown Rat *R. norvegicus* by its generally darker, shaggier coat, more conspicuous ears and longer tail.

DISTRIBUTION The Black Rat is widely distributed throughout Madagascar. It is generally associated with rural villages, degraded areas and wherever native forest cover has been replaced by introduced plants or agriculture. *R. rattus* has also penetrated deep into many pristine native forest areas and throughout the elevational zones to over 2,500m, for example Montagne d'Ambre and the Andringitra Massif, and including offshore islands like Nosy Mangabe.

The Black Rat probably originated in South-East Asia and China and spread westward through India and the Middle East along trade routes. It is now found throughout the world where it lives as a human commensal.

Although *R. rattus* may have arrived on Madagascar as early as the 11th century, evidence suggests that its spread into native forest environs is a relatively recent phenomenon. C. I. Forsyth Major's expedition in 1895/96 to sites in the central-eastern rainforests collected several species of Nesomyinae, but made no mention of introduced rodents. Thus it seems fair to assume that *Rattus* was at least rare in these areas at this time. Some 40 or so years later, C. S. Webb visited rainforest localities near Andasibe (now Analamazaotra Special Reserve), close to sites Forsyth Major had visited, and noted that *R. rattus* (and *R. norvegicus*) 'have multiplied at an alarming rate. The eastern rainforests are now swarming with them, even in the most isolated regions'.

BEHAVIOUR The Black Rat is predominantly nocturnal, its diet consisting mainly of vegetables, fruits, seeds, grains and nuts. It also takes birds' eggs and in native forest areas may predate those of endemic ground-nesters like mesites (Mesitornithidae) and ground-rollers (Brachypteraciidae). *R. rattus* is also very adept at scavenging.

This species is territorial and defends its entire home range, which is usually small. Two or more females are generally subordinate to the dominant male, but are themselves dominant over all other group members.

In many rainforest areas where this species now appears to be widespread, it is probably a severe competitor to sympatric endemic rodents. There is broad dietary overlap between *Rattus* and nesomyine species and direct predation may also occur. Consequently, in some isolated forest patches, native species appear to have been extirpated already, while in other areas where native forests are contiguous *Rattus* may now be the most abundant rodent species. The endemic rodents that are likely to suffer most directly are *Gymnuromys roberti*, *Nesomys* species and to a lesser extent *Eliurus* species. The Black Rat is itself known to be predated by the Fosa *Cryptoprocta ferox*.

VIEWING Often seen in towns and villages around rubbish and where there are rice and grain stores. Also seen scavenging around more permanent forest camps.

BROWN RAT *Rattus norvegicus* (Berkenhout, 1769)

Other names: Common Rat, Norway Rat
Malagasy: Voalavo

MEASUREMENTS Total length: 385-510mm. Head/body length: 215-280mm. Tail length: 170-230mm. Weight: c. 275-520g.

DESCRIPTION The dorsal pelage is generally various shades of brindled brown-grey, giving an overall appearance from mid-brown to dark grey. The ventral pelage is paler grey and sometimes creamy-white on the throat and chest. The ears are short, hairy and partially obscured by the pelage. The tail is relatively short (around 80% head/body length), thick, hairless and bicoloured – dark on top, pale underneath.

Of the endemic rodents, only the Giant Jumping Rat *Hypogeomys antimena* is larger. The Brown Rat appears to have only partially penetrated some native forest areas, mainly those with established field camps. In view of this, confusion with native species seems unlikely. However, small or immature Brown Rats might be confused with *Nesomys*, although these species are generally far more reddish in colour. The Brown Rat is distinguished from the Black Rat *R. rattus* by its often larger size, shorter, fleshier and hairier ears, and a shorter thicker tail.

DISTRIBUTION *R. norvegicus* is found throughout Madagascar, but is mainly restricted to urban environments – refuse tips, sewage systems, food stores, etc. – where it is common. The Brown Rat has been recorded in marginal areas bordering native forests and within these forests where there are permanent field sites. Despite the implications of the Brown Rat's specific name, it may have originated in China (and not Norway). It has now spread throughout the world and generally lives as a human commensal.

BEHAVIOUR This is mainly a nocturnal species, although daytime activity is not uncommon. It is omnivorous, feeding on a variety of seeds, nuts, fruits, invertebrates and smaller vertebrates, and will also eat almost any foodstuff associated with humans, together with oddities like soap and candle wax. Where it occurs in native forests, the Brown Rat may also predate the nests and eggs of native ground-dwelling birds like ground-rollers (Brachypteraciidae) and mesites (Mesitornithidae).

In urban environments their range is small; they rarely move more than 70-80m. In more open areas they may travel three to four kilometres per night. Colonies develop from a pair or single pregnant female, but very large aggregations are usually the result of several of these smaller units (clans) coming together.

In native forest areas, *R. norvegicus* may compete with endemic nesomyine species, for instance, *Gymnuromys roberti*, *Nesomys* species and *Eliurus* species, although its current influence may be far less serious than that of its congener, *R. rattus*.

VIEWING The Brown Rat can be seen at night around waste ground, open sewers and refuse tips in almost any urban area.

Brown Rat

OLD WORLD MICE genus *Mus* Linnaeus, 1758

A large genus containing around 40 species distributed throughout the Old World. As with *Rattus*, most dwell in natural habitats like forests and savannas and have restricted distributions. However, the House Mouse M. *musculus* and a few closely related species, for example M. *cervicolor* and M. *spicilegus*, have spread dramatically in association with man.

HOUSE MOUSE *Mus musculus* Linnaeus, 1758

Malagasy: Totozy

MEASUREMENTS Total length: 150-200mm. Head/body length: 75-100mm. Tail length: 75-100mm. Weight: 12-20g.

DESCRIPTION The upperparts are uniform grey-brown as are the underparts, although they tend to be slightly paler. The ears are rounded and relatively small and the eyes are small. The tail is moderately long, usually equal to the head/body length, and prominently ringed.

The House Mouse is smaller than all the endemic rodents and can only be confused with members of the genus *Macrotarsomys*; however, these species are generally larger and have a proportionally much longer tail (upto 140% head/body length). Confusion with shrew tenrecs is also very unlikely, as *Microgale* species are darker in colour and have very pointed snouts.

DISTRIBUTION Found throughout Madagascar, in association with human habitation from rural villages and agricultural areas to major towns and cities. Its natural range probably extends from Scandinavia to the Mediterranean in Europe, east to Japan and south to Nepal. However, it is now found throughout the world as a human commensal.

BEHAVIOUR The House Mouse is mainly nocturnal and, although omnivorous, shows a preference for cereals and seeds. Home range size varies dramatically with habitat and locality – within farm yards, buildings or similar it may be as little as 4m², while field-dwelling populations may be semi-nomadic and cover 1-2km². These animals live in territorial family units that become aggressive towards one another at higher densities. Breeding can be prolific, with between 5 and 10 litters per year each containing 4-8 young.

VIEWING The House Mouse is often seen in villages, where it is common, especially where there is grain or cereal.

House Mouse

Figure 63. Fosa.

CIVETS AND MONGOOSES
ORDER CARNIVORA

Figure 64. Fosa in rainforest canopy, Mantadia.

Madagascar is home to a remarkable assemblage of carnivores. Remarkable for two reasons: first, there is a smaller number of native species than might be expected – the island's total of eight is impoverished when compared to the diversity shown by the carnivores in Africa and Asia; and second, because of the considerable morphological and ecological diversity that exists amongst them. In addition, the Malagasy carnivores are few in number compared with the radiations that have taken place amongst other mammal groups on the island, most notably the primates (Lemuriformes) and insectivores (Tenrecidae).

There are only two carnivore families that are naturally represented on Madagascar: the civet-like carnivores belonging to the family Viverridae, and the mongooses representing the family Herpestidae. Domestic cats (Felidae) and dogs (Canidae) have been introduced and become feral in some areas.

Debate has surrounded the evolutionary relationships of the civets (Viverridae) to the mongooses (Herpestidae). Some previous authorities have chosen not to recognise the mongooses as a separate family and have included them as a subfamily (Herpestinae) within the Viverridae. This approach has largely been based on tentative evidence relating 'primitive' dental patterns of viverrine civets and herpestine mongooses. However, other taxonomic studies have shown that the mongooses do not share any derived features with viverrids. Various morphological and anatomical features actually suggest that viverrids, felids (cats) and hyaenids (hyaenas) may all share a common ancestry independent of the herpestids. In view of this, the mongooses warrant full distinction at the family level.

Figure 65. Fosa.

Civets and their allies
Family Viverridae

Although restricted to the Old World, the Viverridae is one of the most diverse of all carnivore families and includes the civets, genets, linsangs and their allies. This diversity has long puzzled taxonomists and has presented problems in identifying a common ancestor. Explaining the affinities and peculiarities of the three endemic Malagasy representatives, *Fossa fossana*, *Eupleres goudotii* and *Cryptoprocta ferox*, has been central to these taxonomic difficulties.

The native species are sufficiently different from viverrids in Africa and Asia to warrant subfamily distinction: *Fossa fossana* and *Eupleres goudotii* comprise the subfamily Euplerinae, while *Cryptoprocta ferox* forms the monotypic subfamily Cryptoproctinae. All three species are primarily nocturnal native forest-dwellers and show considerable degrees of morphological and ecological specialisation. They are the largest of the island's endemic carnivores, ranging in size from 1.5kg (*Fossa fossana*) to around 10kg (*Cryptoprocta ferox*).

A single viverrid species, the Small Indian Civet *Viverricula indica* has also been introduced to the island, probably during the early human colonisations from the Indo-Malay region.

There can be misunderstanding regarding the vernacular names of these animals. The generic name of the Malagasy Civet, *Fossa*, often causes confusion with the vernacular for *Cryptoprocta ferox*, the Fosa. Secondly, *Fossa fossana* is generally known by its Malagasy name, 'Fanaloka', which is sometimes interchangeable with 'Falanouc' or a further derivation, 'Fanalouc' depending on region. However, these latter two names are more often used to refer to the Small-toothed Civet *Eupleres goudotii*. Matters are complicated further by the Malagasy themselves, who may use the term 'Fosa' (pronounced foosa – with the 'a' semi-silent) in a way that can refer to a number of the island's endemic carnivores. The vernacular names used in this text are: Fanaloka (*Fossa fossana*), Falanouc (*Eupleres goudotii*) and Fosa (*Cryptoprocta ferox*).

Another Malagasy name that is regularly used for small carnivores is 'jabady' or 'jaboady'. This may refer to several of the island's native species: which particular species varies from region to region. For instance, in the north-east around Marojejy it is *Fossa fossana*; around the Soalala region in the west it is *Eupleres goudotii*, and in central eastern areas it may be the Broad-striped Mongoose *Galidictis fasciata*. Furthermore, 'jabady' or 'jaboady' are also used for the introduced Small Indian Civet over many parts of the island.

Malagasy Civets
Subfamily Euplerinae

The subfamily Euplerinae contains two monotypic genera: *Fossa* and *Eupleres*. Some past authorities have chosen to place both in the subfamily Fossinae, but Euplerinae has precedence. Furthermore, some authors recognise both Euplerinae and Fossinae as monotypic subfamilies, but there is little evidence to support such distinction.

FANALOKA genus *Fossa* Gray, 1865

An endemic genus containing a single species, the Fanaloka *Fossa fossana*. Some dental traits are shared with banded civets and their allies from South-East Asia, so this species has occasionally been classified within the subfamily Hemigalinae. However, the cranial and other anatomical derived features found in the Hemigalinae are absent in *Fossa*.

FANALOKA *Fossa fossana* (Müller, 1776)

Other names: Malagasy Civet, Malagasy Striped Civet
Malagasy: Fanaloka, Tambotsodina

MEASUREMENTS Total length: 610-700mm. Head/body length: 400-450mm. Tail length: 210-250mm. Weight: males up to 2.0kg, females up to 1.5kg.

DESCRIPTION The pelage is dense and light brown in colour with more greyish areas around the head and along the back. The flanks are marked with four irregular rows of black spots which often merge to form broken stripes. There are also a few spots on the thighs. The underparts, including underneath the neck and chin, are very much paler, often light grey or cream, and have few markings. The snout is pointed and the ears rounded. The legs are shortish and delicate with small paws and medium-sized claws. The tail is cylindrical and a similar colour to the main body, with darker areas and diffuse spots sometimes extending along from the back. *F. fossana* is obviously digitigrade (it walks on its toes).

IDENTIFICATION A small fox-like carnivore approximately the size of a domestic cat with conspicuous body markings (figs. 67 & 68). Confusion between this species and the introduced Small Indian Civet *Viverricula indica* is certainly possible as both species are similarly marked and have overlapping size ranges. Generally, the Fanaloka is smaller, with thinner legs, a chunky body and unmarked tail, while *Viverricula* is a larger, longer-bodied animal with a long tail that is clearly ringed. Facially, *F. fossana* has a longer muzzle, so is more fox-like than *Viverricula*. Also the ears of the Fanaloka are far apart at their base, whereas those of the Small Indian Civet are close together.

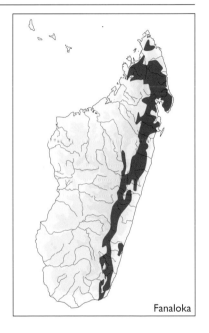

Fanaloka

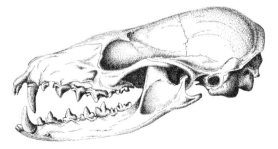

The Fanaloka is distinguished from the Falanouc *Eupleres goudotii* by its less stocky build, spotted/striped flanks and blunter snout. Similarly, the Brown-tailed Mongoose *Salanoia concolor* lacks any markings and is more slender than the Fanaloka. Fanalokas should not be confused with Ring-tailed Mongooses *Galidia elegans* which have russet pelage and a conspicuous black-ringed tail.

DISTRIBUTION The Fanaloka is found throughout the moist rainforest areas of the east and north including those of the Sambirano region in the north-west. This species has also been seen in the isolated humid forests of Montagne d'Ambre and the less humid deciduous forests of the Ankarana Massif in the far north. Its likely strongholds are the largest remaining rainforest blocks on the Masoala Peninsula, the lowland and mid-altitude rainforests at Mananara, Ambatovaky and Zahamena, and in the Andohahela forest block in the extreme south-east.

BEHAVIOUR The Fanaloka is a shy nocturnal creature that forages in low trees and on the forest floor, for rodents, small tenrecs, birds, reptiles, frogs and invertebrates, including freshwater crabs. During the day it sleeps in tree holes, under fallen logs or in rocky crevices. A male and female generally live as a pair and share a territory which may be very large, sometimes several hundred hectares. The boundaries are marked with scent from glands around the anus and on the cheeks and neck. Vocalisations are few, involving the occasional faint cry or groan or the more characteristic *coq-coq* call, only heard when two or more individuals are together.

A brief courtship occurs in August and September with the single young born after a gestation period of three months in the austral winter. Births take place in a secluded den. The young are unusual amongst the majority of carnivores (but similar to *Eupleres goudotii*) in being very well developed at birth. They weigh 60-70g, have their eyes open, and are fully furred. They can walk after three days, but progress relatively slowly after this. Meat can be eaten after a month, but they do not become fully weaned until two to three months. They probably leave their parents when one year of age.

In preparation for the austral winter (June–August), when resources are scarce and foraging more difficult, the Fanaloka is able to lay down fat reserves, especially in its tail. These may constitute 25% of the animal's body weight.

VIEWING It is possible to observe the Fanaloka on night walks in several of the major rainforest reserves (for instance, Analamazaotra, Mantadia, Anjanaharibe-Sud and Montagne d'Ambre) but, being a shy creature, chance encounters of this nature are rare.

Figure 66. Young Fanaloka.

However, members of one family group are regularly seen at Ranomafana National Park near *Belle Vue*. Here, local guides scatter morsels of food on the forest floor and the Fanalokas often approach quite close to take advantage of these free meals.

Figure 67. Fanaloka, Ranomafana.

Figure 68. Fanaloka foraging, Ranomafana.

Figure 69. Falanouc, Montagne d'Ambre.

FALANOUC genus *Eupleres* Doyère, 1835

An endemic monotypic genus represented by the Falanouc *Eupleres goudotii*, which is divided into two subspecies – *E. g. goudotii* and *E. g. major*. This genus poses a number of taxonomic questions which have yet to be satisfactorily answered by those seeking to unravel carnivore ancestry. *Eupleres* exhibits a suite of unique characteristics that make it very difficult to identify any shared derived features with other viverrids. Many of these features are considered primitive and are more typical of the creodonts (early offshoots in carnivore evolution that became extinct around 56 million years ago) than of the true Carnivora. However, other features, such as a highly modified bulla (a bony projection which encases the middle ear), are typical of viverrids.

FALANOUC *Eupleres goudotii* Doyère, 1835

Other name: Malagasy Small-toothed Civet
Malagasy: Falanouc, Falanoucy, Amboa-laolo

MEASUREMENTS Total length: 670-910mm. Head/body length: 450-650mm. Tail length: 220-260mm. Weight: 2.5-4.5kg.

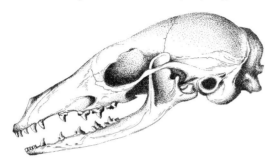

DESCRIPTION The pelage is dense and soft, with long guard hairs. The Eastern Falanouc *E. g. goudotii* has light brown/fawn upperparts with russet spots and tinges around the thighs. The underparts are pale grey-brown. The upperparts of the Western Falanouc *E. g. majori* vary from grey to sombre rufous-brown. The head and tail are generally more grey. The tail is large, broad at its base and taper to a point: it is covered with longer hairs that give it a rather bushy appearance. There may also be faint brown bands down the flanks. The forepaws and claws are formidable and well developed for digging. The western race may be between 25% and 50% larger than its eastern relative.

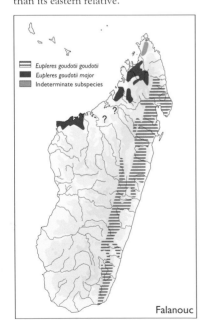

Eupleres goudotii goudotii
Eupleres goudotii major
Indeterminate subspecies

Falanouc

IDENTIFICATION A small- to medium-sized carnivore (larger than a domestic cat) with a stocky body, small delicate head with large ears, elongate snout and highly distinctive fat cylindrical tail (fig. 69). Its larger size and very distinct pointed muzzle should prevent confusion with other species like the Fanaloka *Fossa fossana*, Brown-tailed Mongoose *Salanoia concolor*, Ring-tailed Mongoose *Galidia elegans* or Small Indian Civet *Viverricula indica*.

DISTRIBUTION The Eastern Falanouc *E. g. goudotii* is found in the eastern lowland rainforests and marsh areas dominated by Cyperaceae, *Raphia* and *Pandanus* species, from the Andohahela region in the south to the Marojejy Massif in the north. It seems likely this subspecies's strongholds are the Masoala Peninsula, Mananara and Andohahela regions.

The Western Falanouc *E. g. major* is found from the Tsaratanana Massif in the northwest, south to the northern limits of the Ankarafantsika area including the whole of the Sambirano region. In the Sambirano, the Western Falanouc appears to prefer undisturbed forests and wetland areas dominated by *Raphia* and *Aframomum* species. There are also recent records of *Eupleres* (here assumed to be this subspecies) from deciduous forests to the west of Mahajanga: firstly in the Tsiombikibo forests near Mitsinjo (local name 'falanoucy'), and secondly from the Soalala/Baly Bay region (local name 'jabady'). It is not known whether these populations are continuous with the larger one to the north of Ankarafantsika. These sightings represent a considerable southerly extension to the Western Falanouc's range and may indicate that it is far more widely distributed in western areas than can currently be confirmed.

The Falanouc is also found in the humid forests of Montagne d'Ambre in the far north and has been recorded in the drier deciduous forests of the Ankarana Massif to the south of Montagne. Which of the two subspecies these populations represent has yet to be determined.

BEHAVIOUR The Falanouc is probably Madagascar's most specialised carnivore. Its elongate snout and tiny conical teeth (which resemble those of an insectivore) have evolved to catch earthworms and other small invertebrates on which the Falanouc feeds almost exclusively. It forages in leaf-litter, digging up suitable invertebrates using its strong forepaws and long claws. When walking, these claws are held so as not to make contact with the ground.

The Falanouc is mainly solitary, although small groups (possibly families) have been observed. It is a crepuscular and nocturnal species. The day is spent sleeping under logs or in rock crevices. *Eupleres* is able to defend a large territory; scent glands around the anus and neck are used for this purpose. Very few vocalisations have been recorded.

Courtship and mating take place in July and August, with offspring being born between November and January. The litter size is one or two. In common with *F. fossana*, the Falanouc gives birth to extremely well-developed young. They weigh around 150g, are fully furred (the pelage is much darker than the adult, sometimes almost black) and their eyes are open. They are able to follow their mother on foraging excursions within two days, so maintaining mobility and allowing her to continue the wide-ranging search for food. The young are weaned after nine weeks.

Again like the Fanaloka, *E. goudotii* stores large amounts of fat (up to 800g) in its tail to help see it through the winter months.

VIEWING Although the Falanouc may be locally common in some areas, it appears to be rare or even very rare over most of its range. This, coupled with its shy, secretive and nocturnal habits, makes it a very difficult species to observe. The best place to try is Montagne d'Ambre National Park – here individuals can sometimes be seen at night foraging near the road close to the Station Roussettes. Other possible localities are Ranomafana, Masoala, Verezanantsoro and Mantadia National Parks.

Figure 70. Female Falanouc with young.

Figure 71. Fosa emerging from hollow log.

Figure 72. Adult Fosa at the end of the dry season, Kirindy.

Fosa
Subfamily Cryptoproctinae

An endemic subfamily containing a single species, the Fosa *Cryptoprocta ferox*. Because of some close morphological similarities (for example retractile claws, certain dental traits, facial resemblance), some authorities have excluded this species from the Viverridae and aligned it with the cat family (Felidae). However, the majority of anatomical traits (cranial, post-cranial and soft anatomical features) confirm its alliance to Viverridae. What seems far more likely is that *Cryptoprocta* is a viverrid that has attained a number cat-like traits through convergent evolution.

FOSA genus *Cryptoprocta* Bennett, 1833

Cryptoprocta is a monotypic genus. The Fosa is most often likened to a dark-coloured, short-legged Puma *Felis concolor*, although it is dramatically smaller and more elongate. In some ways *Cryptoprocta* also resembles a Sulawesi Palm Civet *Macrogalidia musschenbroeki*.

FOSA *Cryptoprocta ferox* Bennett, 1833

Malagasy: Fosa, Fossa

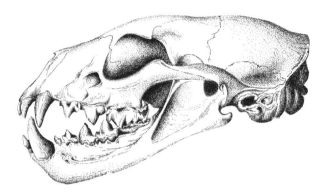

MEASUREMENTS Total length: 140-170cm. Head/body length: 75-80cm (males), 65-70cm (females). Tail length: 70-90cm. Weight: 6-10kg (males), 5-7kg (females).

DESCRIPTION The body is very slender and the legs are short but powerful; the shoulder height is up to about 35cm. The head is relatively small, with a fairly short squarish muzzle and prominent round ears (fig. 63). The feet are large and have curved retractile claws. The tail is very long and slender (fig. 72) and is used as a counter-balance when climbing. The pelage is short, smooth and dense. Upperparts are brown to dark brown and blend to more creamy underparts. In males the underparts often appear quite orange. There are no markings on the coat, but there are unconfirmed reports of melanistic (black) variants from some eastern rainforest areas. The semi-plantigrade gait of this species is quite distinctive when walking. The genitalia of the female are unusual in that they mimic those of the male: the clitoris has a central bone and is penis-like.

IDENTIFICATION A largish sleek low-slung carnivore with a very long slender tail, the Fosa is Madagascar's largest carnivore and one of the largest of all viverrids – only the African Civet *Civettictis civetta*, Binturong *Arctictis binturong* and possibly Sulawesi Palm Civet are larger. Its considerably larger size and distinctive elongate shape should prevent confusion with any other carnivore in Madagascar.

DISTRIBUTION The Fosa is widely distributed throughout Madagascar and has been recorded in native forests and wooded savannas from sea-level to 2,600m (Andringitra Massif). Fosas probably reach their highest densities in some western forests where the availability of potential prey is also high. This species is no longer found in central highland area where virtually all the native forest cover has been removed, but is still known from the Ambohijanahary area on the western high plateau.

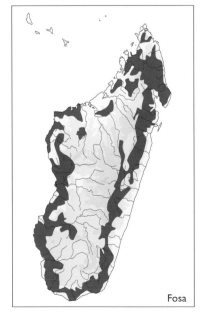

Fosa

BEHAVIOUR Outside the breeding season Fosas are generally solitary creatures. They are active by both day and night (cathemeral). Peak activity is usually under cover of darkness, although this may vary seasonally. They sometimes sleep in caves or hollowed-out termite mounds, but seem to prefer trees, usually resting between large forked branches (fig. 64). They are extremely agile climbers, equally at home hunting in the trees or on the ground, although large distances are rarely covered in the canopy.

Fosas occupy and hunt in large territories – several km². in western dry forests. In areas where prey is scarce individuals may cover considerable distances. In the mountainous Andringitra Massif evidence suggests distances in excess of 7km are covered which include climbs of at least 600m in altitude. Territorial boundaries are regularly marked using pungent scent from glands in the ano-genital region.

Mammals are the mainstay of the Fosa's diet, although the relative abundance and size of the prey species taken reflect habitat and location. In high mountain areas like the Andringitra Massif small prey items such as shrew tenrecs *Microgale* predominate. However, in forested areas larger prey species are preferred. Here lemurs may comprise more than half of the diet – these are often ambushed at night while they are sleeping. Larger species like sifakas *Propithecus* are regularly taken, but also *Eulemur*, *Hapalemur* and *Lepilemur* species and most members of the family Cheirogaleidae. In the deciduous forests near Morondava, the Giant Jumping Rat *Hypogeomys antimena* is a major food source. Here, too, Fosas are known to take introduced Bush Pigs *Potamochoerus larvatus* and even other smaller native carnivores like the Narrow-striped Mongoose *Mungotictis decemlineata*.

Tenrecs (*Tenrec* and *Echinops* spp.) are eaten throughout the year. During the dry season when they are aestivating these animals are excavated from their burrows or hideaways, as are Dwarf Lemurs *Cheirogaleus*. Birds, reptiles, amphibians and invertebrates are also taken on occasion, but constitute a much smaller proportion of the overall diet. In forest areas close to rural villages Fosas have a bad reputation for taking smaller domestic livestock, especially fowl.

The front paws are often used to pin larger prey down before a fatal bite is administered to the throat or back of the head. The victim is often eviscerated and the vital organs eaten first. Observations made in eastern rainforest areas suggest that pairs hunt co-operatively at times, which may allow them to tackle the largest lemurs (*Propithecus diadema* and *Indri indri*).

There is much local folklore surrounding the Fosa, some of which even suggests the species poses a threat to humans. Given the animal's relatively small size there is little probability behind these claims and it seems that they have become considerably exaggerated over the generations. However, the Fosa is certainly known to behave in a highly irregular and erratic manner on occasion and without provocation. For instance, even in remote forest areas far away from regular human habitation, Fosas have walked into temporary field research camps, entered unoccupied tents and proceeded to ransack the contents, in the process chewing metal objects, leather boots, rucksacks and even eating soap and bottles of malaria tablets!

Courtship occurs between September and November. A single female in oestrous may attract the attention of several males which stay in close proximity, although the female herself remains in the same place. Copulations take place over a week or more and tend to be noisy, with both sexes purring, snorting and shrieking. The gestation period is around three months. Females give birth to a litter of between two and four, usually in a den or otherwise secluded site. The young weigh around 100-150g at birth, are fully furred and generally very pale grey, but are toothless and blind. The eyes begin to open after 15 to 16 days and development is relatively slow. After around two months the young leave the den for the first time and make their initial attempts at climbing. They take their first solid food around three months and weaning occurs between four and five months. It takes two years or so for dentition to be complete and a further two years before full maturation and adult weight is reached.

VIEWING Although it is widespread and not uncommon in some localities, the Fosa is not an easy animal to see. The best opportunities occur in western deciduous forests, particularly at Kirindy where it may sometimes be seen during the day, particularly in the dry season when it comes to drink at pools along the Kirindy River. Here, too, the species seems less wary during the breeding season (September to November). Fosas can also occasionally be seen in Ankarana and Analamera Special Reserves. Encounters are possible in many rainforest areas – Ranomafana, Mantadia and Montagne d'Ambre National Parks are perhaps the most likely – but the forest environment generally makes such events difficult and fleeting.

Figure 73. Small Indian Civet.

INTRODUCED SPECIES

Apart from two domesticated species, the dog and the cat, only a single species of wild carnivore has been introduced to Madagascar. It seems likely that the Small Indian Civet *Viverricula indica* arrived from the Indo-Malay region with the early human settlers, around 2,000 years ago. Whether this was accidental or intentional is not known. In all probability, the civet's gradual spread from north to south across the island mirrored that of the human colonists, as the species is regularly associated with human settlement.

What influence the presence of the Small Indian Civet has on the native carnivores is unclear. Where ranges overlap, it would seem logical to assume some competition occurs but to what degree is uncertain. Species endemic to islands are often far more specialist than widespread continental forms and consequently more vulnerable to direct competition from such introduced species. The generalist nature of the Small Indian Civet has allowed it to colonise degraded and secondary forest areas as well as more agricultural and urban environments. As these habitats are not utilised by the native carnivore species, direct competition in these areas is unlikely. Nonetheless, some interaction may occur in marginal areas and where the Small Indian Civet has penetrated tracts of native forest. In these instances, the possibility exists that most of the native carnivore species are impinged upon in some way, whether it be for space, food or den sites.

Civets

Subfamily Viverrinae

This subfamily contains seven genera and 19 species which represent the true civets, linsangs and genets. They are distributed throughout Africa and Asia. The vernacular name civet is derived from the presence of scent glands ('civet') external to the anal region.

CIVETS genus *Viverricula* Hodgson, 1838

Viverricula is a monotypic genus whose single representative is spread widely through southern Asia. It has also been introduced onto a number of islands. Many forms have been described, all of which are regarded as synonyms of *indica*.

SMALL INDIAN CIVET *Viverricula indica* (Desmarest, 1804)

Small Indian Civet

Other names: Lesser Oriental Civet, Rasse
Malagasy: Jabady, Jaboady

MEASUREMENTS Total length: 750-1,060mm. Head/body length: 450-630mm. Tail length: 300-430mm. Weight: 2-4kg.

DESCRIPTION The pelage is short and quite coarse. The upperparts are brownish-grey to beige, while the underparts are slightly paler and generally greyer. The rounded face and head are slightly darker and have few markings, other than dark areas around the eyes. The legs and feet are very dark brown-grey, sometimes almost black. The forequarters are covered in small dark spots which gradually increase in size towards the rear and then fuse to form six to eight longitudinal stripes down the flanks. The tail has between six and nine dark rings, which are broader than the inter-ring spaces.

The Malagasy often mistakenly refer to this species as a cat, their French name for it being *le chat sauvage*.

IDENTIFICATION A small to medium-sized viverrid with conspicuous body markings (fig. 73). This species is generally larger than all but two of the native carnivores, the Fosa *Cryptoprocta ferox* and Falanouc *Eupleres goudotii*. It is considerably smaller than the former and similar in size to the latter. Both native species lack body markings, which should prevent confusion.

Confusion between smaller individuals of *Viverricula* and the Fanaloka *Fossa fossana* is possible as the basic body patterns are broadly similar. The Fanaloka tends to be paler in colour, have fewer and less bold body markings, no rings on its tail and a more pointed face.

DISTRIBUTION The Small Indian Civet originates from the Indian subcontinent, Indochina, mainland South-East Asia and the islands of Sumatra, Java, Bali, Hainan and Taiwan. Apart from Madagascar, it has been introduced to the Comoro Islands and Socotra in the Indian Ocean.

It is widely distributed throughout Madagascar and has been recorded in most of the major habitat types. It does not appear to penetrate dense primary rainforest to any extent, but is more often associated with degraded areas, secondary forests and marshland. This species is also regularly found in and around human settlements and more agricultural areas including those on the high plateau. The population on Madagascar is sometimes regarded as a distinct subspecies *Viverricula indica rasse*.

BEHAVIOUR The Small Indian Civet is usually solitary and primarily nocturnal, but may also be active during daylight hours in areas away from human disturbance. It normally sleeps in shallow burrows that it excavates itself, or in clumps of dense vegetation. In urban areas it is known to frequent disused buildings and drainage ditches and tunnels. It is mainly a terrestrial species, although it is capable of climbing.

The diet is varied and consists of small vertebrates, carrion, insects, grubs, fruits, roots and tubers. In rural areas it regularly predates domestic poultry and in urban areas often scavenges around refuse tips. It is trapped and killed as a pest.

Males and females probably pair during the austral winter when mating occurs. A litter of two to five is then born between September and December in a burrow or similar safe area on the ground.

VIEWING The nocturnal habits of this species make it difficult to see. However, because of its association with human settlement, and sometimes bold nature, it may be encountered at night patrolling the perimeter of rural villages and field camps or urban fringe areas, especially where there is rubbish. It may also be seen on *taxi-brousse* journeys through rural areas, either foraging by the roadside or on the verge as a roadkill.

Mongooses
Family Herpestidae

The mongoose family (Herpestidae) occurs naturally in the Old World and is distributed throughout Africa, Asia and South-East Asia as far as Borneo and the Philippines. It comprises around 37 species, arranged between 18 genera and three subfamilies. As a group they are characterised by the uniquely derived nature of their anal sac and the structure of their auditory bulla.

Malagasy Mongooses
Subfamily Galidiinae

The Malagasy mongooses, of which there are five species, constitute their own subfamily, the Galidiinae. This appears to represent an early offshoot of the herpestine lineage, which confirms a separate evolutionary history from the other Malagasy carnivores (Viverridae). As a group, members of the Galidiinae show a variety of morphological traits that set them apart from mongooses in Africa and Asia (subfamilies Herpestinae and Mungotinae). Galidiinae have broad feet and unfused pads with little hair covering them, and a much reduced anal gland, whereas the anal gland in Herpestinae and Mungotinae is well developed and surrounds the anus in a pouch.

RING-TAILED MONGOOSE genus *Galidia* I. Geoffroy Saint-Hilaire, 1837

The genus *Galidia* contains a single species, the Ring-tailed Mongoose *G. elegans*, which is the most widely distributed and abundant of the Malagasy mongooses. Ring-tailed Mongooses are agile climbers and have glabrous soles with large pads that aid their sure-footedness and agility in trees.

Figure 74. Eastern Ring-tailed Mongoose, Ranomafana.

Figure 75. Northern Ring-tailed Mongoose, Ankarana.

Figure 76. Northern Ring-tailed Mongoose foraging on forest floor, Ankarana.

RING-TAILED MONGOOSE *Galidia elegans* I. Geoffroy Saint-Hilaire, 1837

Malagasy: Vontsira, Kokia

MEASUREMENTS Total length: 600-700mm. Head/body length: 325-380mm. Tail length: 275-320mm. Weight: 700-1,000g.

DESCRIPTION The upperparts are rich russet-chestnut which extends down the thighs and legs. The head, throat and chin slightly more olive-grey to olive-brown. The tail is quite bushy and ringed with four to six alternate bands of russet-chestnut and black. The head is small and pointed with rounded ears. Three subspecies are recognised on the basis of colour variation: the nominate race, *G. e. elegans*, is the darkest and has dark brown to black feet (fig. 74); *G. e. dambrensis* has lighter chestnut upperparts and belly, and the feet are a similar colour to the body (figs. 75 & 76); *G. e. occidentalis* has similar light chestnut upperparts that blend to a very much darker belly, while the legs and paws are almost black.

IDENTIFICATION A small carnivore of 'typical' mongoose shape. The Ring-tailed Mongoose occurs sympatrically with several other Malagasy carnivores: *Fossa fossana*, *Eupleres goudotii*, *Galidictis fasciata* and *Salanoia concolor*. However, the uniform and rich russet-coloured coat, together with the distinctively marked tail, should prevent confusion with any of these species.

DISTRIBUTION This is the commonest and most widespread of the Malagasy mongooses, being found widely in the forests of the east, north and west from sea-level to around 2,000m (Andringitra Massif), although it is more abundant in forests below 1,500m.

The three subspecies occur in distinct areas: the Eastern Ring-tailed Mongoose *G. e. elegans* is found throughout the eastern rainforest belt from Sambava in the north to Tolagnaro in the south; the northern subspecies, *G. e. dambrensis*, is found in the moist forests of Montagne d'Ambre and the drier forests around Ankarana and south into the Sambirano region while the Western Ring-tailed Mongoose *G. e. occidentalis* appears restricted to dry forest areas between Soalala and Antsalova, particularly around the limestone karst formations at Bemaraha and Namoroka.

BEHAVIOUR Ring-tailed Mongooses are diurnal and sociable, often being found in family groups of up to five. At night families shelter in burrows, which they dig themselves, or in hollow logs or similar secluded places. They spend the majority of their time on the ground, but are also capable of climbing nimbly along vines or in the branches of trees. They are adept swimmers.

Their diet includes a variety of prey species: small lemurs (particularly *Microcebus* and *Cheirogaleus* spp.), rodents, small tenrecs (*Hemicentetes* and *Microgale* sp.) adult and young birds, eggs, smaller reptiles, frogs, invertebrates and even fish. Most victims are dispatched by a bite to the back of the neck. Large eggs and snails are broken in typical mongoose fashion – holding the item between the forepaws and kicking it against a hard surface with the hind feet while lying on one side. In some areas where human habitation borders native forest the Ring-tailed Mongoose is reported to be a significant predator of domestic chickens. It is not adverse to scavenging, being a regular visitor to rubbish pits at many forest research camps.

In common with other herpestids scent-marking is important. There are large anal glands from which scent is smeared by rubbing these regions against rocks, tree-trunks and branches. The Ring-tailed Mongoose also has a far more extensive vocal repertoire than other Malagasy carnivores. Contact calls are high-pitched 'peeping' whistles, reminiscent of some tree frogs, that help keep the family unit together while foraging. Muffled 'miaows' and soft 'mews' are emitted during the capture of prey; much louder shrieks and growls are heard when disputes break out; alarm calls are generally low moans or grunts.

Copulation has been observed, lasting about 15 minutes. Most births occur in the austral summer between November and January, after a gestation period of just under three months. New-born Ring-tailed Mongooses weigh around 50g, are fully furred and have the same coloration and markings as their parents. Their eyes are closed and do not open until the seventh or eighth day. The female initially raises the young alone in the burrow and does not allow the male to approach closer than around two metres. Only after a month or so is the male allowed access to the infants.

Development is slow: the young do not take their first steps until 12 to 14 days. They are able to take small amounts of meat at one month, but are not fully weaned until two to three months. Physical maturity is reached in around one year, although the young do not leave their parents until between 18 months and two years, when they attain sexual maturity.

VIEWING Like most small forest carnivores this is not an easy mammal to see. However, being widespread, fairly common and often inquisitive, the Ring-tailed Mongoose is probably the most regularly encountered native carnivore on Madagascar. The eastern subspecies can be seen at Ranomafana National Park around *Belle Vue*, Analamazaotra Special Reserve and Mantadia National Park. The northern race is quite easily seen at Ankarana Special Reserve around the *Campement des Anglais* – here a family group regularly patrols around the camp on the lookout for scraps. The western subspecies is much more difficult to see as the regions it inhabits are remote; the areas around Bemaraha National Park are probably the best places to try.

Galidia elegans elegans
Galidia e. dambrensis
Galidia e. occidentalis

Ring-tailed Mongoose

NARROW-STRIPED MONGOOSE genus *Mungotictis* Pocock, 1915

The genus *Mungotictis* contains a single species, the Narrow-striped Mongoose M. *decemlineata*, which appears to be restricted to seasonal forests in the western regions of the island. Two subspecies have been proposed on the basis of pelage variation.

NARROW-STRIPED MONGOOSE *Mungotictis decemlineata* (A. Grandidier, 1867)

Mungotictis d. decemlineata
Mungotictis d. lineata

Narrow-striped Mongoose

Malagasy: Boky-Boky, Boki-Boki, Teraboky

MEASUREMENTS Total length: 450-620mm. Head/body length: 250-350mm. Tail length: 200-270mm. Weight: 600-700g.

DESCRIPTION The pelage is short and dense, but becomes longer under the belly. The upperparts are grizzled grey-beige and gradually fade to paler beige underparts. The back and flanks are marked with eight to ten longitudinal dark stripes running from behind the ear to the base of the tail. These often fade and become indistinct. The tail is similar in colour to the upper body, though often more grey and flecked with darker and lighter areas; it is very bushy and brush-like. The muzzle is shortish but quite pointed, and the ears are prominent and rounded. The legs are delicate and the feet partially webbed with longish claws (figs. 77 & 78).

Two subspecies are thought to exist, the differences primarily being in colour: M. *d. lineata* differs from the nominate race *decemlineata*, in having a much paler tail that may appear light grey to whitish and more pronounced longitudinal stripes down its back and flanks.

IDENTIFICATION A small elegant carnivore with a pronounced bushy tail, M. *d. decemlineata* should not be confused with any other species within its restricted range. The apparent ranges of M. *d. lineata* and Grandidier's Mongoose *Galidictis grandidieri* are very similar and confusion between the two taxa is possible as they are similarly marked, however, M. *d. lineata* is a smaller and far more delicate animal.

DISTRIBUTION The Narrow-striped Mongoose has a very restricted distribution in western Madagascar. The nominate race is found in the seasonal dry forests between the Tsiribihina river to the north and the Mangoky River to the south inland as far as Mahabo. M. *d. lineata* is known from only a handful of specimens thought to have been collected in Didieraeceae and Euphorbiaceae thickets south of Toliara and around Lac Tsimanampetsotsa, although the exact localities are not known.

BEHAVIOUR The Narrow-striped Mongoose is diurnal and both arboreal and terrestrial. The species's social organisation and activity patterns vary according to the time of year. During the warmer wet season (November–May) groups generally consist of 6 to 8 individuals (although as many as 12 have been observed) including males, females and young, occupying a home range up to 150ha. At this time they are far more arboreal and often spend the night in tree holes several metres off the ground. In the cooler dry season (June–October) these groups subdivide into smaller units of three or four which maintain smaller ranges within the more extensive overall home range. At night they tend to sleep in burrows which are excavated by the group. Group cohesiveness is maintained by a series of short repeated contact calls which sound like bouts of chatter. If disputes arise, the bushy tail is bristled and held erect in threat.

The staple diet appears to be insects, especially larvae, which are dug up or excavated from decaying wood. These are particularly important during the drier months, when little else is available. During the rainy season the diet becomes more varied and may also include small mammals, reptiles, worms and a selection of other invertebrates. Larger prey species, for instance mouse lemurs (*Microcebus*), may be hunted cooperatively.

Most births occur between January and March after a gestation period of 90 to 105 days. Generally, only a single infant is produced; weighs around 50g at birth. The youngster is weaned after two months, but may stay associated with its mother for up to two years.

VIEWING The deciduous forests of Kirindy, north-east of Morondava, offer the visitor the only realistic chance of seeing this species. In these forests the Narrow-striped Mongoose is locally quite common. There is an extensive trail network so during a two- or three-day stay the chances of an encounter are quite good.

Figure 77. Narrow-striped Mongoose, Kirindy.

Figure 78. Narrow-striped Mongoose, Kirindy.

Figure 79. Broad-striped Mongoose, Andringitra.

Figure 80. Grandidier's Mongoose, Tsimanampetsotsa.

BROAD-STRIPED MONGOOSES genus *Galidictis* I. Geoffroy Saint-Hilaire, 1839

A genus that until recently contained just a single taxon, but is now known to include two species, *Galidictis fasciata* and G. *grandidieri*. Both species are strictly nocturnal and have peculiar cranial and dental morphologies that separate them from other Malagasy mongooses.

BROAD-STRIPED MONGOOSE *Galidictis fasciata* (Gmelin, 1788)

Galidictis fasciata fasciata
Galidictis fasciata striata

Broad-striped Mongoose

Malagasy: Vontsirafotsy

MEASUREMENTS Total length: 540-640mm. Head/body length: 300-340mm. Tail length: 240-300mm. Weight: 500-600g.

DESCRIPTION The body colour is grey-beige which extends to the underparts, while the top of the head is darker than the cheeks, chin and throat. The distinctive tail is quite bushy and creamy-white over its distal two-thirds. The grey-beige body coloration continues down the spinal ridge and gradually grades into this over the proximal third of the tail. There are several longitudinal dark brown stripes on the flanks which are broader than the creamy-beige inter-stripe spaces. The muzzle is short and slightly rounded and the ears are small and less prominent than other Malagasy mongooses (fig. 79). The digits and claws on the feet are long, but the webbing between them is less developed than in the Ring-tailed Mongoose *Galidia elegans*.

Two subspecies have been proposed which apparently differ in the number of stripes, although these often fade and become indistinct leading to discrepancies. The nominate race (G. *f. fasciata*) usually has eight stripes and a more bushier tail, while the second subspecies (G. *f. striata*) has only six stripes and a whiter tail. The validity of this differentiation remains questionable.

IDENTIFICATION A small- to medium-sized mongoose with a blunt snout, conspicuous creamy-white tail and distinctive body markings. In the field this species could be mistaken for the Fanaloka *Fossa fossana* with which its shares its range. However, the Broad-striped Mongoose is smaller and more delicate, has a shorter snout, less fox-like appearance and obvious creamy-white tail. Although the spots of the Fanaloka may fuse to become broken stripes, the longitudinal markings of the Broad-striped Mongoose are much more distinct and should serve to differentiate these species.

DISTRIBUTION Both subspecies of Broad-striped Mongoose inhabit the eastern rainforests. The nominate race is found south of the Mangoro River down to the Andohahela region north of Tolagnaro. The distribution of G. *f. striata* appears to lie north of the Mangoro River and extends as far north as the Marojejy Massif.

BEHAVIOUR The Broad-striped Mongoose has yet to be studied in the wild and little is known of its behaviour. It is mainly nocturnal and observations suggest that it lives in pairs and produces a single offspring each year during the austral summer. The peculiar cranial and dental characteristics suggest it is the most specialised flesh-eating member of the subfamily Galidiinae, its diet consisting almost entirely of small vertebrates, especially rodents, and only occasionally invertebrates. Foraging occurs mainly on the forest floor, these mongooses often searching the leaf-litter with their tails held vertically upwards. They have also been observed climbing up and down fallen logs and even into the lower branches of undergrowth.

Opportunist encounters are few and far between, suggesting that the species is either rare or shy or both. However, individuals occasionally seen around some rainforest research camps are often quite tolerant and have been reported raiding camp food stores.

VIEWING The chances of seeing this species are very slim. It has been observed at Ranomafana National Park, occasionally along the road between the park entrance and the village of Ranomafana. Other possible localities are Mantadia and Verezanantsoro National Parks and Anjanaharibe-Sud Special Reserve.

GRANDIDIER'S MONGOOSE *Galidictis grandidieri* Wozencraft, 1986

Other name: Malagasy Giant Striped Mongoose

MEASUREMENTS Total length: 840-900mm*. Head/body length: 450-480mm*. Tail length: 390-420mm*. Weight: 1.2-1.6kg*.
*estimated measurements

DESCRIPTION Grandidier's Mongoose was described in 1986 (name modified in 1987) and until 1989 was known only from two museum specimens. It is the largest member of the subfamily Galidiinae: G. *grandidieri* has proportionally the longest legs and largest feet of any Malagasy mongoose. The cranium is particularly massive and appreciably larger than G. *fasciata*. The underlying body colour is grizzled beige-grey, while the back and flanks are marked with eight dark brown longitudinal stripes running from the neck to the base of the tail the inter-stripe spaces being broader than the stripes themselves. The tail is off-white in colour and bushy in appearance (fig. 80).

IDENTIFICATION A large, distinctively marked mongoose, with a large head, prominent ears and a very pale bushy tail. Grandidier's Mongoose is sympatric with the remarkably similar southern subspecies of the Narrow-striped Mongoose *Mungotictis decemlineata lineata*. However, Grandidier's Mongoose is a more robust and noticeably larger animal with more pronounced stripes and a highly distinctive tail.

The Fosa *Cryptoprocta ferox* is the only other endemic carnivore sympatric with Grandidier's Mongoose. Confusing these two species is extremely unlikely: G. *grandidieri* is appreciably smaller, has obvious body markings (which the Fosa lacks) and has a medium-length bushy tail rather than an extremely long slender tail. The introduced Small Indian Civet *Viverricula indica* is also known from south-west Madagascar, but is larger than G. *grandidieri* and has much bolder longitudinal stripes down its flanks and an obviously ringed tail.

confirmed locality
possible range

Grandidier's Mongoose

DISTRIBUTION The two museum specimens used to describe this species were collected from areas of Didiereaceae thicket around Lac Tsimanampetsotsa in south-west Madagascar. Field research has since confirmed that Grandidier's Mongoose still survives in this region. Although the Lac Tsimanampetsotsa area is currently the species's only confirmed locality, subfossil remains of G. *grandidieri* have been found in caves approximately 50km to the south of the lake. In view of this, and the relative abundance of Grandidier's Mongoose around Lac Tsimanampetsotsa, it has been presumed that the species probably still survives over much of the Mahafaly Plateau in south-west Madagascar.

BEHAVIOUR This species has been the subject of only a very brief study, so information on its behaviour and ecology is limited. It is known to be strictly nocturnal. The day is spent sleeping in a natural cavity, burrow or hole in the peculiar fissured limestone terrain that dominates much of its habitat. Burrows may be as much as 2m deep and probably help keep the mongooses cool during the day when temperatures can be very high. Only after dusk do they emerge, generally returning before dawn. They do not necessarily use the same burrow each night and different mongooses may use the same sleeping site on successive nights.

Grandidier's Mongoose forages either singly or in pairs within a small area (approximately 0.8 to 1.3km²). Invertebrates like hissing cockroaches and scorpions appear to form a major part of the diet, although its powerful skull and massive teeth suggest larger prey like rodents and lizards are also tackled.

The climate in south-west Madagascar is probably the most seasonal on the island – hot and dry during the summer, with a brief rainy season through January and February, and much cooler during the winter months between May and September. In view of this it is somewhat surprising that G. *grandidieri* seems to breed year-round.

Grandidier's Mongoose defecates at specific latrine sites, mostly on exposed rocks or similar prominent places, which suggests that these serve as territorial markers. Evidence indicates that in optimum habitat the species occurs at higher densities than other similar small carnivores. Although wary when approached, Grandidier's Mongoose appears to be a very docile creature and soon becomes accustomed to human presence.

VIEWING The only locality where Grandidier's Mongoose is known to occur is Tsimanampetsotsa Nature Reserve, centred around Lac Tsimanampetsotsa, some 80km due south of Toliara in south-west Madagascar. Although this species probably occurs throughout the reserve and into the surrounding area, the majority of sightings have occurred in Euphorbiaceae scrub growing on limestone on the eastern side of the lake. Here Grandidier's Mongoose appears to be locally common and relatively easy to observe at night.

BROWN-TAILED MONGOOSE genus *Salanoia* Gray, 1865

A genus that contains a single species, *Salanoia concolor*. In the past this species has sometimes been mistakenly referred to as S. *unicolor*, the confusion originating from a typographical error. Some authorities have differentiated two species, S. *concolor* and S. *olivacea*, on the basis of colour differences, but these distinctions are not considered valid.

BROWN-TAILED MONGOOSE *Salanoia concolor* I. Geoffroy Saint-Hilaire, 1839

Malagasy: Salano

MEASUREMENTS Total length: 490-570mm. Head/body length: 300-350mm. Tail length: 190-220mm. Weight: 550-750g*.
*estimated measurement

DESCRIPTION The pelage is short, dense and uniformly reddish-brown to olive-brown. Some individuals have very faint black spots, while others may have paler spots. The tail is the same colour as the body, but is relatively short. The head is small, the snout pointed and the ears rounded and obvious. The claws are long, but not strongly curved.

IDENTIFICATION This species occurs sympatrically with several other carnivores of similar size. Both the Fanaloka *Fossa fossana* and Broad-striped Mongoose *Galidictis fasciata* have obvious body markings which the Brown-tailed Mongoose lacks. The Ring-tailed Mongoose *Galidia elegans* is much more reddish-chestnut in coloration and has a distinctive banded tail. The Falanouc *Eupleres goudotii* is similarly uniform in colour but is generally paler than the Brown-tailed Mongoose. It is also a much larger animal and has a very distinctive pointed snout, which should help prevent confusion.

DISTRIBUTION Information on the distribution of this species is scant. It is probably restricted to the lowland and medium-altitude rainforests of north-east Madagascar, north of the Mangoro River to the Masoala Peninsula and perhaps the Marojejy Massif. Several museum specimens are recorded as being collected from the area north-east of Lac Alaotra in central-eastern Madagascar. Indeed local villagers still occasionally report the presence of a small carnivore in the reedbeds around the lake which may correspond to this species, although the identity of these animals remains a mystery.

Brown-tailed Mongoose

BEHAVIOUR The Brown-tailed Mongoose is diurnal, spending the night in burrows or hollow trees. During the austral summer, when breeding occurs, they are generally found in pairs along with a single offspring. Observations in the winter months suggest males and females are separate at this time of the year.

In common with the Narrow-striped Mongoose *Mungotictis decemlineata* from western Madagascar, the Brown-tailed Mongoose feeds predominantly on insects but will also take small reptiles, frogs and even fruit, and has also been reported to steal domestic fowl.

This species is the least known of the Malagasy carnivores and no other information regarding its behaviour and ecology is available.

VIEWING This species appears to be extremely shy and secretive; consequently casual sightings are very rare indeed. The Masoala and Verezanantsoro National Parks probably offer the best chance of seeing this species. It has been described as relatively common in some areas of forest in these localities.

Figure 81. Brown-tailed Mongoose.

LEMURS
ORDER PRIMATES
INFRAORDER LEMURIFORMES

Figure 82. Ring-tailed Lemur basking, Berenty.

Lemurs are primates and together with the galagos, pottos and lorises form the suborder Strepsirhini (formerly Prosimii). This group is collectively known as prosimians ('before the monkeys') and retain a suite of 'primitive' characteristics that are common to some other mammalian groups but are absent from higher primates (monkeys and apes), which are placed in the suborder Haplorhini (formerly Anthropoidea). These primitive characteristics include: the presence of a tapetum, a reflective layer in the retina of the eye which enhances night-time vision; a rhinarium or 'moist nose' which improves the sense of smell; prominent scent glands for home range demarcation; a bicornuate uterus and epitheliochorial placenta; smaller brain cases; open eye sockets, and different jaw morphology, including a tooth-comb. As such lemurs are closer in evolutionary terms to ancestral primates than to other more recent and extant forms from the suborder Haplorhini.

Evolution is an ongoing process, proceeding in uneven bursts, followed by periods of relative stasis. Ancestral primates may well have been similar in a number of ways to present-day lemurs, but with time some of them altered to better suit and better exploit their environment, eventually evolving into monkeys and apes. Critically, some of the early lemur-like primates became isolated on Madagascar prior to this. Their cousins elsewhere were driven to extinction by the new arrivals, but on Madagascar they found refuge. However, once in residence, the early lemurs continued to evolve to exploit their new home to best advantage. This resulted in a spectacular diversification and speciation. Contemporary lemurs display an extraordinary array of morphologies, behaviours and lifestyles, and it is possible to draw several parallels between these and those of monkeys and their societies.

A number of lemur taxa are differentiated into subspecies, for instance the Brown Lemur *Eulemur fulvus* is split into six, the Black Lemur *E. macaco* has two subspecies, and the Sifaka and Simpona, *Propithecus verreauxi* and *P. diadema*, are each divided into four subspecies. The borders between many of the different populations are obvious, as they are separated by major rivers or similar geographical barriers. But some are not so apparent and gradations exist between one taxon and the next. Analysis of the genetic material from animals at either end of these extremes shows that these populations are still actively diverging. With time, enough differences may accumulate for the separate populations to be regarded as full species.

Today, there are no less than 51 recognised extant taxa within the Lemuriformes, divided between 33 species, 14 genera and five families (Cheirogaleidae, Megaladapidae, Lemuridae, Indriidae and Daubentoniidae), all of which are endemic to Madagascar. Not surprisingly, their precise evolutionary affinities are the subject of considerable debate. Some have argued that such a divergent assemblage can only be the result of multiple colonisations from other landmasses (presumably Africa) during early primate evolutionary history. Others have concluded that the members of the family Cheirogaleidae (mouse and dwarf lemurs) have closer affinities to the Lorisidae (lorises, pottos and galagos) from Africa and Asia than to other Lemuriformes on Madagascar, and are thus derived from an alternative lineage. This hypothesis requires that Malagasy primates dispersed on two separate occasions across the Mozambique Channel. However, recent genetic analysis suggests otherwise. From this, it would appear that all Lemuriformes, including the bizarre Aye-aye *Daubentonia madagascariensis*, are derived from a single ancestor that probably resembled members of the family Cheirogaleidae and may have arrived from Africa on floating mats of vegetation approximately 60 million years ago.

Spectacular as the present-day assemblage of lemurs undoubtedly is, it is only a shadow of the array that once existed on pristine Madagascar. The original lemur fauna included at least 16 other species, arranged between nine genera that are now all sadly extinct (see Appendix I). Without exception these species were larger than extant forms – some attained body weights up to 200kg. What is more, a number of these species survived until the relative recent past (c. 500 B.P.), their demise almost certainly a consequence of overhunting and habitat destruction by the early human colonists.

Lemurs are without question the most intensively studied of Madagascar's mammals. Detailed behavioural and ecological investigation began in the 1960s, when a handful of biologists gained permission to work on the island. However, since the mid 1980s interest in Madagascar has blossomed and the number of biologists conducting lemur-based research has increased dramatically. Encouragingly, this trend shows no sign of abating. Certainly most of our knowledge concerning these unusual and fascinating primates has been gained in the past 15 years. Evidently there is much more to find out: the recent discovery of three completely new species (*Propithecus tattersalli*, *Hapalemur aureus* and *Microcebus ravelobensis*) and relatively recent rediscoveries of three species (*Hapalemur simus*, *Allocebus trichotis* and *Microcebus myoxinus*) are testament to this.

Mouse and Dwarf Lemurs
Family Cheirogaleidae

This family consists of at least eight species of small to small-medium nocturnal lemurs, divided between five genera; *Microcebus*, *Allocebus*, *Cheirogaleus*, *Mirza* and *Phaner*. They are characterised by medium to medium-long bodies, long tails, short legs and a horizontal body posture. All run and jump quadrupedally. They may be both solitary and gregarious when active and will sleep alone or in small groups. The family is represented throughout the various forest types in Madagascar, and in most areas two or more species live sympatrically.

MOUSE LEMURS genus *Microcebus* E. Geoffroy, 1834

At one time this genus was thought to contain just two species that had non-overlapping ranges: the Grey Mouse Lemur M. *murinus* found in the drier regions of the north, west and south, and the Brown Mouse Lemur M. *rufus* of the humid rainforest regions of the east. However, recent research has indicated that the situation is far more complex. Surveys in western forests in particular have revealed a number of distinctive populations, some of which appear to justify full species status. Nevertheless, the overall situation remains uncertain and will only be clarified by further fieldwork and analysis. The systematics of this genus are currently undergoing a major revision.

At present *Microcebus* contains four described species, broadly similar in appearance and habits: characteristic features of their distinctive lifestyle are annual cycles of fat storage, body temperature and activity pattern. They occur in southern, western and eastern regions and prefer leafy areas of forest with tangles of fine branches and lianas. They are without question the most abundant group of primates on Madagascar and, as their vernacular name implies, are quite 'mouse-like' in appearance. They are the smallest members of the family Cheirogaleidae and indeed are the smallest primates in the world.

GREY MOUSE LEMUR *Microcebus murinus* (J. F. Miller, 1777)

Malagasy: Pondiky, Vakiandri, Titilivaha, Tsidy, Koitsiky

MEASUREMENTS Total length: 210-280mm. Head/body length: 80-120mm. Tail length: 130-160mm. Weight: average 60g, seasonal variation 45-85g.

DESCRIPTION The head, dorsal region and flanks are grey to grey-brown with dark hair bases showing through. The tail is of similar coloration, although it may be slightly browner towards the tip. Underparts and throat are cream to white. The ears are relatively long, quite fleshy and protrude noticeably from the head. The face is rounded and the eyes relatively large (figs. 83 & 84).

IDENTIFICATION A small active lemur, with prominent ears and a long tail. Movements tend to be quick and energetic, and are punctuated by brief pauses. This species is distinguished from the Pygmy Mouse Lemur M. *myoxinus* by its larger size, grey rather than rufous-orange coloration, and very obvious ears. The Grey Mouse Lemur is similar in size to the Golden-brown Mouse Lemur M.

ravelobensis, but is more robust in appearance and grey in colour. *M. ravelobensis* also has a relatively longer tail. In areas of sympatry *M. murinus* may possibly be confused with the Fat-tailed Dwarf Lemur *Cheirogaleus medius* and Coquerel's Dwarf Lemur *Mirza coquereli*. However, both these species are noticeably larger and less active than the Grey Mouse Lemur.

HABITAT Dry deciduous, semi-humid deciduous and spiny forest. The Grey Mouse Lemur often appears more abundant in secondary rather than primary vegetation and may even be found in degraded roadside and scrub-type vegetation and gardens on the edge of towns and villages. In most forest types they seem to prefer the lower levels and understorey, where branches and vegetation are dense.

DISTRIBUTION This species is found throughout the dry forests of the western region and spiny forests of the southern region from Tolagnaro in the south to at least the Sambirano River in the north-west. The species's precise northern limits are unclear: it has been reported from the Ankarana and Analamera Special Reserves in the far north, where it may live sympatrically with another *Microcebus* species whose identity has yet to be confirmed (cf. *M. rufus* and *M. myoxinus*). The Grey Mouse Lemur is certainly replaced by the Brown Mouse Lemur *M. rufus* in the Sambirano region of north-west Madagascar.

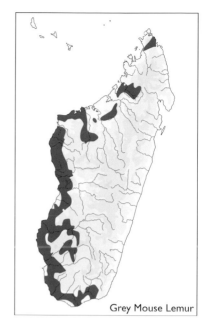
Grey Mouse Lemur

BEHAVIOUR Grey Mouse Lemurs are nocturnal and omnivorous. By day they congregate in communal sleep sites, where up to 15 individuals may gather. These are generally tree holes lined with leaf-litter or purpose-built spherical nests constructed amongst the twigs of dense undergrowth from dead leaves and moss. The composition of the sleeping groups changes seasonally. During the breeding season (September–October) males and females may sleep together. At other times of the year females generally sleep in groups with their dependent offspring, while males sleep alone or in pairs.

Grey Mouse Lemurs are largely solitary foragers and occupy small home ranges: around two hectares for females and three hectares for males. Male home ranges may overlap with one another and always overlap with the home range of at least one female. In some areas two distinct size classes of males have been observed: the home ranges of the smaller males have dramatically reduced areas of overlap with female home ranges, indicating that they may be reproductively suppressed.

Their diet consists mainly of fruit, insects, flowers and young leaves. They will also eat sap and gum from *Euphorbia* and *Terminalia* trees, secretions produced by the nymphs of homopteran insects *Flatidia coccinea* (which are of particular importance during the dry season) and even small vertebrates like tree frogs, geckos and chameleons.

During their day-time period of inactivity Grey Mouse Lemurs may enter temporary torpor and are able to reduce their body temperature to ambient (body temperatures as low as 7°C have been recorded). Furthermore, during the cooler months of the austral winter (May – August) they generally choose tree holes very close to ground level, where ambient temperatures remain slightly lower and more stable. This allows the mouse lemurs to remain torpid for longer. These strategies help conserve valuable body resources.

In the dry season (April/May to September/October) females become totally inactive and may remain dormant within their tree holes for several months – average 176 days – which again conserves energy and helps reduce predation. Males, on the other hand, remain more active at this time and probably establish a hierarchy for future access to breeding females. Prior to the dry season both sexes lay down large reserves of fat in their hind legs and tail – up to 35% of body weight – which helps sustain them through the dry season and their period of aestivation.

Females advertise the onset of oestrous by a distinctive high-frequency call and scent-marking from the ano-genital region. Mating takes place from mid-September until the end of October and, after a gestation period of about 60 days, births are timed to coincide with the onset of the rainy season. Grey Mouse Lemurs generally give birth to twins in a tree hole or leaf nest. The offspring are independent within two months and sexually mature at 18 months.

Major predators of the Grey Mouse Lemur include the Ring-tailed Mongoose *Galidia elegans*, Narrow-striped Mongoose *Mungotictis decemlineata*, Fosa *Cryptoprocta ferox*, Madagascar Long-eared Owl *Asio madagascariensis*, Madagascar Barn Owl *Tyto alba affinis*, Madagascar Tree Boa *Sanzinia madagascariensis* and Madagascar Ground Boa *Acrantophis madagascariensis*.

POPULATION Exact population figures are unknown, but the Grey Mouse Lemur is very abundant, with numbers certainly running into hundreds of thousands and perhaps even millions. The density of populations varies according to habitat. In arid spiny forests up to 360 individuals/km² have been recorded, while in western dry deciduous forests densities can reach 1,300 to 3,600/km², although figures as low as 42/km² have also been recorded for this habitat. It is thought that even in uniform habitat the Grey Mouse Lemur may occur in localised concentrations or 'population nuclei', which would account for the huge variation in these figures.

THREATS This is one of the most widespread and abundant lemur species. It is also quite adaptable, being equally at home in degraded and secondary vegetation as in primary forest. Although overall numbers may be declining because of the extent of forest loss, no major threat to the survival of this species currently exists. It is found in at least 12 protected areas.

VIEWING Due to its abundance, this species can be seen without difficulty throughout its range. The best and easiest places to see Grey Mouse Lemurs are probably Ampijoroa Forestry Station, Kirindy Forest, Beza Mahafaly Special Reserve and Berenty Private Reserve.

Figure 83. Grey Mouse Lemur, Kirindy.

Figure 84. Grey Mouse Lemur, Ampijoroa.

Figure 85. Pygmy Mouse Lemur (left) and
Grey Mouse Lemur (right), Kirindy.

BROWN MOUSE LEMUR *Microcebus rufus* E. Geoffroy, 1834

Malagasy: Tsitsihy, Tsitsidy, Tsidy Savoka

MEASUREMENTS Total length: 170-250mm. Head/body length: 70-90mm. Tail length: 100-160mm. Weight: average 40-45g, seasonal variation 30-55g.

DESCRIPTION The head, upperparts and tail are a characteristic rufous-brown, with a greyish tinge showing through from the hair bases. The face is rounded and often appears more rufous than the rest of the body. The underparts and throat are creamy grey-white. The ears are relatively small and do not protrude noticeably from the head. Eye colour varies from pale green to hazel (figs. 1a & 86).

IDENTIFICATION A very small, particularly active lemur, with a long tail. Movements are quick and often staccato. This species is broadly sympatric with the Greater Dwarf Lemur *Cheirogaleus major*, but is easily distinguished from the latter by its considerably smaller size and more rapid movements. In the north of its range the Brown Mouse Lemur may also be sympatric with the Grey Mouse Lemur *M. murimus*, the former being distinguished by its smaller size, rufous rather than grey coloration, and far less prominent ears.

HABITAT Lowland and montane rainforests and similar habitat, including secondary vegetation and some adjacent plantations. The Brown Mouse Lemur has been observed from ground level to the rainforest canopy.

DISTRIBUTION This species is found throughout the eastern rainforest belt, from Tolagnaro in the south through the Tsaratanana Massif in the north and across into the Sambirano region of the north-west. It is also present at Montagne d'Ambre in the far north. The species's exact distribution in other areas north of the Tsaratanana Massif is unclear. It may be present in some dry forest areas such as Ankarana and Analamera

Brown Mouse Lemur

and, therefore, be sympatric with the Grey Mouse Lemur. However, the exact identity of *Microcebus* species in these forests has yet to be established. An isolated population is also present in the Ambohitantely Special Reserve, a remnant patch of forest on the high plateau.

BEHAVIOUR The Brown Mouse Lemur is nocturnal and omnivorous. It is both solitary and gregarious and occupies a home range of around one hectare. Most foraging takes place in the understorey and low trees. Where resources are concentrated, individuals may gather in small numbers. Their diet consists mainly of fruit (over 40 species are known to be eaten), flowers, young shoots, insects and occasionally small vertebrates like tree frogs.

During the day Brown Mouse Lemurs sleep in groups of one to four in tree holes, leaf nests and sometimes disused birds' nests. Although the composition of sleep groups is unknown, females are known to sleep with small infants. In common with the Grey Mouse Lemur, this species regularly scent-marks with urine and faeces to denote territorial boundaries, although there is still considerable overlap of home ranges. It is suspected that, unlike Grey Mouse Lemurs, Brown Mouse Lemurs remain active during the austral winter (although females may become dormant for short periods; nevertheless, they lay down fat reserves in their tail and probably other areas of the body during the wet season.

Males begin to ready themselves for breeding in mid-August when their testes enlarge. Mating actually takes place between September and November, with births occurring from November to January. Females construct a nest of leaves between one and three metres off the ground and produce one to three young after a gestation period of around 60 days. The young weigh around 5g at birth.

Brown Mouse Lemurs fall victim to a number of different mammalian, avian and reptilian predators: carnivores like the Ring-tailed Mongoose *Galidia elegans* and Fosa *Cryptoprocta ferox* are able to excavate the lemurs from their daytime sleep sites; diurnal raptors, such as the Madagascar Harrier-hawk *Polyboroides radiatus* and other birds, e.g. the Hook-billed Vanga *Vanga curvirostris* have been observed predating *M. rufus*; the Madagascar Long-eared Owl *Asio madagascariensis* and Madagascar Barn Owl *Tyto alba affinis* are significant nocturnal hunters of this species and large snakes like the Madagascar Tree Boa *Sanzinia madagascariensis* are also known to eat Brown Mouse Lemurs.

POPULATION The Brown Mouse Lemur appears abundant throughout the majority of its range. Exact population figures are impossible to calculate, but the species certainly numbers in the hundreds of thousands and possibly millions. Estimates of population density range from around 110 animals/km^2 to over 250 individuals/km^2. In some areas they are more abundant in secondary vegetation than primary forest.

THREATS Because it is so widespread and abundant and is able to adapt to secondary and degraded vegetation, no major threat to this species is currently perceived. However, the ongoing reduction of rainforest areas suggests that numbers are sure to be declining overall. The Brown Mouse Lemur is present in at least 18 protected areas, and probably more.

VIEWING The abundance of this species means it can be seen easily throughout its range. Look principally for their glowing red eyes and darting movements. It is also sometimes possible to hear their irregular high-pitched squeaks and chattery vocalisations, although these can be confused with insect calls. The best places to see the Brown Mouse Lemur are Analamazaotra Special Reserve (Andasibe/ Perinet), Montagne d'Ambre National Park and Ranomafana National Park. The latter site can be particularly rewarding as several individuals regularly visit a feeding station at *Belle Vue*, where exceptionally close views are commonplace.

PYGMY MOUSE LEMUR *Microcebus myoxinus* Peters, 1852

MEASUREMENTS Total length: 170-220mm. Head/body length: 60-70mm. Tail length: 110-150mm. Weight: average 30g, known range 25-40g.

DESCRIPTION The head, upperparts and tail are rufous-brown with a distinct orange tinge, while the underparts are creamy-white (fig. 87). The pelage is short and dense. There is a dark dorsal stripe running down the middle of the back and a short whitish stripe extending from the forehead to the tip of the muzzle. The tail is relatively long compared with the other species of *Microcebus* and it is also more densely furred. This species is the smallest primate in the world.

IDENTIFICATION A tiny active lemur with a very small body and long tail. Within its confirmed range, this species can only be confused with the Grey Mouse Lemur M. *murinus*, the Pygmy Mouse Lemur is distinguished by its noticeably smaller size, brown/orange coloration, small ears and relatively long tail. It also tends to freeze when caught in a torch beam, unlike the Grey Mouse Lemur (fig. 85).

HABITAT Dry deciduous forest. There are reports that this species is also able to survive in coastal mangrove forests.

DISTRIBUTION The Pygmy Mouse Lemur is a recently rediscovered species that can currently be confirmed only from the Kirindy Forest between the villages of Beroboka and Maronfandilia, around 60km north-west of Morondava. However, museum specimens of M. *myoxinus* obtained in the late 1840s suggest a broader distribution: they were collected from diverse localities in the west including St. Augustine Bay near Toliara in the south-west and Bombatoka Bay near Mahajanga in the north-west. Since this species's rediscovery in 1994 there have been several possible sightings from new localities, including the Tsingy de Bemaraha National Park, north of the Tsiribihina river; coastal forests around Baly Bay, south-west of Mahajanga; Ankarafantsika Nature Reserve, south-east of Mahajanga, and even Analamera Special Reserve in the far north-east. However, given the present uncertainty surrounding the taxonomy of *Microcebus* it would be folly to suggest precise identities for these populations: they might be M. *myoxinus*, but potentially could also represent new taxa. It certainly seems likely that the Pygmy Mouse Lemur occurs over a wider range in western forests than is currently conclusively known.

Pygmy Mouse Lemur

BEHAVIOUR Due to the extended period without records (1840 to 1994) very little is known about the behaviour and habits of this species. The Pygmy Mouse Lemur is certainly nocturnal and solitary, and probably omnivorous like the Grey Mouse Lemur with which it shares its known range.

Also like M. *murinus*, the Pygmy Mouse Lemur is able to enter daily and seasonal torpor to conserve vital body resources. Preliminary observations indicate that Pygmy Mouse Lemurs may have larger home ranges than Grey Mouse Lemurs and prefer nests and dense liana tangles, rather than tree holes, as daytime sleep sites.

POPULATION As the precise range of the Pygmy Mouse Lemur has yet to be determined, no reliable population figure can be given. In Kirindy Forest the species is probably common, although not as widespread within the area as the Grey Mouse Lemur.

THREATS Habitat loss and degradation, and possible localised range, are seen as the main threats to this species's survival.

VIEWING The only places where this species can be seen with any degree of certainty are Kirindy Forest and Analabe Private Reserve, north-east of Morondava. At Kirindy, Pygmy Mouse Lemurs are fairly common and often seen in the forest close to the research camp.

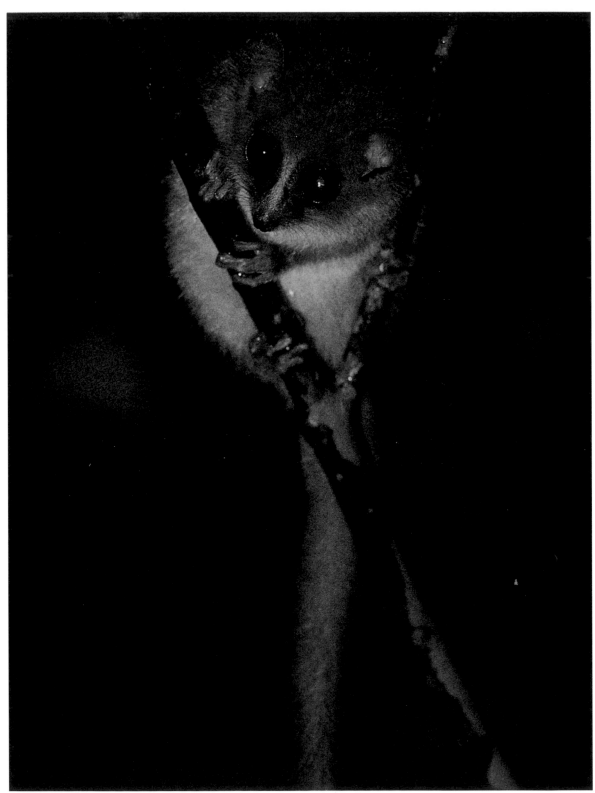

Figure 86. Brown Mouse Lemur, Ranomafana.

Figure 87. Pygmy Mouse Lemur, Kirindy.

Figure 88. Golden-brown Mouse Lemur, Ampijoroa.

149

GOLDEN-BROWN MOUSE LEMUR *Microcebus ravelobensis* Zimmermann *et al.*, 1998

Golden-brown
Mouse Lemur

MEASUREMENTS Total length: 220-305 mm. Head/body length: 90-130mm. Tail length: 130-175mm. Weight: average 55g, known range 40-70g.

DESCRIPTION The pelage is short and dense. The head and upperparts are golden-brown, while the underparts are noticeably paler and yellowish-white. The tail is long, thin and slightly darker brown than the main body, and darkens considerably at the tip. The head is relatively small; there is a faint white stripe extending from the lower forehead to the tip of the muzzle and there are dark brown rings around the eyes. The ears are long, yellow-brown in colour and very sparsely furred.

IDENTIFICATION A small, very active lemur, with long, highly visible ears and a long tail (fig. 88). This species can be distinguished from the similar-sized Grey Mouse Lemur M. *murinus* by its overall more gracile appearance, golden-brown rather than grey pelage and longer tail. Confusion with the Fat-tailed Dwarf Lemur *Cheirogaleus medius* is unlikely since this species is considerably larger than M. *ravelobensis* and grey in colour.

HABITAT Dry deciduous forest.

DISTRIBUTION This recently described species is currently known only from the forests of Ampijoroa, some 120km south-east of Mahajanga in north-west Madagascar. The type specimen was collected adjacent to Lac Ravelobe, a sacred lake at Ampijoroa, hence the specific name, *ravelobensis*. Further research in surrounding areas and elsewhere in north-west Madagascar may reveal new populations and a more extensive range.

BEHAVIOUR The behaviour and ecology of this species have yet to be studied in detail, so information regarding its habits is scant. Initial observations suggest that M.*ravelobensis* is noticeably more active than the sympatric Grey Mouse Lemur. It appears to prefer forest where the canopy is higher, and moves from branch to branch primarily by leaping, rather than quadrupedally like M. *murinus*. Furthermore, this species may remain more active during the dry season as it does not appear to have the same capacity to store fat in its tail as does the Grey Mouse Lemur.

Breeding probably begins in August, prior to that of Grey Mouse Lemur. Nests are often located in tangles of vines and dead leaves, whereas M. *murinus* generally prefers to use tree holes. The gestation length is not known, but it is likely to be similar to that of the Grey Mouse Lemur – around 60 days.

POPULATION No overall population figures are known. In the forests around Lac Ravelobe this species seems to be reasonably abundant.

THREATS The localised range of this species, coupled with continued destruction of dry deciduous forests, is serious cause for concern.

VIEWING The forest around Lac Ravelobe at Ampijoroa Forestry Station is the only known locality where this species can be seen.

Figure 89. Hairy-eared Dwarf Lemur.

HAIRY-EARED DWARF LEMUR genus *Allocebus* Petter-Rousseaux and Petter, 1967

When first described, the Hairy-eared Dwarf Lemur was placed in the genus *Cheirogaleus*. Subsequent research revealed that its closest affinities actually lay within the genus *Microcebus*, although a number of morphological features – particularly aspects of dentition and the cranium – were considered sufficiently distinct to warrant elevation to the monotypic genus *Allocebus*. *Allocebus* was originally known from just five museum specimens, four of which were collected in the late 19th century and the fifth collected in 1965. It was not located again until 1989.

HAIRY-EARED DWARF LEMUR *Allocebus trichotis* (Günther, 1875)

Malagasy: Tsidiala

MEASUREMENTS Total length: 265-355mm. Head/body length: 125-160mm. Tail length: 140-195mm. Weight: 65-90g.

DESCRIPTION The head and upperparts are brownish-grey, sometimes with a slight rosy tinge. The tail is of similar colour, but darkens towards the tip and becomes somewhat bushy. A faint dark dorsal stripe is also apparent on some individuals. The underparts are paler, varying from light grey to almost white, and this coloration extends slightly up the flanks. There are narrow dark rings around the eyes and sometimes a pale whitish stripe extending from between the eyes to the tip of the nose. The ears are small and largely concealed beneath long wavy ear-tufts that extend slightly around the cheeks and give this species both its vernacular and scientific names (figs. 90 & 91).

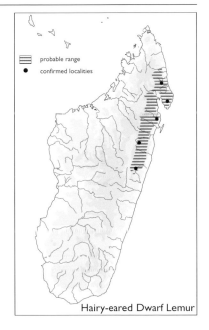

probable range
● confirmed localities

Hairy-eared Dwarf Lemur

On the basis of the limited amount of information currently available, *A. trichotis* would appear to be slightly larger, but with a relatively shorter tail, at the southern end of its range than at its northern limits.

IDENTIFICATION A small, active lemur with a long tail. It is smaller in size than *Cheirogaleus* species, but larger than *Microcebus* species which it closely resembles. Distinguishing *A. trichotis* from the Brown Mouse Lemur *M. rufus* in the field is problematic and requires close observation. However, the larger size and ear-tufts of the Hairy-eared Dwarf Lemur are the obvious features to look for. The pelage of *A. trichotis* is also greyer in colour.

HABITAT Lowland and lower mid-altitude rainforests, including some slightly degraded areas.

DISTRIBUTION The exact range of this species is very poorly understood. When rediscovered in 1989, it was thought to be restricted to the lowland rainforests on both sides of the Mananara River, near the town of Mananara in north-east Madagascar. However, subsequent research has revealed its presence in a number of other localities: Forêt de Vohidrazana just to the east of Andasibe (680-1,235m); Analamazaotra Special Reserve adjacent to Andasibe (900m); Zahamena Nature Reserve; the Masoala Peninsula; and Anjanaharibe-Sud Special Reserve (865m). This certainly indicates that the species is far more widespread than previously thought. Based on this, the known range of *A. trichotis* covers much of the central and north-eastern rainforest areas at lower elevations (below approximately 1,200m) and extends from the region of Andasibe in the south to around the Marojejy Massif in the north and includes the Masoala Peninsula. Future research may well extend this range further.

BEHAVIOUR Minimal research has taken place to establish basic behavioural and ecological data for this species, so very little information is currently available. The Hairy-eared Dwarf Lemur is certainly known to be nocturnal and is probably active from around dusk until dawn. It has been observed both singly and in pairs, probably corresponding to a male and female. Foraging efforts appear to be concentrated in dense tangles of vegetation at lower levels in the forest. The day is spent sleeping in tree holes, generally in groups of two to six individuals. Holes in larger trees appear to be preferred.

The diet of the Hairy-eared Dwarf Lemur is not known. However, its dentition and nails suggest that gum-eating is important and it also has a very long tongue which suggests nectar might be a significant element in its diet. This is reinforced by observations in captivity, where this species feeds avidly on honey, but also eats leaves, fruits and insects.

Little is known of the vocalisations of this species, but it has been heard to emit a series of short whistles and alternating squeals that are similar to those produced by *Microcebus* species. When alarmed it is reported to stand erect on its hind limbs to spot danger.

There is evidence to suggest that the Hairy-eared Dwarf Lemur becomes torpid and aestivates during the austral winter (May–September/October). Prior to the onset of this drier cooler period, *A. trichotis* deposits reserves of fat over its entire body, such that body weight reaches its annual maximum in May and June. Furthermore, testis size in males regresses dramatically during this period and only begins to increase again in September and early October, when the animals emerge and begin to breed. Observations by local people reinforce this: they do not report seeing Hairy-eared Dwarf Lemurs between May and September, but do see the animals between October and early May. This seasonality in general activity and breeding activity is very similar to that found in *Microcebus*.

Births have been reported in January and February. All other aspects of the behaviour and ecology of the Hairy-eared Dwarf Lemur are likely to show similarities to *Microcebus* species.

Figure 90. Hairy-eared Dwarf Lemur, Mananara.

Figure 91. Hairy-eared Dwarf Lemur, Mananara.

Figure 92. Greater Dwarf Lemur, Analamazaotra.

POPULATION Until basic survey work is carried out and the full extent of this species's range understood, estimating total numbers remains impossible. In the areas where it is known to occur, population densities seem to be very low.

THREATS The main danger to this species is the continued destruction of lowland and mid-altitude rainforest. In the Mananara region this species is also trapped and eaten by the local people. *A. trichotis* is currently known to occur in five protected areas (Mananara-Nord Biosphere Reserve, Analamazaotra Special Reserve, Zahamena Nature Reserve, Anjanaharibe-Sud Special Reserve and Masoala National Park). It may also be present in other reserves within its range (e.g. Mantadia National Park and Ambatovaky Special Reserve).

VIEWING The most accessible known locality of the Hairy-eared Dwarf Lemur is Analamazaotra Special Reserve where the species has recently been recorded for the first time. It is almost certain *Allocebus* has been seen in this reserve previously, but has been misidentified as Brown Mouse Lemur. An alternative locality is Forêt de Vohidazana near the village of Fanovana, approximately 12km to the east of Andasibe in the central-eastern rainforests. *A. trichotis* probably also occurs in other areas of rainforest within this vicinity, which includes Mantadia National Park. Indeed, it has been suggested that the boundaries of the park be extended southwards to include the area of primary forest where *Allocebus* has been found.

Alternatively, the forests near Befingitra in Anjanaharibe-Sud Special Reserve or those south-west of Mananara offer a slim chance of seeing this species.

DWARF LEMURS genus *Cheirogaleus* E. Geoffroy, 1812

The genus *Cheirogaleus* includes two species of dwarf lemur: the Greater Dwarf Lemur *C.major* and the Fat-tailed Dwarf Lemur *C.medius*. Both are nocturnal, move quadrupedally and have a horizontal body posture. They are notable for the seasonality of their activity: both become largely inactive during the austral winter and accumulate reserves of fat prior to this time. The two species are largely allopatric throughout their ranges, but in northern areas they appear to be sympatric at some localities.

GREATER DWARF LEMUR *Cheirogaleus major* E. Geoffroy, 1812

Malagasy: Tsidy, Tsitsihy, Hataka

MEASUREMENTS Total length: 500-550mm. Head/body length: 230-250mm. Tail length: 250-280mm. Weight: average 350-400g, seasonal variation 250-500g.

DESCRIPTION The pelage is short and dense. The head, upperparts and broad tail vary from grey-brown to rufous-brown, with an increasing trend towards the latter in the northern part of its range. The underparts are paler grey to white. There are dark rings around the eyes with lighter whitish-grey areas outside these which join between the eyes and extend down the muzzle (figs. 92 & 93). The snout is dark and slightly pointed with a relatively large fleshy nose and pinkish nostrils.

IDENTIFICATION A squirrel-sized lemur, with a horizontal posture. This species is distinguishable from similar-sized *Avahi* and *Lepilemur* species by its horizontal rather than vertical posture. Dwarf lemurs also run quadrupedally, whereas the two other genera are leapers. This species should not be confused with the Fork-marked Lemur *Phaner furcifer* whose face is more elongate and distinctively marked.

In some northern localities, this species may live sympatrically with its congener, the Fat-tailed Dwarf Lemur *C. medius*. Confusion between these two species is certainly possible. In general the Greater Dwarf Lemur is noticeably larger and far more rufous-brown in colour, in contrast to the distinctive grey of *C. medius*.

HABITAT Primary rainforest, well-established secondary forest and some more degraded forests, including coffee and lychee plantations.

DISTRIBUTION This species occurs throughout the eastern rainforest belt, from Tolagnaro in the south to Montagne d'Ambre in the north, including the Tsaratanana Massif and Sambirano region in the north-west. The Greater Dwarf Lemur appears to have a wide elevational tolerance from sea-level to altitudes above 1,600m.

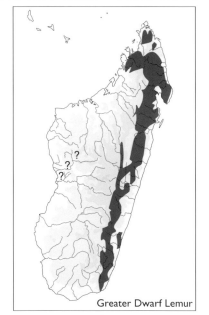

Greater Dwarf Lemur

Interestingly, *C. major* has also been recorded in western Madagascar: sightings have been made to the south and north of the Manambolo River in the region of Bemaraha, and on the Bongolava Massif further to the west. At these sites, this species is sympatric with *C. medius*.

BEHAVIOUR The Greater Dwarf Lemur is nocturnal and forages alone or in small groups of two or three. Home ranges of around four hectares have been estimated. Foraging seems to occur at all levels in the forest from the understorey to the canopy, and the species has even been observed descending to the ground to search for insects in leaf-litter. The day is spent sleeping in small groups in tree holes or dense clumps of tangled vegetation.

It is suspected that this species becomes dormant during the austral winter. Its activity levels are drastically reduced at this time and prior to this period fat reserves are laid down in the tail, which swells in size and then constitutes up to 30% of body weight. From July until around mid-September, the Greater Dwarf Lemur probably conceals itself in leaf-litter at the base of large trees or in tree holes.

The Greater Dwarf Lemur is omnivorous, its diet consisting of ripe fruit, flowers, nectar, pollen, young shoots, insects and perhaps even small vertebrates like chameleons. Recent studies have shown that this lemur may be primarily responsible for pollinating certain species of liana, e.g. *Strongylodon craveniae* (Leguminosae). This is the only lemur not to destroy the inflorescence while feeding and, therefore, trigger the flower's pollen removal/receipt mechanism. Pollen is deposited on the animal's forehead and then transferred to another flower when it moves on to feed elsewhere. There are also many other rainforest plants that have evolved floral traits suggesting that lemur pollination is important.

Mating occurs in late October/early November: at this time much larger aggregations of up to 14 individuals have been seen. These groups are very noisy and highly active, behaving in an agitated manner: they may well be groups of males competing for access to females. Prior to parturition, the female constructs a nest of leaves and vines 6-12m above ground level. A litter of two or three is born in January after a gestation period of around 70 days. Initially the mother carries the young in her mouth, but later they are capable of clinging to her back. When around a month old the infants are able to follow their mother and begin eating soft fruit, although lactation can last up to six weeks.

Predators of the Greater Dwarf Lemur include the Ring-tailed Mongoose *Galidia elegans*, Fosa *Cryptoprocta ferox* and Madagascar Tree Boa *Sanzinia madagascariensis*. A Madagascar Buzzard *Buteo brachypterus* has been observed feeding on C. *major* and it seems likely that other raptors also include this lemur in their diet.

POPULATION This species's large range, small size and nocturnal nature make estimating overall populations virtually impossible. In some areas the Greater Dwarf Lemur has been recorded at densities of around 70 to 110 individuals/km².

THREATS The destruction of its rainforest habitat for timber, fuel and agriculture is the major threat to this lemur. It is also hunted for food throughout its range, being caught in traps or extracted from sleep holes. Although the overall population is probably falling due to habitat loss, no major threat to the species's survival is currently perceived. The Greater Dwarf Lemur is known to occur in at least 15 protected areas and many other forests besides.

VIEWING The best time to see this species is during the austral summer/wet season from November to April, when it is most active. At other times it may be dormant and difficult to locate. It can be seen in all forests within its range. The most accessible sites are Montagne d'Ambre and Ranomafana National Parks and Analamazaotra Special Reserve (Andasibe/Perinet). The forests either side of the road from the village of Andasibe to the entrance of the reserve and between the reserve entrance and the warden's house can be very rewarding during the summer months.

FAT-TAILED DWARF LEMUR *Cheirogaleus medius* E. Geoffroy, 1812

Malagasy: Tsidy, Tsidihy, Kely Be-ohy, Matavirambo

MEASUREMENTS Total length: 400-500mm. Head/body length: 200-230mm. Tail length: 200-270mm. Weight: average 160g, seasonal variation 140-220g.

DESCRIPTION The pelage is short and dense. The head, dorsal region and broad tail are overall pale to mid-grey, but with rufous tints and darker hair bases showing through. The underparts and throat are creamy-white. This paler coloration extends up the flanks from the belly more than in C. *major* and is visible from the side. There are obvious dark rings around the eyes, while the face and cheeks are pale grey-white and the nose is pinkish. The snout and ears may also be slightly darker (figs. 94 & 95).

IDENTIFICATION A small squirrel-sized lemur that adopts a horizontal body posture. In areas of sympatry, confusion with Coquerel's Dwarf Lemur *Mirza coquereli* is distinctly possible as size and pelage colour are broadly similar. However, Coquerel's Dwarf Lemur is larger and more reddish is colour, has much bigger, highly conspicuous ears and lacks the obviously fattened tail of C. *medius*. Furthermore, the movements of *Mirza* tend to be continuous and more rapid than those of the Fat-tailed Dwarf Lemur.

The distinctive facial markings and more rapid movements of the Fork-marked Lemur *Phaner furcifer* should serve to differentiate between it and C. *medius*, while larger size and slower movements of the Fat-tailed Dwarf Lemur should prevent confusion with *Microcebus* species. See also Greater Dwarf Lemur C. *major*.

HABITAT Dry deciduous forest, gallery forest and well-established secondary forest.

DISTRIBUTION This species is found throughout the dry forests of the south and west, from Tolagnaro in the south across to Toliara in the south-west and north to the

Fat-tailed Dwarf Lemur

area south of the Sambirano region in the north-west. It has also been observed north of the Tsaratanana Massif, although its distributional limits within this region have yet to be clarified. The Fat-tailed Dwarf Lemur has been recorded in the dry deciduous forests of Ankarana and Analamera and in the vicinity of Daraina near Vohemar. At this latter locality it is sympatric with C. *major*. There have also been potential observations of the Fat-tailed Dwarf Lemur in the rainforests of Anjanaharibe-Sud Special Reserve in the northeast. If confirmed these would represent a dramatic extension of the species's range into the humid eastern rainforest belt.

During the last century specimens were collected from other northern forest areas, including those of the Sambirano region. This suggests that the species was once more widespread than is currently suspected and lived in much broader sympatry with the Greater Dwarf Lemur, although it is possible that it has simply been overlooked in the north in recent years.

Figure 93. Greater Dwarf Lemur, Analamazaotra.

Figure 94. *Fat-tailed Dwarf Lemur, Ampijoroa.*

BEHAVIOUR Fat-tailed Dwarf Lemurs are nocturnal and omnivorous. They forage alone or in groups of up to three individuals and occupy small home ranges of around four hectares. There is probably a high degree of overlap between adjacent territories. During the day, this species sleeps in tree holes, either alone or in communal groups of up to five individuals.

The diet is varied and consists of fruit, flowers, nectar, pollen, leaf buds, gum, insects and occasionally small vertebrates. *C. medius* may be responsible for pollinating some baobabs *Adansonia* spp.

The Fat-tailed Dwarf Lemur is also an important agent of small seed dispersal and its behaviour in this respect is quite unique: during the rainy season (November to April) it smears its faeces into the branches of trees, which is particularly beneficial to the germination of parasitic plants like mistletoes (e.g. *Viscum* species). In this way *C. medius* fills a role played by birds in other parts of the world.

There is a marked seasonal variation in food availability in their dry deciduous forest habitat. During the wet season, *C. medius* gradually builds up reserves of fat (up to 75g) which are stored in the tail and result in an increase in body weight of up to 40%. At the onset of the dry season (sometimes as early as March) they become inactive for up to six months, spending this time tucked away in a tree hole, sometimes in small groups. However, this period of dormancy does not appear to be continuous, as individuals may occasionally emerge from their torpor. At the end of the dry season between September to October, individuals become active for short periods and then temporarily return to dormancy. By October/November, however, the majority of individuals have emerged fully from dormancy, although there is considerable regional variation linked with climate: towards the north of the species's range they become fully active sooner.

Mating takes place in December and January. After a gestation period of around 60 days, litters of one to four offspring (average two) are born between late January and March. The following April/May, juveniles tend to becoming dormant later into the onset of the dry season than adults and so benefit from a period of reduced competition for food.

Antagonistic interactions between this species and Coquerel's Dwarf Lemur have been observed: *C. medius* appears to be dominant. The Fat-tailed Dwarf Lemur is preyed upon by the Fosa *Cryptoprocta ferox*, which is able to excavate its victims from tree holes; and also by the Madagascar Long-eared Owl *Asio madagascariensis* and occasionally the Madagascar Ground Boa *Acrantophis madagascariensis*.

POPULATION The extensive range of the Fat-tailed Dwarf Lemur, coupled with some high population density estimates, suggests a considerable population size. However, there appears to be variation between areas and habitats. In some primary dry deciduous forests, population densities of 300 to 400 individuals/km^2 have been recorded, although these seem exceptional. Other estimates in similar forests range from 20 to 80 animals/km^2. In riverine gallery forest a density of 37/km^2 has been reported.

THREATS Habitat destruction and, to a lesser extent, hunting for food are the main dangers facing this species. The likelihood is that overall numbers are declining. However, its extensive range and adaptability suggest there is no immediate threat to survival. The Fat-tailed Dwarf Lemur is found in at least seven protected areas and at several other important sites.

VIEWING It is possible to see the Fat-tailed Dwarf Lemur throughout its range, but only during the warm wet season when it is active (November to April). After heavy rain, access to some western areas can be difficult during the middle of this period. The best sites to see this species, and which remain largely accessible throughout the year, are: Ampijoroa Forestry Station (part of Ankarafantsika Nature Reserve), south-east of Mahajanga; Kirindy Forest, north-east of Morondava; and Beza-Mahafaly Special Reserve to the east of Toliara. At all these localities the Fat-tailed Dwarf Lemur is regularly encountered on nocturnal walks.

COQUEREL'S DWARF LEMUR genus *Mirza* Gray, 1870

When first described Coquerel's Dwarf Lemur was placed in the genus *Microcebus* and some authorities still follow this taxonomy. However, on the basis of larger size, morphological differences, dental characteristics and some aspects of behaviour most authorities recognise this species as belonging to the monotypic genus *Mirza*.

COQUEREL'S DWARF LEMUR *Mirza coquereli* (A. Grandidier, 1867)

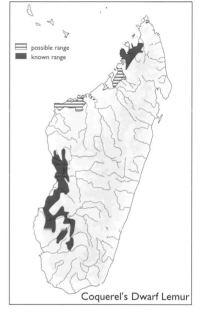

possible range
known range

Coquerel's Dwarf Lemur

Malagasy: Siba, Setohy, Fitily, Tsiba, Tilitilivaha

MEASUREMENTS Total length: 500-550mm. Head/body length: 200-225mm. Tail length: 300-330mm. Weight: 290-320g.

DESCRIPTION The fur is short and dense. The head and upperparts are brown or grey-brown, with some reddish, pinkish or yellowish tinges in places. The underparts are lighter grey, which shows through russet hair tips. The tail is relatively long, bushy in appearance and tends to darken towards the tip. The ears are large, hairless and very distinctive (fig. 96).

IDENTIFICATION A squirrel-sized lemur with a long tail and a horizontal body posture. The movements of *Mirza* are quadrupedal and tend to be rapid scurries, which helps distinguish it from the similar-sized Fat-tailed Dwarf Lemur *Cheirogaleus medius*. Its ears are also very prominent, whereas those of *C. medius* are concealed. In areas of sympatry this species may be confused with the Fork-marked Lemur *Phaner furcifer* which is also of similar size. However, the characteristic facial markings, small ears and loud vocalisations of *Phaner* should be sufficient to distinguish the two.

HABITAT This species inhabits dry deciduous forests, some more humid forests and some secondary forests. In dry forest areas it seems to prefer the slightly taller and thicker vegetation found along riverbanks and by semi-permanent still water. In the Sambirano region, *Mirza* has been observed in secondary forests dominated by cashew trees and coffee plantations.

DISTRIBUTION This species has an apparently discontinuous range along the west and north-west coast of Madagascar, although the exact limits remain a matter of contention. In the south of its range, the species occurs from regions south of the Mangoky River to the vicinity of Antsalova. There have been recent isolated sightings of Coquerel's Dwarf Lemur on the north bank of the Onilahy river some 40km inland from Toliara and in the Zombitse Forest near Sakaraha. These records represent a southerly extension to the range outlined above.

Some 650km to the north a second population of *Mirza* occurs in the Sambirano region, centred around Ambanja and the Ampasindava Peninsula. It has also been suggested that this species occurs in an intermediate area on the west coast between Boriziny in the north and Besalampy to the south.

BEHAVIOUR Coquerel's Dwarf Lemur is nocturnal, spending the day in a spherical nest constructed from interwoven lianas, twigs and leaves. This is usually located in the fork of a branch or amongst dense undergrowth at a height of 2-10m. These nests are generally occupied by solitary adults, but are very occasionally shared by males, females and juveniles. At dusk they leave the nest to begin foraging.

The diet is varied and includes fruit, flowers, shoots, gum, insects and their secretions and other invertebrates. During the dry season (June–August), when resources are scarce, the secretions from homopteran and cochineal nymphs are particularly important. This species is unusual amongst the Cheirogaleidae in that some small vertebrates (baby birds, frogs, lizards and even snakes) are also regularly eaten. Foraging appears to be concentrated in the lower levels of the forest, and this species has also been observed on the ground.

Coquerel's Dwarf Lemur is solitary. Females occupy overlapping home ranges of around three to four hectares, which remain constant in size throughout the year. The home ranges of males vary quite markedly in size between the non-breeding and breeding seasons. For most of the year they are similar in size to those of females and are non-overlapping with one another, but they overlap with the ranges of two or three females. When males and females meet, they may interact and remain together for short periods. During the mating season in October males range over a much wider area – up to 25ha. At this time their ranges overlap with one another and the ranges of up to 15 females.

Some authors have suggested that weak pairbonds are formed and that Coquerel's Dwarf Lemur is monogamous. In light of recent research this appears not to be the case. During the breeding season males have dramatically enlarged testes and females advertise the onset of oestrous with loud calls. This, coupled with the considerable variance in male home range size between breeding and non-breeding season, strongly suggests that competition between males for access to receptive females is intense and that *M. coquereli* is promiscuous.

Mating occurs in October and, after a 90-day gestation period, one or two young are born. At birth they weigh 15-20g. The infants leave the nest after three to four weeks and are initially carried by the mother in her mouth. They are quite vocal and remain in contact with each other during the first stages of independence. Sexual maturity is reached between 18 months and two years.

Aggressive encounters between this species and the Fat-tailed Dwarf Lemur *Cheirogaleus medius* have been observed. Coquerel's Dwarf Lemur is occasionally preyed upon by the Fosa *Cryptoprocta ferox* and Madagascar Long-eared Owl *Asio madagascariensis*.

POPULATION Because the exact range of this species remains uncertain, it is impossible to estimate an overall population figure. Population densities vary enormously with habitat. In dry deciduous forests there are estimates of 50 animals/km², but, if the narrow strips on either side of a river are taken in isolation, this figure may rise to 210 individuals/km². In the Sambirano region, even higher densities of 385/km² have been recorded in humid secondary forests dominated by cashew trees.

THREATS Habitat destruction is the major threat to this species. Hunting probably also occurs but appears to be far less significant. The ability of Coquerel's Dwarf Lemur to adapt to secondary forest suggests it may be able to survive the partial destruction of its natural habitat. However, this species's known range is limited and the habitat within it is becoming increasingly fragmented. Coquerel's Dwarf Lemur is known to occur in only three protected areas although its presence is confirmed in other areas of forest receiving degrees of informal protection.

VIEWING Kirindy Forest, some 60km north-east of Morondava, is probably the best locality to see this species: nocturnal walks along most of the major forest trails should give a reasonable chance of success. Encounter rates are probably higher during the breeding season when males, in particular, are more active. Alternatively, this species can been seen in the secondary forests and abandoned cashew nut groves near Ambanja in the north-west.

Figure 95. Fat-tailed Dwarf Lemur, Ampijoroa.

Figure 96. *Coquerel's Dwarf Lemur, Kirindy.*

FORK-MARKED LEMURS genus *Phaner* Gray, 1871

When first described, the Fork-marked Lemur was placed in the genus *Lemur* (as *Lemur furcifer*). Later study revealed that taxonomic separation was justified. Some authors proposed the creation of its own subfamily, Phanerinae. However, the majority now agree that its true affinities lie with the broad family Cheirogaleidae. Within this, the monotypic genus *Phaner* was proposed and is now widely accepted.

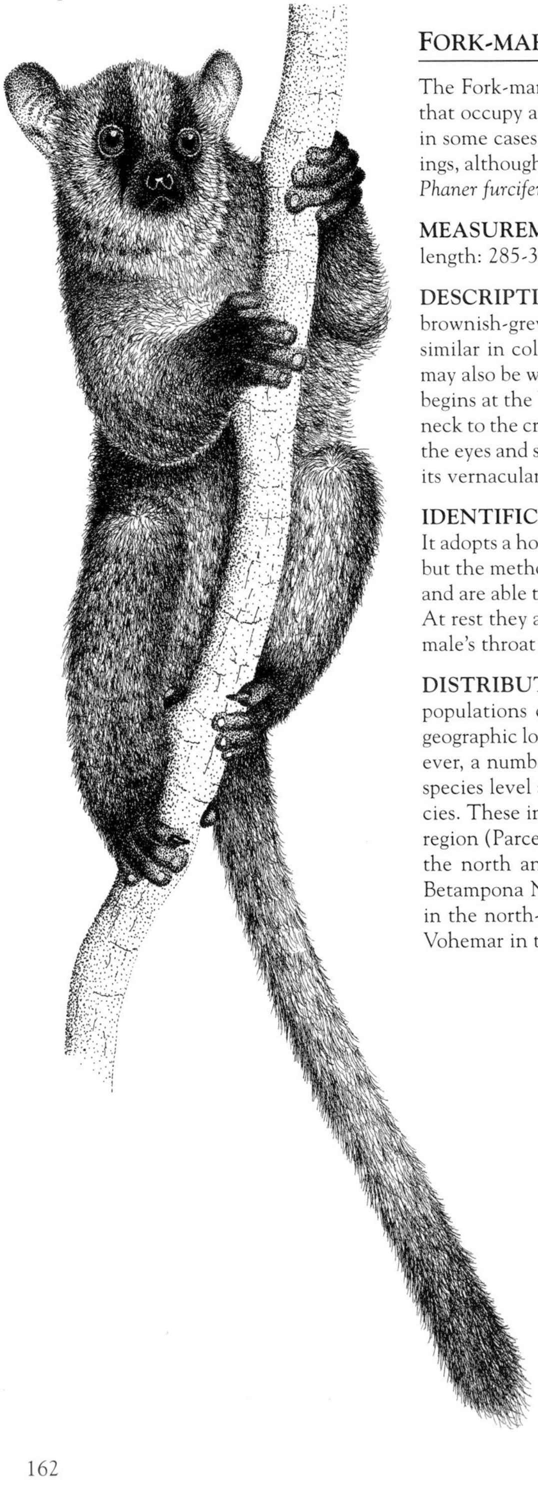

FORK-MARKED LEMUR *Phaner furcifer* (Blainville, 1839)

The Fork-marked Lemur *Phaner furcifer* has recently been divided into four subspecies that occupy apparently discontinuous ranges, the limits of which are poorly understood in some cases. These subspecies are all broadly similar in size, habits and general markings, although some differences in coloration exist between them. A general overview of *Phaner furcifer* is followed by more detailed accounts of each subspecies.

MEASUREMENTS Total length: 500-650mm. Head/body length: 225-285mm. Tail length: 285-370mm. Weight: 350-500g.

DESCRIPTION The pelage is quite dense. Upperparts are various shades of brown to brownish-grey, while the underparts are lighter shades of brown and grey. The tail is similar in colour to the upperparts, but generally darkens towards the tip: the very tip may also be white. The species's most obvious characteristic is the broad dark stripe that begins at the base of the tail and runs right along the dorsal ridge and up the back of the neck to the crown. Here it divides, with the two stripes continuing down the face, around the eyes and sometimes down the muzzle as well. It is this feature which gives the species its vernacular name.

IDENTIFICATION This is probably the largest member of the family Cheirogaleidae. It adopts a horizontal posture and moves quadrupedally like other members of the family, but the method is quite characteristic. Fork-marked Lemurs run at speed along branches and are able to leap from one to the next without pause, making them difficult to follow. At rest they also bob their heads in a distinctive manner. When viewed from below the male's throat gland is quite visible.

DISTRIBUTION Current information suggests there are five major discontinuous populations of *Phaner* which broadly correspond to its subspecific divisions. Indeed geographic location remains the most reliable guide for identifying each subspecies. However, a number of recently discovered populations have yet to be identified to the subspecies level and the possibility exists that some, if not all, of these may be new subspecies. These indeterminate populations occur at the following localities: the spiny forest region (Parcel 2) of the Andohahela Nature Reserve in the extreme south; the region to the north and east of Bombetoka Bay near Mahajanga in the west; Zahamena and Betampona Nature Reserves in the central-eastern rainforests; the Tsaratanana Massif in the north-west; and the dry deciduous and semi-evergreen forests in the vicinity of Vohemar in the north-east.

Figure 97. Eastern Fork-marked Lemur.

Subspecies

Eastern Fork-marked Lemur *Phaner furcifer furcifer* (Blainville, 1839)

Malagasy: Tanta, Tantararaolana

DESCRIPTION The nominate race is probably the largest-bodied and darkest of the subspecies and its pelage is longer and denser. The facial fork and dorsal stripe are very pronounced, although the stripe does not reach to the base of the tail. The tip of the tail is also dark, although the extreme tip may be pale grey.

IDENTIFICATION The distinctive markings and rapid movements of this subspecies should prevent confusion with the Greater Dwarf Lemur *Cheirogaleus major*, the only other species within its range of similar size, colour and posture.

HABITAT Lowland and mid-altitude rainforest.

DISTRIBUTION This subspecies is found on the Masoala Peninsula. The recently reported sightings of *Phaner* in Zahamena and Betampona Nature Reserves to the east of Lac Alaotra may also be attributable to this subspecies.

BEHAVIOUR This lemur is nocturnal. However, it remains unstudied in the wild and no further information is available regarding its habits. See *P. f. pallescens* for details of Fork-marked Lemur behaviour and ecology.

POPULATION Unknown.

THREATS Destruction and degradation of its rainforest habitat is the main threat to this subspecies. This, coupled with a restricted range, gives cause for concern regarding its long-term survival prospects.

VIEWING It is possible to see this subspecies at a number of localities on the Masoala Peninsula, but access is often problematic. Two places that are worth a try are the forests inland from Ambanizana and near Iaraka.

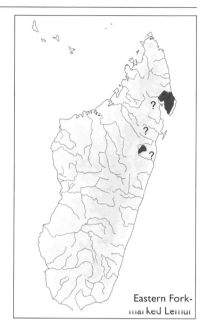

Eastern Fork-marked Lemur

Pariente's Fork-marked Lemur *Phaner furcifer parienti* Groves and Tattersall, 1991

Malagasy: Tanta, Tantaraolana

DESCRIPTION The upperparts are light brown to grey and are darker than *P. f. electromontis* found to the north, and lighter than *P. f. pallescens* that occurs to the south. The facial fork is prominent and the dorsal stripe reaches the base of the tail. There is also a distinct darkening of the tail towards its tip, although the extreme tip is white.

IDENTIFICATION Two sympatric species, the Greater Dwarf Lemur *Cheirogaleus major* and Coquerel's Dwarf Lemur *Mirza coquereli*, are of similar size, colour and posture to this subspecies. However, the distinctive markings and rapid movements of *P. f. parienti* should prevent misidentification.

HABITAT Lowland and mid-altitude humid forests.

DISTRIBUTION This subspecies appears to be restricted to the Sambirano region in north-west Madagascar, between the Andranomalaza River to the south and the Sambirano River to the north and including the Ampasindava Peninsula. *Phaner* has also been observed in the Tsaratanana Massif, at the eastern extreme of the Sambirano region. It seems probable that this population constitutes an extension to the range of this subspecies.

BEHAVIOUR Like other Fork-marked Lemurs, this subspecies is nocturnal and probably omnivorous. No further information is available. See *P. f. pallescens* for details of Fork-marked Lemur behaviour and ecology.

POPULATION Unknown.

THREATS Destruction and degradation of forest habitats for agriculture are the main threat to this subspecies. It also has a very restricted range and is known to occur in only two protected areas.

Pariente's Fork-marked Lemur

VIEWING Areas of well-preserved forest on the Ampasindava Peninsula offer a reasonable chance of seeing this subspecies. Also the forests around the village of Beraty on the western edge of Manongarivo Special Reserve, some 50km south of Ambanja, can be productive.

Pale Fork-marked Lemur *Phaner furcifer pallescens* Groves and Tattersall, 1991

Pale Fork-marked Lemur

Malagasy: Vakivoho, Tanta, Tantaraolana

DESCRIPTION The upperparts are predominantly light grey to grey-fawn, with some silvery tints. The distal two-thirds of the tail are slightly darker than the main body, but unlike other subspecies the tail does not end in an obviously darkened tip. The dorsal stripe and facial fork are less distinct than in the other subspecies. This is the palest, and possibly smallest, of the *Phaner furcifer* subspecies (fig. 98).

IDENTIFICATION This subspecies occurs sympatrically with several other nocturnal lemurs, including the Fat-tailed Dwarf Lemur *Cheirogaleus medius* and Coquerel's Dwarf Lemur *Mirza coquereli*, which are of broadly similar size, colour and posture. However, the unusual markings and more rapid movements of *P. f. pallescens* should prevent confusion with these.

HABITAT Dry deciduous forest and secondary forest.

DISTRIBUTION Confined to western Madagascar, *P. f. pallescens* has the largest range of the four subspecies. The main population extends in a strip, northward from the vicinity of Sakaraha and the Zombitse Forest to around Antsalova, north of the Tsiribihina River.

There is also a second population further north, centred around the Namoroka Nature Reserve and Baly Bay area, which is tentatively ascribed to *P. f. pallescens*. Further north still, to the north and west of the Bombetoka Bay, is a third population. Both of these northerly populations appear to have become isolated and there is speculation as to whether they in fact constitute a fifth subspecies.

BEHAVIOUR All the information on the behaviour and ecology of Fork-marked Lemurs is based on studies of this subspecies in the dry deciduous forests north of Morondava. *P. f. pallescens* is nocturnal although its most active period appears to be around dusk and the first hour or so of darkness. At this time the animals are extremely vocal, their loud calls being a distinctive characteristic of twilight in the forests they inhabit.

The Pale Fork-marked Lemur would appear to be monogamous. A female and male will occupy virtually identical home ranges (of around four hectares) which do not overlap with those of neighbouring males and females. Although the pair do not necessarily forage together, they remain in close proximity to one another and are in constant vocal contact throughout the night, frequently in the form of a duet. Males may also scent-mark their female from a large cutaneous throat gland, and mutual grooming is commonplace. By day, the pair may sleep together in the holes of large trees like baobabs *Adansonia* spp. and occasionally the abandoned nests of Coquerel's Dwarf Lemur.

Mating takes place in June, with the single offspring being born in a tree-hole nest between November and December. When initially leaving the nest, the mother carries the infant in her mouth. Later the offspring is able to ride on her back.

The dentition of this lemur is highly specialised. The lower incisors are modified into an inclined 'dental comb'. This is used to chisel holes in tree bark which stimulates the flow of sap and gums, both very rich sources of sugar and the primary constituents of the Pale Fork-marked Lemur's diet. This practice occurs throughout the year: the gum from *Terminalia* trees is especially favoured. Other food sources include flowers, nectar (*P. f. pallescens* is responsible for pollinating some baobabs) and insects and secretions from homopteran larvae (in particular from the family Machaerotidae). *Phaner* also has a very long extensible tongue, which undoubtedly helps the exploitation of its specialised diet. Interestingly, the two species of needle-clawed bush baby (*Euoticus* spp.: Galagonidae) from the rainforests of West Africa, have very similar adaptations, and also feed predominantly on tree gums and sap.

This subspecies has been seen to be preyed on by two diurnal species of raptor, the Madagascar Buzzard *Buteo brachypterus* and Madagascar Cuckoo-Hawk *Aviceda madagascariensis*.

POPULATION The overall population is unknown. Population densities of 300 to 400/km^2 have been estimated in some western forests. However, these areas of forest were probably particularly 'gum rich' giving an inflated figure. Other estimates range between 50 and 60 individuals/km^2, which would appear to be more realistic.

THREATS The destruction and fragmentation of forest habitat is the main threat to this subspecies. It is thought to occur in four protected areas.

VIEWING Kirindy Forest, Andranomena Special Reserve and Analabe Private Reserve, close to Morondava, probably offer the best chance of seeing this subspecies. Another noteworthy location is Zombitse Forest to the east of Sakaraha. The animals' loud vocalisations at dusk are unmistakable, as is their habit of head-bobbing.

Figure 98. Pale Fork-marked Lemur, Kirindy.

Amber Mountain Fork-marked Lemur *Phaner furcifer electromontis* Groves and Tattersall, 1991

Amber Mountain
Fork-marked Lemur

Malagasy: Tanta, Tantaraolana

DESCRIPTION This is the second largest of the *Phaner* subspecies. The upperparts are light grey to silver with the dark and well-defined broad dorsal stripe extending to the base of the tail. The tip of the tail is also very dark. The facial fork is highly prominent.

IDENTIFICATION The highly distinctive markings and rapid movements of this subspecies should prevent confusion with both *Cheirogaleus* dwarf lemurs, the only two possibly sympatric species that are similar in size and posture to *P. f. electromontis*.

HABITAT Rainforest, dry deciduous forest and secondary forest.

DISTRIBUTION This subspecies is restricted to an area centred around the Montagne d'Ambre complex of protected areas in the far north of Madagascar, including the drier forests of Ankarana and Analamera. Sightings of *Phaner* further to the south-east in the vicinity of Daraina near Vohemar may well correspond to this subspecies.

BEHAVIOUR This subspecies is nocturnal and probably omnivorous, but it has yet to be investigated in the wild. See *P. f. pallescens* for details of Fork-marked Lemur behaviour and ecology.

POPULATION Unknown.

THREATS The destruction of forest habitat by fire for agriculture is the main threat to this subspecies. It also has the most restricted range of the four *Phaner* subspecies and is known to occur in only four protected areas.

VIEWING Montagne d'Ambre National Park is the most accessible place to see this lemur – the botanical garden and areas around the camp site and *Petite Cascade* are good places to concentrate efforts, although the native trees are tall so views are often at a distance. Other potentially productive locations include the nearby Forêt d'Ambre Special Reserve and Ankarana Special Reserve to the south.

165

Sportive Lemurs
Family Megaladapidae
Subfamily Lepilemurinae

Sportive lemurs possess dental and cranial features which indicate that their closest affinities lie not with extant Lemuriformes, but with members of the extinct genus *Megaladapis*, so they are placed in the family Megaladapidae. They are sufficiently different from these very large-bodied extinct lemurs to be classified in their own subfamily, Lepilemurinae.

SPORTIVE LEMURS genus *Lepilemur* I. Geoffroy, 1851

Sportive lemurs all belong to a single genus, *Lepilemur*. There is considerable debate surrounding the taxonomy of this group. In the past, some authorities have regarded all forms as subspecies of *Lepilemur mustelinus*. Majority opinion, based on genetic and slight morphological differences, now suggests that these subspecific divisions warrant full species status. There is further conjecture as to how many valid forms exist, such is the similarity between them. Currently, seven species are recognised. Each appears to occupy a distinct range around Madagascar's periphery, although the boundaries between some of these ranges are unclear. Future research may well prompt revisions to the taxonomy of this group.

Lepilemur species are medium-small to medium-sized lemurs with long tails. They cling vertically to tree trunks and have powerful hind legs that enable them to leap considerable distances. They are strictly nocturnal and are found throughout the varied native forest types of Madagascar. Overall morphology, appearance and pelage coloration are broadly similar in all species, so that geographic location is often the most reliable method of identifying sportive lemurs in the field.

Most studies of *Lepilemur* have taken place in southern and western regions, so the depth of information available for *L. leucopus*, *L. ruficaudatus* and *L. edwardsi* is far greater than for those species inhabiting northern regions and the eastern rainforests. The generic name *Lepilemur* is often used as the vernacular.

WEASEL SPORTIVE LEMUR *Lepilemur mustelinus* I. Geoffroy, 1851

Weasel Sportive Lemur

Malagasy Hataka, Varikosy, Trangalavaka, Kotrika

MEASUREMENTS Total length: 550-640mm*. Head/body length: 300-350mm*. Tail length: 250-290mm*. Weight: 800-1,200g*. *estimated measurements.

DESCRIPTION The pelage is long and dense. Upperparts and head are generally grey-brown to chestnut-brown with a slightly darker stripe sometimes apparent. The tail is similar in colour but tends to darken towards the tip. The face, throat and underparts are a paler grey-brown, while the muzzle is darker (fig. 90). This is probably the largest of the *Lepilemur* species.

IDENTIFICATION A medium-sized, vertically clinging lemur with a tail equivalent in length to its body. This species is most likely to be confused with the Eastern Avahi *Avahi laniger*, which is similar in size, coloration and posture. However, *L. mustelinus* has prominent ears, a more pointed muzzle and an apparently uniform coat coloration, whereas *Avahi* has highly distinctive white thigh patches.

HABITAT Primary and secondary rainforest.

DISTRIBUTION *L. mustelinus* is found over the northern half of the eastern rainforest belt, from the approximate region of the Onibe River near Toamasina in the south to the Tsaratanana and Marojejy Massifs in the north and including the Masoala Peninsula.

At the southern extreme of its range the boundary between this species and the range of *L. microdon* to the south is far from clear. There may well be areas of sympatry or indeed no real boundary may exist at all, as some authors regard these two taxa as synonymous.

BEHAVIOUR As with all *Lepilemur* species this lemur is nocturnal and totally arboreal. During the day in the wet season (November–March), it generally sleeps in nests of leaves, constructed in hanging lianas. In the dry season it prefers to use tree holes 6-12m above the ground.

At dusk the animals emerge and rest at the edge of their tree hole before moving off into the forest at the onset of darkness. At this time they are also very vocal: in any one area of forest the high-pitched calls of several individuals can be heard in rapid succession. The calling soon subsides and generally stops within an hour of nightfall.

This species is solitary while foraging and feeds mainly on leaves, but also some fruit and flowers. Grooming has been observed between mother and young, but never between adults.

L. *mustelinus* is known to be predated in its nests or tree holes by the Madagascar Tree Boa *Sanzinia madagascariensis* and it has been reported that this lemur has a specific alarm call in response to these snakes.

POPULATION This species has not been studied in depth and it is not known what population densities it reaches or approximately how many animals in total there are.

THREATS The continued destruction of the rainforest remains the main threat to this species. In many areas L. *mustelinus* is also trapped and hunted for food. It is known from most protected areas within its range, a total of at least nine, as well as many forest areas outside them.

VIEWING The majority of sites where this species can be seen are relatively inaccessible and well off the major visitor circuits. It is readily encountered on night walks in Anjanaharibe-Sud Special Reserve to the south-west of Andapa. Here individuals may be seen quite low down in vegetation and show little fear when approached. Other potential localities are the forests near Ambanizana on the Masoala Peninsula. Here, however, L. *mustelinus* tends to remain high in the canopy and good views are very difficult to obtain.

SMALL-TOOTHED SPORTIVE LEMUR *Lepilemur microdon* (Forbes, 1894)

Malagasy Fitiliky, Hataka, Varikosy, Trangalavaka, Kotrika

MEASUREMENTS Total length: 550-640mm. Head/body length: 300-350mm. Tail length: 250-290mm. Weight: 800-1000g.

DESCRIPTION The pelage is dense and generally red-brown on the head and dorsal region. The forelimbs and shoulders are a particularly rich chestnut colour and there is a darkish dorsal stripe. The tail is similar in colour to the body and slightly darker towards the tip. The underparts, face and throat are a pale grey-brown (fig. 100). There may be a yellowish-buff wash on the belly. This species, together with L. *mustelinus*, is probably the largest of the sportive lemurs.

IDENTIFICATION A medium-sized vertically clinging lemur with a longish tail. This species is most likely to be confused with the Eastern Avahi *Avahi laniger*, which is similar in size, coloration and posture. The more obvious ears, russet forelimbs and shoulders, and absence of white thighs are the features which distinguish this *Lepilemur*. The species is very similar to L. *mustelinus* and the two are almost impossible to distinguish in the field. Geographic location is often the best guide.

HABITAT Primary and secondary rainforest.

DISTRIBUTION This species is found in the southern half of the eastern rainforest belt, from the region of the Onibe River north of Toamasina south to the Andohahela Massif. Assuming this species and L. *mustelinus* are distinct, the border of their respective ranges, at around 18°S, is unclear and the two taxa may live sympatrically in some areas.

Small-toothed Sportive Lemur

BEHAVIOUR This species is nocturnal and totally arboreal. It appears to be solitary and feeds mainly on leaves, fruit and flowers. Evidence suggests that this and other rainforest *Lepilemur* species lose out in direct competition for food with the Eastern Avahi: *Avahi* feeds primarily on better quality vegetation which restricts *Lepilemur* to leaves of lower nutritional value.

As L. *microdon* has not been studied in detail, further information on its behaviour and ecology is unavailable.

POPULATION Overall population figures and densities are unknown.

THREATS The continued destruction of the rainforest is the main threat to this lemur. The species is probably trapped and hunted for food as well. There are at least eight protected areas that ought to support populations of this lemur, although until survey work is undertaken the status of these cannot be confirmed and commented on.

VIEWING The easiest and most accessible place to see this species is the Analamazaotra Special Reserve to the east of Antananarivo. It is often seen at night in the trees bordering the road that runs from Andasibe village to the park entrance. The local guides are adept at locating their sleep sites, which can be 'staked out' at dusk. Other places to try are the forests at Moromizaha near Andasibe and Mantadia and Ranomafana National Parks.

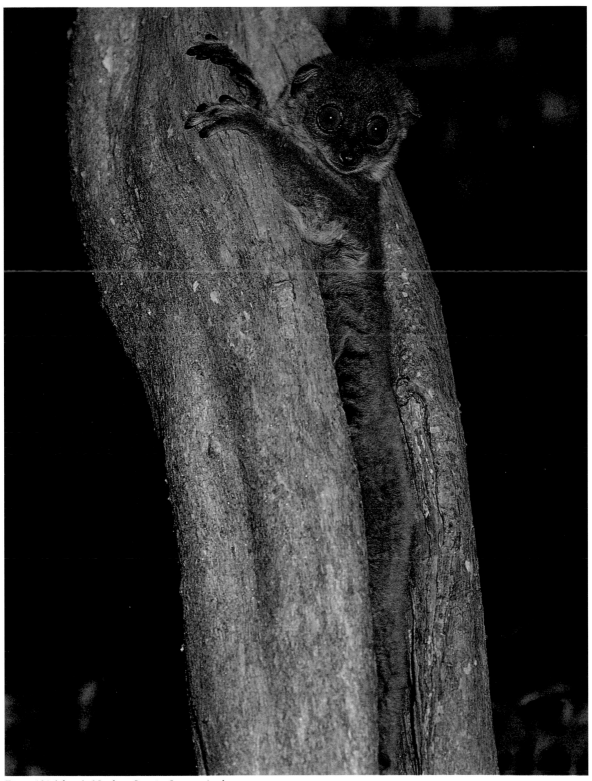

Figure 101 (above). Northern Sportive Lemur, Analamera.

Figure 99 (opposite top). Weasel Sportive Lemur, Anjanaharibe-Sud.

Figure 100 (opposite bottom). Small-toothed Sportive Lemur, Ranomafana.

NORTHERN SPORTIVE LEMUR *Lepilemur septentrionalis* Rumpler and Albignac, 1975

Northern Sportive Lemur

Malagasy Mahiabeala, Songiky

MEASUREMENTS Total length: c. 530mm. Head/body length: c. 280mm. Tail length: c. 250mm. Weight: c. 700-800g.

DESCRIPTION The upperparts are pale grey-brown, becoming slightly darker towards and on the tail, especially towards the tip. Tinges of brown are apparent on the crown and around the shoulders, and there is a darkish stripe running from the head down the dorsal line. The underparts are grey. The ears are less prominent than in other species of *Lepilemur* (fig. 101).

IDENTIFICATION A medium-small vertically clinging lemur; one of the smallest members of *Lepilemur*. Within its range, this species may be confused with *Avahi* which is similar in size and posture, but has much smaller concealed ears, a more rounded 'owl-like' face and distinctive white patches on its thighs. Three other species of broadly similar size are sympatric with *L. septentrionalis*, but the Greater Dwarf Lemur *Cheirogaleus major*, Fat-tailed Dwarf Lemur *C. medius* and Fork-marked Lemur *Phaner furcifer* should be recognisable by their horizontal rather than vertical posture and quadrupedal rather than leaping locomotion.

HABITAT Dry deciduous forests and some more humid evergreen forests.

DISTRIBUTION As its name implies, this species is restricted to the very north of Madagascar. Its range extends from the Montagne d'Ambre region south to the Mahavay River near Ambilobe in the west and south to the vicinity of Vohemar in the east.

BEHAVIOUR This species has not yet been studied to any extent, so information regarding its behaviour and ecology is scant. In common with other *Lepilemur* species, it is nocturnal, with leaves forming the bulk of its diet. The animals are solitary foragers with home ranges covering an area of around one hectare. Adults rarely associate, but mothers and infants have been observed together. The Northern Sportive Lemur spends the day in tree holes or dense tangles of vines. Most sleep sites are 6-8m off the ground, but some may be a low as 1m.

Madagascar Tree Boas *Sanzinia madagascariensis* have been reported to wait in ambush outside the sleep sites of this species. These snakes are also known to take the lemurs from within tree holes.

POPULATION No overall population figures are available but the species appears to reach very high densities in some areas. Figures vary between 150 and 550 animals/km^2, the higher densities being associated with more humid forests. In some very dry forests estimates drop to 60 individuals/km^2.

THREATS Forests destruction, even within protected areas, is widespread in northern Madagascar and constitutes the major threat to this lemur. It is also hunted widely for food. It has been recorded in four protected areas.

VIEWING This species is common in the Ankarana Special Reserve and can be readily seen in the *Canyon Forestière* and the forests around the *Campement des Anglais*. It is also common in Montagne d'Ambre National Park, which is more accessible although the taller trees and denser foliage make good views less likely.

GREY-BACKED SPORTIVE LEMUR *Lepilemur dorsalis* Gray, 1870

Other name: Nosy Be Sportive Lemur
Malagasy Fitsidiky

MEASUREMENTS Total length: 510-540mm. Head/body length: 250-260mm. Tail length: 260-280mm. Weight: c. 500g.

DESCRIPTION The upperparts and tail are medium-brown to grey-brown, while the underparts are a paler grey-brown. There is also a dark brown dorsal stripe. The throat often appears paler still. The head is more grey than brown, while the face tends to be dark grey-brown with a bluntish muzzle. The ears are relatively small and rounded (fig. 102).

IDENTIFICATION A medium-small vertically clinging lemur and one of the smallest members of the genus *Lepilemur*. In the Manongarivo region this species may possibly be confused with the Western Avahi *Avahi occidentalis*, which is similar in posture but noticeably larger. Furthermore, *Avahi* has smaller concealed ears, a rounded 'owl-like' face and distinctive white patches on its thighs. The horizontal posture and quadrupedal locomotion preferred by the Greater Dwarf Lemur *Cheirogaleus major* and Fork-marked Lemur *Phaner furcifer* should be sufficient to prevent confusion with *L. dorsalis*.

HABITAT Humid rainforest and some secondary forest including timber plantations.

DISTRIBUTION This species is restricted to the Sambirano region in north-west Madagascar, including the Ampasindava Peninsula, and the off-shore islands of Nosy Bé and Nosy Komba.

BEHAVIOUR Only brief studies have so far been undertaken. In common with other members of its genus, this species is nocturnal and feeds principally on leaves, some fruits, flowers and occasionally tree bark.

In primary rainforest habitats this species prefers to spend the day in tree holes. In secondary forests, where there are fewer or no large trees, these lemurs spend the day resting curled up on branches or in dense tangles of vegetation. Evidence suggests there is strong site affinity for favoured sleep sites: they may return to the same site for at least 14 consecutive nights. In marginal areas at the edge of primary forest on Nosy Be, this species even utilises purpose-built nestboxes fixed into trees.

Very little is known about the breeding habits of *L. dorsalis*: a single infant is born between September and November.

In secondary habitat close to the village of Ampasindava on Nosy Be, *L. dorsalis* has been seen to be killed by feral dogs. Large raptors like the Madagascar Harrier-Hawk *Polyboroides radiatus* and Madagascar Buzzard *Buteo brachypterus* are also known to take this species and Ring-tailed Mongooses *Galidia elegans* are suspected to be regular predators.

POPULATION No overall population figures or densities are available, but the very restricted range of the Grey-backed Sportive Lemur suggests it is one of the least numerous members of its genus.

THREATS Habitat destruction is the major threat. Even within protected areas the margins are destroyed by 'slash-and-burn' agriculture (for rice and coffee cultivation) and some illegal logging continues. On Nosy Be this species is harassed by children and is often collected as a short-lived pet. On the mainland it is hunted for food. *L. dorsalis* is known to occur in two protected areas: one on the island of Nosy Be (Lokobe) and one on the mainland (Manongarivo).

Grey-backed
Sportive Lemur

VIEWING The Grey-backed Sportive Lemur is most easily observed in the buffer zone on the north-east edge of Lokobe Nature Reserve on the island of Nosy Be. A local guide can be hired in the village of Ambatozavavy. Then take a pirogue around the coast to the village of Ampasipohy. A short walk inland will bring you to areas of secondary forest where *L. dorsalis* is quite common. It is also possible to walk from Ampasipohy to the village of Ambalahonko at the south-east of Lokobe Nature Reserve where *L. dorsalis* is also common in adjacent forests. Here local Malagasy are being trained as guides as part of the community research programme initiated by the Black Lemur Forest Project. They are adept at finding the sleep sites of these lemurs.

MILNE-EDWARDS'S SPORTIVE LEMUR *Lepilemur edwardsi* (Forbes, 1894)

Malagasy Repahaka, Boengy, Boenga

MEASUREMENTS Total length: 540-570mm. Head/body length: 270-290mm. Tail length: 270-290mm. Weight: 600-800g.

DESCRIPTION The upperparts and tail are predominantly grey-brown, with noticeable chestnut-brown areas around the shoulders, on the forelimbs and on the upper thighs (fig. 103). The underparts are paler, generally grey, with some creamy patches. There may also be a darker dorsal stripe down the spine, although this is not always distinct. The head is grey and the muzzle grey-brown. The ears are quite prominent.

IDENTIFICATION A medium-sized, vertically clinging lemur and one of the larger members of its genus. Within its range, this species can only be confused with the Western Avahi *Avahi occidentalis*, which is similar in size and posture. However, *Avahi* has much smaller concealed ears, a more rounded face with larger eyes and distinctive white patches on its thighs. *L. edwardsi* is darker in colour and has a more pointed face.

HABITAT Dry deciduous forest.

DISTRIBUTION This species appears to be restricted to the west and north-west of Madagascar. It is generally thought to occur from the Manambolo River in the west, north to the Sofia River which flows into the Bay of Mahajamba in the north-west. However, the southern limits of this range, where it adjoins the range of *L. ruficaudatus*, are subject to considerable uncertainty and speculation. In fact, it has been suggested by some authorities that *L. edwardsi* and *L. ruficaudatus* are conspecific, although the vocalisations of the two species are quite different.

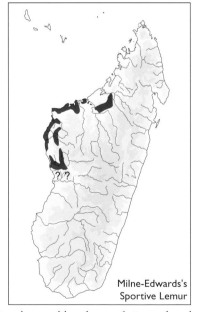

Milne-Edwards's
Sportive Lemur

BEHAVIOUR Milne-Edwards's Sportive Lemur is nocturnal and feeds for the most part on leaves, although some fruits, seeds and flowers are consumed. On occasion they have also been observed opportunistically taking flying insects like moths. Tree holes are the preferred sleep sites: most individuals sleep singly, but at times between two and four individuals of both sexes may share larger holes.

Figure 102. Grey-backed Sportive Lemur, Lokobe.

Figure 103. Milne-Edwards's Sportive Lemur, Ampijoroa.

The majority of sleep holes are 4-5m off the ground, but some are as low as 1m: individuals may utilise a number of different tree holes within their territory, but often return to the same hole for several consecutive nights.

Activity begins around dusk and ends just before daybreak. After emerging, individuals often sit at the entrance to their sleep hole for a short while, before moving off into the forest. The first two hours are the most active. After this, foraging bouts are punctuated by extended periods of rest and grooming on favoured tree branches. They rarely travel more than 300-400m in a single night. Individuals that share sleep sites rarely remain together during the active period, but do sometimes socialise for brief periods with other individuals. Such encounters often include sessions of allogrooming.

Total home ranges cover around one hectare, although *L. edwardsi* appears to spend the majority of time in a core area around half this size. There may be considerable overlap between adjacent ranges, which are defended with loud vocalisations (repeated *chirrups* followed by low *chuck-chuck-chuck* calls) and even branch-shaking. At drier times of the year, when foliage is reduced, several individuals have been seen feeding in the same tree, without apparent aggression.

In the forests of Ankarafantsika this species lives sympatrically with the Western Avahi, the two species being in apparent competition for food. To avoid this, *Avahi* is more active and feeds on leaves of high nutritional value, while *L. edwardsi* tends to minimise its movements and is, therefore, able to subsist on vegetation that is much poorer in quality.

The Fosa *Cryptoprocta ferox* is a major predatory threat to Milne-Edwards's Sportive Lemur. It is capable of excavating the lemurs from their daytime sleep sites.

POPULATION There are no population figures available, but the species is thought to be common within many areas of its range. Densities of up to 60 animals/km^2 have been recorded in fairly typical western dry deciduous forest areas (Ampijoroa Forest Station).

THREATS Habitat loss caused by fires (to create new pasture for livestock), persists in being the main threat to this and so many other lemur species in western Madagascar. In some areas this sportive lemur is also hunted for food. It is found in at least three protected areas and may occur in a number of others that have yet to be surveyed.

VIEWING The best and easiest place to get excellent views of this lemur is at Ampijoroa Forestry Station, part of the Ankarafantsika Nature Reserve. The forests around the campsite provide good opportunities, but better views are often to be had in *Jardin Botanique B* behind the campsite and *Jardin Botanique A*, which is on the northern side of Lac Ravelobe. The local guides know several regular sleep sites within these areas.

RED-TAILED SPORTIVE LEMUR *Lepilemur ruficaudatus* A. Grandidier, 1867

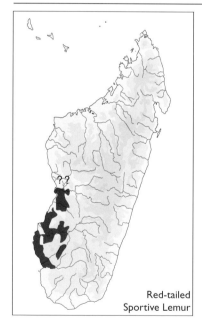

Red-tailed
Sportive Lemur

Malagasy Boengy, Boenga

MEASUREMENTS Total length: 500-560mm. Head/body length: 260-300mm. Tail length: 240-280mm. Weight: 500-800g.

DESCRIPTION The upperparts are grey-brown with chestnut-rufous tinges on the shoulders and forelimbs, while the underparts are much paler grey and the throat is creamy-white. The tail also has a distinct reddish hue. The head is grey, with darker grey regions around the muzzle. The ears are large, rounded and prominent (fig. 104).

IDENTIFICATION A medium-sized, vertically clinging lemur and one of the largest *Lepilemur* species. Within its range, this species is most likely to be mistaken for the Fat-tailed Dwarf Lemur *Cheirogaleus medius*, Coquerel's Dwarf Lemur *Mirza coquereli* or Fork-marked Lemur *Phaner furcifer*. All of these species are smaller, adopt a horizontal rather than vertical posture, and tend to be swifter in their movements.

HABITAT Dry deciduous forest.

DISTRIBUTION The Red-tailed Sportive Lemur is apparently confined to western Madagascar. It occurs from the Onilahy River inland to the forests of Zombitse and Vohibasia and north to the Manambolo River.

The precise limits of the ranges of *L. ruficaudatus* and *L. edwardsi* are ill-defined and some degree of overlap may occur between the Tsiribihina and Manambolo Rivers. Recent sightings of *Lepilemur* in the vicinity of Soalala and Baly Bay, some 300km further north, were identified as *L. ruficaudatus*, although this region falls within the accepted range of *L. edwardsi*. Some authorities do not believe that *L. ruficaudatus* and *L. edwardsi* warrant separate species status.

BEHAVIOUR In common with congeners, *L. ruficaudatus* is nocturnal. It has generally been considered a totally solitary species. However, recent studies in Kirindy Forest, north-east of Morondava, have suggested that a degree of social activity exists. Males and females have overlapping home ranges of around one hectare and are known to associate periodically. Foraging bouts are usually solitary, but night-time resting periods may be synchronised, the pair often meeting to share the same tree hole at this time. Nocturnal foraging bouts are generally punctuated by a single long period of inactivity. When aggressive, individuals bang their hind feet on a branch and shake the tree.

This species is primarily folivorous, although the fruits of some trees (*Diospyros* spp.) are also taken. It can tolerate leaves with high concentrations of potential toxins and during the dry season (May–November) it is even able to subsist on dry leaves. It may in some circumstances re-ingest its own faeces.

During daytime resting periods this species is also known to have one of the lowest metabolic rates of any mammal. This is raised substantially (doubled) prior to the night-time activity phase, although *L. ruficaudatus* achieves this while still resting. This is probably a further adaptation to help this lemur survive on a very poor quality diet and also live at relatively high densities.

Mating has been observed between May and July, with a single young being born after a gestation period of approximately 130 days. At first the infant is carried by its mother in her mouth; it later clings to the fur on her back. When it is older still, the mother may leave or 'park' it in a tree hole or similar 'safe' site while she forages. The offspring continues suckling for at least four months and becomes independent at about one year.

In Kirindy Forest, this species is known to be eaten by the Madagascar Long-eared Owl *Asio madagascariensis*, Madagascar Harrier-Hawk *Polyboroides radiatus* and the Fosa *Cryptoprocta ferox*: the latter two species are known to be capable of excavating the lemurs from their daytime tree holes.

POPULATION This species is thought to be common in many forests within its range, but no overall population estimates are available. In typical dry deciduous forests *L. ruficaudatus* is known to reach very high densities: estimates vary between 180 and 350 individuals/km^2.

THREATS The forest habitats of the west are regularly burned to increase pasture for grazing and this form of habitat destruction and degradation remains the major threat to this lemur and so many others. The Red-tailed Sportive Lemur is also widely hunted for food throughout its range. The species is known to occur in at least two protected areas and other notable forests.

VIEWING Most large areas of dry deciduous forest within its range will provide an opportunity to see this sportive lemur. The best locality is Kirindy Forest north-east of Morondava. This is perhaps the best place in Madagascar to see a number of nocturnal lemur species. There is an extensive network of trails through the forest and even on a short night walk several individuals are normally seen. Local guides also know the whereabouts of their sleep sites.

WHITE-FOOTED SPORTIVE LEMUR *Lepilemur leucopus* (Major, 1894)

Malagasy Songiky

MEASUREMENTS Total length: 460-520mm. Head/body length: 245-260mm. Tail length: 215-260mm. Weight: 500-700g.

DESCRIPTION The head and upperparts are principally pale grey, although there are brownish tinges around the shoulders, upper forelimbs and upper thighs. The tail also tends to be more brownish-grey. The underparts and throat are very pale grey to off-white and this coloration often extends part-way up the flanks. The face is grey-brown and there are whitish 'spectacles' around the eyes. The ears are relatively large and rounded with whitish tufts at their bases (fig. 105).

IDENTIFICATION A small to medium-sized lemur that is probably the smallest member of the genus *Lepilemur*. Within its range, this species can only be confused with the Fat-tailed Dwarf Lemur *Cheirogaleus medius*, although this seems unlikely as *C. medius* adopts a horizontal posture and moves quadrupedally, whereas *L. leucopus* clings vertically to tree trunks and leaps.

HABITAT Xerophytic spiny forest and gallery forest.

DISTRIBUTION This species is restricted to southern and south-west Madagascar from the Tolagnaro region in the south around to the Onilahy River and Toliara area in the south-west.

White-footed Sportive Lemur

BEHAVIOUR The White-footed Sportive Lemur is nocturnal. In spiny forests the bulk of the diet consists of the tough leaves from Didiereaceae and Euphorbiaceae species, together with the leaves and occasionally flowers of the Tamarind or Kily Tree *Tamarindus indica*. During the dry season (May–October), flowers from Didiereaceae species may also be eaten.

In the past it has been suggested that *L. leucopus* may re-ingest its own faeces (a behaviour known as caecotrophy) to maximise the nutrition gained from its meagre diet. However, there is little direct evidence to support this and it now appears more likely that this species copes with the poor quality of its diet by remaining inactive for long periods.

Figure 104. Red-tailed Sportive Lemur, Kirindy.

Figure 105. White-footed Sportive Lemur, Berenty.

During the day either tree holes or tangles of lianas are used as sleep sites: males and females have been reported to share sites as well as sleep separately. There is considerable vocalisation just after dusk when they emerge. During the night only about 30% of the time is spent foraging, these bouts being interspersed with prolonged periods of rest and/or self-grooming. During the cooler dry season these periods of rest increase and shorter distances are travelled when foraging (as little as 200m to 300m per night), although the total time spent foraging per night remains constant throughout the year.

White-footed Sportive Lemurs occupy small territories, around 0.2ha to 0.4ha being the average for both sexes. There seems to be little overlap between the territories of females, but male ranges overlap with those of up to three females. Females share their territories with dependent offspring and adult daughters sometimes remain within their natal range. Territories are defended by calls and displays rather than by scent-marking.

Mating takes place from May to July and the gestation period is around 130 days. A single infant is born between October and November and attains sexual maturity by 18 months of age.

L. leucopus is known to be eaten by the Madagascar Barn Owl *Tyto alba affinis* and Fosa *Cryptoprocta ferox*.

POPULATION No overall population figures are available, but the species is reported to be common throughout its range. In spiny forests population densities vary between 200 and 350 animals/km^2, while in gallery forest, which is more lush and provides a greater concentration of resources, densities may rise to 450/km^2. At one locality in this habitat a figure as high as 810 individuals/km^2 has been estimated.

THREATS Destruction of both spiny and gallery forest by fire is the main threat to the White-footed Sportive Lemur, although the species is also hunted for food. It is found in four protected areas.

VIEWING This species is easily seen at Berenty Private Reserve, two hours drive east of Tolagnaro. Here, *L. leucopus* is abundant and can easily be seen in trees along the path between the reception area and the restaurant. Individuals regularly use a sleep hole in a large tree in the Radiated Tortoise *Geochelone radiata* enclosure and can be seen resting outside at dawn and dusk. Beza-Mahafaly Special Reserve, five hours' drive from Toliara, is also a good place to see this species in both spiny forest and gallery forest.

True Lemurs
Family Lemuridae
Subfamily Hapalemurinae

Bamboo lemurs are the smallest of the diurnal lemur species and, as their vernacular name implies, are generally associated with bamboo. They are considered close enough relatives of the 'true' lemurs (Lemurinae) to be placed in the same family, Lemuridae, but sufficiently different to warrant their own subfamily, Hapalemurinae. Three species are currently recognised, all belonging to the genus *Hapalemur*.

BAMBOO OR GENTLE LEMURS genus *Hapalemur* I. Geoffroy, 1851

Members of the genus *Hapalemur* are all characterised by medium-small to medium-sized bodies, long tails and moderately long back legs designed for leaping. Their muzzles are much shorter than other members of the family Lemuridae (*Lemur*, *Eulemur* and *Varecia*), which gives their faces a rather blunt, rounded appearance. In general *Hapalemur* species prefer to adopt a vertical posture and are capable of quick bounding leaps between the close upright stems of bamboo thickets and similar vegetation. One exception is the Alaotra Reed Lemur *H. griseus alaotrensis* which has evolved a more specialised form of locomotion associated with its unique habitat. It has been suggested that this form may be a full species.

GREY BAMBOO LEMUR *Hapalemur griseus* (Link, 1795)

Three subspecies of Grey Bamboo Lemur are currently recognised, the ranges of which are discontinuous. The nominate race, the Eastern Grey Bamboo Lemur *H. g. griseus* is found throughout the eastern rainforest belt; the Western Grey Bamboo Lemur *H. g. occidentalis* is known from isolated areas in the west and north-west; while the Alaotra Reed Lemur *H. g. alaotrensis* has the most restricted range of the three, being found only in the marshes and reedbeds around Lac Alaotra in central-eastern Madagascar. All subspecies are broadly similar in coloration but there are noticeable size differences between them.

A fourth subspecies of *H. griseus* has been suggested from the humid forests north of Tolagnaro in the far south of Madagascar. This 'southern form' is said to be much darker in colour and apparently only occurs in a very restricted area. However, little information is available and this taxon has yet to be formally described and accepted, so it is not discussed further here.

Subspecies

Eastern Grey Bamboo Lemur *Hapalemur griseus griseus* (Link, 1795)

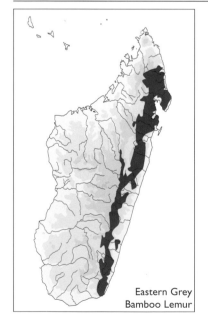

Eastern Grey Bamboo Lemur

Other names: Eastern Grey Gentle Lemur, Eastern Lesser Bamboo Lemur
Malagasy: Bokombolo, Kotrika

MEASUREMENTS Total length: 560-700mm. Head/body length: 240-300mm. Tail length: 320-400mm. Weight: 750-900g.

DESCRIPTION The upperparts are medium-grey to olive-grey with chestnut-russet tinges over the head, around the shoulders and sometimes extending down the dorsum, these areas being more noticeable on individuals from the southern part of the subspecies's range. The tail is generally darker grey. The face and underparts are slightly paler grey, gradually becoming creamy-grey on the belly. The ears are small and rounded, while the muzzle is much shorter than in other diurnal lemur species (figs. 106 & 107).

IDENTIFICATION A medium-sized active lemur, amongst the smallest diurnal lemur species. It is most often seen in a vertical clinging posture not dissimilar to that of nocturnal *Lepilemur* species. The small size, blunt muzzle and rounded face of *H. g. griseus* should prevent confusion with all other non-congeneric diurnal species.

In the very restricted areas of sympatry, confusion between *H. g. griseus* and its two congeners, the Golden Bamboo Lemur *H. aureus* and Greater Bamboo Lemur *H. simus* is possible. *H. g. griseus* is distinguished from *H. aureus* by its smaller size and overall grey, rather than golden-brown, coloration. *H. simus* is of broadly similar coloration, but is significantly larger than *H. g. griseus* and has very distinctive and characteristic ear-tufts.

HABITAT Primary and secondary rainforests with stands of bamboo and bamboo vines.

DISTRIBUTION This subspecies is found throughout the eastern rainforest belt, from Tolagnaro in the south to the Marojejy and Soalala and Baly Bay regions and further east in the Tsiombikibo forest near Mitsinjo have confirmed the existence of this population.

Figure 106. Eastern Grey Bamboo Lemur, Ranomafana.

Tsaratanana Massifs in the north and including the Masoala Peninsula. It is the most widespread of the *H. griseus* subspecies and has a wide elevational tolerance, being found from sea-level to altitudes above 1,600m. For instance, at Anjanaharibe-Sud it has been recorded between 800m and 1,950m and on the Tsaratanana Massif at over 2,000m.

BEHAVIOUR Although often regarded as principally diurnal, *H. g. griseus* is sometimes more active around dawn and dusk (crepuscular) and regular bouts of nocturnal activity have also been observed. Vocalisations may begin around two hours before dawn and have also been heard at night. Evidence suggests that around half the day may be spent foraging at all levels in the forest.

The diet is dominated by various species of bamboo, although there appears to be high plant-part selectivity – the shoots, leaf bases and stem pith are preferred. At certain times of the year these may constitute over 90% of intake: the remainder of the diet is made up of fig leaves, grass stems, other young leaves and some berries. When in season, the proportion of certain fruits in the diet increases. This lemur demonstrates a considerable degree of manual dexterity, especially when feeding on bamboo.

Group size varies between three and six individuals and contains at least one adult pair with their offspring. In some groups a second mature female is present. Home ranges of 6-15ha have been reported, the size probably being correlated with the amount of bamboo within the occupied area. During a typical day's foraging, groups move up to 500m. At night they tend to prefer to sleep in taller trees within the forest.

Females give birth to a singleton between late October and January. A gestation period of around 140 days has been reported, although this seems exceptionally long for a primate weighing less than one kilogram. Until it is capable of climbing and leaping, the infant clings to its mother's fur and rides on her back. On occasion it may also be 'parked' by the mother for brief periods.

Like many other lemur species, the Eastern Grey Bamboo Lemur is known to be predated by the Fosa *Cryptoprocta ferox*. It is known to react evasively towards large raptors, especially the Madagascar Harrier-Hawk *Polyboroides radiatus*, and it is suspected that the Madagascar Long-eared Owl *Asio madagascariensis* also poses a substantial threat. Near Ranomafana National Park there was a reported incident of *H. g. griseus* being consumed by a Madagascar Tree Boa *Sanzinia madagascariensis*.

POPULATION The overall population is unknown. Population densities between 47 and 62 animals/km² have been suggested for a 'typical' area of rainforest (Analamazaotra Special Reserve), but lower estimates are generally regarded as more likely for other areas of primary forest.

THREATS The continuing destruction of the rainforest appears to be the major threat to this lemur. However, areas of forest cleared long ago and now replaced with secondary growth often contain far more bamboo than primary forests. In such areas it has been suggested that *H. g. griseus* attains higher densities. Somewhat paradoxically, this may mean this lemur benefits from the degradation of the original forest cover. The Eastern Grey Bamboo Lemurs are also regularly trapped and kept as pets. This species occurs in at least 12 protected areas.

VIEWING Two accessible rainforests reserves, Analamazaotra Special Reserve (Andasibe/ Perinet) and Ranomafana National Park both offer very good chances of seeing this subspecies. At Analamazaotra, the areas around the orchid garden, close to the warden's house and by the dam at *Lac Vert* support stands of bamboo where these lemurs often feed. Groups may also be encountered along the main ridge, where the habituated *Indri indri*, live and elsewhere within the reserve. At Ranomafana, the bamboo grove near the research cabin on the main path and areas around *Belle Vue* can be good for Grey Bamboo Lemurs, although encounters also occur regularly in other parts of the main trail network.

Western Grey Bamboo Lemur *Hapalemur griseus occidentalis* Rumpler, 1975

Other names: Western Grey Gentle Lemur, Western Lesser Bamboo Lemur
Malagasy: Bokombolo, Ankomba-valiha

MEASUREMENTS Total length: 550-670mm. Head/body length: 270-280mm. Tail length: 360-390mm. Weight: 700-800g.

DESCRIPTION The upperparts are medium to pale grey-brown while the face and underparts are slightly lighter. The overall effect is a more uniform coloration than *H. g. griseus*. The ears are small, while the snout is much shorter than in other diurnal species (fig. 108).

IDENTIFICATION A medium-sized active species, probably the smallest diurnal lemur. It is sympatric with several members of the genus *Eulemur* but this subspecies's small size, uniform grey colour, short muzzle and rounded face should prevent confusion with these other diurnal lemurs.

HABITAT Dry deciduous forests and humid forests containing bamboo and bamboo vines. This subspecies has also been recorded in secondary and degraded forest areas.

DISTRIBUTION This subspecies is known from a number of isolated and apparently discontinuous localities in west and north-west Madagascar. *H. g. occidentalis* occurs throughout the Sambirano region in the north-west, from the Andranomalaza River in the south to the Mahavavy River in the north, including the Ampasindava Peninsula and Ambato Massif. There are also records of *H. griseus* further to the north in the Ankarana Massif which may be attributable to this subspecies.

The second major population is centred around the Tsingy de Bemaraha region in western Madagascar, between the Tsiribihina River to the south and the vicinity of Maintirano to the north and extending inland to the Bongolava Massif. There are also collecting records of this taxon from the Namoroka area, some 300km north of Bemaraha. More recent sightings of *H. g. occidentalis* in the Soalala and Baly Bay regions and further east in the Tsiombikibo forest near Mitsinjo have confirmed the existence of this population. It is currently not known whether this and the population to the south at Bemaraha are continuous.

Figure 107. Eastern Grey Bamboo Lemur, Mantadia.

Figure 108. Western Grey Bamboo Lemur, Sambirano River valley.

BEHAVIOUR Few studies of this subspecies have taken place to date consequently little is known of its behaviour and ecology. In the Sambirano region, group size appears to be between one and four individuals. The animals are active primarily by day, and will forage either on the ground or in understorey vegetation. In common with its eastern relative, the diet of this subspecies probably contain a high proportion of bamboo. However, around Baly Bay local people report that *H. g. occidentalis* does not necessarily feed on bamboo and sightings in forest areas where bamboo is absent would appear to confirm this.

POPULATION No overall population figures are available. However, this taxon is suspected to occur at lower densities than other diurnal lemurs. This, coupled with its restricted range, would indicate that the population is not substantial.

THREATS The major threat to this subspecies is forest clearing and subsequent burning to create pasture for cattle. In some areas it is also hunted for food. The Western Grey Bamboo Lemur is only known to occur in two, or possibly three, protected areas.

VIEWING The known haunts of this subspecies are remote, hence tracking this lemur down can be difficult. *H. g. occidentalis* may be encountered in forests and associated habitats along the Sambirano River valley near the village of Benavony to the southeast of Ambanja. It is also known from the Ambato Massif, part of the Nosy Faly Peninsula, some 30km to the north of Ambanja. These localities both require determination to reach, and a considerable slice of luck is also be needed in order to achieve success.

Other potential sites are Manongarivo Special Reserve, Tsingy de Bemaraha National Park, around Lac Bemamba, and the Soalala region; but once again only a lengthy search is likely to ensure success.

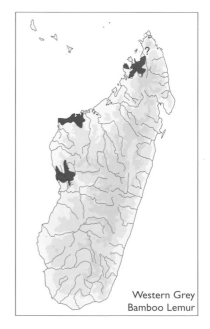

Western Grey
Bamboo Lemur

Alaotra Reed Lemur *Hapalemur griseus alaotrensis* Rumpler, 1975

Other name: Alaotra Gentle Lemur
Malagasy: Bandro

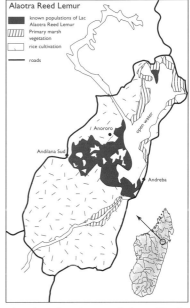

MEASUREMENTS Total length: 770-810mm. Head/body length: 380-400mm. Tail length: 390-410mm. Weight: females average c. 1,550g; males average c. 1,350g.

DESCRIPTION Sexually dimorphic. Females are around 15% heavier than males. The pelage is dense and woolly. Upperparts are medium to darkish grey-brown with the face and underparts slightly paler grey. The crown and nape are more chestnut-brown, this coloration gradually fading over the shoulder region. Overall the head is more rounded than in other *H. griseus* subspecies, while the ears are similarly small and unobtrusive. The Alaotra Reed Lemur is up to 50% larger, and noticeably darker, than the two other *H. griseus* subspecies.

IDENTIFICATION A medium-sized, active lemur with a rotund body and long tail (fig. 109). The Alaotra Reed Lemur cannot be confused with any other species, as it has a very restricted range and is the only lemur found within its chosen habitat.

HABITAT Reed and papyrus beds. This habitat is unique amongst primates.

DISTRIBUTION Today *H. g. alaotrensis* is found only in the reed and papyrus beds and surrounding marshes of Lac Alaotra, in central-eastern Madagascar. The subspecies was probably once present right around the lake (the largest in Madagascar) and is also known to have occurred near Andilamena, at least 35km to the north (but in the 1950s dams were built and the natural marsh vegetation was converted to rice paddies causing the demise of the lemur in this area).

Today the range is further restricted. One population has its stronghold in a large area (around 18,000ha) of primary marsh vegetation at the south-west corner of Lac Alaotra, largely within the triangle formed by the villages of Andreba, Andilana Sud and Anororo. A second much smaller and completely isolated population occurs in a fragment of marsh on the northern shore around the peninsula of Belempona. The Alaotra Reed Lemur has the most restricted range of any lemur taxon.

Figure 109. Alaotra Reed Lemur, Lac Alaotra.

BEHAVIOUR Only recently have any studies of this most unusual lemur taken place. Alaotra Reed Lemurs live in groups of between two and nine individuals, with three to five being average. These groups generally contain one adult of each sex together with offspring. Larger groups may contain two adult females and one or two adult males, although the reproductive hierachy is not clear. Group cohesiveness is maintained by a variety of means. Allogrooming seems to be a particularly important social interaction, animals often sitting facing one another and combing each other's fur with their tooth combs (modified lower front dentition). The hands are used to divide the partner's fur. *H. g. alaotrensis* has an extensive vocal repertoire, and mutual scent-marking also occurs regularly.

Groups occupy a home range of around two hectares, although a substantial proportion of this may be water, the extent of which varies seasonally. Group encounters are frequent and home ranges are defended by vocalisations, scent-marking and display behaviour.

Alaotra Reed Lemurs move in a very different manner from other *Hapalemur* taxa. They are quadrupedal – animals walk up a reed stem until it bends over, then walk along it to reach the next stem (fig.109). In this way, the lemurs may cross narrow water channels, although this is also achieved by jumping across in more conventional bamboo lemur fashion.

This subspecies is cathemeral (active at all times of the day and night) although night-time activity levels are reduced. The two main periods of activity are concentrated around the first and last three hours of daylight. Their diet is strictly folivorous and they have been observed feeding on a wide variety of plant species: the major dietary elements are papyrus *Cyperus madagascariensis* and to a lesser extent reeds *Phragmites communis*, although grasses and ferns are also eaten. These lemurs also demonstrate a high degree of plant part selectivity: from February to April, they feed predominantly on the pith of young papyrus and the new shoots of reeds; later in the year the diet shifts towards older leaves. This diet is low quality, which may explain why the Alaotra Reed Lemur needs to remain active and feed for much of the day.

Although they are permanent inhabitants of reedbeds, these lemurs also spend considerable periods foraging at ground level, particularly during the dry season (June–October) when more solid ground is exposed. During the wet season, water levels rise but the lemurs still descend to ground level in the floating vegetation (fig. 110).

Births have been observed in all months between September and February. Singletons are the norm. The young are relatively well developed and are initially carried on the mother's back. Females have even been seen swimming across open channels while carrying their offspring. When the infants are one to two weeks old they may be 'parked' by their mother in a dense thicket of papyrus and left for up to 30 minutes.

No direct predation of this lemur, other than by humans, has been observed. However, it is suspected that the Madagascar Tree Boa *Sanzinia madagascariensis* and large raptors such as the Black Kite *Milvus migrans* pose a threat. Local villagers around Lac Alaotra also report the presence of a small carnivore in the reedbeds and surrounding cultivated areas which may be a potential predator. Their name for this animal is 'jabady' which in other parts of the island can refer to several of the endemic carnivores, e.g. *Fossa fossana*, *Eupleres goudotii* and *Salanoia concolor* as well as the introduced Small Indian Civet *Viverricula indica*.

Figure 110. Young Alaotra Reed Lemur in papyrus beds, Lac Alaotra.

POPULATION The population of *H. g. alaotrensis* has recently been estimated at between 7,000 and 11,000 individuals, although a figure of 7,500 has been proposed as the most realistic. The vast majority of these animals occur in the large area of marsh around the lake's south-west shore: the isolated population on the north shore is estimated to contain no more than 60 animals and is likely soon to disappear completely. In primary marsh vegetation a population density of around 60 individuals/km² has been estimated.

THREATS This lemur is threatened by a variety of factors, the primary one being destruction of habitat and reduction of its already very limited range. Huge areas of reedbeds are cleared and burned annually to convert to paddies – the Lac Alaotra area is the most important rice-growing region in Madagascar. Run-off from the surrounding deforested hill sides is causing large-scale siltation and choking the reeds, while irrigation schemes are altering the balance of the lake in other ways. Furthermore, the reeds are harvested in substantial quantities for matting, fish traps and screens. This is further fragmenting the habitat. *H. g. alaotrensis* also appears to suffer more direct hunting pressure than most other lemurs. Many are caught for food, often when fleeing dry season fires deliberately started in the reedbeds. Large numbers are also kept as pets by the local people. There are no protected areas within the range of this subspecies and its long-term survival prospects give serious cause for concern. Recommendations have been made to create a small national park to safeguard the habitat of this unique lemur.

VIEWING Due to its unusual lifestyle, very restricted range and elusive nature, this is one of the most difficult lemurs to see in the wild. It is necessary to travel quietly by pirogue through the marginal reedbeds around the south-west shore of the lake and hope for a chance encounter. From the eastern shore set off from the village of Andreba and hire a local fisherman with an intimate knowledge of the area.

GOLDEN BAMBOO LEMUR *Hapalemur aureus* Meier *et al.*, 1987

Other name: Golden Gentle Lemur
Malagasy: Bokombolomena, Varibolomena

MEASUREMENTS Total length: 720-800mm. Head/body length: 340-380mm. Tail length: 380-420mm. Weight: average 1.5-1.65kg.

DESCRIPTION The pelage is dense and soft. Upperparts are rich olive-chestnut with the crown, nape, shoulders, dorsum and upper surface of the tail appearing slightly darker. The tail darkens further towards the tip. The underparts and inner limbs are paler and golden-brown. The inner face around the eyes and extending down the muzzle is dark brown, while the surrounding outer face is the same golden-brown as the underparts. The ears are small and have no tufts, but are noticeable as they are pale golden-brown (fig. 113).

IDENTIFICATION A medium-sized rotund lemur, intermediate in size between its two sympatric relatives, *H. g. griseus* (smaller) and *H. simus* (larger). The golden-brown coloration of *H. aureus* is very distinctive and this, coupled with the size differences between them, should prevent confusion with congeners.

HABITAT Primary mid-altitude rainforest associated with bamboo.

DISTRIBUTION This species was discovered in 1985 at Ranomafana in south-east Madagascar. Ranomafana National Park was the only confirmed locality for this species until 1993 when it was discovered on the Andringitra Massif at elevations between 800m and 1,625m. It is not known whether these two populations are continuous and surveys of intermediate rainforest areas are needed in order to establish this.

confirmed sightings
possible range

Golden Bamboo Lemur

BEHAVIOUR All studies of the Golden Bamboo Lemur have been conducted at Ranomafana National Park. These show the average group size to be between two and six, although three to four appears the norm. Typically, a group consists of an adult male and female, with slightly smaller subadults and juveniles. They occupy territories of up to 80ha, but on average travel less than 400m in a single day. They are most active early in the early morning and evening, but foraging may also extend into the hours of darkness.

At times Golden Bamboo Lemurs can be highly vocal and at least two different calls have been identified. The first is a rather quiet resonant *wuulp* with an inquisitive inflection. This may be repeated by different group members in response to one another and possibly serves as a contact call. The second call is a loud, sharp, staccato 'guttural honk' that is repeated on a slowing, descending scale that also decreases in volume. Only one member of the group appears to issue this call, which may be heard in conjunction with the *wuulp* call from other group members. It is possible the honk has some territorial function.

H. aureus feeds almost exclusively on members of the family Gramineae, in particular the endemic giant bamboo *Cephalostachium viguieri* (fig. 111), but also bamboo creeper and bamboo grass (fig. 112). It is highly selective in relation to which part of the bamboo is consumed: the bases of leaves and new shoots are preferred. This may help reduce competition with the Greater Bamboo Lemur *H. simus* which selects the inner pith. The highly prized young shoots of the giant bamboo are not eaten by any other lemur and have been shown to be very protein-rich, but also contain high levels of cyanide toxins that would normally be lethal. Evidently the Golden

Figure 111. Golden Bamboo Lemur feeding on bamboo, Ranomafana.

Figure 112. Young Golden Bamboo Lemur, Ranomafana.

Bamboo Lemur has evolved a digestive system to cope with these, and in doing so, dramatically reduces competition for food with the other *Hapalemur* species.

Births have been observed in November and December; a single offspring is normally produced.

POPULATION The population at Ranomafana National Park is estimated to be around 1,000 individuals. The status of this species on the Andringitra Massif is not yet known. Surveys of rainforest sites between these two localities are necessary to gauge overall population levels.

THREATS The continued destruction of the rainforests by slash-and-burn remains the major threat to this species. Even the protected forests on the inner periphery of Ranomafana National Park continue to be felled and exploited. Add this to the species's extremely limited range and the prospects for long-term survival are not encouraging. The Golden Bamboo Lemur is now known to occur in two protected areas.

VIEWING Ranomafana National Park is the only accessible locality where this species can be seen. Indeed, the discovery of the Golden Bamboo Lemur brought Ranomafana to the world's attention and prompted the creation of the park in 1991. Searches should be concentrated in and around the stands of giant bamboo close to the research cabin along the main path. It is essential to seek the assistance of one of the local guides to try to find this species. However, even with their expert help, it might take two or three days to ensure success.

Figure 113. Golden Bamboo Lemur.

GREATER BAMBOO LEMUR *Hapalemur simus* Gray, 1870

Other names: Greater Gentle Lemur, Broad-nosed Gentle Lemur
Malagasy: Varibolo

MEASUREMENTS Total length: c. 850-900mm. Head/body length: c. 400-420mm. Tail length: c. 450-480mm. Weight: c. 2.2-2.5kg.

DESCRIPTION The pelage is short and dense. Upperparts and tail are grey-brown, with a slight russet tinge. A more olive-brown coloration is apparent on the head, neck, shoulders and upper arms. There is a noticeable chestnut-brown patch at the base of the tail and the tip of the tail may be very dark grey. The underparts and throat are obviously paler and generally creamy-brown. The inner face, nose bridge and muzzle are dark grey, although the areas just above the eyes may be pale grey. This species's most distinctive features are the large prominent pale grey to white ear-tufts (figs. 114 & 115).

On the Andringitra Massif, a population of *Hapalemur* has recently been discovered that probably represents a very distinct colour morph of the Greater Bamboo Lemur. These individuals are similar in size to *H. simus*, but the head, upperparts, throat and underparts are uniformly deep golden-red. The tail is of similar coloration except at its tip where it is grey. The face and short broad muzzle are dark. The ears are large and prominent, but have no tufts. Specimens have been observed between 700m and 1,200m.

IDENTIFICATION A medium-large, round-bodied lemur, by far the largest of the *Hapalemur* species. Although its coloration is broadly similar to that of *H. g. griseus*, the appreciably larger size and distinctive ear-tufts of this species should prevent confusion. Major colour and size differences and the ear tufts should also be sufficient to distinguish this species from the Golden Bamboo Lemur *H. aureus*. The Greater Bamboo Lemur is similar in size to a number of sympatric *Eulemur* species but its blunt muzzle, rounded face and prominent ear-tufts again ought to prevent confusion.

HABITAT Rainforests associated with giant bamboo. This species has also been observed in agricultural plantations that support giant bamboo adjacent to native forests.

Figure 114. Greater Bamboo Lemur, Ranomafana.

Figure 115. *Greater Bamboo Lemur, in the vicinity of Vondrozo.*

Greater Bamboo Lemur

DISTRIBUTION Subfossil evidence indicates that this species was once widespread in northern, central and eastern Madagascar. Remains have been found at Ampasambazimba in the Itasy Basin to the east of Antananarivo, Andrafiabe in the Ankarana Massif, and Anjohibe north-east of Mahajanga. Furthermore, a number of 19th century expeditions collected specimens from widely dispersed sites in the eastern rainforest belt. More recently the presence of *H. simus* has been suspected in the Mananara region (very close to a known 19th century collection site) on the basis of its distinctive vocalisations but visual confirmation has yet to be obtained.

Today the only localities where *H. simus* can be confirmed are at sites in the south-eastern rainforests. To the east of Fianarantsoa, this species is known to occur in an approximate 50km-wide strip extending from Vohiparara in the west to Kianjavato in the east and centred around the Ranomafana region. It may also occur in the Andringitra Massif, south-west of Fianarantsoa, and has recently been recorded from forests in the vicinity of Vondrozo to the east of Farafangana. Interestingly, village elders from forests near Vondrozo also report the existence of a large red-coloured bamboo lemur fitting the description of the colour morph recently discovered on the Andringitra Massif (see above). Given the paucity of thorough surveys and information relating to this species, it seems quite possible that other isolated populations of *H. simus* are awaiting discovery.

BEHAVIOUR There have been few studies of this species and information regarding its behaviour and ecology is scant. Groups seem to range in number from four to seven and occasionally up to 12; the composition and social structure is unclear. Greater Bamboo Lemurs are active around dawn and dusk and often continue bouts of activity into the night. At Ranomafana National Park one group was recorded to range over an area in excess of 100ha.

H. simus feeds primarily on bamboo (up to 98%), particularly Giant Bamboo *Cephalostachium viguieri*, although in contrast to the Golden Bamboo Lemur, the woody inner pith is preferred. This species is adept at stripping the outer layers off live stalks and breaking through the bamboo pole to reach the pith beneath. Such a foraging technique is quite destructive, and ravaged stands of giant bamboo are clear evidence for the presence of this species. *H. simus* also eats the flowers of the Traveller's Tree *Ravenala madagascariensis*, fruits of *Arctocarpus*, *Ficus* and *Dypsis* as well as some leaves.

POPULATION In the Ranomafana region a population of about 1,000 has been estimated. As yet, no figures are available for the recently discovered populations on the Andringitra Massif and near Vondrozo.

THREATS The continued destruction of the rainforests by slash-and-burn, coupled with extensive cutting of bamboo, are the major threats to this species. Despite its status as a national park the forests inside Ranomafana's borders continue to be exploited. *H. simus* is also known to be hunted with slingshots in some areas. These factors, coupled with the species's limited range, give cause for great concern regarding its long term survival prospects. The Greater Bamboo Lemur is known to occur in two protected areas.

VIEWING Ranomafana National Park is the best place to try to see this species. Groups are sometimes encountered in the patches of giant bamboo around the research cabin adjacent to the main trail. Enlisting the help of a park guide is recommended. Ranomafana is the only accessible locality where all three *Hapalemur* species can be seen (the Andringitra Massif is the only other locality, but is difficult to reach). For this and many other reasons the park is well worth an extended visit but considerable effort and good fortune are generally required to see the Greater Bamboo Lemur.

Subfamily Lemurinae

The subfamily Lemurinae includes the most familiar Malagasy primates which are collectively known as the 'true' lemurs. Three genera are recognised within this division: *Lemur*, *Eulemur* and *Varecia*. They are medium to medium-large lemurs that adopt a horizontal body posture and move and leap quadrupedally. All are skilled climbers, but some are also at home on the ground to varying degrees. In the past they have been regarded as principally diurnal but nocturnal activity is also now known in a number of species. In fact it is clear that this behaviour is probably quite wide-spread and particularly prevalent in the genus *Eulemur*.

There have been a number of recent taxonomic revisions to this subfamily. At one time all species now contained within the genera *Lemur*, *Eulemur* and *Varecia* were ascribed to the genus *Lemur*. The Ruffed Lemurs were then shown to have sufficiently distinct anatomical and be-havioural characteristics to warrant sepa-ration, hence the creation of the genus *Varecia*. Later studies revealed that the Ring-tailed Lemur *Lemur catta* exhibited some unusual traits, including similarities to the bamboo lemurs *Hapalemur*. Hence, the genus *Lemur* was separated into two: *Lemur* now contains a single species, *Lemur catta*, while the new genus *Eulemur* con-tains the five remaining species.

Although some authorities still chal-lenge this series of divisions, the recogni-tion of the genera *Lemur*, *Eulemur* and *Varecia* is now widely accepted.

Figure 116. Ring-tailed Lemur.

RING-TAILED LEMUR genus *Lemur* Linnaeus, 1758

This genus now contains a single species, the Ring-tailed Lemur *Lemur catta*. Although there are some obvious morphological similari-ties between the genera *Lemur* and *Eulemur*, evidence suggests that closer affinities may exist between *Lemur* and the genus *Hapalemur*. *Lemur* is the most terrestrial of all Malagasy primates.

RING-TAILED LEMUR *Lemur catta* Linnaeus, 1758

Malagasy: Maki, Hira

MEASUREMENTS Total length: 950-1,100mm. Head/body length: 385-455mm. Tail length: 560-625mm. Weight: 2.3-3.5kg.

DESCRIPTION The back is usually grey to grey-brown, with the rump, limbs and haunches grey. The underparts are off-white or cream. The neck and crown are charcoal-grey, which contrasts with the white outer face and throat. There are large triangular dark eye-patches which may just reach the crown, and the snout is also dark. The ears are prominent and lighter in colour than the crown.

Figure 117. Ring-tailed Lemur, female and infant, Berenty.

Figure 118. Ring-tailed Lemur, female and infant suckling, Berenty.

Figure 119. Ring-tailed Lemur group calling, Berenty.

Figure 120. Male Ring-tailed Lemur, Beza-Mafahaly.

The tail is long and ringed alternately in black and white, the 13 to 14 black bands generally being broader.

Individuals belonging to an apparently isolated population on the Andringitra Massif vary quite markedly in pelage characteristics and coloration from the typical form described above. The fur of the Andringitra Ring-tailed Lemurs is much more dense and woolly in appearance. The dorsal region, rump and limbs are noticeably darker and more rufous-brown than typical forms. The tail also has fewer dark rings (11 to 12). The taxonomic status of this subpopulation has yet to be determined.

IDENTIFICATION A medium-sized lemur, often seen on the ground and instantly recognisable by its distinctive banded tail. This species cannot be confused with any other (fig. 120).

HABITAT Spiny forest, dry scrub, deciduous forest and gallery forest are used throughout the majority of its range. Exposed rocks, low ericoid bush and subalpine vegetation at higher elevations are the habitat of the population in the Andringitra Massif.

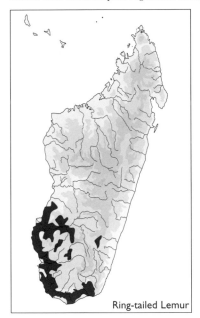

Ring-tailed Lemur

DISTRIBUTION The Ring-tailed Lemur is found in south and south-western Madagascar from Tolagnaro in the south-east to just south of Morondava on the west coast and inland as far as the vicinity of Ambalavao. The species generally occurs at lower elevations. There is also an apparently isolated population remaining in the Andringitra Massif on the south-eastern plateau. Here the species has been recorded above the treeline to altitudes in excess of 2,600m. Today this species ranges further into the interior highlands than any other lemur, but it is patchily distributed throughout its range.

BEHAVIOUR Studies of Ring-tailed Lemur behaviour began in the early 1960s and are ongoing. More information has been gathered on this species of lemur than any other. Ring-tailed Lemurs are diurnal and semi-terrestrial, spending more time on the ground than any other lemur. This tendency is probably dictated by the semi-arid environments they inhabit, where vegetation is not always continuous and resources may be sparse and unevenly distributed.

The diet is very varied and consists of fruit, leaves, flowers, bark, sap and occasionally invertebrates. There has even been an observation of *L. catta* feeding on a small Jewel Chameleon *Furcifer lateralis*. Although fruits are always preferred, their proportion in the diet varies according to the habitat and season; for instance, in gallery forests during October and November the fruits and sap of the Tamarind or Kily Tree *Tamarindus indica* constitute the majority of food intake. Between August and October pregnant and lactating females show a strong preference for energy-rich food items.

L. catta occurs in larger groups than any other Malagasy primate. Group size ranges from three to around 25 individuals, although 13 to 15 is average (fig. 119). Groups contain equal numbers of adult females and males, plus immature and juvenile animals.

There is a well-defined and maintained hierarchy within the troop: females are dominant and the alpha female forms the focal point for the group as a whole. Males also have their own strict hierarchy, but are always subordinate to the females. The 'central' male generally interacts with the females more often than other group males.

Although the groups are not strictly territorial they do have a preferred home range, the size of which is determined by habitat and the resources contained within it. These change seasonally, so the home range can vary from 6ha to over 30ha. Scent-marking is important in demarcating the range. Females leave genital smears, while males use a wrist gland armed with a horny pad to gouge scent into the bark of saplings. Nonetheless, there is a high degree of overlap between the home ranges of neighbouring groups. When groups meet, the dominant females are primarily responsible for defence: they confront members of other groups by staring, lunging approaches and occasional physical aggression. After agonistic encounters, group members normally retreat towards the sanctuary of the centre of their home range.

In the seasonal habitats of the south and south-west, mating is highly synchronous, taking place in a two- to three-week period between mid-April and mid-May. In this way weaning occurs when essential food availability is at a maximum. When females come into oestrous, group males challenge each other for the right of access. They anoint their tails with secretions from their wrist glands, then waft the scent in the direction of opposing males. These 'stink fights' are normally sufficient to establish rank, but physical aggression may ensue.

The young are born after a gestation period of around 135 days, in August and September. Twins are often produced, but a single infant is more common. At first the baby clings to the mother's underside (fig. 118), but moves around to ride on her back after two weeks or so (fig. 117). Infant mortality is high: about 50% of offspring die in their first year and only 30% reach adulthood. Sexual maturity in females is reached after three years, and the majority of females give birth each year. All males leave their natal groups after maturation and established adult males transfer between groups on average every three to five years.

The young of this species are preyed upon by several raptor species, including; the Madagascar Harrier-Hawk *Polyboroides radiatus*, Madagascar Buzzard *Buteo brachypterus* and possibly Black Kite *Milvus migrans* and some *Accipiter* species. Both adults and young are eaten by the Fosa *Cryptoprocta ferox*. Ring-tailed Lemurs have been observed mobbing the introduced Small Indian Civet *Viverricula indica*, but no direct predation has been observed.

POPULATION No overall population figures are available and estimates of population density vary considerably according to habitat. In well-studied areas of gallery forest estimates between 140 and 350 animals/km^2 have been made, although these variations may reflect year-to-year population fluctuations. In more arid or disturbed forests, densities as low as 17 individuals/km^2 have been estimated.

THREATS The two main habitat types preferred by Ring-tailed Lemurs, dense Didieraceae/Euphorbiaceae bush and riverside gallery forest, are already restricted and known to be diminishing alarmingly as a result of fires, overgrazing and wood-harvesting for charcoal production. These lemurs are still hunted in many areas and also trapped and kept as pets. Despite its high-profile image, the long-term survival of this species is undoubtedly in question. Ring-tailed Lemurs are found in all five protected areas within their range, plus two private reserves near Tolagnaro.

VIEWING This species is most easily seen at Berenty Private Reserve to the west of Tolagnaro. Berenty is perhaps Madagascar's best-known reserve and visitors are seldom disappointed. Several troops of Ring-tailed Lemurs have been habituated, which makes for easy viewing. For close encounters of the lemur kind, Berenty is the place. Alternatively, there is another private reserve nearby at Amboasary-Sud, where Ring-tailed Lemurs can also be observed at close quarters. However, the habitat here is not as good as at Berenty, and there is much less in the way of other wildlife to see.

To see Ring-tailed Lemurs in spiny forest it is worth visiting Hazafotsy on the edge of Andohahela Nature Reserve, about four hours' drive from Tolagnaro. Alternatively, Beza-Mahafaly Special Reserve, around six hours east of Toliara, is an excellent place to see this species in both spiny forest and gallery forest. Both these places are visited far less frequently than Berenty and can be highly rewarding.

With patience and a bit of luck, it is also possible to see this species in Isalo National Park. Here the habitat is very different and the lemurs may be seen clambering around over the impressive rock formations, especially early in the morning. However, they tend to be quite shy and it is difficult to get close to them.

TYPICAL LEMURS genus *Eulemur* Simons and Rumpler, 1988

Five species of 'typical' lemur are recognised within the genus *Eulemur*: two of these – *E. fulvus* and *E. macaco* – are further divided into subspecies. *Eulemur* species are characteristically medium-sized, weighing 2-3kg, sexually dichromatic to a varying extent and cathemeral. Scent-marking, particularly with the ano-genital region, is frequent in both sexes.

MONGOOSE LEMUR *Eulemur mongoz* (Linnaeus, 1766)

Malagasy: Gidro, Dredrika

MEASUREMENTS Total length: 750-830mm. Head/body length: 300-350mm. Tail length: 450-480mm. Weight: 1-1.4kg.

DESCRIPTION Sexually dichromatic. **Males:** (fig. 122) Upperparts are grey-brown, with a slightly darker tip to the tail, while the underparts are much paler and creamy-grey. There may be some brownish tinges around the shoulders and there is a dark grey pygal patch. The face is grey and the muzzle pale grey with a dark nose. The cheeks, beard, forehead and back of the neck are rufous-brown and distinctive. In fully mature males there may be a triangular bald patch on the top of the head; this is caused by excessive head rubbing when scent-marking. **Females:** (fig. 121) The upperparts are grey and generally paler than in males, although there may be some faint brownish tinges on the rear flanks and around the rump. There is a dark grey pygal patch. In common with males, the tail tip is darker and the underparts are creamy-grey. The face is dark slate-grey which fades into pale grey or white around the muzzle. The cheeks and beard form a creamy-grey to white ruff and are continuous with the throat and underparts. The eyes in both sexes are reddish-orange.

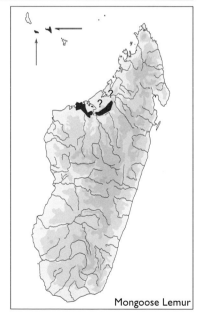

Mongoose Lemur

IDENTIFICATION A medium-sized lemur with a long tail and horizontal body posture; it moves quadrupedally. This species is most easily confused with the Common Brown Lemur *E. fulvus fulvus*, particularly if only a brief glimpse is gained. However, the Mongoose Lemur's pelage is predominantly grey rather than brown and *E. f. fulvus* does not display sexual dichromatism.

HABITAT Dry deciduous forest and secondary forest (Madagascar). Humid forest (Comoros).

DISTRIBUTION The Mongoose Lemur's natural range is restricted to north-west Madagascar, from the region west of the Mahavavy River (in the vicinity of Mitsinjo) to somewhere north of Boriziny, but south of Antsohihy. This species has also been introduced to the Comoros, where populations occur on the islands of Anjouan and Moheli. There are also a few feral individuals on Grande Comoro.

BEHAVIOUR Mongoose Lemurs live in small groups, comprising a monogamous adult pair and one to three dependent offspring. Social bonds within these family units appear to be strong, groups being very cohesive during feeding, travelling, resting and sleeping. Home ranges do not appear to be large and there is extensive overlap between the ranges of neighbouring groups. Despite this, inter-group encounters are infrequent but cause considerable agitation, vocalisation and scent-marking when they occur. In contrast, Mongoose

Figure 121. Female Mongoose Lemur, Tsiombikibo Forest.

Figure 122 (right). Male Mongoose Lemur, Tsiombikibo Forest.

Lemurs appear to tolerate the close proximity of the Common Brown Lemur *Eulemur fulvus fulvus*, which is sympatric in some areas. At times the two species have been seen in mixed groups.

In common with a number of congeners, Mongoose Lemurs appear to be cathemeral thoughout both the wet and dry seasons. However, during the warm wet months (December to April) there is considerably more diurnal (or crepuscular) activity. With the onset of the dry season in May there is a shift towards nocturnal behaviour, which duly becomes predominant. At this time groups travel and feed between dusk and around 22:00 hours, then rest for two to four hours before resuming foraging activity. This continues until just before dawn when they return to their sleep sites in dense foliage or tangled vines at the tops of trees. By foraging at night during the dry season, when temperatures are low, Mongoose Lemurs are able to conserve energy. Also, foliage cover is at its lowest at this time, so nocturnal activity patterns may help reduce the risk of predation from diurnal raptors.

During both wet and dry seasons fruit appears to dominate the diet. In the wet season this is complemented by flowers, particularly Kapok *Ceiba pentandra*, and nectar, which may indicate that Mongoose Lemurs are important pollinators. During the dry season leaves form the other significant dietary element. Beetles and insect grubs are also eaten occasionally.

Females seem capable of giving birth each year, the young being born around October and November. Adult size and coloration is attained between 14 and 16 months, although sexual maturation takes longer.

POPULATION No overall population figures or density estimates are available. However, some authorities have suggested that the Mongoose Lemur is the rarest species in the genus *Eulemur*.

THREATS The dry deciduous forests of the north-west continue to be cleared to create pasture and to produce charcoal. This habitat destruction constitutes the major threat to the Mongoose Lemur on Madagascar. On the Comoros the story is a similar one: habitat destruction continues at an ever-increasing pace and the lemurs are also trapped as pets or killed for food. On Madagascar, the Mongoose Lemur is known to occur in only one protected area – the Ankarafantsika Nature Reserve.

VIEWING Probably the best place on Madagascar to see this species is the area around Mitsinjo, some 90km west of the Betsiboka estuary. The Tsiombikibo Forest to the north-west of the town is the most likely area, and groups are often encountered here. Mongoose Lemurs are even sometimes seen in forest patches adjacent to the town itself and around nearby Lac Kamonjo. Alternatively the forest around Anjamena on the eastern banks of the Mahavavy River is a very good place to see Mongoose Lemurs. This area is around two to three hours' walk from the road between Katsepy and Namakia.

The most readily accessible site to see Mongoose Lemurs is Ampijoroa Forest Station around two hours' drive south-east of Mahajanga. However, Mongoose Lemurs are seen less frequently here than at some remoter sites and require some effort and patience to track down: it is best to seek the help of a local guide from the Forest Station.

CROWNED LEMUR *Eulemur coronatus* (Gray, 1842)

Crowned Lemur

Malagasy: Ankomba, Gidro

MEASUREMENTS Total length: 750-850mm. Head/body length: 340-360mm. Tail length: 410-490mm. Weight: 1.5-1.8kg.

DESCRIPTION Sexually dichromatic. Other than *E. macaco* this is the most obviously sexually dichromatic lemur species and is also the smallest member of the genus *Eulemur*. *Males*: (fig. 123) Upperparts are grey-brown, becoming more brown to chestnut-brown on the flanks and towards the extremities of the limbs. Underparts are paler creamy-grey, often with a brown/chestnut wash. The tail is grey-brown and generally a shade darker than the body. The face and ears are pale grey to white, while the tip of the muzzle is black. There is a conspicuous and distinctive chestnut-orange crown above the eyebrow line and by the side of the ears. This forms a prominent V-shape with the dark charcoal-grey patch on top of the head. The chestnut-orange coloration also extends around the face to form bushy cheeks. *Females*: (fig. 124) The upperparts, flanks and limbs are mid-grey, while the underparts are pale grey to creamy-white. The tail is mid-grey and darkens towards the tip. The face and ears are pale grey to white, the tip of the muzzle is dark grey and the nose black. The top of the head and cheeks are mid-grey and there is a distinctive chestnut-orange crown above the eyebrow line, which forms a V-shape with the mid-grey area on top of the head.

IDENTIFICATION A medium-sized lemur that adopts a horizontal body posture. The Crowned Lemur can only be confused with Sanford's Brown Lemur *Eulemur fulvus sanfordi*, these two taxa being sympatric throughout most of their ranges. However, the distinctive chestnut-orange crown of *Eulemur coronatus* and its very marked sexual dichromatism should prevent misidentification. Also male Sanford's Brown Lemurs have marked pale grey ear-tufts and beards which Crowned Lemurs lack.

HABITAT Dry and semi-dry deciduous forests are preferred, but this species also occurs in some primary and secondary humid forests.

DISTRIBUTION The Crowned Lemur is restricted to the northern tip of Madagascar, but the precise limits of its range are ill-defined. In the north-west its southern limit appears to be the Mahavavy River to the south of Ambilobe, while in the north-east its range extends further southward, probably to the Bemarivo River, just north of Sambava. North of these two apparent boundaries the Crowned Lemur is found all the way to the Cap d'Ambre Peninsula.

BEHAVIOUR Crowned Lemurs appear to be primarily diurnal, although they are also known to be occasionally active at night. They live in groups of 5-15 individuals, although five or six is the norm. These groups contain several adult females and adult males, together with infants and juveniles. In humid forest areas the average group size appears to be smaller than in dry forest areas. During feeding bouts large groups may split into foraging subunits of two to four animals. Characteristic guttural grunts are used to maintain contact with adjacent subgroups. Crowned Lemurs occupy a small home range and there is considerable overlap between the home ranges of neighbouring groups.

Although foraging may take place at all levels of the forest from the ground up

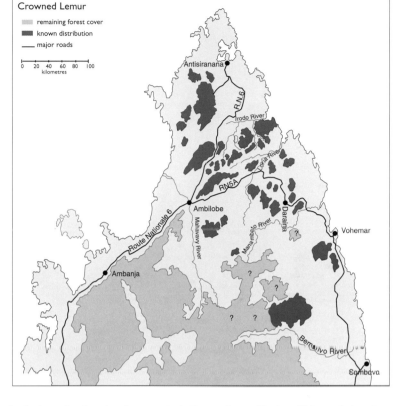

Crowned Lemur

- remaining forest cover
- known distribution
- major roads

0 20 40 60 80 100
kilometres

to the canopy, Crowned Lemurs appear to prefer the lower levels and understorey, including treelets and bushes. This may help reduce competition with Sanford's Brown Lemur, which is largely sympatric but prefers to use the upper levels of the forest. However, the two species are known to aggregate into mixed foraging groups for between 20% and 30% of each day, particularly during the wet season when resources are abundant. During such times there is very little interspecific aggression. When aggressive interactions do occur, Crowned Lemurs are normally displaced by the more forceful Sanford's Brown Lemurs.

During both the wet and the dry seasons, fruit forms the bulk of the Crowned Lemur's diet – around 80% to 90% – and includes *Ficus* spp., *Strychinos* spp., *Pandanus* spp., *Diospyros* spp. and *Tamarindus indica*. In the dry season flowers and young leaves are also taken, together with the occasional invertebrate. In the wet season a greater number of leaves and plant species are utilised. There is circumstantial evidence to suggest that Crowned Lemurs may also predate eggs from birds' nests: an adult Hook-billed Vanga *Vanga curvirostris* in the vicinity of its nest has been seen violently mobbing a female Crowned Lemur with a small infant, such that the infant fell from its mother to the ground.

In both humid and dry regions, mating takes place during late May and June. After a gestation period of around 125 days, births occur from mid-September through October and coincide with the onset of the rainy season. Singletons and twins appear to be equally common. Infants are initially carried on the mother's front, but then move around to ride on her back. Adult size and sexual maturity are not reached until well into the second year.

The Crowned Lemur is regularly predated by the Fosa *Cryptoprocta ferox* and in the Ankarana Massif may also be eaten by crocodiles *Crocodylus niloticus*. The presence of large raptors overhead often provokes agitated alarm calls, which strongly suggests that predation by birds of prey also occurs.

POPULATION No overall population figures are known. Population densities appear to vary widely with habitat type. The highest densities are reported from areas of dry deciduous forest. In Ankarana Special Reserve estimates vary between around 150 and 300 individuals/km^2, while at Sakalava the figure is around 100 individuals/km^2. In the humid forests of Montagne d'Ambre densities around 50 individuals/km^2 have been suggested.

THREATS Throughout much of its range, the Crowned Lemur is threatened by the direct destruction of its habitat. Forest is being cleared and burned to make way for agriculture, and illegal logging also occurs on the periphery of several key reserves. In some areas the Crowned Lemur is also hunted for food. This species is known to occur in four protected areas.

VIEWING The Crowned Lemur is a relatively easy species to see. Several troops are now habituated in Ankarana Special Reserve near the *Campement des Anglais* and *Lac Vert*. There are also easily accessible troops in Montagne d'Ambre National Park near the main campsite, around the *Station Roussettes* and at the viewpoint overlooking the *Grande Cascade*. For the more adventurous, the valley of the Bobakindro River in Analamera Special Reserve is also a particularly rewarding place to see this species.

Figure 123. Male Crowned Lemur, Ankarana.

Figure 124. Female Crowned Lemur, Ankarana.

RED-BELLIED LEMUR *Eulemur rubriventer* (I. Geoffroy, 1850)

Red-bellied Lemur

Malagasy: Barimaso, Soamiera, Tongona

MEASUREMENTS Total length: 780-930mm. Head/body length: 350-400mm. Tail length: 430-530mm. Weight: 1.6-2.4kg.

DESCRIPTION Sexually dichromatic. **Males**: (fig. 125) The pelage is long and dense. Upperparts, chest and underparts are rich dark chestnut-brown, while the tail is noticeably darker, often appearing almost black. The top of the head, face and muzzle are darker, often slate-grey, and there are conspicuous patches of white bare skin forming teardrops beneath the eyes. Although there are no ear-tufts as such, the fur around the ears is particularly dense and gives the head an overall squarish look. **Females**: (fig. 126) The upperparts are rich chestnut-brown as in the males, but the chest and underparts are creamy-white. The tail is dark grey to black. The head is less squarish in shape than in males and the top is not darkened. The face and muzzle are dark slate grey, but the bare patches of white skin are dramatically reduced and in some individuals completely absent. The lower cheeks and beard may be creamy-white like the chest and underparts.

IDENTIFICATION A medium-sized lemur with a horizontal body posture and rich dense coat. Throughout its range, the Red-bellied Lemur occurs sympatrically with a number of Brown Lemur *E. fulvus* subspecies, all of which are broadly similar in size and shape. With a good view, distinguishing *E. rubriventer* should be straightforward. Its coat is much more dense and richly coloured than any *E. fulvus* subspecies and it is far less obviously sexually dichromatic than any except *E. f. fulvus*. Furthermore, the Red-bellied Lemur is generally encountered in small family groups, rather than the larger multi-adult troops seen in *E. fulvus*.

HABITAT Primary and secondary eastern rainforest.

DISTRIBUTION The Red-bellied Lemur appears to be thinly distributed throughout the eastern rainforest belt from the area to the south of the Andringitra Massif in the south to the Tsaratanana Massif in the north, but not including the Masoala Peninsula. Throughout this range, middle to high elevations are preferred – in the Tsaratanana Massif this species has been recorded at altitudes of 2,400m.

BEHAVIOUR The Red-bellied Lemur lives in small family units of two to six animals which generally comprise an adult pair and dependent offspring, although some larger groups do contain more than one adult of each sex. These family groups occupy a home

Figure 125. Male Red-bellied Lemur, Ranomafana.

Figure 126. Female Red-bellied Lemur, Ranomafana.

range of around 10-20 ha which is actively defended, although some observations suggest that neighbouring groups rarely show aggressive behaviour towards one another. Aggressive behaviour between two males apparently belonging to the same group has, however, been observed. On average, the group travels 400-500m per day, but this distance varies seasonally according to food availability. In times of shortage the group may travel more than 1,000m per day. The movements of the unit are instigated and led by the dominant female.

This species is cathemeral, although activity patterns may vary with the seasons and be related to food availability. Fruits appear to be the mainstay of the diet and include introduced species like Chinese Guava *Psidium cattleyanum*. When fruits are unavailable, flowers and leaves are also taken and it is at these times that feeding bouts often continue after dark. The Red-bellied Lemur has been recorded utilising nearly 70 different plant species over the course of the year. It also seems that invertebrates, especially millipedes, constitute an important element in the diet.

The single young are usually born in September and October, and are initially carried on the mother's belly, then later move around to ride on her back. At this stage, infants are also carried by the male, who may form a focus for other infants as well. After around 35 days the female stops carrying the offspring although the male may continue to do so until it approaches 100 days of age.

POPULATION No overall population figures are available. The species is known to be only sparsely distributed throughout its fairly extensive range, so that some authorities believe this to be one of the rarest of the *Eulemur* species. In Ranomafana National Park, a population density of 30 individuals/km² has been estimated.

THREATS The continued destruction of the eastern rainforest remains the primary threat to this species. Each year large areas are lost to shifting agriculture and logging. The Red-bellied Lemur is known to occur in at least nine protected areas.

VIEWING Ranomafana National Park in south-east Madagascar is the best location to see this species. More than one family group has become habituated in the vicinity of the main trail network and these can often be approached with ease. During May and June, when the Chinese Guava are in fruit, the animals can be particularly easy to find around *Belle Vue* (together with *E. fulvus rufus*).

Alternatively, the Red-bellied Lemur can occasionally be seen at Analamazaotra Special Reserve and nearby Mantadia National Park in central-eastern Madagascar, or in Anjanaharibe-Sud Special Reserve in north-east Madagascar.

BROWN LEMUR *Eulemur fulvus* (E. Geoffroy, 1796)

The Brown Lemur is by far the most widespread of the 'typical' lemurs and is divided into no less than six subspecies, each occupying apparently distinct ranges within Madagascar. They occur in all native forest types, with the exception of the arid spiny forest regions of the south and south-west.

All are medium-sized lemurs that live in groups and feed predominantly on fruit, leaves, flowers and sap. They are active during both day and night. The extent of nocturnal activity varies seasonally according to food availability and lunar cycle.

A seventh subspecies of Brown Lemur, *E. f. mayottensis*, from the island of Mayotte in the Comoros has been recognised in the past by some authorities. This population was almost certainly introduced by man from Madagascar several hundred years ago and is now considered to be simply a population of the nominate race of Brown Lemur.

Based on apparent cranial and dental differences, some authorities consider the Brown Lemur to be sufficiently distinct from other members of the genus *Eulemur* to justify its generic separation. These authorities ascribe Brown Lemurs to their own genus, *Petterus*. However, this point of view is not widely accepted and the majority continue to recognise Brown Lemurs as belonging to *Eulemur*.

Subspecies

Common Brown Lemur *Eulemur fulvus fulvus* (E. Geoffroy, 1796)

Malagasy: Varika, Dredrika, Varikosy

MEASUREMENTS Total length: 845-1,010mm. Head/body length: 430-500mm. Tail length: 415-510mm. Weight: 2-3kg.

DESCRIPTION This is the only *Eulemur fulvus* subspecies where both males and females are similarly coloured (fig. 128) – all other subspecies are sexually dichromatic. The pelage is short but quite dense. The upperparts are uniform brown to grey-brown, while the underparts are paler and slightly greyer. The face, muzzle and crown are dark grey to black (females may be slightly paler than males), with slightly paler faint eyebrow patches and paler brown-grey fur around the moderately prominent ears, cheeks and underneath the chin. The eyes are rich orange-red (fig. 127). The tail is long and slightly bushy towards the tip.

IDENTIFICATION A medium-sized lemur with a long tail and horizontal body posture which moves quadrupedally both on the ground and in the canopy. In the eastern part of its range the Common Brown Lemur may be confused with the Red-bellied Lemur *E. rubriventer*, but the latter is very much more reddish in colour and males have distinctive white tear-drops beneath their eyes, while females have a creamy-white throat, chest and belly. In north-western forests, *E. f. fulvus* is distinguished from the Mongoose Lemur *E. mongoz* by its uniform brown coloration: the Mongoose Lemur is mainly grey with slight brownish tinges and is sexually dichromatic.

HABITAT Rainforest, moist montane forest and dry deciduous forest.

DISTRIBUTION Two major populations remain – one in the east, the other in the north-west. In eastern Madagascar the Common Brown Lemur is found in the rainforests north of the Mangoro River to an as yet indeterminate latitude between 16°S and 18°S. Between these latitudes the range of this subspecies meets that of the White-fronted Brown Lemur *E. f. albifrons* but the boundaries

Figure 127. Common Brown Lemur, Ampijoroa.

between the two remain unclear and there may be some overlap where hybridisation occurs. A latitude just to the north of Toamasina (around 18°S) is often quoted as the northern limit for *E. f. fulvus* in the east. However, groups of *E. fulvus* seen in both Zahamena Nature Reserve and Ambatovaky Special Reserve, which respectively lie approximately 40km and 140km to the north of the accepted boundary, appear to resemble the nominate race far more closely than *E. f. albifrons*.

Common Brown Lemur

In the north-west this subspecies is found in the dry deciduous forest north of the Betsiboka River and continues north into the moist evergreen forests of the Sambirano region as far as the Mahavavy River and probably including some of the Tsaratanana Massif.

Between these two main blocks, *E. f. fulvus* also survives in some isolated forest remnants in the central highlands, for example at Ambohitantely Special Reserve, around 130km north-west of Antananarivo. This suggests that the range of this taxon was once continuous when the forests were intact.

There is also an isolated population on the island of Mayotte in the Comoros which is believed to have been introduced by man. However, this population has been described as a separate subspecies, *E. f. mayottensis*, by some authorities.

BEHAVIOUR The Common Brown Lemur is generally encountered in troops of 3-12, with 9-12 being the norm (on the island of Mayotte groups of 30 have been recorded). Groups contain several adult males and females together with subadults, juveniles and infants. Agonistic interactions seem infrequent and there are no discernible dominance hierarchies. They are active for most of the daylight hours, spending virtually all the time in the forest canopy. However, feeding and movement often continues after dark. The extent of their nocturnal activity may well be influenced by the lunar cycle: when the moon is full, nocturnal activity reaches its peak.

The home range size appears to be strongly influenced by habitat. In western dry forests it is around seven to eight hectares, while in eastern rainforests home ranges as large as 20ha have been recorded. Groups continually scent-mark their territory, although some overlap between ranges still occurs: loud vocalisations help groups avoid one another.

The diet is varied and consists of leaves, buds, shoots, flowers and fruits, the proportions of which vary seasonally. In some eastern areas this species has been observed feeding in plantations on the flowers of introduced pine and eucalyptus trees.

Mating takes place in May and June and after a gestation period of around 120 days births occur in September and October at the onset of the rainy season. A single offspring is usual, although twins have been recorded. Weaning occurs between four and five months, and sexual maturity is reached around 18 months.

POPULATION The overall population on Madagascar is not known. On the island of Mayotte in the Comoros there may be around 20,000 Common Brown Lemurs. In western forests, population densities of 170 individuals/km² have been estimated, dropping to 40-60 individuals/km² in eastern rainforests.

THREATS Habitat destruction remains the primary threat. In eastern areas, rainforests are cleared by slash-and-burn to make way for agriculture, while the drier western forests are threatened mostly by fires started to promote new flushes of grass for grazing cattle. The Common Brown Lemur is found in at least eight protected areas. Its presence in others is suspected but cannot be confirmed until thorough surveys are undertaken.

VIEWING The best location to see this subspecies is in the dry deciduous forests at Ampijoroa Forest Station – part of the Ankarafantsika Nature Reserve. This is easily reached by road from Mahajanga. Here a number of troops occupy territories adjacent to the campsite and other groups may be encountered on walks through the forest in *Jardin Botanique A* and *Jardin Botanique B*. Alternatively, the most accessible location in the eastern rainforests is Analamazaotra Special Reserve (Andasibe/Perinet) – here the Common Brown Lemur is readily seen in trees between the main road and the warden's house close to the reserve entrance.

Figure 128. Female (left) and male (right) Common Brown Lemur, Ampijoroa.

Sanford's Brown Lemur *Eulemur fulvus sanfordi* (Archbold, 1932)

Malagasy: Beharavoaka, Ankomba

MEASUREMENTS Total length: 880-950mm. Head/body length: 380-400mm. Tail length: 500-550mm. Weight: 2-2.5 kg.

DESCRIPTION Sexually dichromatic. **Males:** (fig. 130) Upperparts and tail are medium-brown, with slightly darker grey-brown areas along the back and towards the tip of the tail. Underparts are pale brown-grey. The most distinctive feature is the pronounced creamy-grey beard and prominent ear-tufts, which give the male a 'maned' appearance. The crown is also long, but generally brown-grey. The nose bridge and snout are black. Between these dark areas and the mane are patches of creamy-white short hair on the cheeks and above the eyes. **Females:** (fig. 129) The upperparts and tail are grey-brown, with darker areas at the end of the tail, while the underparts are paler grey. The face and head are completely grey – this colour extending over the crown, down the neck and onto the shoulders. The female lacks the ear tufts and beard of the male. Some individuals may have slightly paler areas above the eyes.

IDENTIFICATION A medium-sized lemur with a long tail; it adopts a horizontal body posture and moves quadrupedally. Sanford's Brown Lemur shares its range with the Crowned Lemur *E. coronatus*, which is of very similar size and shape. However, the coloration of the two taxa is completely different. Male Crowned Lemurs are orangy grey-brown, while females are grey and both sexes have a highly distinctive orange-brown V-shape on their crown. Female Sanford's Brown Lemurs are very similar to female White-fronted Brown Lemurs *E. f. albifrons* and where the ranges of the two taxa abut, differentiation can be problematic. However, the males of these two subspecies are quite distinctive.

Figure 129. Female Sanford's Brown Lemur, Montagne d'Ambre.

Figure 130. Male Sanford's Brown Lemur, Ankarana.

Sanford's Brown Lemur

HABITAT Primary and secondary rainforest, dry deciduous forest and partially degraded forest.

DISTRIBUTION Sanford's Brown Lemur is restricted to the far north of Madagascar. Its range extends from the Cap d'Ambre Peninsula west of Antsiranana south to the Manambato River in the east and the Mahavavy River in the west. Populations of Brown Lemurs south of the Manambato River and north of the Bemarivo River appear to be different and probably represent transition forms between *E. f. sanfordi* and *E. f. albifrons*.

BEHAVIOUR Group size is related to habitat. In rainforest areas it is generally between four and seven, while in dry forest regions it may be as large as 15. Troops contain several unpaired adult males and females, together with offspring. Home ranges have been estimated to be around 15ha, and there is often considerable overlap. Agonistic interactions appear to be rare.

Sanford's Brown Lemur is cathemeral and prefers to forage in the middle understorey and forest canopy. Fruit constitutes the mainstay of the diet – up to 90%, together with shoots, flowers and some invertebrates. In the wetter months, when fruit is scarcer, a greater number of plant species are utilised than in the dry season when favoured resources are concentrated on. In the wet season Sanford's Brown Lemurs and Crowned Lemurs regularly form mixed-species foraging groups for up to 30% of the day and there appears to be very little interspecific aggression.

Births occur in late September and early October after a gestation period lasting 120 days. As with other subspecies of Brown Lemur, the infant clings to its mother's belly for the first month before transferring to ride on her back.

POPULATION No overall population figures are available. In dry deciduous forest areas population densities over 200 individuals/km² have been calculated – such a high figure may be a peculiarity of the location (Ankarana Special Reserve). In rainforest areas, densities appear to be appreciably lower than this – between 100 and 125 animals/km².

THREATS Although Sanford's Brown Lemur seems able to survive in secondary and degraded forests, its long-term survival is still threatened by habitat destruction. Having such a small and restricted range accentuates this problem. This lemur is also hunted in many areas. It is known to occur in four protected areas.

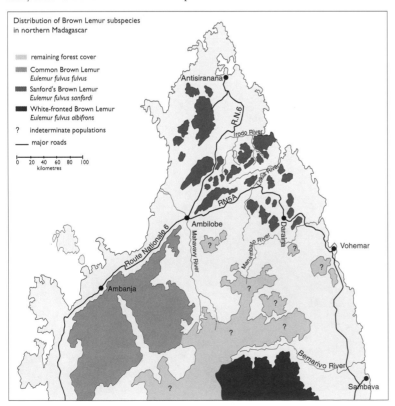

Distribution of Brown Lemur subspecies in northern Madagascar

- remaining forest cover
- Common Brown Lemur *Eulemur fulvus fulvus*
- Sanford's Brown Lemur *Eulemur fulvus sanfordi*
- White-fronted Brown Lemur *Eulemur fulvus albifrons*
- ? indeterminate populations
- — major roads

0 20 40 60 80 100 kilometres

VIEWING Montagne d'Ambre National Park is the most accessible location to see Sanford's Brown Lemur – groups are often encountered close to the *Station Roussettes* and *Petite Cascade* and along the botanical trail. Ankarana Special Reserve is also another rewarding locality; this subspecies is fairly common around the campsite at *Campement des Anglais*.

White-fronted Brown Lemur *Eulemur fulvus albifrons* (E. Geoffroy, 1796)

Malagasy: Varika

MEASUREMENTS Total length: 890-960mm. Head/body length: 390-420mm. Tail length: 500-540mm. Weight: 2-2.6kg.

DESCRIPTION Sexually dichromatic. This subspecies probably exhibits the greatest pelage differences between the sexes in any of the Brown Lemur subspecies. **Males**: (fig. 132) The upperparts and tail are rich mid- to dark brown, often becoming darker and more reddish towards the rear. Underparts are pale grey, sometimes becoming more creamy-white around the chest and throat. The head is completely creamy-white with bushy cheeks, while the muzzle and nose bridge are black. The eyes are red-orange. **Females**: (fig. 133) Upperparts and tail are mid- to dark brown, darkening towards the rear and on the tail, while the underparts are grey. The head, face and muzzle are dark grey, with the nose slightly darker. Unlike the males, the cheeks are not bushy.

IDENTIFICATION A medium-sized lemur with a horizontal body posture and long tail. In the field this subspecies could be confused with the Red-bellied Lemur *E.rubriventer*, although the highly distinctive white head of the male White-fronted Brown Lemur makes this very unlikely. At the southern limit of its range, *E. f. albifrons* may hybridise with *E. f. fulvus*: conclusive identification in this zone is, therefore, difficult.

HABITAT Primary and secondary rainforest.

White-fronted Brown Lemur

DISTRIBUTION This subspecies is restricted to north-eastern Madagascar from the Bemarivo River north of Sambava, south to an ill-defined area between latitudes 16°S and 18°S. Brown Lemurs north of the Bemarivo River, but south of the Manambato River, may represent intermediate forms between *E. f. albifrons* and *E. f. sanfordi*. The southern limit of the White-fronted Brown Lemur's range is also indistinct as it grades with the northern limits of *E. f. fulvus*.

BEHAVIOUR No studies have been undertaken of this subspecies in the wild. Scant behavioural information can only be pieced together from a variety of anecdotal observations. Group sizes of between 3-12 have been observed, although 5-7 seems to be average. They appear to be almost exclusively arboreal and feed on fruits, both ripe and unripe, and to a lesser extent leaves. In some areas the fruits of *Grewia* trees and various *Ficus* species are particularly relished. Nectar is also eaten when fruits are less evident, and these lemurs may as a result act as incidental pollinators.

Vocalisations are often heard around dawn and dusk and have also been recorded well into the night All other aspects of behaviour and ecology are likely to mirror those of other subspecies of Brown Lemur inhabiting eastern rainforest areas (see *E. f. fulvus* and *E. f. rufus*).

On the island of Nosy Mangabe this subspecies has been seen to be preyed on by the Madagascar Ground Boa *Acrantophis madagascariensis*. On the mainland its behaviour strongly suggests that the Fosa *Cryptoprocta ferox* is also a major predator. This subspecies also reacts adversely to the presence of the Madagascar Tree Boa *Sanzinia madagascariensis*.

POPULATION No figures for overall population or population densities are available.

THREATS Destruction of the rainforest in north-eastern Madagascar by slash-and-burn is particularly acute. This constitutes the primary threat to this lemur, which is also widely hunted in many parts of its range. It can be confirmed from just five protected areas, although its presence is highly likely in two or three others that have yet to be surveyed methodically.

VIEWING The island reserve of Nosy Mangabe in the Bay of Antongil, about 5km from Maroantsetra, is the best place to see this lemur. Here groups live in close proximity to the campsite and are often very approachable. Alternatively, the forests near Ambanizana on the Masoala Peninsula or near Befingitra in Anjanaharibe-Sud Special Reserve to the south-west of Andapa are rewarding localities, although these places are more difficult to reach. There is also a free-ranging population at Parc Ivoloina about 12km north-west of Toamasina – here excellent views are assured.

Figure 131. Infant White-fronted Brown Lemur.

Figure 132. Male White-fronted Brown Lemur, Nosy Mangabe.

Figure 133. Female White-fronted Brown Lemur carrying infant, Nosy Mangabe.

212

Red-fronted Brown Lemur *Eulemur fulvus rufus* (Audebert, 1799)

MEASUREMENTS Total length: 800-1,030mm. Head/body length: 350-480mm. Tail length: 450-550mm. Weight: 2-2.75kg.

DESCRIPTION Sexually dichromatic. There are also noticeable variations between individuals and between eastern and western populations. **Males**: (figs. 135 & 136) The upperparts and tail are grizzled grey to grey-brown, while the underparts are paler creamy-grey. The extremities of the limbs may be tinged with brown. The face, muzzle and mid-forehead are dark grey to black, with a thin dark line extending up and dividing the rich russet brown crown. There are prominent white eyebrow patches and distinctive bushy white cheeks and beard. The ears are noticeable but not prominent and the eyes are orange-red. **Females**: (figs. 134 & 137) There is considerable regional variation. The upperparts and tail are grizzled grey-brown to rufous-brown and even orange/cinnamon-brown (western populations tend to be more orange: those around Mitsinjo are very rich orange/cinnamon brown, with the head, cheeks and throat almost totally white), while the underparts are pale grey. The face and muzzle are dark grey to black, with a dark line extending up the forehead to the grizzled grey crown. There are large white eyebrow patches and creamy-coloured cheeks, although these are far less bushy than in males.

IDENTIFICATION A medium-sized lemur with a long tail it adopts a horizontal body posture and generally moves quadrupedally. In eastern rainforest areas this subspecies may be confused with the Red-bellied Lemur *Eulemur rubriventer*, but the latter is far more russet-red in colour and lacks the very pale cheeks and eyebrow patches. In western areas, the Red-fronted Brown Lemur cannot be mistaken as it is not sympatric with another *Eulemur* species.

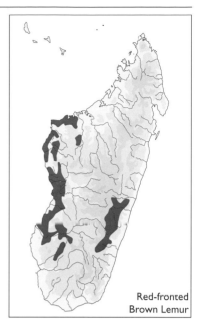

Red-fronted Brown Lemur

HABITAT Primary and secondary rainforest and dry deciduous forest.

DISTRIBUTION The Red-fronted Brown Lemur is now found in two distinct populations in the east and west of Madagascar. In the east it occurs from the Mangoro River south to the Manampatra River, including the western portion of the Andringitra Massif. However, the precise limits of this range remain ill-defined – there are possible records from Kalambatritra Special Reserve which lies outside the above range.

In the west, this subspecies is found from areas just south of the Fiherenana River near Toliara, north as far as the Betsiboka River.

BEHAVIOUR The Red-fronted Brown Lemur is cathemeral and almost totally arboreal, only occasionally descending to the ground, sometimes to lick and eat soil. Troops consist of several adult females and males together with younger animals at various stages of maturation. Group size averages eight to ten individuals, although it may vary between four and 18. In western dry deciduous forests aggregations of between 30 and 100 individuals have been reported feeding in a single large fruiting fig tree (*Ficus grevei*).

Group cohesiveness is maintained through regular grunts, contact calls and vocalisations, but no dominance hierarchies are apparent, although females generally take the lead. Home range size is heavily influenced by habitat and season. During the wet season in western dry forests it may be as small as one hectare and groups rarely move more than 125-150m during a single day. In the dry season when food is scarcer and more dispersed, home ranges expand to 12-15ha, with a corresponding increase in the daily distances travelled.

In eastern rainforests much larger territories up to 100ha, have been estimated, with approximate daily travel distances between 150 and 2,000m: this being correlated with seasonal food availability and in particular the density of fruiting trees. Neighbouring territories overlap extensively and the peaceful movement of individuals between social units has been observed. However, aggressive inter-group encounters may also occur and loud vocalisations help maintain group spatial separation to avoid such confrontations. Like other Brown Lemurs, this subspecies is known to be cathemeral.

Diet varies with habitat, although in both dry deciduous forests and rainforests it is dominated by fruit. *E. f. rufus* are important agents for seed dispersal. In western areas, leaves are also an important dietary element, along with pods, stems, flowers and sap. In eastern areas fruit is the mainstay, including introduced species like Chinese Guava *Psidium cattleyanum*. Leaves are less important, but fungi, insects and other invertebrates like millipedes are also eaten. Millipedes are first tossed from hand to hand to induce the secretion of toxins; these are then washed off with saliva before the millipede is wiped and dried on the lemur's tail – only then is it eaten.

Reproduction is seasonal: infants are generally born in September or early October after a gestation period of about 120 days. At birth they weigh around 75g. At first the infants are carried on the mother's belly and only after a month or so begin to move about and transfer to ride on her back. They are able to travel independently at around three months. Sexual maturity is not reached until two to three years.

There are numerous reports of *E. f. rufus* being predated by the Fosa *Cryptoprocta ferox*, in both rainforest and dry deciduous forest areas. Large raptors like Henst's Goshawk *Accipiter henstii* and the Madagascar Harrier-Hawk *Polyboroides radiatus* may also take this lemur.

POPULATION No overall population figures are available. In western dry deciduous forests this subspecies reaches population densities as high as 100 individuals/km^2 but in eastern rainforests this drops to only 25 individuals/km^2.

Figure 134. Female Red-fronted Brown Lemur, Ranomafana.

Figure 135. Male Red-fronted Brown Lemur, Ranomafana.

THREATS As with the majority of lemur species, habitat destruction is the main threat to the continued survival of this taxon. Fires are the principal danger in the west, while felling and slash-and-burn continue in the east. The Red-fronted Brown Lemur is known to occur in eight protected areas and two private reserves.

VIEWING In the eastern rainforests, Ranomafana National Park is the best place to see this lemur. The established trail network passes through the home ranges of several troops, most of which are now familiar with visitors, so good close views are possible. April and May are a particularly good time, as the Chinese Guava is in fruit, so groups tend to congregate close to *Belle Vue*.

The dry deciduous forests of Kirindy to the north-east of Morondava are probably the best places to see this subspecies in the west. An alternative is the Tsiombikibo forest near Mitsinjo. There is also an introduced population of Red-fronted Brown Lemurs at Berenty Private Reserve near Tolagnaro.

Figure 136. Male Red-fronted Brown Lemur, Kirindy.

Figure 137. Female Red-fronted Brown Lemur, Kirindy.

White-collared Brown Lemur *Eulemur fulvus albocollaris* Rumpler, 1975

White-collared
Brown Lemur

Malagasy: Varika

MEASUREMENTS Total length: 890-950mm. Head/body length: 390-400mm. Tail length: 500-550mm. Weight: 2-2.5kg.

DESCRIPTION Sexually dichromatic. A subspecies that is very similar to the Collared Brown Lemur *E. f. collaris* and whose taxonomic validity remains uncertain. The two can also be separated on the basis of chromosomal differences. **Males**: (fig. 138) Upperparts are grey-brown, with the tail and lower limbs being darker. The underparts are paler grey. The head and face are predominantly grey, with a dark grey crown that grades into paler grey down the neck and onto the shoulders. The cheeks and beard are white, bushy and pronounced. **Females**: (fig. 139) Upperparts and tail are brown-grey and noticeably more rufous than males. Underparts are a similar colour but slightly paler. The feet tend to be darker. The head and face are grey with a darker crown, while the cheeks are less bushy than males and similar in colour to the upperparts.

IDENTIFICATION A medium-sized lemur with a horizontal body posture. The known range of this subspecies does not overlap with any other *Eulemur* species, the range limits of this subspecies and the Collared Brown Lemur remain unclear and where the two meet confusion is certainly possible. Male White-collared Brown Lemurs differ from male *E. f. collaris* in having white rather than cream to browny-orange cheeks. Females of these two subspecies are very similar, although in *E. f. albocollaris* they may be slightly more rufous in colour.

HABITAT Lowland and mid-altitude eastern rainforest.

Figure 138. Male White-collared Brown Lemur.

218

Figure 139. Female White-collared Brown Lemur.

DISTRIBUTION The range of this lemur is the most restricted of any of the Brown Lemur subspecies. It is known to occur only in central south-eastern Madagascar in the thin band of rainforest between the Manampatra River to the north and the Mananara River to the south. However, at the very western edge of this range the picture is far from clear: Brown Lemurs observed on the eastern slopes of the Andringitra Massif appear to be intermediate in appearance between *E. f. albocollaris* and *E. f. collaris*, which may indicate that hybridisation occurs in this region.

BEHAVIOUR This lemur has yet to be studied in the wild, and there have been few anecdotal observations. Its behaviour and ecology are likely to be similar to those of other subspecies of Brown Lemur inhabiting rainforest areas (see *E. f. fulvus* and *E. f. rufus*).

POPULATION No figures for overall population or densities are available.

THREATS As with all lemurs, habitat destruction poses the main threat to this subspecies. This, coupled with its very limited range is cause for considerable concern. In some areas hunting has also been reported. The White-collared Brown Lemur occurs in a single protected area – the Manombo Special Reserve.

VIEWING Seeing this lemur in the wild is a considerable challenge, as its limited range is difficult to reach. The best location to try is probably the Manombo Special Reserve, south of Farafangana on *Route Nationale 12*. Access can be difficult in the wet season when local rivers swell and cut off portions of forest, and visits should be restricted to the drier seasons of the year. Alternatively, the forests to the west of Vondrozo, either side of *Route Nationale 27*, offer a reasonable chance of success.

Collared Brown Lemur *Eulemur fulvus collaris* (E. Geoffroy, 1812)

Malagasy: Varika

MEASUREMENTS Total length: 890-950mm. Head/body length: 390-400mm. Tail length: 500-550mm. Weight: 2.25-2.5kg.

DESCRIPTION Sexually dichromatic, although not as markedly as other *E. fulvus* subspecies, with the exception of *E. fulvus fulvus*. **Males**: (fig. 140) The upperparts are brownish-grey, with the tail being darker. The underparts are pale brown-grey. The muzzle, forehead and crown are dark slate-grey to black, this colour extending and gradually becoming paler down the neck. There is a dark stripe continuing down the spinal ridge. There are pale creamy-grey eyebrow patches, although these vary considerably between individuals. The cheeks and beard are thick, bushy and cream to rufous-brown in colour. **Females**: (fig. 141) Upperparts are browner than in males and sometimes rufous, while the underparts are pale creamy-grey. The head and face are grey, with a faint grey stripe extending over the crown. The cheeks are rufous-brown, but considerably shorter and less bushy than in the males. The eyes of both sexes are orange-red.

IDENTIFICATION A medium-sized lemur that adopts a horizontal body posture and moves quadrupedally. The range of this subspecies does not overlap with any other *Eulemur* species so confusion is unlikely. However, its northern limit abuts the range of White-collared Brown Lemur *E. f. albocollaris*, which is very similar. Male Collared Brown Lemurs differ in having cream to browny-orange rather than white cheeks. The females of these subspecies are often very difficult to differentiate – in *E. f. collaris* they may be more brown than rufous in colour.

HABITAT Lowland and mid-altitude primary and secondary rainforest.

Collared Brown Lemur

DISTRIBUTION The Collared Brown Lemur is restricted to the humid forests of extreme south-eastern Madagascar, from the Mananara River south to the area north of Tolagnaro. The western limits of this range have yet to be firmly established, and at its northern limits the boundaries with the range of *E. f. albocollaris* still need to be clarified. It is possible that *E .f. collaris* and *E. f. albocollaris* interbreed on the eastern slopes of the Andringitra Massif.

BEHAVIOUR No studies have taken place in the wild, so the behaviour and ecology of this subspecies remain unknown. It seems likely it shows close similarities to those of other rainforest subspecies of Brown Lemur (see *E. f. fulvus* and *E. f. rufus*).

POPULATION No population estimates or densities are available for this subspecies.

THREATS In common with the majority of lemurs, habitat destruction, together with hunting and trapping, constitute the major threats to the Collared Brown Lemur. It is known to occur naturally in only one protected area – the rainforest sector (Parcel 1) of Andohahela Nature Reserve. However, this subspecies has also been introduced into two private reserves, Berenty and St. Luce.

VIEWING The St. Luce Private Reserve, north of Tolagnaro, is perhaps the easiest place to see the Collared Brown Lemur. This reserve is administered by the de Heaulme family and visits can be arranged through their hotels in Tolagnaro. There is also a small population at Berenty Private Reserve, but these have probably hybridised with the Red-fronted Brown Lemurs that have also been introduced there. Differentiating these subspecies at Berenty can be problematic. Parcel 1, the rainforest area of Andohahela Nature Reserve, is a good place to see truly wild populations, and this area may become more accessible as ecotourism is developed in the reserve.

Figure 140. Male Collared Brown Lemur.

Figure 141. Female Collared Brown Lemur.

BLACK LEMUR *Eulemur macaco* (Linnaeus, 1766)

Two subspecies of Black Lemur are recognised: the nominate race, simply known as the Black Lemur *E. m. macaco* and the Blue-eyed Black Lemur *E. m. flavifrons*. They are the most extreme sexually dichromatic Malagasy prosimians.

    In the past, some authors have described Brown Lemurs *E. fulvus* as subspecies of the Black Lemur, but genetic and morphological evidence indicates that the two are valid species and the taxonomic arrangement given here is now widely accepted.

Subspecies

Black Lemur *Eulemur macaco macaco* (Linnaeus, 1766)

Malagasy: Ankomba, Komba.

Black Lemur

MEASUREMENTS Total length: 900-1,100mm. Head/body length: 390-450mm. Tail length: 510-650mm. Weight: 2-2.5kg.

DESCRIPTION Sexually dichromatic. **Males**: (fig. 142) The pelage varies from very dark chocolate-brown to almost black (in bright sunlight it may actually appear reddish-brown to dark chocolate-brown). The ears are lavishly tufted with long black hair and the eyes are yellow-orange to deep orange. **Females**: (fig. 143) The upperparts are highly variable from golden-brown to mid-brown or rich chestnut-brown, often becoming slightly paler on the flanks and limbs. The tail is often darker rich chestnut-brown, particularly towards the tip. The feet are slate-grey to dark brownish-black. The throat and chin are pale brown, and gradually change to pale grey-brown and even off-white on the belly. The face and muzzle are dark grey, while the top of the head and temples are pale grey. The ears are extravagantly tufted with long white hair which extends around the cheeks and may gradually change to an orangy-chestnut beard. The eyes are yellow-orange to deep orange.

IDENTIFICATION A medium-sized lemur with a long tail and highly distinctive coloration; it adopts a horizontal body posture. Throughout much of its range, *E. m. macaco* is allopatric with congeners and so is impossible to confuse with any other species. However, at the southern and eastern limits of its range (Manongarivo and Tsaratanana Massifs) this subspecies is sympatric with Common Brown Lemur *E. f. fulvus* and possibly Red-bellied Lemur *Eulemur rubriventer*. Here the distinctive pelage and extreme sexual dichromatism of the Black Lemur should again make confusion virtually impossible.

HABITAT Moist Sambirano forests and similar rainforests on offshore islands, together with some associated modified secondary habitats, including timber, coffee and cashew nut plantations.

DISTRIBUTION The Black Lemur is restricted to the Sambirano region and adjacent offshore islands in north-west Madagascar. Its northern limit is the Mahavavy River and east to the vicinity of Ambilobe, while the southern limit appears to be the Sambirano and Manongarivo Rivers. South of the Sambirano River distributional limits become unclear as *E. m. macaco* is known to hybridise with *E. m. flavifrons*. The extent of this integration has yet to be clarified. To the west the Black Lemur's range includes the Ampasindava Peninsula and the islands of Nosy Be and Nosy Komba. To the east the limits are again unclear, but *E. m. macaco* certainly reaches the Tsaratanana Massif.

BEHAVIOUR Black Lemurs live in groups of between 2-15 individuals, although 7-10 would appear to be normal. Larger groups tend to be associated with modified rather than primary habitats. Group composition is similar to that of other gregarious *Eulemur* species: there are several adult males and females in roughly equal numbers, together with dependent offspring. The activities of the group are dictated by a dominant female, and group cohesiveness is maintained by regular guttural grunts and contact calls from all members. Home ranges average around five to six hectares, but there is considerable overlap between the ranges of neighbouring groups. During daylight these groups remain separate, but may come together after dark.

    Black Lemurs are typical amongst congeners in that they are cathemeral. Daytime activity is concentrated around early morning and late afternoon, while the extent of nocturnal activity may vary with the seasons or the lunar cycle. During the middle of the dry season (June–July) populations on the island of Nosy Be are completely inactive at night and the mornings are spent sunning at the top of the canopy. This contrasts markedly with the end of the dry period (October–December) when nocturnal activity predominates coinciding with the fruiting of favoured large tree species such as Ramy *Canarium madagascariensis*.

    Studies of mainland populations indicate that the phase of the moon is a major influence on activity patterns – when the moon is waxing, full nocturnal activity reaches its peak. This is almost certainly related to the associated increase in light and the lemur's improved night-time visual acuity. In contrast to the Black Lemurs on Nosy Be, nocturnal activity is known to occur year-round, but diurnal activity reaches its peak during the early part of the wet season (December–January).

    Foraging is concentrated in the middle and upper levels of the canopy. The diet is varied, but is dominated by ripe fruit, together with flowers, leaves, fungi and occasionally invertebrates like millipedes. In the dry season nectar from flowers is also an important element. In disturbed and degraded habitats Black Lemurs are known to descend to the ground and forage in the leaf-litter for fallen fruit and fungi, and have even been seen eating soil. During the day Black Lemurs tend to spend longer feeding in the understorey than the canopy and move from one resource patch to the next with greater regularity. At night, however, foraging efforts are concentrated in the canopy (when potential daytime avian predators are not active) and the lemurs travel less.

Figure 142. Male Black Lemur, Lokobe.

Figure 143. Female Black Lemur, Nosy Komba.

Mating occurs in late April and May, with females giving birth between late August and early October, after a gestation period of around 125 days; a single offspring is the norm. Some young infants have also been observed in December, which suggests the birth season may be more protracted in some areas. Infanticide has also been observed in this subspecies: one female killing the infant of another and consequently assuming dominant status within that group. This is thought to be extremely rare and was observed in modified habitat and under stressful circumstances for the troop in question.

E. m. macaco reacts adversely to the presence of large raptors like the Madagascar Harrier-Hawk *Polyboroides radiatus*. The Madagascar Ground Boa *Acrantophis madagascariensis* is known to predate this subspecies.

POPULATION Population densities of 200/km^2 have been calculated in the past, but these are now known to be gross over-estimates. This subspecies is probably far more seriously threatened than has previously been reported, the total population possibly not exceeding 10,000 individuals.

THREATS The remaining native forests of the north-west are threatened by continued slash-and-burn agriculture. *E. m. macaco* appears able to survive in secondary and severely modified habitats, but probably reaches higher densities in undisturbed forests, so habitat destruction remains its principal threat. In marginal areas it may be killed for raiding crops and it is also hunted (using noose traps) towards the east of its range (Tsaratanana). The Black Lemur is known to occur in three protected areas.

VIEWING One of the most accessible sites to see the Black Lemur is in the buffer zone on the north-east edge of Lokobe Nature Reserve on the island of Nosy Be. From the village of Ambatozavavy take a pirogue with a local guide the short distance around the coast to the village of Ampasipohy. The modified forest area (secondary growth and some crops like vanilla) where troops of Black Lemurs can be easily seen is just a short walk inland. This is also a good place to see Grey-backed Sportive Lemur *Lepilemur dorsalis*. From Ampasipohy it is also possible to walk to the village of Ambalahonko (south-east of Lokobe Nature Reserve) where there are troops of Black Lemurs being studied by local Malagasy training to be guides as part of the community research project initiated by the Black Lemur Forest Project based at Ampasindava.

Alternatively, the neighbouring island of Nosy Komba is very good for Black Lemurs. Here, however, groups are totally habituated (and protected by local taboo or *fady*) and live in highly degraded forest on the edge of the main village. The local people sell bananas to tourists to feed the lemurs. These animals are certainly not shy and will immediately leap onto a visitor's shoulders in the scramble to be first to the free meal.

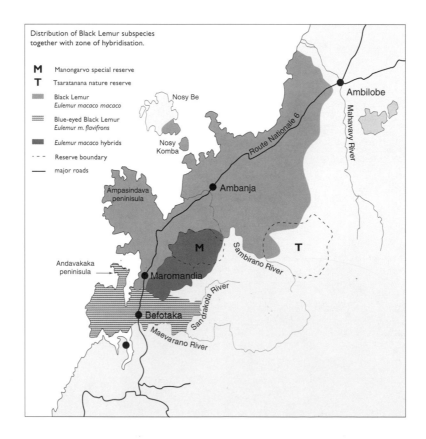

Figure 144. Female and male Black Lemur, Lokobe.

Blue-eyed Black Lemur *Eulemur macaco flavifrons* (Gray, 1867)

Other name: Sclater's Black Lemur
Malagasy: Males – Ankomba Joby. Females – Ankomba Mena.

MEASUREMENTS Total length: 900-1,100mm. Head/body length: 390-450mm. Tail length: 510-650mm. Weight: 2-2.5kg.

DESCRIPTION Sexually dichromatic. As with *E. m. macaco*, the pelage colour differences between the sexes are very marked. **Males**: (fig. 145) The pelage is normally completely black, although there may be dark brown tinges that are apparent. It is shorter in length than in *E. m. macaco* and generally has a softer appearance. There is a distinct ridge of hair on the forehead, which forms a short crest. Unlike *E. m. macaco*, there are no ear-tufts and the eyes are characteristic blue-grey to blue. **Females**: (fig. 146) The upperparts and tail are pale rufous-tan, sometimes approaching rufous-grey, while the underparts are creamy-white to grey. The hands and feet are dark grey. The crown is rufous-tan, while the face is pale grey around the eyes, which darkens to slate-grey around the muzzle and black around the nose. There are no ear-tufts, but there is a short grey-white beard which may have rufous tinges. The eyes are blue-grey to blue. In overall appearance, females of this subspecies are noticeably paler than females of *E. m. macaco*.

IDENTIFICATION A medium-sized lemur with a long tail and highly distinctive coloration; it adopts a horizontal body posture and moves quadrupedally. Throughout its limited range, *E. m. flavifrons* is allopatric with all other members of the genus *Eulemur* and should not be confused with any other species. Other than human beings, this is the only blue-eyed primate.

HABITAT Mixed moist, gallery and dry deciduous forests, secondary forests and plantations.

Blue-eyed Black Lemur

227

Figure 145. Male Blue-eyed Black Lemur.

Figure 146. Female Blue-eyed Black Lemur.

DISTRIBUTION This subspecies is restricted to an area just south of the Sambirano region in north-west Madagascar. Its northern limit appears to be the Andranomalaza River, while its southern limit is the Maevarano river. To the east its range appears to be bounded by the Sandrakota River. Within the southern limits of the Sambirano region (north of the Andranomalaza River, but south of the Manongarivo River, including part of the Manongarivo Special Reserve), *E. m. flavifrons* and *E. m. macaco* are known to hybridise; the resulting animals are similar in appearance to pure-bred *E. m. flavifrons*, but have pale brown eyes.

BEHAVIOUR This subspecies has yet to be studied in the wild so little is known about its behaviour and ecology. Group sizes ranging from six to ten individuals have been reported. In other major respects the behaviour and ecology of the Blue-eyed Black Lemur probably resembles that of the nominate race.

POPULATION Although no calculated figures for overall population size or density are available, it is suspected that less than 1,000 individuals survive in the wild. Throughout most of its very limited range this subspecies has been reported as being patchily distributed.

THREATS The Blue-eyed Black Lemur suffers from the destruction of its habitat. It is also hunted in many parts of its very restricted range. Pure-bred forms of *E. m. flavifrons* are not known to occur in any protected area, although a national park within its range has been proposed. *E. m. flavifrons*/*E. m. macaco* hybrids are found in the southern part of the Manongarivo Special Reserve.

VIEWING Because of its very limited and rather inaccessible range, the Blue-eyed Black Lemur is a difficult subspecies to see in the wild. Efforts are best concentrated in the forests to the south-west of Maromandia, between the main road and the coast in the vicinity of Marovato-Sud. This area, together with the adjoining Andavakaka Peninsula, is the focus of the newly proposed national park which will protect around 380km² of dry forests and mangroves where the largest populations of *E. m. flavifrons* live.

Figure 147. Infant Blue-eyed Black Lemur.

RUFFED LEMUR genus *Varecia* Gray, 1863

Ruffed lemurs are confined to eastern rainforest regions and appear to be uncommon to rare throughout their ranges. They are the largest extant members of the family Lemuridae and the most frugivorous. Their large size and distinctive coloration should prevent confusion with all other lemur taxa.

RUFFED LEMUR *Varecia variegata* (Kerr, 1792)

Currently a single species of ruffed lemur is recognised, *Varecia variegata*, which is divided into two visually distinct subspecies, the Black-and-white Ruffed Lemur *V. v. variegata* and the Red Ruffed Lemur *V. v. rubra*. However, recent systematic research (based on genetic analysis) strongly suggests that these two forms merit reclassification as distinct species with additional differentiation at the subspecific level.

Subspecies

Black-and-white Ruffed Lemur *Varecia variegata variegata* (Kerr, 1792)

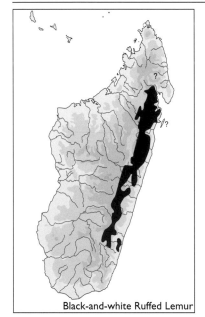

Black-and-white Ruffed Lemur

Malagasy: Varikandra, Vari, Varikandana, Varijatsy

MEASUREMENTS Total length: 1,100-1,200mm. Head/body length: 500-550mm. Tail length: 600-650mm. Weight: 3-4.5kg.

DESCRIPTION The pelage is long and luxuriant, and predominantly consists of different-sized patches of black and white. In general, the tail, hands and feet, inner surfaces of the limbs, shoulders, face, long muzzle and top of the head are black, while the back, flanks, rump and majority of the hindlimbs are white. The ears are white and lavishly tufted, this long hair forming a continuous white 'ruff' around the cheeks and under the chin (fig. 148). However, the overall pattern varies considerably throughout the species's range and as many as four distinct varieties have been recognised, some even being proposed as 'subspecies' (e.g. *variegata, editorum, subcincta*). Towards the south of the range the pelage is mostly white, large black patches only occurring on the shoulders and sometimes the tops of the thighs. At the northern extremity of the range, individuals tend to appear darker as the black areas dominate, large white patches being restricted to the forearms, saddle and rear surface of the hindquarters.

IDENTIFICATION This subspecies cannot be confused with any other lemur. The utterly distinctive black-and-white coloration distinguishes it from all sympatric quadrupedal species like Brown Lemur *Eulemur fulvus* and Red-bellied Lemur *E. rubriventer*. Its long tail and horizontal body posture distinguish it from the black and white Indri *Indri indri*.

HABITAT Primary and secondary lowland and mid-altitude rainforest.

DISTRIBUTION The distribution of this subspecies is poorly known, particularly at the northern limits. Its approximate range extends from the Antainambalana River to the north-west of Maroantsetra south to the Mananara River south of Farafangana, and includes the Andringitra Massif. There is also an introduced population on the island of Nosy Mangabe in the Bay of Antongil. There are reported sightings from near Antsahaberaoka towards the north of the Marojejy Massif, which represent a considerable northerly extension to the known range. However, recent surveys of Marojejy and Anjanaharibe-Sud just to the south-west have not recorded *Varecia*. This subspecies apparently occurs patchily and at relatively low densities throughout its range.

BEHAVIOUR The Black-and-white Ruffed Lemur is almost exclusively diurnal, being most active early in the morning and in the late afternoon/evening, although occasional bouts of nocturnal activity have also been reported. The diet consists primarily of fruit and nectar, supplemented with small amounts of leaves and seeds. Nectar is only available for short periods each year but constitutes the dominant food source when flowers are in bloom. Three flower species appear particularly important, *Ravenala madagascariensis*, *Labramia costata* and *Mammea* sp. These Lemurs use their long snouts and tongues to reach deep inside the flowers and lick the nectar. In doing so, they do not destroy the inflorescence, but collect pollen on their muzzles and fur and transport this between flowers on different plants.

The size and structure of *Ravenala* inflorescence, coupled with the Ruffed Lemur's selectivity and method of feeding, strongly suggest that *Varecia* is the primary pollinator of *Ravenala* and that this pollination system has co-evolved. Further weight is added to this theory as the distributions of *Varecia* and *Ravenela* in eastern Madagascar mirror one another very closely.

Group size and social system appear to vary considerably. In the mainland rainforests of the south-east (Ranomafana), single females and single males have been observed as cohesive pairs occupying very large home ranges (up to 200ha) and ranging up to one kilometre each day. However, at the same site longer-term studies have revealed mean group sizes of between five and seven individuals. Within these, males appear to defend the group's territory. Elsewhere group sizes of between two and five individuals have been reported. On the island of Nosy Mangabe group size appears to be much larger – 8-16 animals – these consisting of several adult

Figure 148. Black-and-white Ruffed Lemur, Nosy Mangabe.

females and males together with subadults and juveniles. Although both females and males in these larger groups (communities) share home ranges, unlike at Ranomafana National Park only the females defend them from intrusion by neighbouring groups.

Black-and-white Ruffed Lemurs are highly vocal, their raucous barking calls allowing groups to communicate with one another and maintain spacing in the forest. Ano-genital scent-marking is also an important means of communication. Within a group, the strongest social bonds develop between females, while those between males are much weaker. On Nosy Mangabe, group composition and ranging behaviour is seasonally variable: during the warm wet season (November–April) females tend to range widely either singly or in groups of up to six, while in the cool dry season (May–October) smaller, more stable subgroups occupy concentrated areas. At Ranomafana National Park social organisation appears to be much less fluid: here Black-and-white Ruffed Lemurs live in discrete multi-male, multi-female groups which do not vary seasonally.

Varecia reproduces seasonally. Mating occurs between May and July, with most offspring being born in September and October, after a gestation period of 90-102 days. Twins appear to be the norm but litter sizes of up to four have been reported in captivity. Unlike the majority of other lemur species, Ruffed Lemurs give birth in well-concealed nests constructed of twigs, leaves and vines, generally 10-20m above the ground. Between one and two weeks the mother begins to move her young; initially they are carried in her mouth and later 'parked' in trees, sometimes for several hours, allowing her to forage more efficiently during this high-cost period of lactation.

Infant *Varecia* develop more rapidly than many other lemur species. At around three weeks of age they are capable of following their mother, the two regularly exchanging contact calls. By four months they are as active and mobile as adults. Infant mortality is very high, around 65% of offspring failing to reach three months of age and many dying from accidental falls and related injuries.

POPULATION No overall population figures are available. This subspecies appears to occur at relatively low densities at the majority of mainland localities: at Ranomafana a figure around 5.5 individuals/km^2 has been calculated. On Nosy Mangabe densities are much higher, estimates varying between 20 and 30 individuals/km^2.

THREATS Ruffed Lemurs are heavily hunted for food throughout their range and are also collected as pets, both of which constitute major threats. Nonetheless, as with all other lemur species, habitat destruction remains the primary cause for concern. *Varecia* is also susceptible to habitat disturbance to a far greater degree than most other lemur taxa. Black-and-white Ruffed Lemurs are known to occur in at least ten protected areas in eastern Madagascar and possibly two more that have not been thoroughly surveyed.

VIEWING The only locality where Black-and-white Ruffed Lemurs can be readily seen is Nosy Mangabe Special Reserve, an island 5km off Maroantstra in the Bay of Antongil. The island can easily be reached by boat and a number of the hotels in Maroantsetra can arrange this. Guides are available from the Masoala Project offices in the town. It is necessary to camp and there are only basic facilities. There is an extensive network of trails, although the slopes are often steep and slippery. However, groups of Black-and-white Ruffed Lemurs are often encountered only short distances from the campsite along the path running parallel to the beach.

At rainforest reserves on the mainland this lemur tends to be more difficult to see as it occurs at lower densities and is generally very shy. The two most likely sites are Ranomafana and Mantadia National Parks. Here V. v. variegata is quite often heard, but less often seen. A considerable amount of patience, strenuous hiking and luck are usually needed to catch a glimpse.

Figure 149. Black-and-white Ruffed Lemur, 'suspension feeding' on flowers and nectar.

Figure 150. Red Ruffed Lemur, Masoala Peninsula.

Red Ruffed Lemur *Varecia variegata rubra* (E. Geoffroy, 1812)

Malagasy: Varimena, Varignena

MEASUREMENTS Total length: 1,100-1,200mm. Head/body length: 500-550mm. Tail length: 600-650mm. Weight: 3-4.5kg.

DESCRIPTION The Red Ruffed Lemur is very similar in size and shape to the Black-and-white Ruffed Lemur, however as its name suggests its coloration is dramatically different. The pelage is dense and luxuriant. The majority of the upperparts, legs and belly are deep chestnut-red, as are the distinctive ear-tufts and ruff around the cheeks and throat (fig. 151). The inside of the limbs, feet, tail, top of head, face and muzzle are black (fig. 150). There is a large white patch over the back of the neck, sometimes extending onto the shoulders. In some individuals there are further white areas around the wrists and ankles, rump and muzzle. As with its congener, *V. v. variegata*, these pelage differences show a degree of correlation with locality, although once again insufficient information is available to draw any taxonomic conclusions.

Red Ruffed Lemur

IDENTIFICATION This subspecies occurs sympatrically with only one other diurnal quadrupedal species, the White-fronted Brown Lemur *Eulemur fulvus albifrons*. The larger size and very distinctive coloration of the Red Ruffed Lemur should prevent confusion with this or any other species.

HABITAT Primary and secondary rainforest.

DISTRIBUTION This subspecies appears to be restricted to the Masoala Peninsula, to the east of Maroantsetra in north-east Madagascar. Its western limit may be the Antainambalana River, which separates its range from *V. v. variegata*, although it is known to be very scarce in this region. The northern limit of the range is poorly under stood, but is generally thought to extend as far as the Ankavanana River. However, there are reported sightings in the forests of Besariaka, south-west of Andapa, where this subspecies may be sympatric with Indri *Indri indri* and Silky Sifaka *Propithecus diadema candidus*. This represents a northerly extension to the Red Ruffed Lemur's previously recorded range.

BEHAVIOUR Little is known of the behaviour and ecology of the Red Ruffed Lemur as few field studies have so far been undertaken. What research has taken place suggests there is considerable variation in social structure, organisation and home range size of this subspecies from one locality to the next.

In the Ambatonakolahy Forest area of the Masoala Peninsula this subspecies lives in groups of five to six adult animals, which occupy home ranges of around 25ha, although there appears to be a core area that the lemurs spend the majority of time in, which constitutes around 10% of the overall home range. The position of home ranges shows close correlation to the location of the largest fruiting trees within the forest. Daily travel distances up to 1,200m have been recorded. During the cool wet season groups tend to range less than at other times, but may fragment into subunits that utilise different core areas within the home range.

Elsewhere on the peninsula (the Andranobe River region) it has been suggested that Red Ruffed Lemurs live in large 'communities' of between 18 and 32 animals that occupy total home ranges of around 60ha. The number of animals in, and structure of, these communities appears to vary seasonally. Males reside year-round within the core area of their home range, while females remain within the core area during the cool wet season (May–October), but range far more widely through the communal territory during the hot rainy season (November–April).

The Red Ruffed Lemur is highly vocal. An individual's raucous calls are answered by animals from neighbouring groups very promptly. Together with scent-marking, this is an efficient way of establishing territories and avoiding direct confrontations.

Red Ruffed Lemurs are primarily frugivorous: around 75% of their diet is fruit. The remainder is made up of leaves, nectar and to a lesser extent flowers. A wide variety of plant species are utilised throughout the year: over 40 species have been recorded in the diet, although a marked preference is shown for less than ten of these. For instance, at one study site, Ambatonakolahy, two members of the family Moraceae – Ammotana *Ficus lutea* and Nonosay *F. reflexa* – accounted for nearly 60% of all fruit-eating observations.

In similar fashion to *V. v. variegata*, female Red Ruffed Lemurs construct a nest of twigs, leaves and mosses and give birth to litters of between one and five infants, although twins and triplets are most common. Once again, the young are 'parked' in the nest during the early stages of development. At 20 to 25 days of age they are capable of leaving the nest and moving around independently. Most other aspects of the behaviour and ecology of this subspecies are probably similar to those of *V. v. variegata*.

POPULATION No population figures are available. The Red Ruffed Lemur only occurs at low densities and appears to be rare throughout its limited range. The highest densities probably occur on the western side of the Masoala Peninsula, where estimates of 20-25 individuals/km² have been proposed. In some of the more heavily disturbed areas on the Masoala Peninsula this animal is already known to have disappeared.

THREATS The Masoala Peninsula supports the largest undisturbed tracts of rainforest left on Madagascar, yet forest destruction still continues at an alarming rate and this remains the principal threat to *V. v .rubra*. This subspecies is particularly susceptible to habitat disturbance, which is linked to its high dependence on large fruiting trees in primary forest. The animals are also widely hunted for food and collected as pets. The Red Ruffed Lemur occurs in a single protected area, Masoala National Park.

Figure 151. Red Ruffed Lemur, Masoala Peninsula.

VIEWING This is a difficult lemur to see in the wild. It is only found on the Masoala Peninsula, which can be awkward to reach. It is possible to arrange a boat trip to Andranobe or Ambanizana, about half-way down the peninsula, through some of the hotels in Maroantsetra. It is necessary to camp and all supplies must be taken. There are trails leading into the forest, although the terrain is steep and tough: Red Ruffed Lemurs will certainly be heard, although finding them requires considerable effort, patience and some luck. A minimum stay of three days is recommended to increase the chances of success.

It is also possible to walk into the peninsula from Maroantsetra, but this is arduous and requires considerable planning. When visiting Masoala National Park, the services of local guides from the Association des Guides Ecotouristiques de Maroantsetra (AGEM) should always be sought.

Figure 152. Eastern Avahi, Ranomafana.

Avahis, Sifakas and Indri
Family Indriidae

This family contains six species arranged between three genera. Two genera *Indri* and *Propithecus*, are diurnal and the largest extant Malagasy prosimians; and *Avahi*, which is considerably smaller in size, is nocturnal. All indriids are saltatory: they are characterised by long powerful hindlimbs (around 35% longer than their forelimbs) and prefer to cling to, and leap between, vertical trunks and branches. From finer branches they may also hang, using both their arms and legs. The hands and feet are narrow and elongate and the thumb and big toe are both slightly opposed to the other digits, providing good grasping ability. The palms and soles are padded. Females have a single pair of mammary glands on the upper chest and males possess a penis bone. Indriids have fewer teeth than other primates (30) and are strictly vegetarian.

AVAHIS OR WOOLLY LEMURS genus *Avahi* Jourdan, 1834

This is the only nocturnal genus within the family Indriidae and contains two species with distinct ranges – the Eastern Avahi *Avahi laniger* and the Western Avahi *A. occidentalis*. Previously these two forms were considered to be conspecific. Due to their small size and nocturnal habits, members of this genus cannot be mistaken for any other indriid.

The generic name *Avahi* is derived from one of the calls given by these species – *ava hee* – and is often also used as the vernacular name as it is here.

EASTERN AVAHI *Avahi laniger* (Gmelin, 1788)

Other name: Eastern Woolly Lemur
Malagasy: Avahy, Fotsifaka, Fotsife, Ampongy

MEASUREMENTS Total length: 590-675mm. Head/body length: 250-295mm. Tail length: 315-370mm. Weight: 900-1,200g (males), 1,000-1,300g (females).

DESCRIPTION The pelage is thick and woolly in texture. Upperparts are greyish-brown with reddish tinges, becoming paler towards the rump. The tail is noticeably more rufous than the body. The chest and underparts are pale grey, while the insides of the thighs have distinctive white patches. The muzzle is short and dark, and the head is rounded with small hidden ears. The facial disc is brown and there may be lighter cream eyebrow patches. The eyes are large and the overall effect of these features gives *Avahi* a rather 'owl-like' appearance (fig. 152).

IDENTIFICATION This is a medium-small lemur that adopts a vertical posture. Confusion between *Avahi laniger* and rainforest *Lepilemur* species is possible, as they are of similar size and also cling vertically. However, *Avahi* is generally slightly larger and has concealed ears, whereas those of *Lepilemur* are more prominent. *Avahi* also has characteristic and very noticeable white thigh patches, which *Lepilemur* species lack. Confusion with the Greater Dwarf Lemur *Cheirogaleus major* should not occur as this species is smaller and moves horizontally.

HABITAT Primary and secondary rainforest.

DISTRIBUTION The Eastern Avahi is found throughout the eastern rainforest belt, from around Sambava in the north (Marojejy Massif) to near Tolagnaro in the south (Andohahela Massif). A remnant population also remains in a fragment of native ever-green forest in the central highlands at Ambohitantely Special Reserve, 130km north-west of Antananarivo.

Eastern Avahi

Avahi has also been reported from the deciduous forests of Ankarana towards the island's northern tip. Which species this population represents has yet to be clarified. This record is farther north than the known range of *A. laniger* and, if validated, suggests the species may also occur at intermediate localities like the Tsaratanana Massif, although no authentic records yet exist.

BEHAVIOUR The Eastern Avahi is nocturnal and lives in monogamous pairs. Small groups of up to five have been reported and probably consist of an adult pair plus their offspring and other related animals. The day is spent concealed in thick foliage three to four metres off the ground, usually sitting on a branch and lodged against a vertical trunk. Individuals occasionally rest alone, but more usually the pair sleeps tightly huddled together (fig. 153).

Activity begins just after dusk, the pair normally spending some time grooming themselves or each other before moving off to forage. Most foraging takes place alone and during the first and last two hours of darkness, and although it may continue for short periods in-between, the majority of the intervening time is spent resting and grooming when the pair re-unite. When apart the pair keep in close contact with regular high-pitched whistles which enable them to locate each other. They return to their chosen sleep site just before first light.

A pair occupies a home range of between one and two hectares. This territory is aggressively defended by calling (often the distinctive *ava hee* call) and then chasing away intruders. Eastern Avahis do not appear to range widely, on average travelling around 300-500m per night. Their diet consists almost exclusively of young and mature leaves from a variety of different tree species, and only small quantities of fruit and flowers are very occasionally taken. In many areas *Avahi* probably competes directly with *Lepilemur* for food but *Avahi* tend to concentrate on better-quality vegetation, restricting *Lepilemur* to leaves of lower nutritional value.

A single infant is born in August or September. This is initially carried on the mother's underside, but when older prefers to ride on her back. Females are probably able to produce offspring each year.

POPULATION Overall population figures are unknown. Some short-term studies suggest this species can attain quite high population densities – at Analamazaotra Special Reserve (mid-altitude central-eastern rainforest) figures of between 72 and 100 individuals/km^2 have been estimated. However, the species may not be so abundant throughout its entire geographic range.

THREATS The principal threat to this species is the continuing destruction of its habitat. Being small and nocturnal, it suffers considerably less hunting pressure than other indriids, but is nonetheless trapped for food in some areas. The Eastern Avahi occurs within at least 12 and possibly 16 protected areas.

VIEWING The most accessible place to see the Eastern Avahi is Analamazaotra Special Reserve next to the village of Andasibe (Perinet), 140km east of Antananarivo. Here, a night walk along the road between the village and park entrance often produces several sightings (and views of other nocturnal lemurs as well). Along the main ridge of the reserve proper and around *Lac Vert* are alternative productive areas. Another equally good venue is Ranomafana National Park. Local guides at both reserves are adept at finding Eastern Avahis resting at the daytime sleep sites. With care they can often be approached quite close.

Figure 153. Eastern Avahis, Ranomafana.

WESTERN AVAHI *Avahi occidentalis* Lorenz, 1898

Other name: Western Woolly Lemur
Malagasy: Tsarafangitra, Fotsife

MEASUREMENTS Total length: 560-650. Head/body length: 250-285. Tail length: 310-365. Weight: 700-900g.

DESCRIPTION The pelage is dense and woolly. Upperparts are light to medium-grey with tinges of sandy-brown or olive-brown that fade towards the rear. The tail is greyish with increasing reddish-ochre tinges towards the tip. The underparts and throat are pale grey. The face is rounded and pale with a dark muzzle. The ears are small and unobtrusive (fig. 154). In overall appearance this species is very similar to its eastern relative, but is smaller in size and much paler.

IDENTIFICATION A medium-small lemur invariably seen clinging vertically to trunks or branches. The only species likely to cause confusion are *Lepilemur*, which are of similar size and posture. *Avahi* has a round face and almost totally concealed ears, while *Lepilemur* species have very noticeable ears and a more pointed snout. Confusion between the Western Avahi and Fat-tailed Dwarf Lemur *Cheirogaleus medius* is very unlikely as this species moves horizontally and is much smaller.

Western Avahi

Figure 154. Western Avahi, Ampijoroa.

HABITAT Dry deciduous forests and moist forests in the Sambirano region.

DISTRIBUTION The Western Avahi seems to be restricted to western and north-western Madagascar, although the precise limits of the range are unclear. The area north of the Betsiboka River from Ankarafantsika Nature Reserve to the Bay of Narinda appears to be its stronghold. Apparently isolated populations have also been found further north around Manongarivo Special Reserve in the Sambirano region, and to the south in the Tsingy de Bemaraha National Park. Recent reports of *Avahi* from the dry forests of Ankarana in the extreme north could represent another isolated population of *A. occidentalis.*

BEHAVIOUR This species has only been studied in the dry deciduous forests of Ankarafantsika. Here the Western Avahi appears to live in small family groups of two to four individuals, normally consisting of an adult pair with their dependent offspring, which may be up to two years of age (groups of five individuals have been seen, but their composition remains unclear). These family units occupy home ranges of around two hectares, which contain a central core area that is used predominantly. There is a small degree of overlap between the ranges of adjacent social units, but territories are defended with a piercing *ava hee* call.

A. *occidentalis* is almost exclusively nocturnal. The family unit spend the day

Figure 155. Female Western Avahi with infant, Ampijoroa.

resting huddled close together in dense clumps of foliage at heights 3-13m above the ground. Each family has several favoured sleep sites within its range and may move during the day if the one initially chosen becomes particularly exposed to the sun.

Western Avahis become active around dusk or just before, but spend time grooming themselves prior to vacating their sleep site. The family unit largely remains together while foraging, individuals maintaining contact with gentle purring calls produced by vibrating their nostrils, although males do sometimes temporarily leave the female and offspring and forage singly for periods. A large proportion of the night is spent travelling. The average distance covered is 900-1,400m. Feeding activity tends to be concentrated into the first half of the night. The bulk of the diet consists of young leaves and buds taken from a variety of plants – in Ankarafantsika this species is known to feed on at least 20 different plant species. *A. occidentalis* generally return to their sleep sites before dawn but during the dry season (May–October), when foliage is reduced, they sometimes remain active until after after sunrise.

A single offspring is born generally between September and October. The youngster clings to its mother's belly (fig. 155) for the first three weeks or so and then moves round to ride on her back.

POPULATION No overall population figures are available. At Ampijoroa in the deciduous forests of Ankarafantsika population densities have been estimated at around 70 individuals/km², but such a high figure is unlikely to be repeated throughout this species's range.

THREATS Forest-felling and burning to create new agricultural land is the principal threat. In some areas hunting also occurs. These factors, coupled with this species's restricted range, give cause for concern. The Western Avahi is confirmed from only three protected areas, with one other (Ankarana Special Reserve) a possibility.

VIEWING The Western Avahi is common and fairly easy to find on night walks at the Ampijoroa Forest Station (part of Ankarafantsika Nature Reserve), two hours drive south-east of Mahajanga. Being a dry deciduous forest area, the canopy is lower and the branches and foliage less dense, so views can be good. If a 'sleep-tree' is located, pairs or family units can also be seen huddled together during the day.

SIFAKAS genus *Propithecus* Bennett, 1832

All sifakas (often called simponas in eastern rainforest regions) are diurnal and primarily arboreal. Three species are recognised: *P. diadema* is distributed in the wetter forests of the north and east, while *P. verreauxi* is found in the drier regions of the south and west; each of these species is divided into four subspecies that have apparently distinct ranges. The third species, *P. tattersalli*, is restricted to a small enclave of forest in north-eastern Madagascar.

DIADEMED SIFAKA *Propithecus diadema* Bennett, 1832

Diademed Sifaka has four subspecies that apparently have distinct ranges.

Subspecies

Diademed Sifaka *Propithecus diadema diadema* Bennett, 1832

Malagasy: Simpona, Simpony

MEASUREMENTS Total length: 940-1,050mm. Head/body length: 500-550mm. Tail length: 440-500mm. Weight: 6-7.25kg.

DESCRIPTION The pelage is moderately long and silky. The head is principally white with a black crown that may extend down the nape. The face is bare and dark-grey to black with rich red-brown eyes. The shoulders and upper back are deep slate-grey fading to silver-grey on the lower back. The lower body and tail are pale grey to white and there is often a golden-yellow area around the pygal region (base of the tail). The arms and legs are rich orange to yellow-gold and the hands and feet are black. The chest and belly areas are normally off-white to pale grey (figs. 156 & 157). This subspecies is widely regarded as the most beautiful of Malagasy primates.

IDENTIFICATION A large, vertically clinging and leaping lemur. Together with the Indri *Indri indri*, the Diademed Sifaka is the largest extant lemur. Although both species are sympatric over most of their ranges, confusion between the two is highly unlikely. There are marked differences in coloration and morphology – the Indri is black and white with virtually no tail – which are sufficient to make confusion improbable.

HABITAT Primary mid-altitude rainforest. Elevations above 800m are preferred.

Figure 156. Diademed Sifaka, Mantadia.

Figure 157. Diademed Sifaka, Mantadia.

Diademed Sifaka

DISTRIBUTION The Diademed Sifaka is restricted to the rainforests of east and north-east Madagascar. It is certainly the most widely distributed of the *P. diadema* subspecies, although the precise limits are unclear. Evidence suggests the range extends from the Mangoro River in the south to the region south of the Antainambalana River in the north. Populations of *P. diadema* further to the north are ascribed to the subspecies *P. d. candidus*, which is all white. However, some individuals from areas at the borders of their respective ranges show intermediate coloration.

BEHAVIOUR The Diademed Sifaka is diurnal and lives in multi-male/multi-female groups of up to eight or so individuals. Males immigrate into a group from neighbouring groups and are unrelated, whereas females remain within their natal group and so constitute a matriline. These groups occupy home ranges of up to 35 ha, which are defended primarily by scent-marking. Unlike the Indri, vocalisations are not used as a means of territorial defence, but rather to maintain group cohesion. The daily distance travelled within territories can be several hundred metres. During the course of these movements the group will spend time both at higher elevations within the canopy and lower down in the understorey. At times they even descend to the ground to search for fallen fruits and indulge in prolonged bouts of play-wrestling.

The diet consists primarily of leaves, flowers and fruits, the respective proportions of which vary according to seasonal abundance. Over 25 different plant species are regularly utilised each day. There is only a small degree of overlap in the plant species eaten by the Diademed Sifaka and the broadly sympatric Indri, which reduces competition for food to a minimum.

Females give birth to a single offspring which initially clings to the mother's underside and switches to riding on her back when older. Infants and younger animals may fall prey to the Fosa *Cryptoprocta ferox* or even large raptors like the Madagascar Harrier-Hawk *Polyboroides radiatus* and Henst's Goshawk *Accipiter henstii*.

When alarmed by a ground predator the adults give an intense sneeze-like *tzisk-tzisk-tzisk* call, whereas for aerial predators the alarm call is a loud resonant *honk-honk-honk*.

POPULATION No overall population figures are available. Evidence suggests that even in pristine primary rainforest the Diademed Sifaka exists only at low densities.

THREATS This subspecies is threatened by the continued destruction of its rainforest home due to agricultural clearance and timber extraction. The Diademed Sifaka appears now to be absent from many areas that have suffered only minor degradation, which suggests that it is particularly susceptible to disturbance. In many parts of its range this lemur is also hunted for food, even within the boundaries of national parks and reserves. It is known to occur for certain in five, and possibly six, protected areas.

VIEWING This is one of the more difficult lemur species to see, but such is its beauty that the effort is well worthwhile. At one time the Diademed Sifaka was found in Analamazaotra Special Reserve near Andasibe (Perinet) but that no longer appears to be so. However, in the nearby unprotected forests of Maromizaha it can occasionally be seen from the ridge. There are also trails that descend into the forest for those wishing to conduct a more thorough search.

The best locality is Mantadia National Park, which lies around 25km to the north of Andasibe. The forests here are superb, but there are no facilities and the few trails are often steep, making conditions difficult. Even with several days of searching, sightings of the Diademed Sifaka are by no means guaranteed. It is imperative that anyone making the effort to see this species, either at Maromizaha or Mantadia, do so in conjunction with a local guide from Andasibe.

Milne-Edwards's Sifaka *Propithecus diadema edwardsi* A. Grandidier, 1871

Malagasy: Simpona, Simpony

MEASUREMENTS Total length: 830-995mm. Head/body length: 420-520mm. Tail length: 410-475mm. Weight: 5-6.5kg.

DESCRIPTION The pelage is soft and dense and varies from dark chocolate-brown to almost black on the head, upper body, limbs and tail. The chest and belly are also dark, but with far less fur. The face is bare and dark grey to black, with orange-red eyes. The lower flanks and back form a creamy-white saddle with reddish-brown areas at the margins grading into the main dark brown regions (figs. 158 & 159). A thin dark area often remains running down the spine to the base of the tail.

IDENTIFICATION A large, dark, vertically clinging and leaping lemur that should not be mistaken for any other species within its range. Only the Indri *Indri indri* is of similar size and coloration, but is allopatric, so confusion should not be possible for anyone familiar with the species' respective distributions.

HABITAT Primary and secondary mid-altitude rainforest.

DISTRIBUTION Milne-Edwards's Sifaka is restricted to the southern portion of the eastern rainforest belt: its range extends from

Figure 158. Milne-Edwards's Sifaka, Ranomafana.

the Mangoro River in the north to the Mananara River in the south and includes the eastern slopes of the Andringitra Massif.

BEHAVIOUR Like all sifakas, this subspecies is diurnal and arboreal. Milne-Edwards's Sifaka lives in groups of three to nine animals. Evidence suggests these are more than simple family units: they often contain two or more mature members of each sex. Females are resident and appear to be dominant, while adult males are known to migrate between groups. It seems likely that these groups represent mutually familiar foraging parties, rather than fixed reproductive units, although some breeding relationships may be stable over six to ten years.

The diet is varied and consists mainly of leaves (around 60%), together with fruits (25%) and flowers (15%) – over 25 different species have been seen to be eaten each day. In the spring (October–November) new leaves and shoots are preferred as they are rich in protein. For females, the timing of these high-quality resources is vital as it corresponds to the late lactation/early weaning period when their energetic costs are highest. During foraging bouts the sifakas move and feed at all heights within the forest canopy and even descend to ground level on occasion to eat soil – this may provide them with vital trace nutrients or help detoxify poisons accumulated from some of the leaves in their regular diet.

Groups maintain exclusive home ranges with virtually no overlap. These are large – 100 to 250ha – and the boundaries consistent, even if group size fluctuates up or down. Within these territories the daily distances travelled are also considerable, usually between 650m and 1,250m. At the boundaries of home ranges, neighbouring groups sometimes approach within a few metres of one another with no apparent aggression or vocalisations, and group intermingling has even been observed. Sleep sites are normally associated with ridgetops, the sifakas preferring branches eight to ten metres above the ground.

Milne-Edwards's Sifaka

Figure 159. Milne-Edwards's Sifaka, Ranomafana.

Infants are born in the winter months – May to July,with the peak in June – after a gestation period of 180 days. They weigh around 160g at birth. Their first month of life is spent holding onto their mother's belly; they then transfer to ride on her back. Weaning begins after two to three months, and by six months more than half the infant's nourishment comes from foods other than milk. Mothers continue to sleep with their offspring for up to two years. On average females breed every other year. Infant mortality is very high – over 40% die within the first year – and around 65% fail to reach sexual maturity. Most infants are predated, mainly by the Fosa *Cryptoprocta ferox*, or possibly large raptors. Some are the victims of infanticide by immigrating adult males.

At one year of age, individuals weigh around 50% of adult body weight. Sexual maturity is reached at four years in females and five years in males. Females may either remain in their natal group and begin breeding or move to an adjacent group, while newly matured males always move out of their natal area to take up residence elsewhere.

POPULATION The total population of this subspecies is unknown. From observations made at Ranomafana National Park, population densities are low – around 8 individuals/km².

THREATS Slash-and-burn clearance of the rainforest and timber extraction are the principal threats to this sifaka. Even forests adjacent to protected areas suffer severe encroachment. Milne-Edwards's Sifaka is found in three protected areas.

VIEWING Ranomafana National Park is by far the best place to see this lemur. It has been intensively studied at this site for several years and some groups are now well habituated. It is often possible to approach individuals quite closely and get excellent views. The local guides at the national park are expert at finding the sifakas and many other lemurs and their services should always be sought.

Silky Sifaka *Propithecus diadema candidus* A. Grandidier, 1871

Malagasy: Simpona, Simpony

MEASUREMENTS Total length: 930-1,050mm. Head/body length: 480-540mm. Tail length: 450-510mm. Weight: 5-6kg.

DESCRIPTION The pelage is long, silky and uniformly creamy-white in colour. Some individuals have tints of silver-grey around the crown, back and limbs. The area around the lower back and base of the tail may also be darker and slightly discoloured. The face is bare and slate-grey black, while the eyes are deep orange-red. Some individuals seen in the Marojejy Massif seem to lack skin pigment on their faces, which appear either totally pink or a mixture of pink and slate-grey (fig. 160).

IDENTIFICATION A large, vertically clinging and leaping lemur with very distinctive all-white coloration. The silky sifaka cannot be mistaken for any other lemur within its range.

HABITAT Primary mid-altitude and montane rainforest. Elevations above 800m are preferred and this subspecies has been observed up to approximately 1,500m.

DISTRIBUTION The Silky Sifaka is only found at the northern end of the eastern rainforest belt. Its range extends from the Antainambalana River close to Maroantsetra in the south to the Marojejy Massif in the north, but it does not apparently extend eastward into the Masoala Peninsula, although it is unclear why this should be. In the southern part of this subspecies's range, the coloration of some individuals appears intermediate between *P. d. candidus* and *P. d. diadema*.

Silky Sifaka

BEHAVIOUR No formal studies have been undertaken, so information on this subspecies's behaviour and ecology is limited. Most brief observations have been made in Anjanaharibe-Sud and the Marojejy Massif. Group size appears to vary between three and seven. Smaller groups of three to four probably consist of an adult pair plus their offspring, while larger groups of five to seven probably constitute mutually familiar foraging units that may contain more than one breeding pair together with juveniles.

Home range size would appear to be fairly large although no estimates have been calculated and scent-marking is evidently an important behaviour in its demarcation. The alarm call is the familiar *tzisk-tzisk-tzisk* that is common to all simponas.

Infants are probably born around August and initially grasp the fur on their mother's belly. When older they prefer to ride on her back.

It seems probable that other aspects of the Silky Sifaka behaviour and ecology resemble that of the Diademed Sifaka *P. d. diadema*.

POPULATION No population figures are available, but this lemur is known to be extremely rare throughout its range. In the Marojejy Massif an approximate population density of just eight to ten individuals/km² has been estimated.

THREATS The Silky Sifaka is threatened primarily by the destruction of its rainforest habitat. It is also known to be hunted for food, particularly in the Marojejy Massif and Andapa Basin area. This lemur is known to occur in just two protected areas.

Figure 160. Silky Sifaka, Marojejy.

VIEWING This is a very difficult lemur to see. The most readily accessible site (although still quite remote) is the Befingitra Forest, which lies within Anjanaharibe-Sud Special Reserve, around 15km south-west of the town of Andapa. Efforts are best concentrated at higher elevations, although even here these animals are very wary and difficult to locate. The alternative is the forest area close to the town of Doany at the western edge of Marojejy Nature Reserve. This area is far more remote and requires considerable planning and effort to reach.

The Silky Sifaka can readily be seen in some parts of the Marojejy Nature Reserve, although these areas have until now been inaccessible to visitors. However, Marojejy is due to become a new national park in the near future. Once officially gazetted, visitor access seems sure to improve and tracking down the Silky Sifaka may become a more realistic proposition.

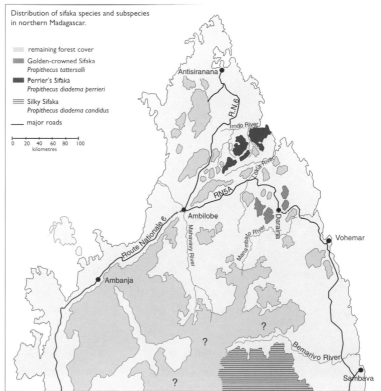

247

Perrier's Sifaka *Propithecus diadema perrieri* Lavauden, 1931

Perrier's Sifaka

Malagasy: Ankomba Joby, Radjako

MEASUREMENTS Total length: 850-920mm. Head/body length: 430-470mm. Tail length: 420-450mm. Weight: 5-5.5kg.

DESCRIPTION Sexes similar. The pelage is dense and uniformly black (figs. 161 & 162), although it is sometimes tinged brown around the chest and lower abdomen. The face is bare and dark grey-black and the eyes are deep orange-red. Perrier's Sifaka is probably the smallest of the *P. diadema* subspecies.

IDENTIFICATION A large, vertically clinging and leaping lemur with silky black pelage. Not only is this the largest lemur within its range, it is also the most distinctive in terms of coloration. Confusion with any other species should not be possible.

HABITAT Dry deciduous and semi-humid forests.

DISTRIBUTION Perrier's Sifaka has the most restricted range of the *P. diadema* subspecies. It occurs only in north-east Madagascar in the area lying between the Lokia River to the south and Irodo River to the north, centred around the Analamera and Andrafiamena Massifs. To the west its range just reaches the north-eastern limits of the Ankarana Massif, although it is known to be particularly rare in these localities.

BEHAVIOUR Very few observations and studies have been made so information on the behaviour and ecology of this lemur is scant. The maximum group size appears to be six, probably consisting of four or so adults and their offspring. A home range size around 30ha has been suggested. The diet consists of mature leaves, unripe fruit, leave petioles, young shoots and flowers. When feeding group members may be spread out in trees more than 50m apart, but individuals maintain contact with one another through regular quiet calls.

Figure 161. Perrier's Sifaka, Analamera.

Figure 162. Perrier's Sifaka, Analamera.

Towards the end of the dry season (November) groups of Perrier's Sifakas may move into ribbons of more humid forest that border dry river beds. Within some of these areas introduced mango trees *Mangifera indica* flourish and the sifakas spend considerable periods feeding on the fruit.

The distinctive simpona alarm call – *tzisk-tzisk-tzisk* – is given to human intruders and the Fosa *Cryptoprocta ferox*. Perrier's Sifaka reacts in a highly agitated manner to the presence of the Fosa: when the predator is on the ground all group members gather into adjacent trees, watch intently and give the alarm call. They then quickly leave the area.

POPULATION This is certainly the rarest of the Diademed Sifaka subspecies – evidence suggests its total population is less than 2,000. In Analamera Special Reserve the population density is estimated to be around 20 individuals/km².

THREATS Continued habitat destruction within the range of Perrier's Sifaka constitutes the major threat. Wood-cutting for charcoal and forest clearance to make way for agriculture remain common practices in the area, while deliberate fires annually encroach into the remaining forest margins, even within protected areas. The majority of the Perrier's Sifaka population is found within Analamera Special Reserve, the only protected area where its presence can still be confirmed. Until recently (early 1990s) a small population was also known from Ankarana Special Reserve to the west of Analamera, but its continued survival is now questionable.

VIEWING This is one of the most challenging of lemurs to see. The more humid forests along the Bobakindro River which flows through Analamera Special Reserve offer the best chance, particularly during the months of October and November when the mango trees are in fruit. This is a remote area and requires considerable time and planning to reach. It is best approached from the village of Menagisy at the northern edge of the reserve. Here it is essential to hire a local guide. The best areas are a day's walk away and lie around 15-20km south of the village. This area is also very good for Crowned Lemurs *Eulemur coronatus* and Sanford's Brown Lemurs *E. fulvus sanfordi*.

VERREAUX'S SIFAKA *Propithecus verreauxi* A. Grandidier, 1867

Verreaux's Sifaka has four subspecies that apparently have distinct ranges.

Subspecies

Verreaux's Sifaka *Prop]ithecus verreauxi verreauxi* A. Grandidier, 1867

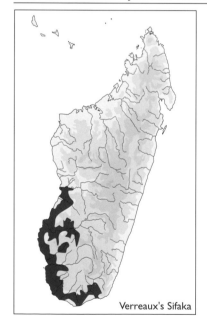

Verreaux's Sifaka

Malagasy: Sifaka, Sifaka-avahi (dark variant), Sifaka-bilany (Isalo area)

MEASUREMENTS Total length: 900-1,075mm. Head/body length: 400-475mm. Tail length: 500-600mm. Weight: 3-4kg.

DESCRIPTION The pelage is longish, thick and soft in texture. The overall coloration, including the tail, is white, with a dark brown crown that extends down the nape. The ears are white, tufted and reasonably prominent. The face and muzzle are very dark grey to black and the large eyes vivid yellow (figs. 164 & 165). The fur on the chest, belly and underarms is more sparse, allowing the grey skin to show through. This often gives the underparts a darker appearance. In males the upper chest area is sometimes tinged with reddish-brown due to a gland at the base of the throat.

Considerable colour variations are known in this subspecies. Some individuals have dark brown areas on their backs, chest, upper arms, upper thighs and tail (this distinctive variant has sometimes been called *P. v. 'majori'*), while others are almost completely white. Mixed groups containing both 'normal' individuals and these variants have been observed at several localities.

IDENTIFICATION A large, vertically clinging and leaping lemur. The large size and distinctive coloration of Verreaux's Sifaka make it impossible to confuse with any other species within its range.

HABITAT Dry deciduous forest in the west. Xerophytic spiny forest and gallery forests in the south. Humid rainforest at the extreme south-eastern limit of its range.

DISTRIBUTION Verreaux's Sifaka occurs in forested regions from the Tsiribihina River in the west, south to the Tolagnaro area in the south-east and inland as far as the Isalo Massif. At the very eastern limits of its range, in the Andohahela Nature Reserve to the north-west of Tolagnaro, this species has been observed in humid rainforests (Parcel 1), some individuals here conforming to the *P. v. 'majori'* colour variant.

BEHAVIOUR Verreaux's Sifaka is diurnal and lives in mixed (multi-male/multi-female) groups of up to 14 individuals, although four to eight members is average. In the larger groups more than one female breeds each year, although it is unusual for more than one infant to survive. Smaller groups (six or less) may represent family units, while the larger groups probably comprise mutually familiar animals united into foraging parties. Within these, females appear to be dominant, and always displace adult males at favoured feeding sites.

Figure 163. Verreaux's Sifaka, Berenty.

Figure 164. Verreaux's Sifaka, Kirindy.

In spiny forest areas group home ranges are around seven to eight hectares, while in gallery forests, where resources are more abundant, home range size is considerably smaller, around two to three hectares. Towards the northern limits of this subspecies' range, where it lives in dry deciduous forests, home ranges appear larger, between 12 and 25ha. This increase in range size may be correlated with more intense competition as these deciduous forests also support a greater density and diversity of other lemur species compared to spiny and gallery forests. Home ranges tend to constrict when females are giving birth. Ranges do overlap, often considerably, but there is always a core territory which remains exclusive to the group. Territories are defended by scent-marking and boundary disputes are generally resolved with few or no vocalisations.

Activity patterns vary seasonally and with habitat. During the cool dry season Verreaux's Sifakas often remain inactive for up to two hours after sunrise then move high into the canopy to sunbathe. After this they forage almost continuously until mid-afternoon before settling down for the night; rarely do they travel more than 500m in a day. During the warm wet season they are regularly active before sunrise and stop foraging by mid-morning. They then rest during the heat of the day and resume foraging in the late afternoon and may continue until after sunset – often having travelled more than 1,000m in the day.

Being arboreal, most movement involves leaping between vertical trunks. The animals are even able to do this amongst the viciously thorned Didiereaceae trees of the spiny forest without injury. When necessary, Verreaux's Sifakas may also descend to the ground and cross open spaces by bounding on their hind legs with arms held aloft for balance in a very balletic manner (fig. 163).

Leaves, fruits and flowers constitute the diet, although there is seasonal variation in the proportions that are eaten. In general, leaves predominate during the dry season, with a shift to fruit and flowers during the wet season. Verreaux's Sifakas also seem able to tolerate prolonged drought conditions – groups exclusively inhabiting spiny forest areas appear to gain necessary moisture from the leaves of the Didiereaceae. At the height of the dry season, when heavy dews are common, they have also been observed licking moisture from their coats.

The mating season is brief and highly synchronous, females all coming into oestrous between late January and early February. Around 45% of females breed each year, the remainder every other year. Males move from female to female in the group to find a receptive mate and sometimes roam between neighbouring groups. Fights between rival males are common and consist of bouts of cuffs and bites, which occasionally result in serious injury.

Figure 165. Verreaux's Sifaka in gallery forest, Beza-Mahafaly.

A single offspring is born between August and September after a gestation period of around 155-165 days. Initially infants ride on their mother's belly, then shift to ride on her back after a month or so. Independence is reached shortly after six months. Adults are particularly vigilant when the group contains young, always keeping a keen eye out for predators. If potential danger is spotted on the ground adults call with a characteristic repeated nasal bark – *si-fak, si-fak, si-fak* – (from which these animals take their name), at the same time throwing back their heads in a jerky motion. Interestingly, the call is different for aerial predators, which induce a loud bellow or roar, especially the Madagascar Harrier-Hawk *Polyboroides radiatus*. Nonetheless, infant predation is high: in some dry deciduous forest areas around 30% of each year's offspring are lost to the Fosa *Cryptoprocta ferox* and a smaller percentage may be taken by large raptors.

Sexual maturity is not reached for at least three and sometimes five years. Adult females tend to remain in their natal group, whereas males are encouraged by established group members to leave when they mature and transfer to a neighbouring group. New groups may be slow to accept incoming males, which are forced to spend time on the periphery. Resident males also tend to be initially hostile towards newcomers. Males generally move between groups several times within their lifetime.

POPULATION This is the most widely distributed *Propithecus* species and probably the most abundant, but total population figures are unknown. In disturbed gallery forests densities of 47 individuals/km² have been estimated. In the less disturbed gallery forests at Berenty Reserve densities reach between 150 and 200 individuals/km², but these are almost certainly abnormally high and a result of the 'hard-edged' and 'artificial' nature of the reserve. The densities reached in gallery and dry deciduous forests are higher than those in Didiereaceae forest.

THREATS The various habitat types (spiny, gallery and dry deciduous forest) this subspecies occupies are becoming increasingly fragmented, due to cutting for timber, firewood and charcoal production. Hunting takes place in some areas (in the Isalo region the animal is known as *sifaka-bilany* or 'sifaka of the cooking pot'), but in other tribal areas (Antandroy and Mahafaly) hunting Verreaux's Sifaka is taboo or *fady*. This subspecies occurs in at least seven protected areas.

VIEWING Berenty Reserve to the west of Tolagnaro is the best place to see this lemur. Here groups are completely habituated and even during a single day's visit close encounters are guaranteed. Most groups live in the gallery forest, although there are occasional sightings in the adjacent parcels of spiny forest. This is also the best place to see them 'dancing' across open spaces. The nearby reserve of Amboasary-Sud is an alternative.

Beza-Mahafaly Special Reserve south-east of Toliara and Hazafotsy on the western edge of Andohahela Nature Reserve (Parcel 2) are good places to see Verreaux's Sifakas in spiny forest, where they leap impressively between the stands of Didiereaceae.

At Kirindy Forest to the north-east of Morondava, this subspecies can easily be seen in dry deciduous forest.

Coquerel's Sifaka *Propithecus verreauxi coquereli* Milne-Edwards, 1871

Coquerel's Sifaka

Malagasy: Sifaka, Tsibahaka

MEASUREMENTS Total length: 925-1,100mm. Head/body length: 425-500mm. Tail length: 500-600mm. Weight: 3.5-4kg.

DESCRIPTION The dense pelage is mostly white on the head, body and tail, with distinctive deep maroon patches on the thighs and arms and extending across the chest. Some individuals have a brown to silvery-grey area at the base of the back. The inner face is black, surrounded by white fur around the cheeks and crown extending from the forehead down the nose bridge to the muzzle. The ears are black and prominent and the eyes are vivid yellow (fig. 166).

IDENTIFICATION A large, vertically clinging and leaping lemur with highly distinctive coloration. Coquerel's Sifaka cannot be confused with any other species within its range.

HABITAT Dry-deciduous and semi-evergreen forest.

DISTRIBUTION Coquerel's Sifaka is restricted to north-west Madagascar. Its range extends from the region of Ambato-Boeni and the Betsiboka River north to around Antsohihy in the north-west and Befandriana Nord in the north-east.

BEHAVIOUR Coquerel's Sifaka is diurnal and lives in groups of three to ten individuals, although groups with four or five members appear most common. Smaller groups consist of family units and rarely contain more than one infant, but larger groups have a variable age and sex composition. In common with Verreaux's Sifaka, these probably represent mutually familiar foraging units rather than stable family groups.

Home ranges are between four and eight hectares, although within these the animals utilise an exclusive core area of two to three hectares for more than 60% of the time. There is considerable overlap of home ranges around the periphery, where encounters between neighbouring groups occur. These rarely lead to aggressive defence, but rather mutual avoidance.

Figure 166. Coquerel's Sifaka, Ampijoroa.

During the dry season the diet consists primarily of mature leaves and buds and occasionally bark: in the wet season the proportion of young leaves (in particular), flowers and fruits increases. Coquerel's Sifaka has been recorded eating nearly 100 different plant species; however only 12 of these form two-thirds of the diet. Foraging activities occupy between 30% and 40% of the day, although there are seasonal changes to the times of principal activity. During the wet season feeding bouts regularly begin before sunrise and peak before mid-morning. After a rest period, activity begins again in the afternoon and continues until early evening. The average daily distance travelled is around 1,000m. In the dry season feeding begins later and ends earlier, and there is a little rest period either side of midday, the daily distance covered being around 750m.

Generally single births occur in June and July after a gestation period of around 160 days. At first the infant clings to its mother's front, then after three to fours weeks transfers to riding on her back. This may continue to the age of six months, although it is more normal for the offspring to be independent by this stage. Adult size is reached at around one year of age.

POPULATION Total population figures are unknown, but are certainly declining. In Ankarafantsika Nature Reserve population densities of 60 individuals/km^2 have been estimated.

THREATS Habitat destruction is the main threat to this species. Not only is forest being felled for agriculture and charcoal, but deliberately started bush fires, lit to encourage new grass shoots to grow, continually encroach on remaining habitat. This, in conjunction with its restricted range, gives severe cause for concern. Hunting occurs in some areas, although in others (around Ankarafantsika for instance), this subspecies is protected by taboo or *fady*. Coquerel's Sifaka occurs in only two protected areas.

VIEWING A trip to Ampijoroa Forestry Station (part of Ankarafantsika Nature Reserve) is strongly recommended for anyone wanting to see this stunningly beautiful lemur. Several groups live within close proximity of the campsite, the trail network is well maintained and good views are almost guaranteed.

Figure 167. Coquerel's Sifakas in suspensory posture, Ampijoroa.

Decken's Sifaka *Propithecus verreauxi deckeni* Peters, 1870

Decken's Sifaka

Malagasy: Sifaka, Tsibahaka

MEASUREMENTS Total length: 925-1,075mm. Head/body length: 425-475mm. Tail length: 500-600mm. Weight: c. 3.5-4.5kg.

DESCRIPTION Typically the pelage is creamy-white all over, sometimes washed with tinges of yellow-gold, silver-grey or pale brown on the neck, shoulders, back and limbs. The face is entirely black and appears slightly more rounded and blunt-muzzled than in other subspecies of *P. verreauxi* (fig. 168).

A melanistic variant (identified from the Analabe region to the west of the Maha-vavy River and east of Lac Kinkony) differs from the typical form in that the entire head and dorsal regions of the neck are dark brown to black. Further, the dorsal areas of the upper arms and shoulders, as well as the upper back, are light brown to silvery-grey. The ventral surface of the arms and the chest are dark brown and the legs light brown or silvery-grey ventrally. The upper surfaces of the forearms and legs are white.

IDENTIFICATION A large, vertically clinging and leaping lemur. The size and al-most pure white coloration of *P. v. deckeni* are distinctive and make confusion with any other lemur highly improbable. However, at the southern and eastern boundary of its range (Bongolava) distinction may have to be made from the Crowned Sifaka *P. v. coronatus*; this subspecies is also white, but has a dark brown to black head.

HABITAT Dry deciduous forest.

DISTRIBUTION This subspecies is restricted to western Madagascar, between the Manambolo River to the south and the Mahavavy River to the north, including the western edge of the Bongolava Massif. The precise limits of this range, and how they relate to the distribution of *P. v. coronatus*, are unclear, particularly to the south and east of the Manambolo River. In this area it is possible that the two subspecies are sympatric and may intergrade.

BEHAVIOUR Decken's Sifaka has yet to be studied in the wild so very little information is available. Observations suggest group sizes range from two to ten individuals, although units of between three and six animals appear most common. Groups containing two adult females with young have also been seen (pers. obs.). In some areas this subspecies seems able to survive in quite degraded habitat, for instance around Mitsinjo and the Tsiombikibo Forest. It seems likely that all aspects of behaviour and ecology show close similarities to other subspecies of *P. verreauxi* inhabiting dry deciduous forest.

POPULATION No overall population figures are available. Density estimates varying between 23 individuals/km^2 (Anlabe) and 3 individuals/km^2 (Anadabomandry) have been calculated, the lower figures being in heavily deforested regions. These figures are based on brief surveys and probably underestimate numbers, particularly for areas with intact native forest, so they should be treated with caution.

THREATS The dry deciduous forests within the range of Decken's Sifaka are already severely fragmented and it seems likely that many subpopulations are already isolated from one another. Habitat destruction continues as forests are cleared and burned to create fresh pasture for livestock. It is probable that hunting occurs in at least some parts of this subspecies's range. Five protected areas lie within the range of Decken's Sifaka, although its presence can only be confirmed in two of these.

VIEWING The majority of this subspecies's range is inaccessible, so seeing it requires some effort. The Tsiombikibo Forest to the north-west of Mitsinjo, around four hours' drive from Katsepy west of the Betsiboka River estuary, is perhaps the best place to try. Here Decken's Sifaka is quite tolerant and can be easily observed. Groups may sometimes also be encountered in and around the town of Mitsinjo itself and in the forests adjacent to nearby Lac Kamonjo. A local guide is always recommended.

At the southern extreme of its range this subspecies can be seen in the Tsingy de Bemaraha National Park, where it is locally quite common and relatively easily located. The forests close to Bekopaka, north of the Manambolo River, are well worth exploring. The local guides associated with the national park will be able to assist. Further to the north, in the region of Antsalova, Decken's Sifaka is readily encountered, but this locality takes a considerable amount of effort to reach.

Figure 168. Decken's Sifakas, near Mitsinjo.

Figure 169. Crowned Sifaka, near Katsepy.

Crowned Sifaka *Propithecus verreauxi coronatus* Milne-Edwards, 1871

Crowned Sifaka

Malagasy: Sifaka, Tsibahaka

MEASUREMENTS Total length: 870-1,020mm. Head/body length: 395-455mm. Tail length: 475-565m. Weight: 3.5-4.3kg.

DESCRIPTION In common with other *P. verreauxi* subspecies, the overall colour is creamy-white. However, the head, neck and throat are dark chocolate-brown to black. The upper chest, shoulders, upper forelimbs and upper back are variably tinted with golden-brown that lightens to golden-yellow lower down the torso and fades out completely to creamy-white by the abdomen. The hindlimbs and tail are creamy-white. The face is bare and mainly dark grey to black: there is sometimes a paler grey to white patch across the bridge of the nose and whitish ear-tufts. The muzzle may be more blunt and the face more squarish than in other subspecies (fig. 169).

IDENTIFICATION A large, predominantly white, vertically clinging and leaping lemur. The 'typical' form of the Crowned Sifaka (as described above) cannot be confused with any other lemur in its range. However, some colour variation has been observed and the relationships and distinctions between this subspecies and Decken's Sifaka *P. v. deckeni* have yet to be fully established.

HABITAT Dry deciduous forest.

DISTRIBUTION After initial collections and surveys the range of the Crowned Sifaka was thought to lie between the Mahavavy and Betsiboka Rivers in north-west Madagascar. It was assumed that at the south-western limit, the Mahavavy acted as a boundary between this subspecies and Decken's Sifaka, while in the north-east the Betsiboka separated the Crowned Sifaka from Coquerel's Sifaka. However, it is now known that *P. v. coronatus* also occurs on the Bongolava Massif and in areas south of the Manambolo River, which suggests its range forms a crescent-shape that encircles the range of *P. v. deckeni*. Recent observations confirm that the lower reaches of the Mahavavy River acts as a clear boundary between the two subspecies. However, the situation in the Bongolava where their respective ranges meet will remain enigmatic until thorough surveys are undertaken.

BEHAVIOUR There have been only brief studies of the Crowned Sifaka in the wild, which have taken place mainly during the dry season. Group size seems variable. At Anjamena groups of between two and eight individuals have been observed; these have variable sex and age composition, and in common with *P. v. verreauxi*, probably represent mutually familiar foraging parties rather than stable family groups.

Home ranges appear to be very small – 1.2 to 1.5ha – and even within this range group members spend around 75% of time in a core area little more than 0.3ha in extent. Groups are territorial and defend their home ranges aggressively. This behaviour appears to resemble more closely that of *P. verreauxi* subspecies inhabiting arid southern forests rather than equivalent western dry deciduous forests.

Most foraging takes place in the upper canopy; Crowned Sifakas are rarely seen on the forest floor, although they do occasionally eat soil. During the dry season the diet consists primarily of buds and unripe fruits, but also includes a significant proportion of mature leaves that have a high fibre content. No dietary data is available for the wet season. In the dry season, the daily activity period lasts over nine hours; foraging occupies 30-40% of the day and the average distance covered is around 600m. The remainder of the day is principally spent resting with some time also devoted to grooming and other interactions with group members. At Anjamena, groups choose tall trees (over 20m), optimally exposed to sunlight and located close to a major river (the Mahavavy) in which to sleep.

POPULATION The population is unknown, but is likely to be low due to this subspecies' very restricted range. Density estimates of 5 individuals/km² (Katsepy) and 173 individuals/km² (Anjamena) suggest that these differences probably reflect the variation in quality of habitat (and also surveying methods) with very low values corresponding to heavily deforested areas and/or regions where sifakas are still hunted.

THREATS Continued habitat destruction is the main threat to this sifaka. Forests are being cleared for new pasture and charcoal production. Its presence cannot be confirmed from any protected area.

VIEWING Most of this lemur's range falls outside regularly visited locations, so it is not an easy animal to see. Perhaps the most accessible site is the forest below the lighthouse north of Katsepy (opposite side of the Betsiboka estuary from Mahajanga). There are few trails through the forest and sifakas are sparsely distributed and can be difficult to locate. However, with luck they can be seen by walking along the shore. Visiting this area involves a full day trek from Katsepy.

An alternative location, which is more difficult to reach but far more rewarding, is the forest around Anjamena on the eastern banks of the Mahavavy River. This area is around two to three hours walk from the road between Katsepy and Namakia, but Crowned Sifakas are common and quite easy to see.

Figure 170. Golden-crowned Sifaka.

GOLDEN-CROWNED SIFAKA *Propithecus tattersalli* Simons, 1988

Other name: Tattersall's Sifaka
Malagasy: Simpona, Ankomba Malandy

MEASUREMENTS Total length: 870-940mm. Head/body length: 450-470mm. Tail length: 420-470mm. Weight: c. 3.5kg.

DESCRIPTION The pelage is moderate in length and predominantly creamy-white on the head and body. The crown is rich yellow-orange and there may also be tinges of this colour on the shoulders and upper arms, across the chest and on the rump. The ears sport prominent tufts, which give the head an overall triangular shape. The face is mainly bare and dark grey-black with some white hairs extending underneath the eyes onto the cheeks. The eyes are orange (fig. 170). This is the smallest member of the genus.

IDENTIFICATION A medium-large, vertically clinging and leaping lemur. Distinctive coloration and posture make this lemur impossible to confuse with any other species within its very limited range.

HABITAT Dry deciduous, gallery and semi-evergreen forests.

DISTRIBUTION The Golden-crowned Sifaka is confined to a very small area between the Manambato and Loky Rivers in north-east Madagascar. The town of Daraina, 55km north-west of Vohemar, lies at the centre of this range which, is perhaps only 30km to 35km in diameter (see p.247).

Golden-crowned Sifaka

BEHAVIOUR Like all sifakas, this species is primarily diurnal, although it has been observed moving before dawn and after dusk during the rainy season (December–March). At night the sifakas sleep in the taller trees. The group size appears to vary considerably between three and ten, although most contain five or six members. These often consist of two or more mature members of each sex, although only one female within each group seems to breed successfully each year. Males have been seen to move between neighbouring groups during the mating season.

Golden-crowned Sifakas inhabit a mosaic of forest types. The dry deciduous forests are very similar to those that characterise western areas, while semi-evergreen forest still survives on some higher ground within the range and gallery forest follows the watercourses. Territories are around 6-12ha and within these the group ranges between 400 and 1,200m daily – the distances moved being greater during the drier months when food is less abundant.

P. tattersalli feeds on a variety of unripe fruits, seeds, shoots, mature leaves and flowers. Bark may also be eaten during the dry season. Immature leaves are particularly relished, and the sifakas are prepared to forage over a wider area than normal in search of them.

This species responds to large raptors like the Madagascar Harrier-Hawk *Polyboroides radiatus*, with characteristic 'mobbing' alarm calls, while the more familiar *si-fak, si-fak, si-fak* call is directed at terrestrial predators like the Fosa *Cryptoprocta ferox* and even large boas (*Acrantophis* and *Sanzinia* sp.).

Mating takes place in January and births occur, after a gestation period of around 180 days, in July. The infants are sparsely covered in hair when born and are initially carried by the mother on her belly, before moving around to ride on her back. They are weaned at around five months of age (November–December), which coincides with an increased abundance of high-quality immature leaves. Following weaning, the mother repeatedly refuses all attempts by the infant to suckle and only rarely tolerates dorsal riding for brief periods, for instance during predator scares. By one year of age young animals have attained around 70% of normal adult body weight.

POPULATION The total population is estimated to be no more than 8,000 individuals and may be considerably less. This total population is spread between a number of discontinuous forest fragments – the largest single population of *P. tattersalli* is estimated to be around 2,500 individuals. Within areas of good-quality forest population densities may reach 60-70 individuals/km².

THREATS The forests throughout the Golden-crowned Sifaka's very limited range are already severely fragmented and the species only occurs in isolated remnants that are surrounded by agriculture. Timber-felling and bush fires continue to encroach on the patches that remain and the species is known to be hunted in some areas. *P. tattersalli* does not occur in any protected area, although a three-parcel national park covering 20,000ha has been proposed in the Daraina area to try and safeguard the species in the wild.

VIEWING Anyone wishing to try and see this beautiful lemur should head for the town of Daraina. From here it is possible to visit various patches of forest where the sifaka occurs. Perhaps the best forests are those close to the village of Antsahampano which is 10km east of Daraina. None of these areas is easily reached and attempts are best limited to the dry season when the dirt roads are passable.

Figure 171. Golden-crowned Sifaka, near Daraina.

261

INDRI genus *Indri* E. Geoffroy and G. Cuvier, 1796

A monotypic genus containing one of the most familiar lemurs. The Indri is probably the largest extant prosimian, although the sympatric Diademed Sifaka *Propithecus diadema diadema* is of a similar size and weight.

INDRI *Indri indri* (Gmelin, 1788)

Malagasy: Babakoto, Endrina, Amboanala

MEASUREMENTS Total length: 640-720m. Head/body length: 600-670mm. Tail length: 40-50mm. Weight: 6-7.5kg.

DESCRIPTION The pelage is very dense and the coloration a mixture of black and white. There is considerable variation through the species's range. Towards the southern limits, the basic colour is black with creamy-white patches on the crown, nape and throat, base of the back, fore-arms, thighs and lower legs – these areas may also be tinged with silver-grey or pale creamy-yellow. The face and muzzle are black and the ears are round, tufted and prominent. The eyes are yellow-green (figs. 172 & 173).

At the northern extreme of the Indri's range pelage pattern is very different. Again the base colour is black, but pale grey and white regions are far less evident. The inner face is black, surrounded by a white facial disc which extends down the throat (fig. 182). There are white areas on the sides of the abdomen which extend under the armpits and there is a white pygal triangle at the base of the back which continues to the rump and includes the vestigial tail; the heels may also be pale grey or yellowish-white. White areas are completely absent on the forearms and upper hindlimbs.

In some localities towards the centre of the Indri's range, for instance around Mananara, a mixed pattern occurs which is intermediate between the two extremes outlined above.

The hindlimbs are proportionally very long (equivalent to the head/body length), but the tail is vestigial (this is the only virtually tailless lemur).

IDENTIFICATION A large, highly distinctive, vertically clinging and leaping lemur. Within the Indri's range, only the Diademed Sifaka is of comparable size, but is very much paler in colour and has a long tail. The Black-and-white Ruffed Lemur *Varecia variegata variegata* is similarly coloured, but it is considerably smaller in size and adopts a horizontal body posture.

HABITAT Primary and secondary lowland and mid-altitude rainforest.

DISTRIBUTION Today the Indri is confined to the central-eastern and north-eastern rainforests from sea-level to around 1,500m, although elevations below 1,000m appear to be preferred. Its range extends from the Mangoro River in the south to the area just south-west of Andapa in the north (Anjanaharibe-Sud), but does not reach the Marojejy Massif; nor does its range extend into the Masoala Peninsula in the north-east. Subfossil evidence indicates that the Indri's range was once

Figure 172. Indri, Mantadia.

Figure 173. Indri, Analamazaotra.

Indri

more extensive than this: remains have been found in caves in the Ankarana Massif towards Madagascar's northern tip and in the Itasy Massif in the central highlands.

BEHAVIOUR Indris are probably the most strictly diurnal lemurs (although they are known to call at night). They are active for 5-11 of the daylight hours, depending on the season and weather conditions. Group size varies between two and six, and normally comprises an adult pair with their dependent offspring of varying ages. Within the pair, the female tends to be dominant and has priority at food resources. These family units occupy territories of 8-30ha which are defended by the Indri's characteristic eerie wailing song (fig. 175). Smaller territories appear typical of isolated pockets of forest like Analamazaotra Special Reserve, while larger territories are associated with more expansive undisturbed tracts of forest like Mantadia National Park.

The Indri's call is loud enough to carry two to three kilometres and is generally answered by neighbouring groups; this maintains group distribution in the forest and prevents significant overlap of home ranges. Most calling bouts occur in the morning: the first ones between 05:30 and 07:00hr, the second between 08:00 and 09:00hr and the final major bout between 10:30 and 13:00hr. However, at certain times of the year (normally October–November) groups may also call at night, between 02:30 and 04:30hr. Individual calls may last up to 2.5 minutes and pairs often synchronise their calls and sing as a 'duet'. Some elements of the Indri's song closely resemble those of the White-handed Gibbon *Hylobates lar* from South-East Asia. A second call, akin to a klaxon-like repeated *honk, honk, honk* is used to warn of potential danger from aerial or ground predators.

The Indri's daily range is between 300m and 700m. The animals move through the canopy with spectacular bounds of up to ten metres between vertical branches and trunks.

Figure 174. Female Indri with infant, Analamazaotra.

Figure 175. Female Indri calling, Analamazaotra.

Prior to dusk, the group settles in a sleep tree, 10-30m off the ground. Females generally sleep in contact with their infants or subadult offspring, but males typically sleep 2-50m away. If males approach too close to the sleeping female, they often get cuffed.

The diet consists largely of young leaves and leaf buds, but also some flowers and both ripe and unripe fruits. Foraging may take place at all levels within the canopy. Bouts of feeding are punctuated by periods of rest, before the group moves on to the next feeding site. Very occasionally, the animals descend to the forest floor to eat soil, which may help detoxify poisons accumulated from the leaves they feed on or provide some vital trace elements.

Indris do not reach sexual maturity until between seven and nine years of age, and females are probably only capable of giving birth every second or third year. Therefore, their capacity for population growth is very slow. Mating generally occurs between December and March with a single offspring being born in May or June, but sometimes as late as August. The gestation period is between 120 and 150 days. Initially, the infant is carried on the mother's lower stomach (fig. 174), but transfers to ride on her back after four months. The young is capable of moving independently at eight months, but remains in close proximity to the mother until well into its second year. Mother and infant always sleep together for the first year, but afterwards do so only sporadically.

POPULATION No accurate population figures are available, and even rough estimates are difficult as it is not known to what extent populations have been fragmented by habitat destruction. Population densities of 9-16 /km^2 have been estimated.

THREATS The survival of this species is severely threatened by habitat destruction. Even forests lying within the bounds of protected areas continue to be felled and disturbed. Indris are not hunted by the local people as it is considered taboo or *fady* – the Betsimisaraka tribal name 'Babakoto' means 'Ancestor of Man'. However, there are reports of immigrants from other tribal groups and even some foreign immigrants hunting Indri. This species is known to occur in seven protected areas.

VIEWING No visit to Madagascar would be complete without seeing this spectacular creature. Fortunately this can be easily accomplished. At Analamazaotra Special Reserve near the village of Andasibe (Perinet) two family groups have been habituated and good sightings are virtually guaranteed. Andasibe is only four hours' drive from Antananarivo (about six hours by train) and a two-night stay in one of the local hotels/lodges should be ample. The local guides are excellent and provide a thorough and organised service. Try to be in the forest between 08:00hr and noon in order to hear the Indri call.

A worthwhile alternative is to visit the nearby forests at Maromizaha – along the ridge you will be fortunate to see Indri, but in the morning you are almost certain to hear them. Several groups inhabit the area and their combined duets and choruses are a memorable experience. Indri are also relatively common in Mantadia National Park to the north of Andasibe, but they tend to be very wary and difficult to approach.

It is also well worth trying to see the very dark Indri at the northern limit of the species's range, as this form is dramatically different to that found at Analamazaotra Special Reserve. The best place to try is Anjanaharibe-Sud Special Reserve, around 15km south-west of the town of Andapa. Here the Indri are not habituated so are much more difficult to find. Ideally a two- to three-night camping trip is necessary.

Figure 176. Indri feeding in rainforest canopy, Analamazaotra.

Figure 177. Aye-aye.

Aye-ayes
Family Daubentoniidae

This family contains a single extant species, the Aye-aye *Daubentonia madagascariensis*. Such is the bizarre appearance of the Aye-aye that, when first discovered, it was classified as a squirrel-like rodent: not until around 1850 was the species widely accepted as a primate.

AYE-AYE genus *Daubentonia* E. Geoffroy, 1795

Daubentonia exhibits a variety of peculiar morphological traits that set it apart from all other lemurs: an unusual dentition – incisors that grow continually (unique amongst primates), very large ears and a skeletally thin middle finger. Furthermore, the Aye-aye's morphology is so unusual that determining its closest relatives amongst other lemurs and primates is also proving extremely difficult. This species has to be regarded as one of the most unusual mammals on earth.

A second species, the Giant Aye-aye *D. robusta* is known only from subfossil remains found in southern and south-western Madagascar. From the post-cranial and dental material discovered, it is estimated to have been 2.5-5 times heavier than *D. madagascariensis*.

267

AYE-AYE *Daubentonia madagascariensis* (Gmelin, 1788)

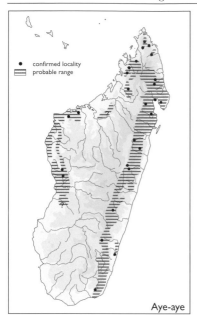

confirmed locality
probable range

Aye-aye

Malagasy: Hay-hay, Ahay, Aiay.

MEASUREMENTS Total length: 740-900mm. Head/body length: 300-370mm. Tail length: 440-530mm. Weight: 2-3kg.

DESCRIPTION Sexes similar. The overall colour of the head, upperparts, legs and tail is brindled dark slate grey-brown with white flecks. This effect is produced by long coarse dark grey-black guard hairs with white tips, overlaying a dense but short pale grey to creamy-white undercoat. The black ears are very large, leathery in appearance and mobile. The snout is very short and blunt and the nose is pink. The striking yellow/orange eyes are surrounded by dark rings, while the rest of the face and throat are pale grey. The tail is long and very bushy. The hands are also highly distinctive: all the digits are elongated with curved claw-like nails (only the first toe has a flat nail): the middle finger is extraordinarily thin – nothing more than skin, tendons and bone (figs. 177 & 178). The incisors are particularly long and rodent-like (and grow continually). Both of these remarkable features are similarly exhibited, but to a lesser extent, by the Long-fingered Triok *Dactylopsila palpator* (Petauridae) from New Guinea. Female Aye-ayes have two inguinal mammary glands located abdominally, and males have a penis bone.

IDENTIFICATION The suite of peculiar features that amalgamate to form an Aye-aye – huge ears, bushy tail, long shaggy coat and skeletal 'probe-like' middle finger – make this lemur unmistakable. It is by far the largest nocturnal species (twice the size of *Avahi* or *Lepilemur*), and confusion with either of these should not be possible.

HABITAT Low and mid-altitude rainforests, dry deciduous forests and some cultivated areas like coconut and lychee plantations.

DISTRIBUTION This species was once thought to be confined to the lowland rainforests of the north-east in the vicinity of Mananara. However, it is now known to be widely distributed in a variety of native forest types. It has been recorded at localities covering the entire extent of the eastern rainforest belt, from near Sambava (Marojejy) in the north all the way south to near Tolagnaro (Andohahela) in the far south. It has also been recorded in the moist forests of the Sambirano region in the north-west and the drier forests to the south in the vicinity of the Manasamody hills, the deciduous forests of Ankarana and Analamera and rainforests of Montagne d'Ambre in the far north. Evidence also indicates its presence at isolated localities in the west, most notably the Tsiombikibo Forest near Mitsinjo, the region south-east of Soalala, the Tsingy de Bemaraha National Park and the Kirindy Forest.

BEHAVIOUR The Aye-aye is nocturnal and largely solitary. The day is spent tucked away in a nest constructed from interwoven twigs and dead leaves, usually towards the canopy (above 7m) in a dense tangle of vines or branches. There is a high nest turn-over rate: in one study, eight Aye-ayes used over 100 nests in a two-year period, with different Aye-ayes using the same nest on different occasions. Large trees may contain as many as six nests.

Male Aye-ayes have large home ranges, between 100 and 200ha. These can overlap considerably with one another and the common area may be occupied by both males simultaneously: interactions occur and are sometimes agonistic. The males are also capable of travelling between two and four kilometres in a single night. Female home ranges are much smaller, generally between 30 and 50ha and do not overlap with one another, but do overlap with the home range of at least one male. Females interact rarely but are then invariably aggressive towards one another. Males and females occasionally come together and interact for brief periods, often when foraging. When they are active, Aye-ayes scent-mark regularly through urination and also by rubbing their ano-genital region, neck and cheeks directly onto branches.

Activity begins up to 30 minutes before sunset, although it may not begin until three hours after. Males are generally active before females. Vocalisations are most frequent at this time, typically a short sonorous *cree* lasting two to three seconds.

Up to 80% of the night is spent travelling and foraging in the upper canopy, when distances in excess of 2,500m may be covered. These foraging bouts are punctuated by rest periods that may last up to two hours. Aye-ayes are able to move quite nimbly around the branches and can leap and climb vertically with ease: horizontal movements are more deliberate, but they do descend to the ground and sometimes cover quite large distances. Outside breeding periods groups of three to four individuals have been seen travelling together and feeding at favoured foraging sites.

The Aye-aye's diet is quite specialised and consists mainly of the interior of ramy nuts *Canarium madagascariensis*, nectar from the Traveller's Tree *Ravenala madagascariensis*, some fungus and insect grubs. They are also known to raid coconut plantations and have been seen eating lychees and mangoes. The hard outer covers of Ramy nuts and coconuts are first gnawed through with their chisel-like incisors, before the thin middle digit is used to scoop out the pulp (fig. 179). In a similar fashion, insect grubs are winkled out of bark and rotting wood, their cavities having first been located by the Aye-aye tapping on the wood with its middle finger and then listening for any movements beneath. Aye-ayes spend considerable periods of time in search of insect grubs, which suggests they are particularly nutritious and energy-rich.

Aye-ayes do not have a fixed breeding season: at the onset of oestrous females move rapidly around their home range advertising their condition with distinctive calls. These attract the attention of several males simultaneously, which then gather around the female and fight one another for access. Copulation lasts around an hour and afterwards the female moves to another location and repeats her advertisement call. In this way both males and females may mate with several partners.

Figure 178. Aye-aye.

A single offspring is generally produced after a gestation period of around 160 to 170 days. At birth the infant weighs approximately 100g. There are indications that females have a two- to three-year interval between births.

POPULATION Although it is impossible to estimate the Aye-aye population, this species is now known to be far more wide-spread and numerous than previously thought, although it is always elusive. This is not to say that the Aye-aye is common as it has only ever been recorded at low densities in all the localities where it occurs. The fact remains that the Aye-aye is still a very rare animal whose population is almost certainly declining. It therefore warrants continued vigilance by all seeking to ensure its survival.

THREATS As with the majority of other lemurs, the main threat to the Aye-aye's survival is habitat destruction, although the species does make forays into certain cultivated areas. As the species only occurs at low densities, large tracts of forest are needed to maintain viable populations.

The Aye-aye is central to many superstitious beliefs, although they vary from region to region. In some areas they are thought to embody ancestral spirits and bring good luck. However, elsewhere they are considered ill omens and may be killed, villagers sometimes then erect the tails of slaughtered Aye-ayes on poles outside their dwellings. The meat is also sometimes eaten. Furthermore, the species often falls victim to angry farmers whose coconut or lychee plantations have been raided. The Aye-aye has been reported from at least 16 protected areas.

VIEWING This is certainly one of the most difficult lemur species to see in the wild, and usually a great deal of patience and a considerable slice of luck are needed for success. The two best places to try are Verezanantsoro National Park (Mananara-

Figure 179. Aye-aye feeding.

Nord Biosphere Reserve) south of Maroantsetra (especially Ile mon Désir) and Nosy Mangabe Special Reserve off Maroantsetra in the Bay of Antongil. Aye-ayes were introduced to the island of Nosy Mangabe in 1966 and have since thrived. Camping here for two or three nights would give a reasonably good chance of success. This species is also very, very occasionally seen at other popular rainforest localities, like Analamazaotra Special Reserve (Andasibe/Perinet), Montagne d'Ambre National Park and Ranomafana National Park. In all localities, seeing evidence of Aye-aye presence – gnawed holes in tree trunks and branches or nests in the canopy – is far more likely than seeing the animal itself.

Alternatively, this is such an unusual creature that it is worth making the effort to see one at close quarters in captivity. There are three individuals at Parc Botanique et Zoologique de Tsimbazaza in Antananarivo which can be viewed after dark by prior arrangement (not during the day). Also Jersey Zoo (UK) and Duke University Primate Centre (USA) have excellent nocturnal features where these animals can be seen (the latter again by prior arrangement).

NON-ENDEMIC MAMMALS
EVEN-TOED UNGULATES
ORDER ARTIODACTYLA

Figure 180. Bush Pigs.

Unlike many other island biotas, the fauna of Madagascar has not (yet) suffered a major intrusion of species, accidentally or intentionally, introduced by man. Aside from three domesticated species – Dogs *Canis familiaris*, Cats *Felis catus* and Zebu Cattle *Bos taurus* – which will not be treated further, only seven non-endemic mammals have found their way to Madagascar: three rodents, the Black Rat *Rattus rattus*, Brown Rat *R. norvegicus* and House Mouse *Mus musculus*; two insectivores, the Musk Shrew *Suncus murinus* and Pygmy Musk Shrew *S. etruscus*; one viverrid, the Small Indian Civet *Viverricula indica* and one ungulate, the Bush Pig *Potamochoerus larvatus*.

It is known that the Bush Pig is a relatively recent arrival on Madagascar, although there is some conjecture as to how it arrived and whether it is actually introduced at all. On mainland Africa, the Bush Pig is known to venture regularly into extensive papyrus beds, which may become detached, float down river and out to sea. In this manner it has been suggested that Bush Pigs might have reached Madagascar as a natural process. However, introduction by human agency seems more probable and is assumed to be the case here.

Pigs
Family Suidae

This family of Old World wild pigs contains ten species, arranged between five genera. As a family they are found throughout Europe, Asia, South-East Asia, the East Indies and Africa. Family members have also been introduced to North and South America, Australia, New Guinea and New Zealand. One species, the Wild Boar *Sus scrofa* has given rise to the domestic pig, which now occurs worldwide in association with humans.

BUSH PIGS genus *Potamochoerus* Gray, 1854

This genus contains just two species, the Red River Hog *P. porcus* and the Bush Pig *P. larvatus*. They are distributed through the equatorial regions of sub-Saharan Africa, the Red River Hog being found in West Africa from Senegal to eastern Zaïre and as far south as northern Angola, while the Bush Pig's range is limited to eastern and south-eastern Africa and Madagascar. Some authorities do not believe differentiation is warranted and regard all populations as belonging to the same species, the name *P. porcus* taking priority.

271

BUSH PIG *Potamochoerus larvatus* (F. Cuvier, 1822)

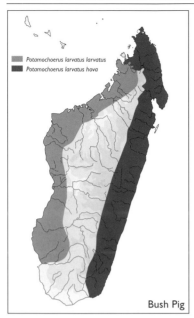

Potamochoerus larvatus larvatus
Potamochoerus larvatus hova

Bush Pig

Malagasy: Lambo, Antsanga

MEASUREMENTS Head/body length: 900-1200mm*. Tail length: 300-400mm*. Shoulder height: 600-800mm*. Weight: females upto 55kg*, males up to 70kg*.
*estimated measurements for Malagasy specimens.

DESCRIPTION The pelage over the entire body, including the head and face, is long and bristly but relatively sparse. From between the ears running down the length of the back, the hairs are longer and form a distinct dorsal crest. The snout is very elongate and the ears have extended pinnae which are tufted. The cheeks of males in particular are often quite bushy and beard-like. Males also have small tusks which are barely visible. Pelage coloration can be quite variable: generally the face and head are predominantly grey with this extending over the nape and part-way down the dorsal crest. There is a darker broad band around the muzzle. The upperparts of the body are reddish-brown to greyish-brown and these grade to darker grey-brown underparts and limbs.

IDENTIFICATION A medium-sized wild pig with a rather shaggy appearance. This is the only wild ungulate on Madagascar. It is by far the largest free-living mammal on the island and cannot be confused with any other species.

HABITAT On Madagascar this species is known to occur in all major habitat types from rainforests to dry deciduous forests and spiny forests. It is also common in many secondary and degraded habitats and cultivated areas, wherever the level of cover is sufficient. It appears to be absent from the deforested central highlands and within the proximity of major urban areas.

DISTRIBUTION The Bush Pig is currently divided into four subspecies: despite probably being introduced, the nominate race, *P. l. larvatus* is described from western Madagascar and the Comoros; a second Malagasy race, *P. l. hova* is recognised from eastern regions of the island, although some regard this division as questionable; while mainland Africa populations comprise *P. l. hassama* from East Africa as far north as Ethiopia and *P. l. koiropotamus* from northern Tanzania, east to Angola and south to Mozambique. There is also an apparently isolated population of this race on the Cape coast in South Africa.

The recognition of two races in Madagascar is contentious. Few specimens have been examined from either population, so differentiation may not withstand closer scrutiny. However, populations from eastern rainforest regions appear to be larger in size and greyer in colour, while those from the west are smaller and distinctly reddish. These distinctions are supported by observational evidence from the Malagasy people, who recognise two forms.

BEHAVIOUR The Bush Pig has not been studied in detail in Madagascar. The information presented here is based on anecdotal accounts and observations, and behavioural and ecological information inferred from studies on mainland Africa.

Bush Pigs live in groups of between two and ten individuals, although four to six is average in Madagascar. Each group appears to contain a dominant male. They are predominantly nocturnal, although there may be a tendency towards diurnal activity in remote areas away from human disturbance. The day is often spent in a self-excavated burrow or similar natural secluded hideaway like large roots systems (pers. obs.). In forested areas average home range size appears to be between four and ten square kilometers.

Births occur between October and December, a litter of one to four young being produced after a gestation period of around 120 days. Females may construct a deep nest of vegetation in order to protect the piglets. They are given a considerable amount of care and attention not only by the sow but also by the dominant boar.

The catholic diet consists mainly of roots, tubers, berries and fallen fruit, but also animal matter like reptile eggs, small vertebrates, a variety of invertebrates, carrion and excrement. At times groups may take advantage of fruit discarded by lemurs feeding in the canopy. When feeding, the powerful snout is used as a plough to dig up subsoil matter the tusks may also be used to help dig deeper. This is a highly destructive method of feeding and in short periods of time a group can strip an area of most plants; they may also do considerable damage to crops.

It is known that the Bush Pig has been a highly influential factor contributing to the rapid decline of some native tortoise species in Madagascar. For instance, the nests of the Anogonoka *Geochelone yniphora* are regularly predated (both eggs and hatchlings). This species is now probably the world's most endangered tortoise and is restricted to a small area in the region of Soalala in western Madagascar. It is highly likely that other endemic reptiles and possibly ground nesting birds suffer in a similar fashion.

Bush Pigs are widely hunted by humans in Madagascar, sometimes with the aid of dogs. Smaller individuals are also known to be predated by the island's largest native carnivore, the Fosa *Cryptoprocta ferox*.

VIEWING Although Bush Pigs are widespread and common, they are rarely seen during the day due to their shyness and mainly nocturnal habits. However, indications of their presence are often to be found in forested regions, in the form of large excavated areas of the forest floor. The animals can occasionally be encountered on forest walks at night, but soon disappear when startled.

CONSERVATION AND PROTECTED AREAS

Figure 181. Malagasy children with pet infant Red-fronted Brown Lemur, Mitsinjo.

Madagascar's unique biological heritage faces a barrage of serious and ever increasing threats, the most immediate being habitat destruction and degradation – alas, problems that impinge upon floral and faunal communities throughout the tropical forests of the world.

In Madagascar habitat destruction is particularly acute. The majority of the human population live in rural communities that depend heavily on the land and native forests for their livelihood. Methods of traditional subsistence agriculture involve slash-and-burn (*tavy*) cultivation, where forests are felled and then torched to clear the land and subsequently plant crops – mainly rice and manioc, but also coffee, vanilla, cloves and other spices. Madagascar's lateritic soils are poor in quality and cannot sustain food crops for more than two or three years. Without the protection of the trees above, the soil is quickly eroded and washed away, especially on slopes, resulting in rivers and streams becoming clogged with silt. Within a short space of time, the cleared land is reduced to a sterile and barren moonscape, so farmers move on to clear more forest, and the unfortunate destructive cycle is repeated.

Evidence suggests that humans are comparative newcomers to Madagascar: they arrived mainly from South-East Asia, Arabia and later mainland Africa, as recently as 1,500 to 2,000 years ago. It is bewildering to contemplate that in the relatively short time that our species has been resident on the island, around 80% of the native forest cover has been lost. In the second half of the 20th century alone, there has been a 50% decline in the extent of the eastern rainforests. It has been estimated that more than 110,000ha of rainforest are felled each year, a total area approximately half the size of the largest national park within that region! These figures are made all the more staggering in that this destruction has been achieved largely with hand tools and back-breaking human endeavour rather than the efficient machinery of commercial logging concerns.

As if the destruction of the forests were not enough, some of Madagascar's wildlife faces a more direct threat from hunting. With an ever-expanding human population there is an increased demand for food, and protein in particular, a demand that the beleaguered agricultural system cannot meet. In many remaining forests tracts a variety of species, especially mammals, are hunted for food, their skins, the captive animal trade or even for superstitious reasons, despite being officially protected by law. This particularly affects many of the large lemur species, but also some of the carnivores, larger tenrecs, rodents and fruit bats.

So what can be done to try and stem the tide of depletion? In the past the simple gazetting of a protected area has not been enough. More often than not this has been little more than a line-drawing exercise on a map. The local people have continued to cut wood, clear forests and hunt wildlife within the area, unaware that legislation had been implemented. And even if they were aware, it has made little difference since they have had no alternatives to supplement their livelihood.

In many past instances in other parts of the world, the human populations living adjacent to protected areas have been regarded as the first line of attack. Exclusion was seen as the answer, leaving the area as a preserve solely for wildlife. However, attempts to exclude local people from these areas have proved futile and disastrous in the long term. When the people's very survival is dependent on utilising the natural environment, no protective force will be sufficient to stop them, and they will find ways to circumvent even the strictest laws. Consequently, there has been a growing realisation amongst the conservation community that the answer perhaps lies on the opposite side of the fence: if conservation activities are to succeed in the long run, they must *involve* the local people.

273

In essence the principles are simple. Conservation needs to be linked to incentives that help improve the standards of living for local people, but in ways that reduce the pressures they place on their local environment to the point where they ultimately become sustainable. In this way the destructive downward spiral may be slowed and eventually halted. However, if these projects are to succeed, they must above all else give the local people both a say and a personal stake in the project. By becoming aware that their very existence is inextricably linked to the quality and integrity of their environment, local people have the strongest possible incentive to help ensure that its conservation is a success. No longer are they considered the first line of attack, but rather the last line of defence.

These principles now widely inform conservation efforts in Madagascar. The Malagasy government, working in conjunction with a number of international conservation agencies and funding organisations, has now implemented several projects that integrate the conservation of biodiversity with the development of local communities (Integrated Conservation and Developments Projects, or ICDPs). The World Wide Fund for Nature (WWF) is focusing its attention on the Montagne d'Ambre and Ankarana, Beza-Mahafaly, Andohahela, Andringitra, Marojejy and Anjanaharibe-Sud reserves; Conservation International (CI) is directing its attention to the Ankarafantsika and Zahamena reserves; the recently created Masoala National Park is a cooperative effort involving the Wildlife Conservation Society (WCS), CARE International and the Peregrine Fund; the Institute for the Conservation of Tropical Environments (ICTE) and State University of New York (SUNY) at Stony Brook oversee the Ranomafana National Park Project; UNESCO manages the biosphere reserve at Mananara-Nord, while Jersey Wildlife Preservation Trust (JWPT) concentrates its efforts around Lac Alaotra, in the Soalala region and further south at Lac Bemamba. These are all relatively new initiatives and it is clear there are no simple formulae to solve the many complex problems and issues that exist.

However, certain fundamental elements underpin the majority of ICDPs. In order to devise sustainable (long-term) economic alternatives to forest clearance it is vital to understand the interrelationships of the fauna and flora within the forest. To this end biodiversity research, involving a wide spectrum of taxonomic groups, focuses on how each species fits into the forest community as a whole and its interdependency on other species. This information can then be integrated with indigenous knowledge from the local communities.

Armed with this knowledge, it is then possible to devise, implement and support sustainable agricultural techniques that are sympathetic to the local environment. For instance, in rainforest areas alternatives such as aquaculture, apiculture and horticulture of important native species have been encouraged, whilst attempting to find ways of maximising production from existing land under rice cultivation (by application of fertilisers, using more suitable seed varieties, and improved irrigation systems). This then reduces the need for the expansion of *tavy* cultivation and hence maintains the integrity of the remaining forests and watershed.

Healthcare is also a vital component. Local communities generally acknowledge this to be their primary concern. It involves improved preventative measures, sanitation and family planning, and whereever possible incorporates both traditional medicinal methods based on forest products (those that can be cultivated or sustainably harvested) as well as modern western techniques. If improved health results in better child survivorship, then there is less incentive to have a large family, eventually leading to a slowing of population growth.

Of course education and training run hand-in-hand with all of these. Education and conservation awareness programmes are designed to increase literacy and provide access to educational facilities for local residents. Local people also work closely with both Malagasy and western scientists to gain a better understanding of the precarious nature of their environment: some become full-time researchers and others park rangers.

Figure 182. Captive Indris being kept for the 'pot'.

Once all the above are in place, the final piece of the jigsaw can be slotted in – ecotourism. The recreational use of forests creates more jobs for the local people and increases revenue for the community. Local people who may have once relied for their livelihood on harvesting forest products are then able to earn a living as park guides or maintenance personnel. Furthermore, tourists require accommodation, so employment is created in local hotels and other secondary service industries.

This is not to say that ecotourism is a panacea for Madagascar's environmental ills. It is not. There is always a great danger of identity and integrity being lost when simple indigenous communities are exposed to materialistic western cultures. However, if the approach is cautious and the system carefully managed, there is every reason to believe that ecotourism has a vital role to play in the conservation of Madagascar's natural heritage.

Parks and Reserves

Madagascar has an extensive network of protected areas, the origins of which date back to 1927 and French colonial administration. For years the system was ill-funded, inadequately manned and stagnant, offering only cursory protection against habitat destruction, disturbance and hunting. However, the situation has changed over recent years. In the mid-1980s Madagascar was identified as the world's major conservation priority. This galvanised the Malagasy government and the international community into action. A number of major initiatives have been undertaken and are still in progress.

The management of the island's protected areas now falls under the remit of the National Association for Management of Protected Areas (ANGAP); further conservation and forestry issues are dealt with by the Department of Waters and Forests (DEF), with the entire environmental programme being administered by a National Environmental Office (ONE). The DEF and ANGAP now work in concert with a number of high-profile international conservation agencies to enhance the management of Madagascar's protected areas network.

Today the protected areas are divided into several categories, based on management strategy, main purpose, degree of protection and visitor access. The major areas incorporate eight national parks (with at least two more due to be declared in the near future), 10 'strict nature reserves', 23 'special reserves' and a small number of 'private reserves' (see Appendix II). Together, these cover just over 1.3 million hectares (national parks: 534,740ha; strict nature reserves: 417,542ha; special reserves: 376,580ha; private reserves: around 8,000ha), which still only represents 2% of the island's surface area. In addition, there are 267 areas of partial protection (forestry stations, classified forests and forest reserves) which cover in excess of four million hectares or 7% of Madagascar's land area. Therefore, a total area amounting to 9% of Madagascar's surface areas can be considered protected to some degree.

Because of Madagascar's large size and modest road infrastructure, only a few of these areas of biological interest are easily accessible. This can be a frustrating limitation to the visiting naturalist. However, development is taking place and the transport network slowly improving, partially subsidised by revenue from the flow of visitors that come to see the island's natural riches. Several of the island's major 'wildlife hotspots' are now within easy reach for the traveller and so receive a constant influx of eager and expectant visitors.

All state-run parks and reserves require an entry ticket (permit). These are issued by ANGAP and are easily obtainable from their main offices in Antananarivo (see Appendix IV) or from the various regional offices close to the protected area in question. Some of the more frequently visited parks and reserves issue tickets at the entrance. It is vital that a ticket be obtained every time an area is visited, as 50% of the money is ploughed back into conservation and local community development around the protected area. In this way the local population becomes aware of the sustainable benefits to be gained by maintaining the integrity of their forest areas.

Top Mammal-watching Sites

In this section the major sites of interest to the mammal-watcher are outlined. They have been chosen first because they offer superb wildlife experiences, second because they represent a cross-section of the different regions and habitat types, and third because access to them is feasible for the independent traveller or organised group.

Each account contains a list of the main mammal species that have been recorded. Species given in **bold** indicate that observations can be particularly rewarding, and correspond to the recommended sites suggested in the 'Viewing' section of the individual species accounts.

Rainforest Areas

The eastern rainforest belt is perhaps the most exciting region for naturalists as it supports the greatest diversity of animal and plant species. Furthermore, around 80% of species are endemic to this region. It can also be the most infuriating, as animals, and in particular mammals, can be very difficult to find. No fewer than 25 major protected areas are located within rainforest areas, but the majority of these are either remote and difficult to reach or off-limits for all except government officials and scientists with permission. However, several key reserves in widely distributed localities are accessible. Visits to three or four of these would offer ample mammal-watching opportunities for a wide cross-section of species.

LOWLAND RAINFOREST RESERVES

Masoala National Park

Permits: Obtainable from the Masoala Project offices in Maroantsetra and Antalaha or the ANGAP offices in Antananarivo.

Location and Access: 15°12'–15°50'S, 49°55'–50°20'E (approximate).
The Masoala Peninsula lies to the east of Maroantsetra and forms the northern coastline of the Bay of Antongil. The western side of the park is best reached by boat from Maroantsetra. This takes around three to four hours to the village of Ambanizana, the point of easiest access. From here good areas of forest can be reached in less than an hour. It is also possible to take a boat from Antalaha on the east side of the Peninsula down to Cap Est. Here it is possible to arrange boat trips and guided forest walks into the park.

Elevation: sea-level to around 1,100m.

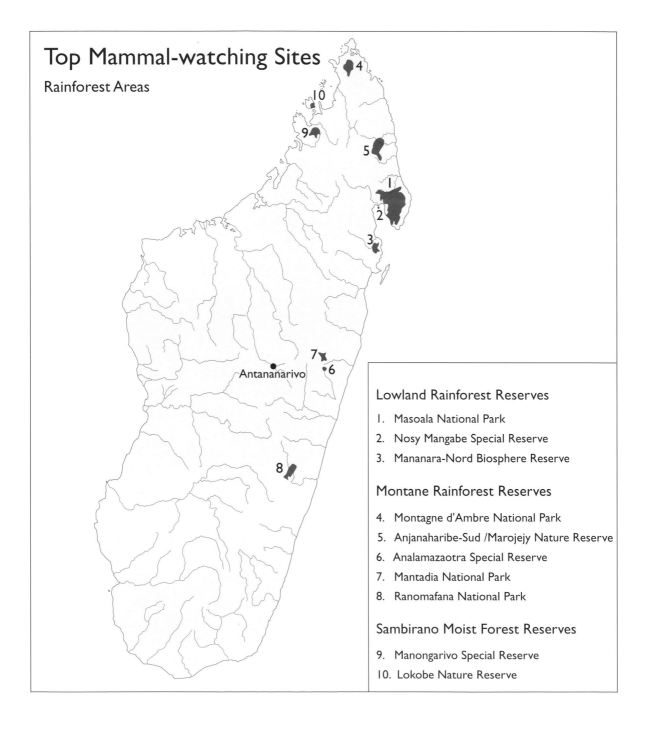

Top Mammal-watching Sites

Rainforest Areas

Lowland Rainforest Reserves

1. Masoala National Park
2. Nosy Mangabe Special Reserve
3. Mananara-Nord Biosphere Reserve

Montane Rainforest Reserves

4. Montagne d'Ambre National Park
5. Anjanaharibe-Sud /Marojejy Nature Reserve
6. Analamazaotra Special Reserve
7. Mantadia National Park
8. Ranomafana National Park

Sambirano Moist Forest Reserves

9. Manongarivo Special Reserve
10. Lokobe Nature Reserve

Antananarivo

Habitat and Terrain: This is the largest and best remaining area of coastal/lowland rainforest on Madagascar, often extending right down to the shore. The peninsula covers a total area in excess of 400,000ha, with the park occupying 210,200ha of pristine forest primarily on the western side. The height of the canopy is between 25m and 30m and there are few emergent trees. The understorey is characterised by abundant palms and tree ferns and there are many epiphytes and orchids. The slopes are often very steep, and there are numerous clear, fast flowing streams and small rivers. This is the wettest part of Madagascar: annual rainfall exceeds 3,500mm and there is no discernible dry season.

KEY MAMMAL SPECIES

Bats: **Madagascar Flying Fox** *Pteropus rufus*, Madagascar Straw-coloured Fruit Bat *Eidolon dupreanum*, Madagascar Rousette *Rousettus madagascariensis*, Sucker-footed Bat *Myzopoda aurita*, long-fingered bat *Miniopterus manavi* and Commerson's Leaf-nosed Bat *Hipposideros commersoni*.

Tenrecs: Common Tenrec *Tenrec ecaudatus* Greater Hedgehog Tenrec *Setifer setosus*, Lowland Streaked Tenrec *Hemicentetes semispinosus*, rice tenrecs *Oryzorictes* spp. and shrew tenrecs *Microgale* spp.

Rodents: Eastern Red Forest Rat *Nesomys rufus*, **Lowland Red Forest Rat** *Nesomys audeberti* and tuft-tailed rats *Eliurus* spp.

Carnivores: Fanaloka *Fossa fossana*, Falanouc *Eupleres goudotii*, Fosa *Cryptoprocta ferox*, Broad-striped Mongoose *Galidictis fasciata*, Ring-tailed Mongoose *Galidia elegans elegans* and **Brown-tailed Mongoose** *Salanoia concolor*.

Lemurs: **Red-ruffed Lemur** *Varecia variegata rubra*, White-fronted Brown Lemur *Eulemur fulvus albifrons*, Eastern Grey Bamboo Lemur *Hapalemur griseus griseus*, **Weasel Sportive Lemur** *Lepilemur mustelinus*, Eastern Avahi *Avahi laniger*, Greater Dwarf Lemur *Cheirogaleus major*, **Eastern Fork-marked Lemur** *Phaner furcifer furcifer*, Brown Mouse Lemur *Microcebus rufus*, Hairy-eared Dwarf Lemur *Allocebus trichotis* and Aye-aye *Daubentonia madagascariensis*.

Season: The Masoala Peninsula is wet throughout the year. Avoid the cyclone season (January to March) as the sea can be rough, the boat journey is treacherous and the rainfall, temperatures and humidity are at their highest, making conditions very trying.

Facilities: Hotels in Maroantsetra (Relais du Masoala and Coco Beach) can arrange boat trips with their own support personnel and guides. There are only camping facilities on the peninsula: all equipment and provisions must be taken. The trail network is limited and paths are often steep. The most accessible areas are around the village of Ambanizana. The Residence du Cap at Cap Est is able to organise boat trips, guides and forest walks into the eastern side of the park. A Park Education and Interpretive Centre is planned at the Masoala Project offices in Maroantsetra in the future.

Visiting: Masoala takes time and effort to reach. A visit of at least four days, and preferably more, is recommended for this wonderful area. A local guide from the Association des Guides Ecotouristiques de Maroantsetra (AGEM) is essential at all times. They can be arranged through the Masoala Project office in Maroantsetra.

Nosy Mangabe Special Reserve

Permits: Available from the Masoala Project offices in Maroantsetra or the ANGAP offices in Antananarivo. Guides from the Association des Guides Eco-touristiques de Maroantsetra (AGEM) are also available from the offices in Maroantsetra.

Location and Access: 15°30'S 49°46'E. The island of Nosy Mangabe lies 5km off the coast in the Bay of Antongil in north-east Madagascar. The boat ride from Maroantsetra takes about 45 minutes.

Elevation: Sea-level to 332m.

Habitat and Terrain: A good example of lowland rainforest which covers the entire island, an area of some 520ha. This forest has largely regenerated after considerable human activity around 200 to 300 years ago. There are large buttress-rooted trees reaching 35m or more in height. Species are typical of this type of forest: *Ravensara*, *Canarium*, *Ocotea*, *Ficus* and *Tambourissa*. Tree ferns, ferns, epiphytes and orchids are also common. The island's slopes rise steeply from the sea to the summit.

Figure 183. Aye-aye.

277

KEY MAMMAL SPECIES

Bats: **Madagascar Flying Fox** *Pteropus rufus*, Malagasy Mouse-eared Bat *Myotis goudoti* and Commerson's Leaf-nosed Bat *Hipposideros commersoni*.

Tenrecs: Greater Hedgehog Tenrec *Setifer setosus* and rice tenrec *Oryzorictes talpoides*.

Rodents: Black Rat *Rattus rattus*.

Carnivores: none.

Lemurs: **Aye-aye** *Daubentonia madagascariensis*, **Black-and-white Ruffed Lemur** *Varecia variegata variegata*, **White-fronted Brown Lemur** *Eulemur fulvus albifrons*, Greater Dwarf Lemur *Cheirogaleus major* and Brown Mouse Lemur *Microcebus rufus*.

Season: Accessible all year round, although it is best to avoid the cyclone season (January to March) as the sea can be choppy and rainfall, temperatures and humidity are at their highest. The best time to see Aye-ayes on their favoured trees near the beach is between April and June.

Facilities: There is an established campsite, with a limited number of covered tent platforms, a shower (fed from a waterfall) and toilets. All equipment and provisions must be taken from Maroantsetra. An old research laboratory has been converted into an interpretive centre. An extensive network of footpaths, which is gradually being improved, winds through the forest. Some of the trails, particularly those up to the summit, are steep: there are flat trails with wooden walkways/bridges around the campsite and behind the beach.

Visiting: A day trip from Maroantsetra, leaving early in the morning, is possible and will be rewarding. However, Nosy Mangabe is such a beautiful island that a longer camping trip of two or three days is recommended, particularly if trying to see Aye-ayes is a priority.

Mananara-Nord Biosphere Reserve *(Verezanantsoro National Park)*

Permits: Issued at the Biosphere Office in the town of Mananara Avaratra (Mananara-Nord).

Location and Access: 16°14'–16°32'S 49°38'–49°50'E.
The reserve is located on the east coast close to the entrance to the Bay of Antongil. It lies to the south of the town of Mananara Avaratra, approximately 225km north of Toamasina. The roads to Mananara Avaratra are very poor and often impassable after heavy rain. The easiest way to reach the town is by air. From Mananara Avaratra the small town of Sandrakatsy is a two-hour drive. It is then necessary to walk to Ivavary and then on to the best area of the park.

Elevation: Sea-level to around 570m.

Habitat and Terrain: Mananara-Nord Biosphere Reserve covers a total area of 140,000ha. Contained within this is Verezanantsoro National Park, which is divided into two parcels, 1,000ha covering coastal and reef environments (Nosy Atafana) and 23,000ha covering primary and secondary lowland rainforests. These are the largest and best remaining fragments of lowland east coast rainforest. The canopy is high (25-30m) and closed. There are numerous very large trees with buttress roots. This is probably the richest site on the island for endemic palm species (Palmae). The area is very wet with many rivers and streams. Some of the slopes are steep.

KEY MAMMAL SPECIES

Bats: Madagascar Flying Fox *Pteropus rufus*, Madagascar Straw-coloured Fruit Bat *Eidolon dupreanum*, Sucker-footed Bat *Myzopoda aurita* and free-tailed bats *Tadarida* spp.

Tenrecs: Common Tenrec *Tenrec ecaudatus*, Greater Hedgehog Tenrec *Setifer setosus*, Lowland Streaked Tenrec *Hemicentetes semispinosus*, rice tenrec *Oryzorictes hova* and various shrew tenrecs *Microgale* spp.

Rodents: **Lowland Red Forest Rat** *Nesomys audeberti* and the tuft-tailed rats, *Eliurus minor*, *E. ellermani* and *E. webbi*.

Carnivores: Falanouc *Eupleres goudotii*, Fanaloka *Fossa fossana*, Fosa *Cryptoprocta ferox*, Eastern Ring-tailed Mongoose *Galidia elegans elegans*, Broad-striped Mongoose *Galidictis fasciata* and Brown-tailed Mongoose *Salanoia concolor*.

Lemurs: Black-and-white Ruffed Lemur *Varecia variegata variegata*, White-fronted Brown Lemur *Eulemur fulvus albifrons*, Indri *Indri indri*, Diademed Sifaka *Propithecus diadema diadema* Eastern Grey Bamboo Lemur *Hapalemur griseus griseus*, Weasel Sportive Lemur *Lepilemur mustelinus*, Eastern Avahi *Avahi laniger*, Greater Dwarf Lemur *Cheirogaleus major*, Brown Mouse Lemur *Microcebus rufus*, **Hairy-eared Dwarf Lemur** *Allocebus trichotis* and Aye-aye *Daubentonia madagascariensis*.

Season: Not accessible during the rainy season between December and March. Best from September to November.

Facilities: These are very limited. The Hotel Aye-Aye in Mananara Avaratra (Mananara-Nord) can arrange excursions with guides, cooks and porters. There is basic accommodation in Ivavary for visitors to the park. Camping is possible, but all equipment and provisions must be taken. The trails are limited and often arduous.

Visiting: This is a difficult reserve to reach. A minimum stay of three nights is recommended. Mammal-watching is difficult, there are no habituated groups of lemurs, and glimpses are likely to be brief. However, this is such a spectacular area of primary rainforest that all efforts are worthwhile.

MONTANE RAINFOREST RESERVES

Montagne d'Ambre National Park

Permits: Available from WWF Montagne d'Ambre Project Office in Antsiranana or at the park entrance. Guides can also be hired here.

Location and Access: The park is located some 30km south from Antsiranana (Diego Suarez) at the island's northern tip. It is less than one hour's drive along a metalled road to Ambohitra (Joffreville) and then a well-maintained dirt road for the last 7km to the park entrance.

Elevation: Between 850m and 1,475m.

Habitat and Terrain: An isolated patch of montane rainforest covering an area of 18,200ha. Montagne d'Ambre derives it name from the resin that oozes from the trunks of large trees like 'Ramy' *Canarium madagascariense* and 'Rotra' *Eugenia rotra*. The canopy height averages 25m to 30m, but in places reaches 40m. There are numerous Bird's Nest Ferns *Asplenium nidus*, tree ferns *Cyanathea* spp., orchids *Angraecum* spp. and lianas.

Two waterfalls – *La Grande Cascade* and *La Petite Cascade* – form the focal points of the park. There are also crater lakes (*Lac de la Coupe Verte* and *La Grande Lac*) and several viewpoints over the forest and surrounding area.

KEY MAMMAL SPECIES

Bats: Madagascar Flying Fox *Pteropus rufus*, Madagascar Straw-coloured Fruit Bat *Eidolon dupreanum*, Madagascar Rousette *Rousettus madagascariensis* and **Commerson's Leaf-nosed Bat** *Hipposideros commersoni*.

Tenrecs: Common Tenrec *Tenrec ecaudatus*, Greater Hedgehog Tenrec *Setifer setosus*, **Lowland Streaked Tenrec** *Hemicentetes semispinosus* and various shrew tenrecs *Microgale* spp.

Rodents: Eastern Red Forest Rat *Nesomys rufus*.

Carnivores: Falanouc *Eupleres goudotii*, Fanaloka *Fossa fossana*, Fosa *Cryptoprocta ferox* and Northern Ring-tailed Mongoose *Galidia elegans dambrensis*.

Lemurs: **Sanford's Brown Lemur** *Eulemur fulvus sanfordi*, **Crowned Lemur** *Eulemur coronatus*, **Northern Sportive Lemur** *Lepilemur septentrionalis*, **Amber Mountain Fork-marked Lemur** *Phaner furcifer electromontis*, Greater Dwarf Lemur *Cheirogaleus major*, **Brown Mouse Lemur** *Microcebus rufus* and Aye-aye *Daubentonia madagascariensis*.

Season: Accessible all the year round. The austral summer (October to April) is the more rewarding time for the wildlife, but avoid January to March because of potential heavy rain. Best compromise, September to December.

Facilities: There is no permanent accommodation within the park, only a well-maintained campsite. All equipment and provisions must be taken. There is an extensive network of trails through all the best areas within the park. Those less frequently used tend to become overgrown. Some of the trails follow steep slopes, so walking can be difficult and tiring.

Visiting: A day trip from Antsiranana is possible, but to get the most from the park it is necessary to camp for at least one night and preferably two or three. The forests around, and within easy walking distance from, the campsite are good for the majority of accessible mammals. Nocturnal walks can be very good. It is recommended to employ the services of a park guide.

Anjanaharibe-Sud Special Reserve/ Marojejy Nature Reserve

Permits: Available from the WWF Anjanaharibe-Sud – Marojejy Project Office in Andapa. Advice on local guides is also available here.

Location and Access: 14°35'–14°50'S 49°26'–49°31'E.
The reserve lies 25km to the west of the town of Andapa, which is situated around 120km south-west of Sambava at the northern end of the eastern rainforest belt. The reserve is around an hour by road from Andapa.

Elevation: Between 500m and 2064m.

Habitat and Terrain: Montane and high montane rainforest covering an area of 32,100ha. These forests, along with those on the adjacent Marojejy Massif, are particularly rich, with a high proportion of locally endemic species. The Anjanaharibe-Sud Massif spans a wide elevational range: at lower altitudes the forest is similar to lowland rainforests with the canopy reaching 30m and many large buttress trees like *Canarium*; the majority of the reserve is typical mid-altitude montane rainforest, the canopy averaging 20m to 25m; above 1,500m this gives way to high montane rainforest, and where altitudes exceed 1,800m the vegetation is mainly stunted bush dominated by the family Ericaceae. At lower elevations annual rainfall averages around 2,000mm, rising to over 3,000mm at higher altitudes. The slopes are often steep and there are many deep valleys with fast-flowing streams.

KEY MAMMAL SPECIES

Bats: Madagascar Flying Fox *Pteropus rufus*.

Tenrecs: Common Tenrec *Tenrec ecaudatus*, Greater Hedgehog Tenrec *Setifer setosus*, Lowland Streaked Tenrec *Hemicentetes semispinosus* and various shrew tenrecs *Microgale* spp., including M. *dobsoni*, M. *talazaci*, M. *soricoides* and M. *gymnorhyncha*.

Rodents: Eastern Red Forest Rat *Nesomys rufus*, White-tailed Tree Rat *Brachytarsomys albicauda*, tuft-tailed rats *Eliurus* spp.

Carnivores:Fanaloka *Fossa fossana*, Fosa *Cryptoprocta ferox*, Eastern Ring-tailed Mongoose *Galidia elegans elegans* and **Broad-striped Mongoose** *Galidictis fasciata*.

Lemurs: **Indri** *Indri indri* (black variant), **Silky Sifaka** *Propithecus diadema candidus*, White-fronted Brown Lemur *Eulemur fulvus albifrons*, Red-bellied Lemur *Eulemur rubriventer*, Eastern Grey Bamboo Lemur *Hapalemur griseus griseus*, Eastern Avahi *Avahi laniger*, **Weasel Sportive Lemur** *Lepilemur mustelinus*, **Greater Dwarf Lemur** *Cheirogaleus major*, Brown Mouse Lemur *Microcebus rufus*, **Hairy-eared Dwarf Lemur** *Allocebus trichotis* and Aye-aye *Daubentonia madagascariensis*.

Season: The rainy season between late December and March is best avoided. The months prior to this (September to November) offer the best combination of good wildlife-watching and tolerable conditions.

Facilities: There are no visitor facilities within the reserve or close by. The nearest suitable accommodation consists of small hotels in Andapa. Small cleared campsites are located at specific points along some trails. The trail network itself is not extensive and the hills are often steep. Walking can be difficult.

Visiting: Trips to the reserve can be arranged through the Hotel Vatosoa in Andapa. It is recommended to camp for at least two nights, preferably longer, and arranged to be picked up. A local guide is essential.

Analamazaotra Special Reserve

Permits: These may be obtained at the park entrance or at the ANGAP offices in Antananarivo. Local guides from the Association des Guides d'Andasibe are always on hand to offer assistance.

Location and Access: 18°58'S 48°28'E.
The reserve lies adjacent to the village of Andasibe, which is 30km east of Moromanga (45 minutes' drive) and approximately 145km east of Antananarivo (three to four hours' drive). Andasibe is also on the main Antananarivo to Toamasina railway line; it takes around 6 hours in either direction.

The nearby unprotected forests of Maromizaha lie to the south of *Route Nationale 2*, some 8km from Andasibe. They can be reached by car or on foot from Andasibe along RN 2. The final 2km, up a steep dirt track and past a stone quarry, is best on foot.

Elevation: Between 930 and 1,040m.

Habitat and Terrain: This is a reasonable example of mid-altitude montane rainforest and covers an area of 810ha. Many of the largest trees have been removed and the canopy averages 20m to 25m. Dominant trees include, *Tambourissa*, *Symphonia*, *Dalbergia* and *Weinmannia* species. There are also numerous tree ferns (*Cyathea* spp.) and epiphytes. The reserve is centred around a small dammed lake, *Lac Vert*, with moderately steep forested slopes rising around it. Average annual rainfall is around 1,700mm.

The forests at Maromizaha are less disturbed, but have still been subject to logging and the pressures continue to increase. Nonetheless, there are numerous large buttress-rooted trees, festooned with mosses and epiphytes. The slopes are steep and often difficult. However, views out over the rainforest from the ridge are superb.

KEY MAMMAL SPECIES

Bats: **Madagascar Rousette** *Rousettus madagascariensis* and Commerson's Leaf-nosed Bat *Hipposideros commersoni*.

Tenrecs: **Common Tenrec** *Tenrec ecaudatus*, Greater Hedgehog Tenrec *Setifer setosus*, **Lowland Streaked Tenrec** *Hemicentetes semispinosus*, rice tenrec *Oryzorictes hova* and several shrew tenrecs *Microgale* spp., including M. *cowani*, M. *talazaci*, M. *melanorrhachis* and M. *gracilis*.

Rodents: **Eastern Red Forest Rat** *Nesomys rufus*, **Voalavoanala** *Gymnuromys roberti*, White-tailed Tree Rat *Brachytarsomys albicauda* and tuft-tailed rats *Eliurus* spp.

Carnivores:Fanaloka *Fossa fossana*, Fosa *Cryptoprocta ferox* and Eastern Ring-tailed Mongoose *Galidia elegans elegans*.

Lemurs: **Indri** *Indri indri*, **Common Brown Lemur** *Eulemur fulvus fulvus*, Red-bellied Lemur *Eulemur rubriventer*, **Eastern Grey Bamboo Lemur** *Hapalemur griseus griseus*, **Small-toothed Sportive Lemur** *Lepilemur microdon*, **Eastern Avahi** *Avahi laniger*, **Greater Dwarf Lemur** *Cheirogaleus major*, **Hairy-eared Dwarf Lemur** *Allocebus trichotis*, **Brown Mouse Lemur** *Microcebus rufus* and Aye-aye *Daubentonia madagascariensis*. Diademed Sifaka *Propithecus diadema diadema* and Black-and-white Ruffed Lemur *Varecia variegata variegata* at Maromizaha only.

Season: Accessible all year round, although the best times for wildlife are September to December and April to May.

Facilities: There are two adequate hotels in Andasibe (Hotel Buffet de la Gare and Hotel Orchidées) and a third close to the reserve entrance (Hotel Feon'ny'ala). There is also a better hotel (Vakona Lodge) to the north of Andasibe, but it is an awkward distance from the reserve. An extensive network of paths runs throughout the main reserve, some of which are labelled. There are maps available. The trails at Maromizaha are much more steep and demanding.

Visiting: One full day and evening is adequate to see the main reserve, although two days are better. For those with patience, really good views of Indri are almost guaranteed. A full day is necessary to explore the forests at Maromizaha, where taking a guide is advisable. If possible camp overnight on the ridge.

Mantadia National Park

Permits: It is better to get these in advance from the ANGAP offices in Antanan-arivo. A local guide from the Association des Guides d'Andasibe is absolutely necessary.

Location and Access: 18°46'–18°56'S 48°28'–48°32'E.
Mantadia is a relatively new park that lies approximately 25km north of Andasibe. Access is along the road from Andasibe and past the graphite mine. This stretch of road is privately owned and permission must be sought from the mine to use it either by vehicle or on foot. Trucks connected with the mine may pick up those trying to hitch-hike.

Elevation: Between 800m and 1,260m.

Habitat and Terrain: This is an excellent example of primary mid-altitude montane rainforest which covers an area of 10,000ha. There are numerous huge trees and the canopy averages 25m to 30m. The understorey is dominated by tree ferns (*Cyathea* sp.), while orchids and other epiphytes are common. This is a hilly area with virtually no flat ground. Some of the slopes are very steep and difficult. Rainfall averages between 1,500mm and 2,000mm per year.

KEY MAMMAL SPECIES

Bats: Madagascar Flying Fox *Pteropus rufus*, Madagascar Rousette *Rousettus madagascariensis* and Commerson's Leaf-nosed Bat *Hipposideros commersoni*.

Tenrecs: Common Tenrec *Tenrec ecaudatus*, Greater Hedgehog Tenrec *Setifer setosus*, Lowland Streaked Tenrec *Hemicentetes semispinosus*, and several shrew tenrecs *Microgale* spp., including *M. soricoides*.

Rodents: **Eastern Red Forest Rat** *Nesomys rufus*, **Voalavoanala** *Gymnuromys roberti* and tuft-tailed rats *Eliurus* spp.

Carnivores: Fanaloka *Fossa fossana*, Falanouc *Eupleres goudotii*, Fosa *Cryptoprocta ferox*, Broad-striped Mongoose *Galadictis fasciata* and Eastern Ring-tailed Mongoose *Galidia elegans elegans*.

Lemurs: **Diademed Sifaka** *Propithecus diadema diadema*, Indri *Indri indri*, **Black-and-white Ruffed Lemur** *Varecia variegata variegata*, Common Brown Lemur *Eulemur fulvus fulvus*, Red-bellied Lemur *Eulemur rubriventer*, Eastern Grey Bamboo Lemur *Hapalemur griseus griseus*, **Small-toothed Sportive Lemur** *Lepilemur microdon*, Eastern Avahi *Avahi laniger*, Greater Dwarf Lemur *Cheirogaleus major*, Brown Mouse Lemur *Microcebus rufus* and Aye-aye *Daubentonia madagascariensis*.

Figure 184. Black-and-white Ruffed Lemur.

Season: Avoid the really rainy season from January to March. The periods either side of this are best.

Facilities: There are no facilities within or near the park. Camping is permitted by the side of the road or just inside the forest. Within the forest there are very few areas flat enough to pitch a tent. All provisions must be carried from Andasibe. Paths are limited and traverse difficult, steep and often muddy and slippery terrain.

Visiting: As the park is only 40 minutes' drive north of Andasibe, those staying in the town's various hotels can visit Mantadia for the day. If doing so it is best to set off before dawn and arrive just as it is getting light. Many of the species this area is renowned for can be seen relatively close to the road. For those wishing to explore the park more fully a two- or three-day camping trip is necessary. Taking a local guide is absolutely essential.

Ranomafana National Park

Permits: Available from the Ranomafana National Park Office in Ranomafana, at the park entrance, or from the Hotel Soafia in Fianarantsoa. Local guides are also available in Ranomafana and at the park gate.

Location and Access: 21°21'–21°23'S 47°27'–47°29'E.
The park lies approximately 65km north-east of Fianarantsoa and is adjacent to the village of Ranomafana. Access is along *Route Nationale 25* which bisects the park and continues on to Mananjary on the east coast. The journey takes between one and two hours depending on road conditions. It is possible to drive from Antananarivo to Ranomafana in a day, but this generally takes more than ten hours.

Elevation: Between 650m and 1,417m.

Habitat and Terrain: An excellent example of mid-altitude montane rainforest which covers an area of 39,200ha. The area is dominated by the river Namorona, which is fed by many streams flowing from the hills, and plunges off the eastern escarpment close to the park entrance. The park's steep slopes are covered with a mixture of primary and secondary forest, where the canopy averages 30m. Much of the secondary growth is dominated by dense areas of introduced Chinese Guava *Psidium cattleyanum*. Stands of giant bamboo *Cephalostacyum viguieri* are also a prominent feature. The average annual rainfall is 2,600mm.

KEY MAMMAL SPECIES

Bats: Madagascar Straw-coloured Fruit Bat *Eidolon dupreanum*, Madagascar Rousette *Rousettus madagascariensis*, Malagasy Mouse-eared Bat *Myotis goudoti* and members of the genera *Eptesicus*, *Miniopterus*, *Mormopterus*, *Tadarida* and possibly others.

Tenrecs: Aquatic Tenrec *Limnogale mergulus*, Greater Hedgehog Tenrec *Setifer setosus*, Lowland Streaked Tenrec *Hemicentetes semispinosus* and several shrew tenrecs *Microgale* spp.

Rodents: **Eastern Red Forest Rat** *Nesomys rufus*, Lowland Red Forest Rat *Nesomys audeberti*, Voalavoanala *Gymnuromys roberti*, White-tailed Tree Rat *Brachytarsomys albicauda* and tuft-tailed rats *Eliurus* spp.

Carnivores: Fanaloka *Fossa fossana*, Falanouc *Eupleres goudotii*, Fosa *Cryptoprocta ferox*, **Eastern Ring-tailed Mongoose** *Galidia elegans elegans* and **Broad-striped Mongoose** *Galidictis fasciata*.

Lemurs: **Golden Bamboo Lemur** *Hapalemur aureus*, **Greater Bamboo Lemur** *Hapalemur simus*, **Eastern Grey Bamboo Lemur** *Hapalemur griseus griseus*, **Milne-Edwards's Sifaka** *Propithecus diadema edwardsi*, **Red-bellied Lemur** *Eulemur rubriventer*, **Red-fronted Brown Lemur** *Eulemur fulvus rufus*, Black-and-white Ruffed Lemur *Varecia variegata variegata*, **Eastern Avahi** *Avahi laniger*, Small-toothed Sportive Lemur *Lepilemur microdon*, **Greater Dwarf Lemur** *Cheirogaleus major*, **Brown Mouse Lemur** *Microcebus rufus* and Aye-aye *Daubentonia madagascariensis*.

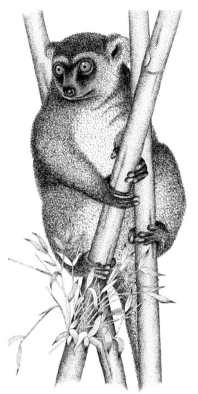

Figure 185. Golden Bamboo Lemur.

Season: The forests are at their most vibrant during the austral summer rainy season from December to March, but access and conditions at this time can be difficult. Otherwise, the periods either side of the main rains are most rewarding – April and September to November.

Facilities: The rather rustic Hotel Thermale in Ranomafana offers basic accommodation with good food. A second hotel, the Domaine Nature, is situated between the village and the park entrance. There are a small number of self-catering rooms available at the park gate, together with a pleasant campsite. An extensive system of well-maintained trails and paths runs through the best wildlife areas, but many are up and down steep and often muddy slopes.

Visiting: A minimum trip of two or three days is recommended, with at least two daytime excursions to the park and one night-time visit to *Belle Vue*. Camping at the entrance offers the best nocturnal watching experiences. The local guides are generally very knowledgeable (many of them are also involved in research projects within the park), but it is wise to settle all plans and financial arrangements at the beginning to avoid ambiguity.

SAMBIRANO MOIST FOREST RESERVES

Manongarivo Special Reserve

Permits: Available from the ANGAP offices in Antananarivo.

Location and Access: 13°53'–14°07'S 48°15'–48°32'E.
This reserve lies around 40km south of Ambanja and east of the Ampasindava Peninsula in north-west Madagascar. The villages of Djangoa and Anjiabory, situated on *Route Nationale* 6 probably provide the best points of access. From these the reserve can be reached on foot, the walk taking at least two hours. It can also be reached from Ankaramihely on *Route Nationale* 6, by walking approximately 17km to the village of Beraty. However, this takes considerable planning and effort.

Elevation: Between 155m and 1,876m.

Habitat and Terrain: The reserve lies at the heart of the Manongarivo Massif and also, with the Tsaratanana Massif to the east, protects some of the best remaining areas of Sambirano humid forests. The forests vary considerably with altitude. At lower elevations (below 800m) the largely closed canopy reaches 30m, with some large trees like 'Ramy' *Canarium madagascariense* reaching 35m. Palms and epiphytes are also diverse and abundant. At higher altitudes the forest canopy is lower, generally less than 15m, and the vegetation less dense. Here mosses and lichens abound. The terrain is often difficult and annual rainfall averages over 2,000mm.

KEY MAMMAL SPECIES

Bats: Madagascar Flying Fox *Pteropus rufus*.

Tenrecs: Common Tenrec *Tenrec ecaudatus*, Greater Hedgehog Tenrec *Setifer setosus*, Short-tailed Shrew Tenrec *Microgale brevicaudata* and Talazac's Shrew Tenrec *Microgale talazaci*.

Rodents: Tuft-tailed rats *Eliurus* spp. (possibly *E. myoxinus*, *E. webbi* and *E. minor*).

Carnivores: Falanouc *Eupleres goudotii*, Fanaloka *Fossa fossana*, Fosa *Cryptoprocta ferox*, and Northern Ring-tailed Mongoose *Galidia elegans dambrensis*.

Lemurs: Black Lemur *Eulemur macaco macaco*, Common Brown Lemur *Eulemur fulvus fulvus*, Western Grey Bamboo Lemur *Hapalemur griseus occidentalis*, Western Avahi *Avahi occidentalis*, Grey-backed Sportive Lemur *Lepilemur dorsalis*, Greater Dwarf Lemur *Cheirogaleus major*, **Pariente's Fork-marked Lemur** *Phaner furcifer parienti*, Brown Mouse Lemur *Microcebus rufus* and Aye-aye *Daubentonia madagascariensis*.

Season: The heart of the rainy season between January and March is to be avoided. The austral spring between September and December is perhaps the best time for wildlife, but there can be heavy rain at night during November and December.

Facilities: There are none. Camping is possible but all equipment and provisions must be taken. There is a limited path network in some areas but the majority of the rainforest terrain is hilly and difficult.

Visiting: This is a difficult reserve to reach and is best left to those with prior experience of rainforest environments and independent travel in Madagascar.

Lokobe Nature Reserve

Permits: Lokobe is a strict nature reserve (Réserve Naturelle Intégrale), so permits are only issued to approved scientists and government officials. However, the buffer zones around the edge of the reserve can be visited and no permits are required.

Location and Access: 13°25'S 48°20'E.
Lokobe is situated on the island of Nosy Be of the north west coast. The reserve itself lies on a peninsula at the south east corner of the Nosy Be, only 5km from Andoany (Hell Ville). There are regular flights to Nosy Be from either Antananarivo or Antsiranana. Alternatively, the island is easily reached by ferry from Ambohimena on the mainland, near the town of Ambanja.

Elevation: Sea-level to 430m.

Habitat and Terrain: Although, strictly, Lokobe does not lie within the Sambirano domain, the forest composition and structure is very similar. Aspects of the fauna are also largely typical of the Sambirano and this reserve offers a chance to see species far more easily than is possible on the mainland. Lokobe is the last remaining stand of lowland rainforest on Nosy Be and covers an area of 740ha. The forest appears very similar to eastern rainforests, the canopy reaching around 20m to 25m, but there are a number of locally endemic species including various palms from the genera *Chrysalidocarpus, Ravenea, Dypsis* and *Neodypsis*. The buffer zones are a mixture of native vegetation and cultivated species like, mango, banana, papaya, jackfruit, breadfruit and coffee. Yearly rainfall averages over 2200mm, although there is marked dry period between June and August.

KEY MAMMAL SPECIES

Bats: **Madagascar Flying Fox** *Pteropus rufus*.

Tenrecs: Greater Hedgehog Tenrec *Setifer setosus*.

Rodents: not known.

Carnivores: none.

Lemurs: **Black Lemur** *Eulemur macaco macaco*, **Grey-backed Sportive Lemur** *Lepilemur dorsalis* and Brown Mouse Lemur *Microcebus rufus*.

Season: Accessible all year round. Wildlife-watching is best between September and December, and in April and May.

Facilities: There are numerous hotels in Andoany and around the coast at Ambatoloaka. There is also basic hotel accommodation much nearer the reserve at Ambatozavavy and Ampasipohy on the north-east side of the Lokobe peninsula. The best areas to see lemurs are a short walk inland from Ampasipohy and at Ambalahonko*, which is around 40 minutes' walk away. The paths are reasonable and none of the hills particularly steep.

Visiting: Arrangements can be made for day trips to the buffer zones around Lokobe from many of the main hotels. At Ambatozavavy guides can be hired, to take you around the coast by pirogue to Ampasipohy.

* THE BLACK LEMUR FOREST PROJECT

This is a long-term, community-orientated conservation, research and education project based at Ampasindava on the south-west side of Lokobe. The project has encouraged the training of local guides at Ambalahonko, who are studying populations of Black Lemurs and Grey-backed Sportive Lemurs. At Maradokana the project has opened a community conservation centre, which provides basic information for visitors. There are future plans to accommodate visitors and build a new information centre close to the project's headquarters at Ampasindava.

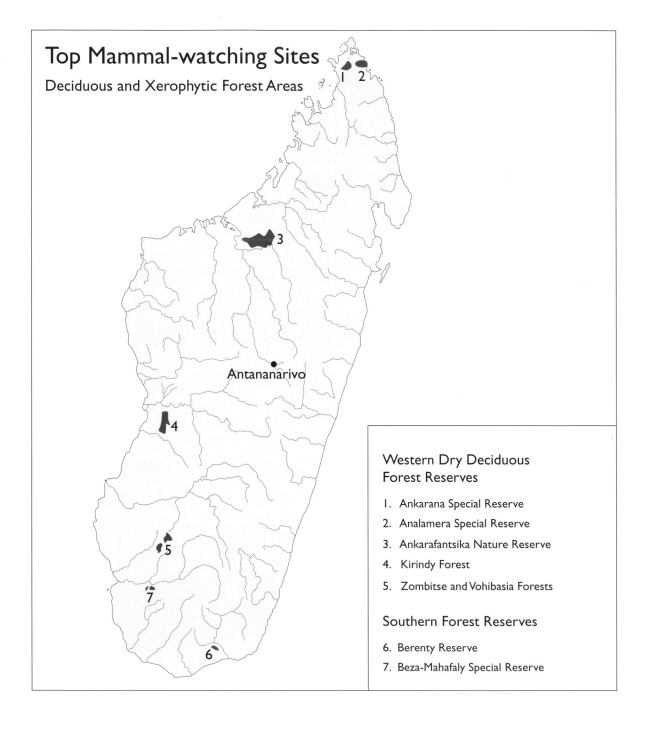

Top Mammal-watching Sites

Deciduous and Xerophytic Forest Areas

Antananarivo

Western Dry Deciduous Forest Reserves

1. Ankarana Special Reserve

2. Analamera Special Reserve

3. Ankarafantsika Nature Reserve

4. Kirindy Forest

5. Zombitse and Vohibasia Forests

Southern Forest Reserves

6. Berenty Reserve

7. Beza-Mahafaly Special Reserve

Deciduous Forest Areas

The deciduous forests of western Madagascar are less diverse than the rainforests of the east, but nonetheless contain a wealth of fauna and flora that is of great importance, because the levels of endemicity are so high (around 90%). The height of the canopy and density of the trees is lower than in eastern rainforests, which gives western deciduous forests a more 'open' feel. This of course makes wildlife watching a little easier. There are a total of 12 major protected areas in deciduous forest regions. While some of these are remote and remain inaccessible to visitors, several are amongst the most popular and rewarding wildlife-watching localities on the island.

Perhaps of particular note are those reserves incorporating limestone massifs that have been eroded into spectacular pinnacle formations known as karst or locally as 'tsingy' (the sound the rock is said to make when it is struck). Rivers flowing through these limestone areas have eroded underground passages and caves, some of which have collapsed to form canyons. Within these canyons, dry deciduous forest flourishes, often supporting isolated faunal assemblages unlike any others on the island. Mammal-watching can be particularly rewarding in such areas: the main examples are at Ankarana (see below), Namoroka and Bemaraha, although only the former is readily accessible.

WESTERN DRY DECIDUOUS FOREST RESERVES

Ankarana Special Reserve

Permits: Available from WWF Montagne d'Ambre Project Office in Antsiranana. Guides are absolutely essential and can also be arranged through the office.

Location and Access: 12°50'–13°01'S 49°01'–49°16'E.
Situated approximately 110km south of Antsiranana down *Route Nationale* 6. The reserve lies predominantly to the west of the main road. Just south of Anivorano Avaratra take the turn west: four-wheel drive is necessary to negotiate the final 30km or so. The journey from Antsiranana takes around four hours. Alternatively, it is possible to approach from Ambilobe in the south, but the road is often worse and four-wheel drive essential.

Elevation: Between 50m and 410m.

Habitat and Terrain: The reserve is centred around the Ankarana Massif and covers an area of 18,225ha. It is dominated by impressive formations of 'tsingy' that form an almost impenetrable fortress in places. There is an extensive system of caves, with underground rivers and canyons. Dry deciduous forest grows around the periphery of the massif and penetrates up into the larger canyons. In some areas there are isolated pockets of forest growing within the 'tsingy' where caves have collapsed. The canopy reaches 25m where the dominant trees include *Cassia* sp., *Dalbergia* sp., *Ficus sp.* and the baobab *Adansonia madagascariensis*. In the canyon bottoms the terrain is reasonably level but most areas, especially the 'tsingy' are very rugged and potentially hazardous. The yearly rainfall for the area averages 1,800mm.

KEY MAMMAL SPECIES

Bats: The wealth of caves in Ankarana make it one of the richest bat sites on the island. Recorded species include: Madagascar Flying Fox *Pteropus rufus*, **Madagascar Straw-coloured Fruit Bat** *Eidolon dupreanum*, Madagascar Rousette *Rousettus madagascariensis*, Madagascar Slit-faced Bat *Nycteris madagascariensis*, Commerson's Leaf-nosed Bat *Hipposideros commersoni*, Trouessart's Trident Bat *Triaenops furculus*, Malagasy Mouse-eared Bat *Myotis goudoti* and the long-fingered bat *Miniopterus manavi*.

Tenrecs: Common Tenrec *Tenrec ecaudatus* and Greater Hedgehog Tenrec *Setifer setosus*.

Rodents: Western Tuft-tailed Rat *Eliurus myoxinus*.

Carnivores:**Northern Ring-tailed Mongoose** *Galidia elegans dambrensis*, Fosa *Cryptoprocta ferox*, Fanaloka *Fossa fossana* and Falanouc *Eupleres goudotii*. Also introduced Small Indian Civet *Viverricula indica*.

Lemurs: **Crowned Lemur** *Eulemur coronatus*, **Sanford's Brown Lemur** *Eulemur fulvus sanfordi*, Western Grey Bamboo Lemur *Hapalemur griseus occidentalis*, possibly Perrier's Sifaka *Propithecus diadema perrieri* and Western Avahi *Avahi occidentalis*, **Northern Sportive Lemur** *Lepilemur septentrionalis*, **Ambre Mountain Fork-marked Lemur** *Phaner furcifer electromontis*, Fat-tailed Dwarf Lemur *Cheirogaleus medius*, Grey Mouse Lemur *Microcebus murinus*, possibly Brown Mouse Lemur *Microcebus rufus*, and Aye-aye *Daubentonia madagascariensis*.

Season: Only accessible during the dry season from May to November. Ankarana can be very hot during the day, but cool at night.

Facilities: There are no facilities in or near the reserve and camping is the only option: all equipment and provisions must be taken. The two main campsites are the *Campement des Anglais* in the *Canyon Grande* and the *Campement des Americains* at the foot of the western escarpment. Water is scarce within the reserve, but available from underground streams near the main camps. There is a reasonable path system around the *Canyon Grande* but the remote areas are much more challenging to explore.

Visiting: Camping excursions can be arranged through a number of operators based in Antsiranana. A minimum stay of two or three nights is recommended, although longer is better. To explore the reserve more fully it is best to spend nights at different campsites. A local guide is absolutely essential.

Analamera Special Reserve

Permits: Available from WWF Montagne d'Ambre Project Office in Antsiranana. Guides are essential and can be hired at the village of Menagisy on the way into the reserve.

Location and Access: 12°39'–12°54'S 49°19'–49°36'E.
Analamera lies between the north-east coast and *Route Nationale* 6, approximately 80km south of Antsiranana. At the village of Sadjoavato turn east and drive along the track following the Irodo River: four-wheel drive is essential. Near Ankarongana cross the river to the village of Menagisy which is situated at the northern boundary of the reserve. It is best to go into the reserve on foot from this point. The journey from Antsiranana to Menagisy takes around three hours.

Elevation: Between 10m and 610m.

Habitat and Terrain: Analamera is a limestone karst plateau adjacent to the Indian Ocean but stretching inland for around 35km; however, it is not continuous with the Ankarana Massif further to the west. The reserve is divided by the Bobakindro River valley, which runs north–south, into two main blocks that cover a total area of 34,700ha. Most of the reserve is covered in deciduous type forest where the canopy reaches 15m. These formations resemble 'typical' western forests, but because Analamera tends to be more humid, also show characteristics of eastern forests. Along the watercourses, the vegetation is more lush and resembles riverine forest. Here larger trees like 'Ramy' *Canarium madagascariense* grow along with a wide variety of palm species. The average annual rainfall is 1,250mm, the majority of which falls between November and April.

KEY MAMMAL SPECIES
Bats: Madagascar Flying Fox *Pteropus rufus*.
Tenrecs: Common Tenrec *Tenrec ecaudatus* and Greater Hedgehog Tenrec *Setifer setosus*.
Rodents: not known.
Carnivores:Northern Ring-tailed Mongoose *Galidia elegans dambrensis* and Fosa *Cryptoprocta ferox*. Also introduced Small Indian Civet *Viverricula indica*.
Lemurs: **Perrier's Sifaka** *Propithecus diadema perrieri*, **Crowned Lemur** *Eulemur coronatus*, Sanford's Brown Lemur *Eulemur fulvus sanfordi*, **Northern Sportive Lemur** *Lepilemur septentrionalis*, Amber Mountain Fork-marked Lemur *Phaner furcifer electromontis*, Fat-tailed Dwarf Lemur *Cheirogaleus medius*, Grey Mouse Lemur *Microcebus murinus* and Aye-aye *Daubentonia madagascariensis*.

Season: Analamera is only accessible during the dry season between May and November. During the austral spring and summer temperatures can be very high.

Facilities: Camping only: there are no set campsites and all equipment and provisions, including drinking water, must be taken. During the dry season tents can be pitched around dry riverbeds. There are some trails running through the reserve, particularly along the valley of the Bobakindro River. Away from this area there are few trails, although it is possible to follow dry riverbeds.

Visiting: This reserve requires a considerable amount of effort to reach. It is recommended to go for at least three or four nights, particularly if seeing Perrier's Sifaka is a priority, as these animals can take some time to track down. The help of a local guide is essential.

Ankarafantsika Nature Reserve (*Ampijoroa Forestry Station*)

Permits: Permits are not issued for Ankarafantsika as it is a strict nature reserve (Réserve Naturelle Intégrale). However, it is possible to visit the forestry station at Ampijoroa which lies within the main reserve. Permits are available from the Water and Forest Department (DEF) in Antananarivo or at the station itself.

Location and Access: 16°15'S 46°48'E (Ampijoroa).
The Ampijoroa Forestry Station lies either side of *Route Nationale* 4 approximately 120km south-east of Mahajanga. The road from Mahajanga is well maintained and the journey takes around two hours. It is also possible to drive directly from Antananarivo, but this takes 14 to 16 hours.

Elevation: Between 80m and 330m.

Habitat and Terrain: Ankarafantsika is a mixture of dry deciduous forest and a karstic limestone plateau covering a total area of 65,520ha. Ampijoroa is located towards the centre of the reserve and covers an area of 20,000ha. The immediate area is dominated by Lac Ravelobe which lies on the northern side of *Route Nationale* 4. Around the lake, on sandy soils, grows typical dry deciduous forest where the canopy reaches 15m to 20m. The understorey is sparse, with virtually no epiphytes. On the higher plateau areas the canopy averages 5m to 10m and there is very little understorey. In the more open rocky areas succulents like the Elephant's Foot Plant *Pachypodium rosulatum rosulatum* and *Aloe* species grow. The terrain is gently undulating or flat, with the occasional shallow ridge. Annual rainfall is between 1,000mm and 1,500mm.

KEY MAMMAL SPECIES
Bats: Madagascar Flying Fox *Pteropus rufus* and Commerson's Leaf-nosed Bat *Hipposideros commersoni*.
Tenrecs: Common Tenrec *Tenrec ecaudatus* and **Greater Hedgehog Tenrec** *Setifer setosus*.

Rodents: **Western Tuft-tailed Rat** *Eliurus myoxinus*, **Western Forest Mouse** *Macrotarsomys bastardi* and *Macrotarsomys ingens*.

Carnivores: Fosa *Cryptoprocta ferox*. Also introduced Small Indian Civet *Viverricula indica*.

Lemurs: **Coquerel's Sifaka** *Propithecus verreauxi coquereli*, Mongoose Lemur *Eulemur mongoz*, **Common Brown Lemur** *Eulemur fulvus fulvus*, **Western Avahi** *Avahi occidentalis*, **Milne-Edwards's Sportive Lemur** *Lepilemur edwardsi*, **Fat-tailed Dwarf Lemur** *Cheirogaleus medius*, **Grey Mouse Lemur** *Microcebus murinus* and **Golden-brown Mouse Lemur** *Microcebus ravelobensis*.

Project Angonoka

Ampijoroa is the site of a joint Jersey Wildlife Preservation Trust and World-Wide Fund for Nature captive-breeding programme to help save two of the world's most endangered tortoises. Both the Angonoka or Plowshare Tortoise *Geochelone yniphora* and Kapidolo or Flat-tailed Tortoise *Pyxis planicauda* have been raised successfully with the intention of releasing individuals back to suitable areas in the wild.

Season: It is possible to visit Ampijoroa all year round, but the roads can be difficult at the height of the wet season (January to March), especially from Antananarivo. The reptiles are more prominent after the first rains in November. During the austral summer it can be very hot indeed.

Facilities: There is a large, reasonably maintained campsite at Ampijoroa, with a water well and small toilet block. All equipment and provisions must be taken. The campsite can become crowded. It is possible to wash and swim in the lake. These facilities are due to be improved. Permanent visitor accommodation is planned. In the nearby village of Andranofasika there are several small shops for basic supplies. The trails through the forest are wide and the walking is easy on both sides of the road. Forestry staff are usually available to guide.

Visiting: Ampijoroa is one of the best remaining examples of dry deciduous forest. A stay of at least two or three days is recommended to explore this wonderful area fully.

Kirindy Forest

Permits: The Kirindy Forest is administered by the Coopération Suisse (Swiss Aid) and permits are available from the offices of the Centre de Formation Professionnelle Forestière (CFPF) in Morondava. Several of the hotels in Morondava are also able to assist with permits.

Location and Access: 20°01'–20°04'S 44°32'–44°44'E.
Kirindy Forest lies approximately 60km north-east of Morondava and 20km inland from the west coast. It is situated to the east of the road to Belo Tsiribihina, north of the village of Marofandilia. The drive from Morondava takes about 1.5 hours.

Elevation: Between 18m and 40m.

Figure 186. Giant Jumping Rat.

287

Habitat and Terrain: Kirindy is an area of typical dry deciduous forest growing on sandy soils and covering around 10,000ha. The tree species are similar to those found in other deciduous forests of the west: the canopy normally averages 12m to 15m, but may reach 20m to 25m in the more humid areas along watercourses. There is often a dense understorey and intermediate layer before the canopy. These forests support three species of baobab, *Adansonia fony*, *A. za* and *A. grandidieri*. The latter species dominates the landscape in some areas; it is the largest baobab in Madagascar and reaches heights in excess of 30m. Annual rainfall averages 700mm to 800mm, with the majority of this falling between the months of December and March.

KEY MAMMAL SPECIES

Bats: Madagascar Flying Fox *Pteropus rufus*, Madagascar Straw-coloured Fruit Bat *Eidolon dupreanum*, **Commerson's Leaf-nosed Bat** *Hipposideros commersoni*, Rufous Trident Bat *Triaenops rufus*, the house bat *Scotophilus borbonicus*, Little Free-tailed Bat *Tadarida* (*Chaerephon*) *pumila*, the greater mastiff bat *Tadarida* (*Mops*) *leucostigma* and two members of the genus *Pipistrellus*.

Tenrecs: **Common Tenrec** *Tenrec ecaudatus*, Greater Hedgehog Tenrec *Setifer setosus*, Lesser Hedgehog Tenrec *Echinops telfairi* and **Large-eared Tenrec** *Geogale aurita*.

Rodents: **Giant Jumping Rat** *Hypogeomys antimena*, Western Tuft-tailed Rat *Eliurus myoxinus* and **Western Forest Mouse** *Macrotarsomys bastardi*.

Carnivores: Fossa *Cryptoprocta ferox* and **Narrow-striped Mongoose** *Mungotictis decemlineata*. Also the introduced Small Indian Civet *Viverricula indica*.

Lemurs: **Verreaux's Sifaka** *Propithecus verreauxi verreauxi*, **Red-fronted Brown Lemur** *Eulemur fulvus rufus*, Pygmy Mouse Lemur *Microcebus myoxinus*, **Grey Mouse Lemur** *Microcebus murinus*, **Red-tailed Sportive Lemur** *Lepilemur ruficaudatus*, **Pale Fork-marked Lemur** *Phaner furcifer pallescens*, **Coquerel's Dwarf Lemur** *Mirza coquereli* and **Fat-tailed Dwarf Lemur** *Cheirogaleus medius*.

Season: There is a marked dry season from May to October when virtually no rain falls. The wettest months are in the austral summer. Wildlife-watching is best in the spring and summer October to April, particularly after rain. However, the road conditions can be difficult during the wetter months and temperatures very high. In winter the forests sometimes appear quite lifeless and nights can be cold.

Facilities: There is a field camp, with basic accommodation and permanent tent pitches. When camping all equipment must be taken. A snack bar serves cool drinks and simple good value meals. The paths through the forest are wide and the walking flat and easy. The trails are arranged in a grid system which makes navigation straightforward. Local forestry staff can be hired as guides.

Visiting: Day trips can be organised by a number of hotels in Morondava. However, two or three nights camping is recommended to make the most of the nocturnal wildlife watching for which Kirindy is renowned. Between Morondava and Kirindy is the famous avenue of giant baobabs (*Baobab Allée*) which is well worth stopping at.

Zombitse and Vohibasia Forests

Permits: The government in conjunction with WWF have plans to create a national park to protect these areas. At present, however, Zombitse and Vohibasia are classified forests and no permit is required to visit.

Location and Access: 22°45'–22°49'S 44°37'–44°45'E.
The Zombitse Forest straddles *Route Nationale* 7, some 25km east of Sakaraha. The drive north-east from Toliara takes around three hours. South-west from Ranohira it takes just over one hour. Vohibasia Forest lies to the north-east of Zombitse and is accessible only on foot from the main road.

Habitat and Terrain: These two areas constitute the last remnants of transition forest between the western and southern floristic domains. They are similar in appearance to western deciduous forests and share many tree species with this forest type along with some species normally associated with areas further south. Two baobabs, *Adansonia madagascariensis* and *A. za*, are present, but the canopy generally averages 15m. Zombitse covers an area of 21,500ha – in the past the edges and forest margins were continually being eroded by fires and the spread of agriculture, but thankfully this has now been halted. The soil is sandy and the terrain fairly flat. There is a long dry season from May to October, annual rainfall averages 700mm (the majority falling between December and February), and there are no permanent watercourses.

KEY MAMMAL SPECIES

Bats: Mauritian Tomb Bat *Taphozous mauritianus*, the house bat *Scotophilus robustus*, Peters's Goblin Bat *Mormopterus jugularis* and Midas Free-tailed Bat *Tadarida* (*Mops*) *midas*.

Tenrecs: Common Tenrec *Tenrec ecaudatus*, Greater Hedgehog Tenrec *Setifer setosus*, Lesser Hedgehog Tenrec *Echinops telfairi* and Large-eared Tenrec *Geogale aurita*.

Rodents: Western Tuft-tailed Rat *Eliurus myoxinus* and Western Forest Mouse *Macrotarsomys bastardi*.

Carnivores: Fosa *Cryptoprocta ferox*. Also the introduced Small Indian Civet *Viverricula indica*.

Lemurs: Verreaux's Sifaka *Propithecus verreauxi verreauxi*, Ring-tailed Lemur *Lemur catta*, Red-fronted Brown Lemur *Eulemur fulvus rufus*, Red-tailed Sportive Lemur *Lepilemur ruficaudatus*, **Pale Fork-marked Lemur** *Phaner furcifer pallescens*, **Coquerel's Dwarf Lemur** *Mirza coquereli*, Fat-tailed Dwarf Lemur *Cheirogaleus medius* and Grey Mouse Lemur *Microcebus murinus*.

Season: Accessible year round. At its best during the austral spring and summer, October to April. The forests can appear relatively lifeless during the winter months.

Facilities: There are no facilities. Those wishing to camp will need to be entirely self-sufficient (including water supplies). There are no formal paths and trails at present. However, plans to develop Zombitse as a park include the provision of basic facilities and the training of guides.

Visiting: Its proximity to the road makes Zombitse an easy place to visit. Most visitors stop for brief periods *en route* between Isalo National Park and Toliara. For the enthusiast, it is worth camping for one or two nights, to see the best the forest has to offer.

Xerophytic Forest Areas

These areas are perhaps the most bizarre and unusual in Madagascar. They occupy the most harsh and arid region on the island and consequently the faunal and floral diversity is much reduced in comparison to other areas, but the rates of endemicity remain very high. The vegetation comprises a type of deciduous thicket dominated by members of the Didiereaceae and Euphorbiaceae families. This is commonly referred to as 'spiny forest'.

It follows that mammal diversity is also reduced in this region, but that is not to say the south is an area the mammal-watcher should overlook. There are five protected areas in the south, and although some of these remain off-limits to the visitor, others offer some of the closest and most intimate mammal-watching experiences Madagascar has to offer, particularly with two of the species the island is perhaps most famous for, the Ring-tailed Lemur and Verreaux's Sifaka.

SOUTHERN FOREST RESERVES

Berenty Reserve

Permits: Berenty is a private reserve owned by the de Heaulme family, who also run the two main hotels in Tolagnaro (Dauphin and Miramar). It is necessary to arrange an excursion to the reserve through one of these.

Location and Access: 25°00'S 46°17'E.
The reserve is located on the banks of the Mandrare River, some 80km west of Tolagnaro and approximately 10km north of Amboasary-Sud. The road from Tolagnaro is in reasonable condition and the journey from Tolagnaro takes around 2 hours

Elevation: Around 50m.

Habitat and Terrain: The reserve primarily consists of a small (25ha) isolated patch of riverine gallery forest dominated by huge Tamarind Trees *Tamarindus indica*, which may exceed 20m. Adjacent to the gallery forest are much smaller parcels of spiny forest dominated by *Alluaudia procera*. The terrain is flat and walking very easy.

KEY MAMMAL SPECIES
Bats: **Madagascar Flying Fox** *Pteropus rufus*.
Tenrecs: Common Tenrec *Tenrec ecaudatus* and Greater Hedgehog Tenrec *Setifer setosus*.
Rodents: not known.
Carnivores:Small Indian Civet *Viverricula indica*.
Lemurs: **Verreaux's Sifaka** *Propithecus verreauxi verreauxi*, **Ring-tailed Lemur** *Lemur catta*, Red-fronted Brown Lemur *Eulemur fulvus rufus* (introduced), **White-footed Sportive Lemur** *Lepilemur leucopus*, Fat-tailed Dwarf Lemur *Cheirogaleus medius* and **Grey Mouse Lemur** *Microcebus murinus*.

Season: Enjoyable and accessible all year round. September and October are good for baby Ring-tailed Lemurs.

Facilities: Pleasant complex of bungalows with a good restaurant adjacent to the reserve. There is an excellent network of wide paths and trails throughout the gallery forest. Guides can easily be arranged, through the hotel.

Visiting: Day trips from Tolagnaro are possible, but a stay of at least one full day and night is recommended.

Beza-Mahafaly Special Reserve

Permits: Permits and guides are available at the reserve.

Location and Access: 23°38'–23°42'S 44°31'–44°34'E.
Beza-Mahafaly is located around 35km north-east of Betioky-Sud, to the south of the Onilahy River and adjacent to the west bank of the Sakamena River. Betioky-Sud lies on *Route Nationale* 10 and is around five hours' drive from Toliara. Both *Route Nationale* 10 and the track from Betioky-Sud to the reserve are poorly maintained and four-wheel drive is necessary. It is also possible to take a *taxi-brousse* from Toliara to Betioky-Sud, then hire a zebu cart and guide to get to the reserve. This trip takes a full day.

Elevation: Between 75m and 200m.

Habitat and Terrain: The reserve is divided into two separate blocks. Parcel 1 consists of around 100ha of riverine gallery forest bordering the Sakamena River. This is dominated by large Kily or Tamarind Trees *Tamarindus indica* that can reach a height of 30m. Parcel 2 protects an excellent area of spiny forest dominated by members of the Didiereaceae, particularly *Alluadia procera*, together with Euphorbiaceae and *Acacia* species. There are also large specimens of *Pachypodium geayi* and *P. rutenbergianum*. Parcel 2 covers an area of 480ha incorporating a rocky ridge. The annual rainfall in the area is around 550mm.

KEY MAMMAL SPECIES

Bats: not known.

Tenrecs: Common Tenrec *Tenrec ecaudatus*, Greater Hedgehog Tenrec *Setifer setosus*, **Lesser Hedgehog Tenrec** *Echinops telfairi* and **Large-eared Tenrec** *Geogale aurita*.

Rodents: no endemic species recorded.

Carnivores: Fosa *Cryptoprocta ferox*.

Lemurs: **Verreaux's Sifaka** *Propithecus verreauxi verreauxi*, **Ring-tailed Lemur** *Lemur catta*, **White-footed Sportive Lemur** *Lepilemur leucopus*, **Fat-tailed Dwarf Lemur** *Cheirogaleus medius* and **Grey Mouse Lemur** *Microcebus murinus*.

Season: During the heaviest of the rains, between January and April, the area can become flooded and access is extremely difficult. The best time to visit is between June and November. In September many of the Ring-tailed Lemurs will have young.

Facilities: These are very basic. There is rudimentary accommodation, which is generally reserved for official scientists, and a toilet. Self-sufficient camping is the only practical option. There is an extensive grid of pathways through the forest and the walking is generally flat and easy.

Visiting: Beza-Mahafaly requires a considerable amount of effort to reach, but it is well worth it. In remote and totally natural surroundings, it is an excellent place to observe at close quarters some of the mammals that characterise the south, especially Ring-tailed Lemurs and Verreaux's Sifakas (which can be seen leaping through the spiny forest. A minimum stay of three days is recommended.

Figure 187. Ring-tailed Lemur.

GLOSSARY

Adaptive Radiation
A burst of evolution, where an ancestral form undergoes rapid diversification into many new forms, resulting in the exploitation of an array of habitats (cf. Convergent Evolution).

Aestivate
In tropical environments where animals seasonally enter a state of dormancy or torpor in response periods of water and/or food shortage usually corresponding with hot dry climatic conditions (cf. Hibernate).

Agouti
Referring to pelage: a grizzled coloration resulting from alternate light and dark barring of each hair.

Allopatry
The occurrence of populations of different species (or higher taxonomic units) in different geographical areas i.e. with non-over-lapping ranges or distributions (cf. Sympatry).

Altricial
Applied to young animals that are born in a rudimentary state of development and, therefore, require an extended period of nursing by the parents (cf. Precocial).

Anthropogenic
Applied to habitats and environments that are primarily a consequence of interference by man.

Arboreal
Refers to animals that spend the majority of their lives living in trees.

Austral
Of the southern hemisphere.

Caecotrophy
Where animals re-ingest their own faeces to extract further nutrients.

Cathemeral
Applied to animals that are active both day and night. The relative proportions of daytime and night-time activity may vary with the seasons (cf. Diurnal and Nocturnal).

Carnivore
Generally applied to any primarily flesh-eating organism. More specifically refers to members of the taxonomic order Carnivora.

Class
A taxonomic category that is subordinate to phylum and superior to order, e.g. the mammals are class Mammalia in phylum Chordata (see Taxonomy).

Cline
A graded sequence of differences within a species across its geographical distribution.

Commensal
Refers to an animal that lives side by side with another species, sharing its food. Often applied to species that live in close association with man, e.g. rats and mice.

Congener
Individuals from the same or different species that belong to the same genus.

Conspecific
Individuals that belong to the same species.

Convergent Evolution
The independent acquisition through evolution of similar characteristics in unrelated taxonomic groupings that lead similar ways of life, as opposed to the possession of similarities by virtue of descent from a common ancestor.

Crepuscular
Of twilight: the term applies to animals that are primarily active around dusk.

Cursorial
Applied to an animal possessing limbs adapted for running.

Dichromatic
Where individuals of the same species exhibit two noticeably different colour patterns e.g. sexually dichromatic refers to differences between adult males and females, while maturationally dichromatic refers to differences between immature and adult individuals.

Digitigrade
Applied to the gait in which only the digits, and not the heel, make contact with the ground (cf. Plantigrade).

Diurnal
Applied to animals that are primarily active during the day time (cf. Nocturnal and Cathemeral).

Dorsal
The upper or top side or surface of an animal (cf. Ventral)

Endemic
Where a species or other taxonomic grouping is naturally restricted to a particular geographic region: such a taxon is then said to be

endemic to that region. In this context, the size of the region will usually depend on the status of the taxon: thus, all other factors being equal, a family will be endemic to a larger area than a genus or a species. For instance the family Lemuridae is endemic to the island of Madagascar as a whole, while the Crowned Lemur is endemic to the very northern tip of the island (cf. Indigenous and Exotic).

Exotic
Refers to a taxonomic grouping (usually a species) that has been accidentally or deliberately introduced to a region in which it does not occur naturally (cf. Indigenous).

Family
A taxonomic category that is subordinate to order and superior to subfamily, e.g. the mongooses – family Herpestidae (see Taxonomy).

Folivore
Applied to an animal that feeds primarily on leaves.

Fossorial
Applied to an animal with a burrowing lifestyle.

Frugivore
Applied to an animal that feeds primarily on fruit.

Genus (plural Genera)
A taxonomic category that is subordinate to subfamily and superior to species, e.g. the sifakas – genus *Propithecus* (see Taxonomy).

Gestation
The period of development within the uterus.

Glabrous
Smooth and lacking hairs.

Hallux
The 'great toe'. In mammals: on the pentadactyl hind-limb, the digit on the tibial side which is often shorter than the other digits.

Hibernate
In cold environments where animals become dormant over the winter months: during this deep sleep the metabolic rate is dramatically reduced and the animal survives on stored fat reserves that have been built up during the favourable summer months (cf. Aestivate).

Hybrid
An offspring produced by parents which are genetically unlike, e.g. belonging to different species or subspecies.

Indigenous
Applies to species or other taxonomic groupings that occur naturally in a specified area or region and have, therefore, not been introduced either deliberately or accidentally by man. This term is synonymous with Native (cf. Endemic and Exotic).

Monogamy
A mating system where individuals have only one partner per breeding season. This is often extended to mean the pair mate for life (cf. Polygamy and Polygyny).

Niche
The functional position or role of an organism (usually applied to a species) within its community and environment, defined in all aspects of its lifestyle e.g. food, competitors, predators and other resource requirements. Also referred to as Ecological Niche.

Nocturnal
Applied to animals that are primarily active during the night (cf. Diurnal and Cathemeral).

Omnivore
Applied to an animal with a varied diet that feeds on both flesh and vegetation.

Order
A taxonomic category that is subordinate to class and superior to family, e.g. the rodents – order Rodentia (see Taxonomy).

Pelage
The hair covering the body of a mammal. Coat is a synonymous and more popular term.

Pencillate
Applied to the tails of mammals that end in a conspicuous brush-like terminal tuft.

Plantigrade
Applied to the gait in which the soles of the feet, including the heels, make contact with the ground (cf. Digitigrade).

Polygamy
A mating system where individuals of either sex have more than one partner per breeding season (cf. Monogamy and Polygyny).

Polygyny
A mating system where males mate with more than one (and generally several) females during a single breeding season (cf. Monogamy and Polygamy).

Post-cranial
Refers to all parts of the skeleton behind/below the cranium (skull).

Precocial
Applied to young animals that are born in a relatively advanced state of development and, therefore, require only a brief period of nursing by the parents (cf. Altricial).

Prosimian
Literally meaning 'before the monkeys': used as a collective term referring to the relatively primitive primates belonging to the suborder Strepsirhini (formerly Prosimii) which includes the lemurs, galagos, pottos and lorises.

Pygal
The region at the base of the back around where the tail joins the main body.

Quadrupedal
Applied to an animal that walks on all four limbs.

Saltatory
Applied to animals whose primary mode of movement is leaping.

Scansorial
Applied to an animal that is adapted to climbing.

Sclerophyllous
Applied to vegetation, typically scrub, but also woodland, in which the leaves of the trees and shrubs are small, hard, thick, leathery with a waxy cuticle and evergreen,. These adaptations allow the vegetation to survive a pronounced hot, dry season.

sp. (plural spp.)
When considering a species, an abbreviation indicating that the genus is known, but not the specific species, e.g. *Eulemur* sp. refers to an unspecified member of the genus *Eulemur*.

Species
A taxonomic category that is subordinate to genus and superior to subspecies e.g. the Ring-tailed Lemur (*Lemur catta*). This is the fundamental unit of taxonomy and is broadly defined as a population of organisms with like morphology that are able to interbreed and produce viable offspring, i.e. they have compatible gametes and share a common fertilisation technique (see Taxonomy).

Speciation
The process by which new species arise by evolution. It is widely accepted that this occurs when a single species population becomes divided and then different selection pressures acting on each new population cause them to diverge.

Subfamily
A taxonomic category that is subordinate to family and superior to genus, e.g. the Malagasy mongooses – subfamily Galidiinae (see Taxonomy).

Subspecies
A taxonomic category that is subordinate to species and denotes a recognisable sub-population within a single species that typically has a distinct geographical range, e.g. The Broad-striped Mongoose (*Galidictis fasciata*) is divided into a southern subspecies, *Galidictis fasciata fasciata* (the nominate form) and a northern subspecies, *Galidictis fasciata striata*. Subspecies is interchangeable with the term race (see Taxonomy).

Sympatry
The occurrence of populations of different species (or higher taxonomic units) in the same geographical areas, i.e. with overlapping ranges or distributions (cf. Allopatry).

Taxon (plural Taxa)
A general term for a taxonomic group whatever its rank, e.g. family, genus, species or subspecies.

Taxonomy
The science of classifying organisms. In this classification system organisms which share common features are grouped together and are, therefore, thought to share a common ancestry. Each individual is thus a member of a series of ever-broader categories (individual – species – genus – family – order – class – phylum – kingdom) and each of these categories can be further divided where convenient and appropriate (e.g. subspecies, subfamily, superfamily or intraorder).

Terrestrial
Refers to animals that spend the majority of their lives living on the ground.

Ventral
The lower or bottom side or surface of an animal.

Vibrissae
Stiff, coarse hairs, richly supplied with nerves that are especially found around the snout and have a sensory (tactile) function. More commonly referred to as whiskers.

Xerophytic
Applies to vegetation, typically a forest, that grows in areas that receive relatively little rainfall. The trees and plants of such forests are generally adapted to protect themselves against browsing animals by having well-developed spines, and reduce water loss through transpiration by having small, leathery leaves with a waxy cuticle.

APPENDIX I
THE EXTINCT MAMMALS OF MADAGASCAR

RODENTS
ORDER RODENTIA
Family Muridae

Hypogeomys australis

This species of jumping rat was first described in 1903 from jaw material around 4,400 years old, collected in the Andrahomana Cave some 40km west of Tolagnaro. In the intervening years its validity has been questioned by some who have argued that specific differentiation of *Hypogeomys australis* and its extant congener *H. antimena* is unwarranted. However, recent detailed comparison of the two taxa have confirmed that *H. australis* is a good species and was considerably larger in size than *H. antimena*.

Further subfossil material collected from the Antsirabe region in the central highlands has been identified as *H. australis*, which suggests that this species was once widely distributed, its range at least covering much of the southern half of the island.

Nothing is known about the natural history of *H. australis*, although it is presumed to have lived in burrows excavated in areas of sandy soil, much as *H. antimena* does today.

EVEN-TOED UNGULATES
ORDER ARTIODACTYLA
Family Hippopotamidae

Three species of dwarf hippopotamus have been described from Madagascar, all of which show considerable similarities to the extant hippopotamuses that remain on mainland Africa – the Common Hippopotamus *Hippopotamus amphibius* and the Pygmy Hippopotamus *Choeropsis liberiensis* (formerly genus *Hexaprotodon*).

Material from these species has been dated to the Holocene and not before, indicating that they were all relatively recent arrivals on Madagascar and the result of three independent colonisations. The early human colonisation of the island c. 2,000 years B.P. is implicated in the extinction of these species, although climatic change may also have been a factor.

MALAGASY DWARF HIPPOPOTAMUS *Hippopotamus lemerlei*

Estimated measurements: Total length: 2,000mm. Height at the shoulder: 800mm.

This species resembled a small *H. amphibius* and probably had a similar lifestyle; its remains have principally been recovered from coastal lowland sites. Adult skulls are markedly different in size, presumably indicating that this species was sexually dimorphic. *H. lemerlei* survived on the island at least until 980 ± 200 years B.P.

MALAGASY HIPPOPOTAMUS *Hippopotamus laloumena*

This species, described in 1990, is known only from a lower jaw and limb bones found near Mananjary on the south-east coast of the island. It was the largest of the three Malagasy hippopotamuses, but did not approach the size of the Common Hippopotamus, which it otherwise appears to have resembled closely.

MALAGASY PYGMY HIPPOPOTAMUS *Hexaprotodon madagascariensis*

Hexaprotodon madagascariensis was considerably smaller than *Hippopotamus lemerlei*, with no appreciable size differences between the sexes. Until recently these two species were regarded as congeners, but a reassessment of the evidence has concluded that *Hexaprotodon madagascariensis* was more terrestrial in its habits and lifestyle than *Hippopotamus lemerlei*, thus warranting generic separation. In common with the extant Pygmy Hippopotamus from equatorial West Africa, *Hexaprotodon* was probably secretive, nocturnal, favouring forested regions and possibly living singly or in pairs. It was exclusively vegetarian.

ORDER BIBYMALAGASIA

An extinct mammal assigned to the genus *Plesiorycteropus* and known only from the Quaternary of Madagascar has conventionally been regarded as a primitive aardvark (Order Tubulidentata) and, therefore, a close relative of the extant genus *Orycteropus*. Indeed some features do show affinities with contemporary aardvarks – e.g. obvious adaptations for digging – but similarities can also be drawn with pangolins, armadillos and vermilinguans.

More recent analysis of the evidence (skull fragments) has concluded that while *Plesiorycteropus* is a eutherian mammal that justifies overall placement in the superorder Ungulata, it is distinguishable from all other known eutherians (including all recognised tubulidentates) and so warrants separation into a new mammalian order Bibymalagasia.

There is a significant size variation in the skull fragments that have been recovered to date, which suggests that two species existed.

In common with *Hippopotamus*, *Palaeopropithecus*, *Megaladapis* and many other extinct taxa that once lived in central and south-western Madagascar, species of *Plesiorycteropus* seem not to have been inextricably tied to native forest environments. It may be that much of the Quaternary fauna was largely confined to narrow belts in and around major wetland areas – swamps, river margins and lakes – that were widespread in the interior (although not necessarily with the association of native forests). This is supported by the fact that the only subfossil localities found in the interior of Madagascar are in wetland settings. It is suspected that both species of *Plesiorycteropus* became extinct approximately 1,000 years B.P.

Plesiorycteropus madagascariensis

This species was described from a partial skull found in alluvial sands near Belo Tsiribihina in central western Madagascar.

Plesiorycteropus germainepetterae

Again this species is known only from incomplete skull fragments, probably recovered from Ampasambazimba in the central highlands. This evidence indicates that *P. germainepetterae* was smaller than *P. madagascariensis* and that there were cranial differences between the two species.

LEMURS
ORDER PRIMATES

The impressive adaptive radiation of Malagasy primates includes many species of lemur that are today extinct and known only from subfossil records. To date the remains of at least 16 such species have been documented. The majority of these have been recovered from Holocene cave, marsh or riverside sites in the western and south-western regions of the island.

It is interesting to note that the bones of these extinct lemurs have been found alongside those of extant species, yet only one of the subfossil species (*Daubentonia robusta*) has a congener that survives to this day, although the two extinct *Pachylemur* species are known to be very close relatives of the extant genus *Varecia* and indeed are sometimes included within it.

The remaining species, arranged between seven genera and into three families, were totally unlike any living lemur. All were diurnal and larger (often dramatically so) than the largest extant species (*Indri indri* and *Propithecus diadema*) and most were primarily arboreal. However, although they obviously share a number of basic and defining prosimian and primate features, their nearest ecological equivalents (ecotypic analogues) often lie outside the order Primates. For instance, various species have been compared with cave bears, tree sloths, ground sloths, koalas, possums and lorises. There are also similarities to higher primates like macaques, baboons, orang-utans and gorillas.

Radiocarbon dates associated with all known extinct lemur taxa range from approximately 26,000 years B.P. to around 500 years B.P.

Family Lemuridae

Pachylemur jullyi
Pachylemur insignis

Estimated body weight: 8-10kg.

Pachylemur species are the only extinct representatives of the prolific family Lemuridae. Some early authorities proposed several different species, based on subfossil material recovered from widely distributed sites. However, more recent analysis indicates that all the material collected to date is referable to just two species, *Pachylemur jullyi* and *P. insignis*.

It has been suggested that *Pachylemur* species might be more appropriately placed in the extant genus *Varecia* and although some similarities do exist, there are striking post cranial differences between the two genera which serve to differentiate them. *Pachylemur* was primarily an arboreal quadruped – the major limb bones are robust and the fore- and hindlimbs are subequal in length. It probably climbed more slowly and was capable of less bounding and leaping and more hindlimb suspension than *Varecia*. The dentition of *Pachylemur* is very similar to that of *Varecia*, suggesting a similar diet based on fruit and foliage.

Pachylemur remains have been found at many subfossil sites distributed widely around Madagascar, including Antsirabe and Ampasambazimba on the High Plateau, and the Ankarana Massif towards the island's northern tip.

Family Megaladapidae

The family Megaladapidae contains two extinct morphological variants that are now recognised as subgenera of the genus *Megaladapis* (subgenera *Megaladapis* and *Peloriadapis*), together with the seven extant members of the genus *Lepilemur* which comprise their own subfamily Lepilemurinae. Indeed, *Megaladapis* is thought to be derived from a *Lepilemur*-like ancestor.

Megaladapis species were large-bodied animals, with skulls similar in size to those of gorillas. Their skulls were highly elongate (to a degree seen in no other primates), while the body in relation to the head was comparatively small.

Some of the first *Megaladapis* remains to be found in the Ankarana Massif have been dated to the late Pleistocene, $26,150 \pm 400$ years B.P., while later discoveries from nearby caves were dated at $12,760 \pm 70$ years B.P. However, more recently collected specimens from caves on the Manamby Plateau to the north of Toliara in the south-west suggest a date of 630 ± 50 years B.P., raising the possibility that these lemurs continued to survive long after the first humans arrived on the island and perhaps lending weight to the argument that humans were largely responsible for their eventual demise.

Megaladapis (*Megaladapis*) *madagascariensis*
Megaladapis (*Megaladapis*) *grandidieri*

Estimated body weight: 35-70kg

These large bodied lemurs had long forelimbs with huge grasping hands and feet. The hallux or great toe was enormous and widely divergent promoting sufficient grip to support the animals' considerable weight. *Megaladapis* were principally vertical clingers and climbers, although it is clear they were also capable of hindlimb-only suspension while feeding, somewhat similar to extant *Propithecus* and *Varecia* species.

Although primarily arboreal, these species also descended to ground level where they moved quadrupedally, perhaps in a similar fashion to the orang-utan. The dentition is reminiscent of *Lepilemur* species, indicating a folivorous diet, and although upper incisors are absent, a leaf-cropping adaptation such as a mobile proboscis has been suggested. Remains of these species have been found at subfossil sites throughout Madagascar.

Megaladapis (*Peloriadapis*) *edwardsi*

Estimated body weight: 75+kg

This species was appreciably larger than the two congeners belonging to the subgenus *Megaladapis*. The forelimbs were longer than the hindlimbs and had very large grasping hands and feet. In common with M. *madagascariensis* and M. *grandidieri*, this species was primarily a vertical clinger, although suspensory behaviour was dramatically reduced in comparison with its two congeners. It also seems likely that M. *edwardsi* was far more terrestrial, where it moved quadrupedally, again in an 'orang-like' fashion.

The diet was leaves and the dentition similar to that of *Lepilemur*. There were no upper incisors, although a cropping pad was present. Subfossil remains of M. *edwardsi* have been found at sites in south-east and south-west Madagascar.

Family Palaeopropithecidae

This family includes species ascribed to four genera, *Palaeopropithecus*, *Archaeoindris*, *Babakotia* and *Mesopropithecus*. Due to their extraordinary post-cranial adaptations for suspension (especially in the hindlimbs, hands and feet) members of this family are commonly referred to as the 'sloth lemurs'.

In common with the Archaeolemuridae, members of this family are also included in the superfamily Indrioidea. In these giant lemurs it is their dentition which is similar to extant members of the family Indriidae (*Propithecus*, *Indri* and *Avahi*) while, unlike indriids, their skulls are heavily built and specialised. Their diets appear to have been dominated by leaves, perhaps with the addition of some fruits and seeds.

Palaeopropithecus ingens
Palaeopropithecus maximus

Estimated body weight: 40-55kg

Members of this genus are the most 'sloth-like' of the palaeopropithecid lemurs. All anatomical features are indicative of a highly developed four-limbed suspensory lifestyle. Examples from this genus have been recovered from subfossil sites throughout the island; some from the south-west have been dated as recently as 510 ± 80 years B.P.

Archaeoindris fontoynontii

Estimated body weight: 200 ± 50kg

This species is perhaps the least known of the subfossil lemurs. *Archaeoindris* has a gorilla-sized skull and dentition and long bone dimensions that also suggest a body size approaching that of a gorilla, making it the largest of all known Lemuriformes. Despite this very large size, evidence from the humerus and femur indicate that this species may have been, at least in part, scansorial.

Archaeoindris has been found at only one site – Ampasambazimba – in the central highlands. These remains have been dated at 8,245 ± 215 years B.P.

Babakotia radofilai

Estimated body weight: approximately 15kg

Babakotia had a very *Indri*-like skull, but in contrast to *Indri*, the forelimbs, hands and feet were long, while the hindfoot was reduced, thus indicating a movement away from leaping behaviour towards more suspensory behaviour. The adaptations of the spinal column, pelvis, forelimbs, hindlimbs and digits of *Babakotia* suggest an intermediate position between *Mesopropithecus* and *Palaeopropithecus*, i.e. *Babakotia* was probably more suspensory in its behaviour than *Mesopropithecus*, but less so than *Palaeopropithecus*.

This species is known only from sites in north and north-west Madagascar – the Ankarana Massif and Anjohibe.

Mesopropithecus globiceps
Mesopropithecus pithecoides
Mesopropithecus dolichobrachion

Estimated body weight: 10kg

Members of the genus *Mesopropithecus* are known to have been arboreal quadrupeds, adapted for slow climbing and to a lesser extent suspension. Their skulls closely resemble those of extant *Propithecus* species, especially the more delicate *Propithecus verreauxi*. However, the post-cranial skeleton is quite different – in *Mesopropithecus* it is the forelimbs, rather than the hindlimbs (as with *Propithecus*) that are greatly elongated – emphasising the importance of suspensory behaviour. These species have been found in deposits throughout the island.

Family Archaeolemuridae

Members of this family are thought to be relatively close relatives of the living indriids (and are therefore included in the superfamily Indrioidea). However, while the structure of their skulls is considered primitive (and thus indriid-like), their dentition is highly specialised and non-indriid-like (in fact the molars bear resemblance to those of Old World monkeys).

Archaeolemur majori
Archaeolemur edwardsi

Estimated body weight: 15-25kg

The two members of this genus are considered to be semi-terrestrial quadrupeds and generally rather baboon-like in their behaviour. However, they were almost certainly less cursorial than contemporary baboons, with shorter limbs and digits and a wider trunk.

The dentition of *Archaeolemur*, which included enlarged incisors, suggests these species were dietary generalists, feeding on fruits and tough seeds. They may also have fed on savanna as well as forest species.

Subfossil remains have been recovered from widely dispersed localities throughout Madagascar, and they often appear to have been the most abundant species.

Hadropithecus stenognathus

Estimated body weight: approximately 17kg

H. stenagnathus is the sole member of its genus. It is thought to have been more terrestrial than *Archaeolemur* (probably filling a similar niche to that of the Gelada *Theropithecus gelada* from central Ethiopia), since its unusual dentition implies that grasses and small seed formed a significant element in the diet.

Hadropithecus is a rarely recovered species, current knowledge being based on only partial skeletal remains that have been found at sites in the south-east, south-west and central highlands.

Family Daubentoniidae

Daubentonia robusta

Estimated body weight: approximately 10kg

Daubentonia is the only lemuriform genus known to contain both an extinct and an extant species. The massive and robust limb bones of *D. robusta* indicate that it was some 2.5-5 times heavier than the living species *D. madagascariensis*. However, dental evidence (large isolated incisors), together with the arrangement of the hand bones, suggests a lifestyle, mode of locomotion and foraging behaviour similar to that of the Aye-aye *D. madagascariensis*.

Classification

Order Rodentia

Family **Muridae**
    Subfamily **Nesomyinae**
        Genus *Hypogeomys*
            Hypogeomys australis

Order Artiodactyla

Family **Hippopotamidae**
    Genus *Hippopotamus*
        Malagasy Dwarf Hippopotamus *Hippopotamus lemerlei*
        Malagasy Hippopotamus *Hippopotamus laloumena*
    Genus *Hexaprotodon*
        Malagasy Pygmy Hippopotamus *Hexaprotodon madagascariensis*

Order Bibymalagasia

Family **unknown** (false aardvarks)
    Genus *Plesiorycteropus*
        Plesiorycteropus madagascariensis
        Plesiorycteropus germainepetterae

Order Primates

Infraorder Lemuriformes

Family **Lemuridae**
    Genus *Pachylemur*
        Pachylemur jullyi
        Pachylemur insignis

Family **Megaladapidae**
    Genus *Megaladapis*
        Megaladapis (Megaladapis) madagascariensis
        Megaladapis (Megaladapis) grandidieri
        Megaladapis (Peloriadapis) edwardsi

Family **Palaeopropithecidae** (sloth lemurs)
    Genus *Palaeopropithecus*
        Palaeopropithecus ingens
        Palaeopropithecus maximus
    Genus *Archaeoindris*
        Archaeoindris fontoynontii
    Genus *Babakotia*
        Babakotia radofilai
    Genus *Mesopropithecus*
        Mesopropithecus globiceps
        Mesopropithecus pithecoides
        Mesopropithecus dolichobrachion

Family **Archaeolemuridae**
    Genus *Archaeolemur*
        Archaeolemur majori
        Archaeolemur edwardsi
    Genus *Hadropithecus*
        Hadropithecus stenognathus

Family **Daubentoniidae**
    Genus *Daubentonia*
        Daubentonia robusta

APPENDIX II
NATIONAL PARKS AND RESERVES

Madagascar has an established system of protected areas which are divided into several categories. The four main divisions are: national parks (Parcs Nationaux), strict nature reserves (Réserves Naturelles Intégrales), special reserves (Réserves Spéciales) and private reserves (Reserves Privées). These divisions correspond to the varying degree of protection, utilisation and access that the legislation allows. In addition to these areas, there is an extensive network of classified forests and forest reserves which receive cursory levels of protection: most of these areas have yet to be surveyed, so little is known of the mammalian fauna that exists within them.

National Parks

National parks are gazetted to allow the integration of conservation and development within the local communities. As such, they tend to have core areas for protection of primary and secondary habitats, surrounded by buffer zones where the local communities are encouraged to utilise natural resources sustainably. National parks are open to visitors, but access to specific areas is controlled.

Eastern Domain

Masoala	lowland/mid-altitude rainforest	210,000ha
Isalo	sandstone massif/palm savanna	81,540ha
Ranomafana	mid-altitude rainforest	39,200ha
Verezanantsoro	lowland rainforest	23,000ha
Montagne d'Ambre	mid-altitude rainforest	18,000ha
Mantadia	mid-altitude rainforest	10,000ha
Nosy Atafana	marine	1,000ha

Western Domain

Tsingy de Bemaraha	limestone karst/deciduous forest	152,000ha

PROPOSED NATIONAL PARKS

Eastern Domain

Marojejy	lowland/mid- and high-altitude rainforest	60,150ha
Andohahela – parcel 1	low and mid-altitude rainforest	63,100ha

Western Domain

Zombitse	deciduous forest	21,500ha

Southern Domain

Andohahela – parcels 2 and 3	spiny forest	12,920ha

Strict Nature Reserves

Strict nature reserves have been set aside solely for the purpose of protection and research. Access to them is restricted to government officials, representatives of the Water and Forest Department (DEF), and scientists with specific research permission from the relevant government ministries.

Eastern Domain

Zahamena	lowland/mid-altitude rainforest	73,160ha
Andohahela – parcel 1	lowland/mid-altitude rainforest	63,100ha
Marojejy	lowland/mid- and high-altitude rainforest	60,150ha
Tsaratanana	lowland/mid- and high-altitude rainforest	48,622ha
Andringitra	lowland/mid- and high-altitude rainforest	31,160ha
Betampona	lowland rainforest	2,228ha

Sambirano Domain

Lokobe	Sambirano humid forest	740ha

Western Domain

Ankarafantsika	deciduous forest	60,520ha
Namoroka	limestone karst/deciduous forest	21,742ha

Southern Domain

Tsimanampetsotsa	spiny forest	43,200ha
Andohahela – parcels 2 and 3	spiny forest	12,920ha

Special Reserves

These reserves have been created with the specific intention of protecting a particular species of plant or animal. Visitors are allowed to enter special reserves with prior permission and a permit from ANGAP. Traditional rights of access and exploitation are also allowed.

Eastern Domain

Ambatovaky	lowland/mid-altitude rainforest	60,050ha
Marotandrano	mid-altitude rainforest	42,200ha
Anjanaharibe-Sud	lowland/mid- & high-altitude rainforest	2,100ha
Kalambatrita	mid-altitude rainforest	28,250ha
Analamaitso	mid-altitude rainforest	17,150ha
Mangerivola	lowland rainforest	11,900ha
Ambohitantely	mid-altitude rainforest	5,600ha
Manombo	lowland rainforest	5,020ha
Forêt d'Ambre	mid-altitude rainforest	4,810ha
Pic d'Ivohibe	mid- & high-altitude rainforest	3,450ha
Analamazaotra	mid-altitude rainforest	810ha
Nosy Mangabe	lowland rainforest	520ha

Sambirano Domain

Manongarivo	Sambirano humid forest	35,250ha

Western Domain

Analamera	semi-humid/deciduous forest	34,700ha
Ambohijanahary	semi-humid/deciduous forest	24,750ha
Kasijy	deciduous forest	18,800ha
Ankarana	deciduous forest	18,220ha
Bemarivo	deciduous forest	11,570ha
Maningozo	deciduous forest	7,900ha
Andranomena	deciduous forest	6,420ha
Bora	deciduous forest	4,780ha

Southern Domain

Cap Sainte-Marie	spiny forest	1,750ha
Beza-Mahafaly	gallery and spiny forest	580ha

Private Reserves

At present four private reserves have been established on the island. These are all owned and administered by the de Heaulme family from Tolagnaro. Although it is possible to visit all three, only one of them, Berenty, currently has the facilities to receive regular visitors.

Eastern Domain

Sainte Luce	lowland rainforest	200ha

Western Domain

Analabe	deciduous forest	2,000-12,000ha

Southern Domain

Berenty	gallery and spiny forest	265ha
Amboasary-Sud	gallery and spiny forest	100ha

Appendix III
Useful Addresses and Contacts

A number of major European and American research and conservation organisations are focusing their attention on Madagascar and may be able to provide further information relating to the status of the island's fauna. As indicated, some also have offices in Madagascar. Some other useful addresses are also given.

EUROPE

Jersey Wildlife Preservation Trust
Les Augrès Manor
Trinity
Jersey JE3 5BP
Channel Islands, U.K.
http://www.jersey.co.uk/jwpt

World Wide Fund for Nature – U.K.
Panda House
Weyside Park
Godalming
Surrey GU7 1XR
U.K.
http://www.wwf-uk.org

World Wide Fund for Nature – International
Avenue du Mont-Blanc
CH-1196 Gland
Switzerland
http://www.panda.org

German Primate Centre
DPZ - Deutsches Primatenzentrum GmbH
Kellnerweg 4
D - 37077 Göttingen
Germany
http://www.dpz.gwdg.de

World Conservation Monitoring Centre,
219 Huntingdon Road
Cambridge CB3 0DL
U.K.
http://www.wcmc.org.uk

NORTH AMERICA

World Wildlife Fund – U.S.
1250 24th Street N W
Washington
D.C. 20037-1175
U.S.A.
http://www.wwf.org

Institute for the Conservation of Tropical Environments
State University of New York at Stony Brook
SBS Building, 5th Floor
Stony Brook
New York 11794-4364
U.S.A.

Wildlife Conservation Society
International Wildlife Conservation Park
Bronx
New York 10468–1099
U.S.A.
http://www.wcs.org

Duke University Primate Centre,
Lemur Lane,
3705 Erwin Road,
Durham,
North Carolina 27705-5000,
U.S.A.
http://www.duke.edu/web/primate

Conservation International
1015 18th Street N.W.
Suite 1000
Washington
D.C. 20036
U.S.A.
http://www.conservation.org

Wildlife Preservation Trust International
34th Street and Girard Avenue
Philadelphia
Pennsylvania 19104
U.S.A.
http://www.columbia.edu/cu/cerc/wpti.html

Madagascar Fauna Group
A consortium of 26 zoological institutions in the United States, United Kingdom and mainland Europe. Their aim is to promote the conservation of all classes of Malagasy fauna, particularly those species whose populations appear to be falling below viable levels.
c/o David Anderson
San Francisco Zoo
1 Zoo Road
San Francisco
California 94132-1098
U.S.A.
http://www.aza.org/aza/advisory/madfig.htm

MADAGASCAR

WORLD WIDE FUND FOR NATURE
Aires Protégées
B.P. 738
Antananarivo 101
Madagascar.
Tel: (261) 202 234 885/638
Fax: (261) 202 234 888
e-mail: wwfrcp@dts.mg

RANOMAFANA NATIONAL PARK PROJECT
111 L-102 Tsimbazaza
P.O. Box 3715
Antananarivo 101
Madagascar
Tel/Fax: (261) 202 232 123
e-mail: MICET@dts.mg

CONSERVATION INTERNATIONAL
B.P. 5178
Antananarivo 101
Madagascar

JERSEY WILDLIFE PRESERVATION TRUST
B.P. 8511
Antananarivo 101
Madagascar
Tel/Fax: (261) 202 235 748
e-mail: jwpt@bow.dtd.mg

WILDLIFE CONSERVATION SOCIETY
B.P. 8500
Antananarivo 101
Madagascar

DIRECTION DES EAUX ET FORÊTS (Directorate of Water and Forests)
B.P. 243
Antananarivo 101
Madagascar
Tel: (261) 202 240 610

ASSOCIATION NATIONALE POUR LA GESTION DES AIRES PROTEGÉES (ANGAP)
(National Association for the Management of Protected Areas)
B.P. 1424
Antananarivo 101
Madagascar
Tel: (261) 202 230 518
Fax: (261) 202 231 994

BIBLIOGRAPHY
General Bibliography

Battistini, R. and Richard-Vindard, G. (1972) *Biogeography and Ecology in Madagascar*. Dr W. Junk, The Hague.

Bradt, H. (1997) *Guide to Madagascar* (5th ed.). Bradt Publications, U.K.

Bradt, H., Schuurman, D. and Garbutt, N. (1996) *Madagascar Wildlife – A Visitor's Guide*. Bradt Publications, U.K.

Dransfield, J. and Beentje H. (1996) *The Palms of Madagascar*. Royal Botanic Gardens, Kew, U.K.

Glaw, F. and Vences M. (1994) *A Fieldguide to the Amphibians and Reptiles of Madagascar*.

Harcourt, C. and Thornback, J. (1990) *Lemurs of Madagascar and the Comoros*. IUCN Red Data Book. IUCN, Gland, Switzerland and Cambridge, U.K.

IUCN/UNDP/WWF (1990) *Madagascar: Profil de l'environnement*. Jenkins, M.D. (ed.). IUCN, Cambridge, U.K. and Gland, Switzerland.

Jolly, A. (1980) *A World Like Our Own: Man and Nature in Madagascar*. Yale University Press, Connecticut.

Jolly, A., Oberle, P. and Albignac R. (eds.)(1984) *Key Environments: Madagascar*. Pergamon Press, Oxford, U.K.

Langrand, O. (1990) *Guide to the Birds of Madagascar*. Yale University Press, U.S.A.

Mittermeier, R.A., Konstant, W.R., Nicoll, M.E. and Langrand, O. (1992) *Lemurs of Madagascar: An Action Plan for their Conservation, 1993-1999*. IUCN/SSC Primate Specialist Group, Gland, Switzerland.

Mittermeier, R.A., Tattersall, I., Konstant, W.R., Meyers, D. and Mast, R.B. (1994) *Lemurs of Madagascar*. Conservation International Tropical Field Guide. Conservation International, Washington, D.C.

Morris, P. and Hawkins, F. (1998) *Birds of Madagascar: A Photographic Guide*. Pica Press, U.K.

Nicoll, M.E. and Langrand O.(1989) *Madagascar: Revue de la Conservation et des Aires Protégées*. WWF, Gland, Switzerland.

Preston-Mafham, K. (1991) *Madagascar: A Natural History*. Facts on File, U.K.

Quammen, D. (1996) *The Song of the Dodo: Island Biogeography in an Age of Extinction*. Hutchinson, London, U.K.

Tattersall, I. (1982) *The Primates of Madagascar*. Columbia University Press, N.Y.

Wilson, D.E. and Reeder, D.M. (eds.)(1993) *Mammal Species of the World: a taxonomic and geographic reference*. 2nd edition. Smithsonian Inst. Press. Washington, D.C.

Specific Bibliographies

Biogeography and Biogeographic Regions

Agrawal, P.K., Pandey, O.P. and Negi, J.G. (1992) Madagascar – a continental fragment of the Paleo-Super Dharwar Craton of India. *Geology* 20: 543-546.

Bassias, Y. (1992) Petrological and geological investigation of rocks from the Davie-Fracture Zone (Mozambique Channel) and some tectonic implications. *J. African Earth Sci. Mid. East* 15: 321-339.

Coffin, M.F. and Rabinowitz, P.D. (1987) Reconstruction of Madagascar and Africa: evidence from the Davie Fracture Zone and the western Somali basin. *J. Geophysical Research* B92: 9385- 9406.

Dewar, R.E. (1984) Recent extinctions in Madagascar: the loss of the subfossil fauna. In: Martin, P.S. and Klein R.G. (eds.) *Quaternary Extinctions: a Prehistoric Revolution*, pp. 574-593. Uni. Arizona Press.

Du Puy, D.J. and Moat, J. (1996) J. A refined classification of the vegetation types of Madagascar, and their current distribution. In: Lourenco, W.R. (ed.) *Biogéographie de Madagascar*, pp. 205-218. Editions de l'ORSTOM, Paris.

Green, G.M. and Sussman, R.W. (1990) Deforestation history of the eastern rainforests of Madagascar from satellite images. *Science* 248: 212-215.

Koechlin, J., Guillaumet, J.-L. and Morat, P. (1974) *Flore et Vegetation de Madagascar*. J. Cramer Verlag, Vaduz.

Krause, D.W., Hartman, J.H. and Wells, N.A. (1997) Late Cretaceous vertebrates from Madagascar: implications for biotic change in deep time. In: Goodman, S.M. and Patterson, B.D. (eds.) *Natural Change and Human Impact in Madagascar*, pp. 3-43. Smithsonian Inst. Press, Washington, D.C.

Lowry II, P.P., Schatz, G.E. and Phillipson, P.B. (1997) The classification of natural and anthropogenic vegetation in Madagascar. In: Goodman, S. M. and Patterson, B.D. (eds.) *Natural Change and Human Impact in Madagascar*, pp. 93-123. Smithsonian Inst. Press, Washington, D.C.

Malod, J.A., Mougenot, D., Raillard, S. and Maillard, A. (1991) New constraints on the kinematics of Madagascar – tectonic structure of the Davie ridge. *Comptes Rendus de l'Academie des Sciences Serie II*, 312: 1639-1646.

Martin, R.D. (1993) Primate origins: plugging the gaps. *Nature* 363: 223-234.

Paulian, R. (1984) Madagascar, a micro-continent between Africa and Asia. In: Jolly, A., Oberle, P. and Albignac R. (eds.) *Key Environments: Madagascar*, pp. 1-26. Pergamon Press, Oxford, U.K.

Pavoni, N. (1992) Rifting of Africa and pattern of mantle convection beneath the African plate. *Tectonophysics* 215: 35-53.

Rabinowitz, P.D., Coffin, M.F. and Flavey, D. (1983) The separation of Madagascar and Africa. *Science* 220. 67-69.

Reeves, C.V., Karanja, F.M. and MacLeod, I.N.(1987) Geophysical evidence for a failed Jurassic rift and triple in Kenya. *Earth and Planetary Science Letters* 81: 299-311.

Storey, M.J., Mahoney, J.J., Saunders, A.D., Duncan, R.A., Kelley, S.P. and Coffin, M.F. (1995) Timing of hot-spot related volcanism and the break up of Madagascar and India. *Science* 267: 852-855.

Warren, R.D. and Crompton, R.H. (1996) Lazy leapers: energetics, phylogenetic inertia and the locomotor differentiation of the Malagasy primates. In: Lourenco, W.R. (ed.) *Biogéographie de Madagascar*, pp. 259-266. Editions de l'ORSTOM, Paris.

White, F. (1983) The vegetation of Africa, a descriptive memoir to accompany the UNESCO/AETFAT/UNSO vegetation map of Africa. UNESCO, *Natural Resource Res*. 20: 1-356.

Yoder, A. (1996) The use of phylogeny for reconstructing lemuriform biogeography. In: Lourenco, W.R. (ed.) *Biogéographie de Madagascar*, pp. 245-258. Editions de l'ORSTOM, Paris.

Order Chiroptera

Andersen, K. (1912) *Catalogue of Chiroptera in the Collection of the British Museum* (2nd Ed.), 1: Megachiroptera. Brit. Mus. (Nat. Hist.).

Bergmans, W. (1977) Notes on new material of *Rousettus madagascariensis* Grandidier, 1929 (Mammalia, Megachiroptera). *Mammalia* 41: 67-74.

Bergmans, W. (1990) Taxonomy and biogeography of African fruit bats (Mammalia, Megachiroptera) 3. The genera *Scotonycteris* Matschie 1894, *Casinycteris* Thomas 1910, *Pteropus* Brisson 1762 and *Eidolon* Rafinesque 1815. *Beaufortia* 40(7): 111-117.

Bergmans, W. (1994) Taxonomy and biogeography of African fruit bats (Mammalia, Megachiroptera) 4. The genus *Rousettus* Gray 1821. *Beaufortia* 44(4): 79-126.

Butler, D.M. (1978) Insectivora and Chiroptera. In: Maglio, V. J. and Cook, H.B.S. (eds.) *Evolution of African Mammals*, pp. 56-66. Harvard University Press.

Cheke, A.S. and Dahl, J.F. (1981) The status of bats on Western Indian Ocean islands, with special reference to *Pteropus*. *Mammalia* 45: 205-238.

DeFrees, S.L. and Wilson, D.E. (1988) *Eidolon helvum*. *Mammalian Species* 312.

Eger, J.L. and Mitchell, L. (1996) Biogeography of the bats of Madagascar. In: Lourenco, W.R. (ed.) *Biogéographie de Madagascar*, pp. 321-328. Editions de l'ORSTOM, Paris.

Freeman, P.W. (1981) A multivariate study of the family Molossidae (Mammalia, Chiroptera): morphology, ecology and evolution. *Fieldiana Zoology* 7: 1-173.

Goodman, S.M. (1996) Results of a bat survey of the eastern slopes of the Réserve Naturelle Intégrale d'Andringitra, Madagascar. *Fieldiana Zoology* 85: 284-288.

Göpfert, M.C. and Wasserthal, L.T. (1995) Notes on the echolocation calls, food and roosting behaviour of the Old World sucker-footed bat *Myzopoda aurita* (Chiroptera, Myzopodidae). *Int. J. Mammalian Biol.* 60: 1-8.

Göpfert, M.C., Heller, K.-G., Volleth, M. and Wasserthal, L.T. (1995) Madagascar Microchiropteran bats: new records including new species. *Bat Research News* 36(4): 68-69.

Grandidier, G. (1929) Nouvelle espèce de chauve-souris frugivore, *Rousettus madagascariensis*, G. Grandidier. *Bull. Acad. Malgache N.S.* 11 (1928): 91-93.

Harrison, D.L. (1959) A new subspecies of lesser long-winged bat, *Miniopterus minor* Peters 1867, from the Comoro Islands. *Durban Mus. Novit.*, 5: 191-196.

Hayman, R.W. and Hill, J.E. (1977) Order Chiroptera. In: Meester, J. and Setzer, H.W. *The Mammals of Africa: an identification manual*. Smithsonian Inst. Press, Washington, D.C.

Hill, J.E. (1993) Long-fingered bats of the genus *Miniopterus* (Chiroptera: Vespertilionidae) from Madagascar. *Mammalia* 57: 401-405.

Kingdon, J. (1974) *East African Mammals: An Atlas of Evolution in Africa*, II (A). (Insectivores & Bats). Academic Press, London and N.Y.

Kock, D. (1978) A new fruit bat of the genus *Rousettus* Gray 1821 (Mammalia: Chiroptera) from the Comoro Islands, Western Indian Ocean. In: Olembo, R.J. (ed.) *Proc. 4th Int. Bat Research Conf.* pp. 205-216. Kenya Inst. Bureau, Nairobi.

Koopman, K.F. (1984) A synopsis of the families of bats. Part VII. *Bat Research News* 25: 25-27.

Koopman, K.F. (1984) Bats. In: Anderson, S. and Jones, J.K. (eds.) *Orders and Families of Recent Mammals of the World*, pp. 145-186. John Wiley & Sons, N.Y.

Koopman, K.F. (1993) Order Chiroptera. In: Wilson, D.E. and Reeder, D.M. (eds.), *Mammal Species of the World: A Taxonomic and Geographic Reference*, 2nd edition, pp. 137-241. Smithsonian Inst. Press, Washington, D.C.

Long, E. (1995) Some aspects of the feeding ecology of *Pteropus rufus* in north east Madagascar. In: Wells, M., Long, E., Palmer, G., Taylor, A., Tedd, J. and Grant, I. (eds.) Project Madagascar 1994: Final Report of University of Aberdeen Expedition to Zahamena Nature Reserve, Madagascar, pp. 30-35. Dept. Zoology, University of Aberdeen. Unpublished report.

Long, E. (*in litt.*) Comments on the behaviour and ecology of Madagascar Fruit Bats (*Pteropus rufus*) at Berenty Reserve in southern Madagascar. University of Aberdeen (unpublished PhD research).

McHale, M. (1987) The Bats. In: Wilson, J. (ed.), The crocodile caves of Ankarana: Expedition to northern Madagascar 1986, pp. 14. *Cave Sci.: Trans. British Cave Res. Ass.* 14: 107-119.

Mickleburgh, S.P., Hutson, A.M. and Racey, P.A. (1992) *Old World Fruit Bats: An Action Plan for their Conservation*. IUCN/SCC Chiroptera Special Group. IUCN Gland, Switzerland and Cambridge, U.K.

Nowak, R.M. (1995) *Walker's Bats of the World*. Johns Hopkins Uni. Press.

Peterson, R.L. Eger, J.L. and Mitchell, L. (1995) Chiroptères: *Faune de Madagascar*. Vol. 84. Nat. Hist. Mus. Paris.

Pont, S.M. and Armstrong, J.D. (1990) A study of the bat fauna of the Réserve Naturelle Intégrale de Marojejy in north east Madagascar. Report of the Aberdeen University Expedition to Madagascar 1989. Dept. Zoology, University of Aberdeen. Unpublished report.

Racey, P.A. (1982) Ecology of bat reproduction. In: Kunz, T.H. (ed.) *Ecology of Bats*, pp. 57-104. Plenum Press, London & N.Y.

Rasolozaka, I.N. (1994) Les Micro-Chiroptères. In: Goodman, S.M. and Langrand, O. (eds.) *Inventaire Biologique Forêt de Zombitse, Recherches pour le Developpement, Série Science Biologiques*, pp. 64-67. No.Spécial 1994. Centre d'Information et de Documentation Scientifique et Technique, Antananarivo, Madagascar.

Safford, R.J. and Duckworth, J.W. (1990) A wildlife survey of Marojejy Nature Reserve, Madagascar. *Int. Council Bird Preserv. Study Report* No. 40.

Schliemann, H. and Maas, B. (1978) *Myzopoda aurita. Mammalian Species* 116.

Thomas, O. (1904) On the osteology and systematic position of the rare Malagasy bat *Myzopoda aurita. Proc. Zool. Soc.* (London) 1904: 2-6.

Van Cakenberghe, V. and DeVree, F. (1985) Systematics of African *Nycteris* (Mammalia: Chiroptera). *Proc. Int. Symp. Afr. Vert.*, Bonn, pp. 53-90.

Wells, M. (1995) The roost ecology of the Malagasy flying fox (*Pteropus rufus*). In: Wells, M., Long, E., Palmer, G., Taylor, A., Tedd, J. and Grant, I. (eds.) Project Madagascar 1994: Final Report of University of Aberdeen Expedition to Zahamena Nature Reserve, Madagascar, pp. 36-44. Dept. Zoology, University of Aberdeen. Unpublished report.

Order Insectivora

Report, Special Issue, 46-1(June 1996).

Genest, H. and Petter, F. (1977) Subfamilies Tenrecinae and Oryzorictinae. In Meester, J. and Setzer, H.W. *The Mammals of Africa: an Identification Manual*. Smithsonian Inst. Press, Washington, D.C.

Goodman, S.M. and Ganzhorn, J.U. (1994) Les petites mammifères. In: Goodman, S.M. and Langrand, O. (eds.) *Inventaire Biologique Forêt de Zombitse, Recherches pour le Developpement, Série Science Biologiques*, pp. 58-63. No.Spécial 1994. Centre d'Information et de Documentation Scientifique et Technique, Antananarivo, Madagascar.

Goodman, S.M, Parrillo, P.P., James, S. and Sierwald, P. (1996) Elevational variation in soil macroinvertebrates on the eastern slopes of the Réserve Naturelle Intégrale d'Andringitra, Madagascar. *Fieldiana Zoology* 85: 144-151.

Goodman, S.M., Raxworthy, C.J. and Jenkins, P.D. (1996) Insectivore ecology in the Réserve Naturelle Intégrale d'Andringitra, Madagascar. *Fieldiana Zoology*, 85: 218-230.

Goodman, S.M., Jenkins, P.D. and Langrand, O. (1997) Exceptional records of *Microgale* species (Insectivora: Tenrecidae) in vertebrate food remains. *Kunde: Bonn. Zool. Beiträge* 47: 1-2.

Goodman, S.M. and Jenkins, P.D. (in press) The Insectivores of the Réserve Speciale d'Anjanaharibe-Sud, Madagascar. *Fieldiana Zoology*.

Goodman, S.M., Andrianarimisa, A., Olson, L.E. and Soarimalala, V. (in press) Patterns of elevational distribution of birds and small mammals in the humid forests of Montagne d'Ambre, Madagascar. *Ecotropica*.

Gould, E. and Eisenberg, J.F. (1966) Notes on the biology of the Tenrecidae. *J. Mammal.* 47: 660- 686.

Grandidier, G. (1934) Deux nouveaux mammifères insectivores de Madagascar, *Microgale drouhardi* et *Microgale parvula. Bull. Mus. Natn. Hist. Nat. Paris* (Zool.) 6: 474-477.

Hasler, M.J., Hasler, J.F. and Nalbandov, A.V. (1977) . Comparative breeding biology of musk shrews (*Suncus murinus*) from Guam and Madagascar. *J. Mammal.* 58: 285-290.

Heim de Balsac, H. (1972) Insectivores. In Battistini, R. and Richard-Vindard, G. (eds.) *Biogeography and Ecology of Madagascar*. Dr W. Junk, The Hague.

Hutterer, R. and Tranier, M. (1990) The immigration of the Asian house shrew (*Suncus murinus*) into Africa and Madagascar. In Peters and Hutterer, R.

(eds.) *Vertebrates in the Tropics*, pp.309-321. Museum A. Koenig, Bonn.

Jenkins, P.D. (1988) A new species of *Microgale* (Insectivora: Tenrecidae) from north eastern Madagascar. *Ame. Mus. Novitates* 2910.

Jenkins, P.D. (1992) Description of a new species of *Microgale* (Insectivora: Tenrecidae) from north eastern Madagascar. *Bull. Brit. Mus. Nat. Hist.* (Zool.) 58 (1): 53-59.

Jenkins, P.D. (1993) A new species of *Microgale* (Insectivora: Tenrecidae) from eastern Madagascar with an unusual dentition. *Amer. Mus. Novitates* 3067.

Jenkins, P.D., Goodman, S.M. and Raxworthy, C.J. (1996) The shrew tenrecs (*Microgale*)(Insectivora: Tenrecidae) of the Réserve Naturelle Intégrale d'Andringitra, Madagascar. *Fieldiana Zoology*, 85: 191-217.

Jenkins, P.D., Raxworthy, C. J. and Nussbaum, R.A. (1997) A new species of *Microgale* (Insectivora, Tenrecidae), with comments on the status of four other taxa of shrew tenrec. *Bull. Nat. Hist. Mus. Lond.* (Zool.) 63(1): 1-12.

MacPhee, R.D.E. (1987) The shrew tenrecs of Madagascar: systematic revision and Holocene distribution of *Microgale* (Insectivora: Tenrecidae). *Amer. Mus. Novitates* 2889.

MacPhee, R.D.E. (1987) Systematic status of *Dasogale fontoynonti* (Tenrecidae: Insectivora). *J. Mammal.* 68(1): 133-135.

Major, C.I. Forsyth (1896) Diagnoses of new mammals from Madagascar. *Annals & Magazine of Natural History*, series 6, 18: 318-325.

Major, C.I. Forsyth (1896) Descriptions of four additional new mammals from Madagascar. *Annals & Magazine of Natural History*, series 6, 18: 461-463.

Mallinson, J. (1973) Establishing mammalian gestation periods. *J.W.P.T. Report* 9: 62-65.

Malzy, P. (1965) Un mammifère aquatique de Madagascar: le *Limnogale. Mammalia* 29: 399-411.

Morrison-Scott, T.C.S. (1948) The insectivorous genera *Microgale* and *Nesogale* (Madagascar). *Proc. Zool. Soc.* (London), 118: 817-822.

Nicoll, M.E. (1984) Tenrecs. In Macdonald, D. (ed.) *The Encyclopaedia of Mammals*. pp. 744-747. Unwins, London.

Nicoll, M.E. (1985) Responses to Seychelles tropical forest seasons by a litter foraging mammalian insectivore, *Tenrec ecaudatus*, native to Madagascar. *J. Anim. Ecol.* 54: 71-88.

Ade, M. (1996) Examination of the digestive tract contents of *Tenrec ecaudatus* Schreber, 1777 (Tenrecidae, Insectivora) from western Madagascar. In: Ganzhorn, J.U. and Sorg, J.-P. (eds.) Ecology and Economy of a Tropical Dry Forest in Madagascar, pp. 233-249. *Primate Report*, Special Issue, 46-1(June 1996).

Ade, M. (1996) Morphological observations on a *Microgale* specimen (Insectivora, Tenrecidae) from western Madagascar. In: Ganzhorn, J.U. and Sorg, J.-P. (eds.) Ecology and Economy of a Tropical Dry Forest in Madagascar, pp. 251-255. *Primate Report*, Special Issue, 46-1(June 1996).

Barden, T.L., Evans, M.I., Raxworthy, C.J., Razafimahimodison, J.C. and Wilson, A. (1991) The mammals of Ambatovaky Special Reserve. In, Thompson, P.M. and Evans, M.I. (eds.) *A Survey of Ambatovaky Special Reserve, Madagascar*. Madagascar Environmental Research Group. Chapter 5, pp. 1-22.

Coquerel, C. (1848) Note sur une espèce nouvelle de musaraigne trouvée à Madagascar. *Annales de Sciences Naturelles Zoologie* 9: 193-198.

Duckworth, J.W. and Rakotondraparany, F. (1990) The mammals of Marojejy. In Safford, R. J. and Duckworth, J.W. (eds.) *A Wildlife Survey of Marojejy Nature Reserve, Madagascar*, pp.54-60. *Int. Council Bird Preserv. Study Report No. 40*.

Eisenberg, J.F. and Gould, E. (1967) The maintenance of tenrecoid insectivores in captivity. *Int. Zoo Yearbook* 7: 194-196.

Eisenberg, J.F. and Gould, E. (1970) The tenrecs: a study in mammalian behaviour and evolution. *Smithsonian Contrib. Zool.* 27: 1-137.

Fowler, P.A. (1986) Aspects of reproduction and heterothermy in seasonally breeding mammals. PhD thesis, University of Aberdeen, Aberdeen, U.K.

Ganzhorn, J.U., Ganzhorn, A.W., Abraham, J.-P., Andriamanarivo, L. and Ramanandjatovo, A. (1990) The impact of selective logging on forest structure and tenrec populations in western Madagascar. *Oecologia* 84: 126-133.

Ganzhorn, J.U., Sommer, S., Abraham, J.-P., Ade, M., Raharivololona, B.M., Rakotovao, E.R., Rakotondrasoa, C. and Randriamarosoa, R. (1996) Mammals of the Kirindy Forest with special emphasis on *Hypogeomys antimena* and the effects of logging on the small mammal fauna. In: Ganzhorn, J.U. and Sorg, J.-P. (eds.) Ecology and Economy of a Tropical Dry Forest in Madagascar, pp. 251-255. *Primate*

Nicoll, M.E. (1986) Diel variation in body temperature in *Tenrec ecaudatus* during seasonal hypothermia. *J. Mammal.* 67: 759-762.

Nicoll, M.E., Rakotondraparany, F. and Randrianasolo, V. (1988) Diversité des petits mammifères en forêt tropicale humide de Madagascar: analyse préliminaire. In: Rakotovao, L., Barre, V. and Sayer, J. (eds.) *L'Equilibre des Ecosystèmes Forestiers à Madagascar: actes d'un séminaire international*, pp. 241-52. IUCN, Gland, Switzerland.

Nicoll, M.E. and Rathbun, G.B. (1990) *African Insectivora and Elephant Shrews: An Action Plan for their Conservation*. IUCN, Gland, Switzerland.

Nowak, R.M. (1991) *Walker's Mammals of the World* (5th edition). Johns Hopkins U.P. Baltimore and London.

Paulian, R., Betsch, J.M., Guillaumet, J.L., Blanc, C. and Griveaud, P. (1971) Etudes des écosystèmes montagnards dans la région Malgache. I. Le Massif de l'Andringitra, 1970-1971. Géomorphologie, climatologie et groupements végétaux. RCP 225. *Bulletin de la Société d'Ecologie* 11(2-3): 198-226.

Paulian, R., Blanc, C., Guillaumet, J.L., Betsch, J.M., Griveaud, P. and Peyrieras, A. (1973) Etudes des écosystèmes montagnards dans le région Malgache. II. Les Chaînes anosyennes. Géomorphologie, climatologie et groupements végétaux. Campagne RCP 225, 1971-1972. *Bull. Mus. Nat. Hist. Paris* III, Séries 118 Ecol. 1: 1-40.

Poppitt, S.D., Speakman, J.R. and Racey, P.A. (1994) Energetics of reproduction in the lesser hedgehog tenrec, *Echinops telfairi*. *Physiol. Zool.* 976-994.

Raxworthy, C.J. and Rakotondraparany, F. (1988) Mammals Report. In Quansah, N. (ed.) *Manongarivo Special Reserve, Madagascar 1987/88 Expedition Report*. Madagascar Environmental Research Group. Chapter 7, pp. 121-131.

Raxworthy, C.J. and Nussbaum, R.N. (1994) A rainforest survey of amphibians, reptiles and small mammals at Montagne d'Ambre, Madagascar. *Biol. Conserv.* 69: 65-73.

Stephenson, P.J. (1993) The small mammal fauna of Réserve Speciale d'Analamazaotra, Madagascar: the effects of human disturbance on endemic species diversity. *Biodiv. & Conserv.* 2: 603-615.

Stephenson, P.J. (1993) Reproductive biology of the large eared tenrec, *Geogale aurita* (Insectivora: Tenrecidae). *Mammalia* 57: 553-563.

Stephenson, P.J. (1994) Small mammal species richness in a Madagascar rainforest. *African J. Ecol.* 32: 255-258.

Stephenson, P.J. (1994) Notes on the biology of the fossorial tenrec, *Oryzorictes hova* (Insectivora: Tenrecidae). *Mammalia* 58: 312-315.

Stephenson, P.J. (1994) Resting metabolic rate and body temperature in the aquatic tenrec, *Limnogale mergulus* (Insectivora: Tenrecidae). *Acta Theriologica* 39: 89-92.

Stephenson, P.J. (1995) Taxonomy of shrew-tenrecs (*Microgale* spp.) from eastern and central Madagascar. *J. Zool.* (Lond.) 235: 339-350.

Stephenson, P.J. (1995) Small mammal micro-habitat use in lowland rainforest of north east Madagascar. *Acta Theriologica* 40(4): 425-438.

Stephenson, P.J. and Racey, P.A. (1992) Basal metabolic rate and body mass in the Tenrecidae: the influence of phylogeny and ecology on the energetics of the Insectivora. *Israel J. Zool.* 38: 426.

Stephenson, P.J. and Racey, P.A. (1993) Reproductive energetics of the Tenrecidae (Mammalia: Insectivora), I: the large eared tenrec, *Geogale aurita*. *Physiol. Zool.* 66: 643-663.

Stephenson, P.J. and Racey, P.A. (1993) Reproductive energetics of the Tenrecidae (Mammalia: Insectivora), II: the shrew tenrecs, *Microgale* spp. *Physiol. Zool.* 66: 664-685.

Stephenson, P.J. and Racey, P.A. (1994) Seasonal variation in resting metabolic rate and body temperature of streaked tenrecs, *Hemicentetes nigriceps* and *Hemicentetes semispinosus* (Insectivora: Tenrecidae). *J. Zool.* (Lond.) 232: 285-294.

Stephenson, P.J. and Racey, P.A. (1995) Resting metabolic rate and reproduction in the Insectivora. *Comp. Biochem. & Physiol.* 112A: 215-223.

Stephenson, P.J., Randriamahazo, H., Rakotoarison, N. and Racey, P.A. (1994) Conservation of mammalian species diversity in Ambohitantely Special Reserve, Madagascar. *Biol. Conserv.* 69: 213-218.

Stephenson, P.J., Speakman, J.R. and Racey, P.A. (1994) Field metabolic rate in two species of shrew tenrec, *Microgale dobsoni* and *Microgale talazaci*. *Comp. Biochem. & Physiol.* 107A: 283-287.

Stephenson, P.J., Racey, P.A. and Rakotondraparany, F. (1994) Maintenance and reproduction of tenrecs (Tenrecidae) in captivity at Parc Tsimbazaza, Madagascar. *Int. Zoo Yearbook* 33.

Taylor, A. (1995) The abundance and distribution of small mammals in a Malagasy rainforest in relation to micro-habitat. In Wells, M. *et al.*, Project Madagascar 1994 – Final Report of the 1994 Aberdeen University Expedition to Zahamena Special Reserve, Madagascar. pp. 20-28. Aberdeen University 1995.

Order Rodentia

Bartlett, E. (1879) Second list of mammals and birds collected by Mr. Thomas Waters in Madagascar. *Proc. Zool. Soc.* (London) 1879: 767-770.

Carleton, M.D. (1994) Systematic studies of Madagascar's endemic rodents (Muroidea: Nesomyinae): revision of the genus *Eliurus*. *Amer. Mus. Novitates* 3087.

Carleton, M.D. and Musser, G.G. (1984) Muroid rodents. In Anderson, S. and Jones, J.K. (eds.) *Orders and Families of Recent Mammals of the World*, pp. 289-379. John Wiley & Sons, N.Y.

Carleton, M.D. and Schmidt, D.F. (1990) Systematic studies of Madagascar's endemic rodents (Muroidea: Nesomyinae): an annotated gazetteer of collecting localities of known forms. *Amer. Mus. Novitates* 2987.

Carleton, M.D. and Goodman, S.M. (1996) Systematic studies of Madagascar's endemic rodents (Muroidea: Nesomyinae): a new genus and species from the Central Highlands. *Fieldiana Zoology* 85: 231-256.

Carleton, M.D. and Goodman, S.M. (in press) Systematic studies of Madagascar's endemic rodents (Muroidea: Nesomyinae): a new genus and species from the north east. *Fieldiana Zoology*.

Chaline, J., Mein, P. and Petter, F. (1977) Les grandes lignes d'une classification évolutive des Muroidea. *Mammalia* 41: 245-252.

Cook, J.M., Trevelyan, R., Walls, S.S., Hatcher, M. and Rakotondraparany, F. (1990). *Final report of Votsotsa '88. An Oxford University Expedition to Madagascar.* Bull. Oxford Uni. Exp. Club (N.S.) 12.

Cook, J.M., Trevelyan, R., Walls, S.S., Hatcher, M. and Rakotondraparany, F. (1991) The ecology of *Hypogeomys antimena*, an endemic Madagascan rodent. *J. Zool.* (London) 224: 191-200.

Duckworth, J.W. and Rakotondraparany, F. (1990) The mammals of Marojejy. In Safford, R. J. and Duckworth, J.W. (eds.) *A Wildlife Survey of Marojejy Nature Reserve, Madagascar. Int. Council Bird Preserv. Study report* No.40 : 54-60.

Ellerman, J.R. (1940) *The Families and Genera of Living Rodents. Vol. 1, Rodents other than Muridae.* London: British Museum (Natural History).

Ellerman, J.R. (1941) *The Families and Genera of Living Rodents. Vol. 2, Family Muridae.* London: British Museum (Natural History).

Ellerman, J.R. (1949) *The Families and Genera of Living Rodents. Vol. 3, Appendix II* [Notes on the rodents from Madagascar in the British Museum, and on a collection from the island obtained by Mr. C. S. Webb]. London: British Museum (Natural History).

Ganzhorn, J.U., Sommer, S., Abraham, J.-P., Ade, M., Raharivololona, B.M., Rakotovao, E.R., Rakotondrasoa, C. and Randriamarosoa, R. (1996) Mammals of the Kirindy Forest with special emphasis on *Hypogeomys antimena* and the effects of logging on the small mammal fauna. In Ganzhorn, J.U. and Sorg, J.-P. (eds.) Ecology and Economy of a Tropical Dry Forest in Madagascar, pp. 251-255. *Primate Report*, Special Issue, 46-1(June 1996).

Goodman, S.M. (1994) A description of the ground burrow of *Eliurus webbi* (Nesomyinae) and case of cohabitation with an endemic bird (Brachypteraciidae, *Brachypteracias*). *Mammalia* 58(4): 670-672.

Goodman, S.M. (1995) *Rattus* on Madagascar and the dilemma of protecting the endemic rodent fauna. *Conservation Biology*, 9(2): 450-453.

Goodman, S.M. and Ganzhorn, J.U. (1994) Les petites mammifères. In Goodman, S.M. and Langrand, O. (eds.) *Inventaire Biologique Forêt de Zombitse, Recherches pour le Developpement, Série Science Biologiques*, pp, 58-63. No. Spécial 1994. Centre d'Information et de Documentation Scientifique et Technique, Antananarivo, Madagascar.

Goodman, S.M. and Carleton, M.D. (1996) The rodents of the Réserve Naturelle Intégrale d'Andringitra, Madagascar. *Fieldiana Zoology* 85: 257-283.

Goodman, S.M. and Sterling, E.J. (1996) The utilisation of *Canarium* (Burseraceae) seeds by vertebrates in the Réserve Naturelle Intégrale d'Andringitra, Madagascar. *Fieldiana Zoology* 85: 83-89.

Goodman, S.M. and Rakotondravony, D. (1996) The Holocene distribution of *Hypogeomys* (Rodentia: Muridae: Nesomyinae) on Madagascar. In Lourenco, W.R. (ed.) *Biogéographie de Madagascar*. pp. 283-293. Editions de l'ORSTOM, Paris.

Goodman, S.M. and Carleton, M.D. (in press) The Rodents of the Réserve Speciale d'Anjanaharibe-Sud, Madagascar. *Fieldiana Zoology*.

Goodman, S.M, Andrianarimisa, A., Olson, L.E. and Soarimalala, V. (in press) Patterns of elevational distribution of birds and small mammals in the humid forests of Montagne d'Ambre, Madagascar. *Ecotropica*.

Grandidier, G. (1928) Description d'une nouvelle espèce de *Nesomys*, le *N. lambertoni*, G. Grand. *Bulletin de l'Academie Malgache, NS*, 11: 95-99.

Jentink, F.A. (1879) On a new genus and species of *Mus* from Madagascar. *Notes from the Leyden Museum* 1879: 107-109.

Lavocat, R. (1978) Rodentia and Lagomorpha. In Maglio, V.J. and Cooke, H.B.S. (eds.) *Evolution of African Mammals*. Harvard Uni. Press.

Letellier, F. and Petter, F. (1962) Reproduction en captivité d'un rongeur de Madagascar – *Macrotarsomys bastardi*. *Mammalia* 26: 132-133.

Major, C.I. Forsyth (1896) Diagnoses of new mammals from Madagascar. *Annals & Magazine of Natural History*, series 6, 18: 318-325.

Major, C.I. Forsyth (1896) Descriptions of four additional new mammals from Madagascar. *Annals & Magazine of Natural History*, series 6, 18: 461-463.

Milne-Edwards, A. (1885) Description d'une nouvelle espèce de rongeur provenant de Madagascar. *Annales des Sciences Naturelles, Zoologie et Paleontologie* (Paris), 20: Article 1 bis.

Nowak, R.M. (1991). *Walker's Mammals of the World* (5th edition). Johns Hopkins Uni. Press.

MacPhee, R.D.E. (1986) Environment, extinction and Holocene vertebrate localities in southern Madagascar. *National Geographic Research* 2: 441-455.

Malzy, P. (1964) Zoologie Malgache: sur deux rongeurs

importés à Madagascar. *Bulletin de Madagascar* 14: 619-623.

Miller, G.S. and Gidley, J.W. (1918) Synopsis of the supergeneric groups of rodent. *J. Washington Acad. Sci.* 8: 431-448.

Musser, G.G. and Carleton, M.D. (1993) Family Muridae. In Wilson, D.E. and Reeder, D.H. (eds.) *Mammal Species of the World: a taxonomic and geographic reference* (2nd ed.). Smithsonian Inst. Press. Washington, D.C.

Peters, W. (1870) Uber *Nesomys rufus*, eine neue Gattung und Art madagascarischer Nager. *Sitzungsberichte der Gesellschaft naturforschender Freunde,* Berlin 1870: 54-55.

Petter, F. (1962) Un nouveau rongeur Malgache: *Brachytarsomys albicauda villosa. Mammalia* 26: 570-572.

Petter, F. (1972) The rodents of Madagascar. In Battistini, R. and Richard-Vindard, G. (eds.) *Biogeography and Ecology of Madagascar,* pp. 661-665. Dr W. Junk, The Hague.

Petter, F. (1977) Rodentia: Cricetidae: Nesomyinae. In Meester, J. and Setzer, H.W. *The Mammals of Africa: an identification manual.* Part 6.2, pp. 1-4. Smithsonian Inst. Press, Washington, D.C.

Rakotondravony, D.A. (1987) Les rongeurs à Madagascar. In *Priorités en Matière de Conservation des espèces à Madagascar.* pp. 93-94. Occasional papers IUCN SSC No. 2.

Rakotondravony, D.A. (1996) Biogéographie des rongeurs. In Lourenco, W.R. (ed.) *Biogéographie de Madagascar,* pp. 303-306. Editions de l'ORSTOM, Paris.

Rakotozafy, L.M.A. (1996) Étude de la constitution du régime alimentaire des habitants du site de Mahilaka du XIè au XIVè Siècle à partir des produits de fouilles archéologiques. Doctorat de Troisième Cycle des Sciences Naturelles. Departement de Paléontologie et d'Anthropologie Biologique, University of Antananarivo.

Raxworthy, C.J. and Nussbaum, R.N. (1994) A rainforest survey of amphibians, reptiles and small mammals at Montagne d'Ambre, Madagascar. *Biol. Conserv.* 69: 65-73.

Ryan, J.M., Creighton, G.K. and Emmons, L.H. (1993) Activity patterns of two species of *Nesomys* (Muridae: Nesomyinae) in a Madagascar rainforest. *J. Tropical Ecol.* 9: 101-107.

Schlitter, D.A. (1989) African rodents of special concern: a preliminary assessment. In Lidicker, W.Z. (e.d.) *Rodents: a world survey of species of conservation concern.* pp. 33-39. Occasional Papers, IUCN/

SSC No.4.

Sommer, S. (1996) Ecology and social structure of *Hypogeomys antimena,* an endemic rodent of the dry deciduous forest in western Madagascar. In Lourenco, W.R. (ed.) *Biogéographie de Madagascar,* pp. 295-302. Editions de l'ORSTOM, Paris.

Sommer, S. (*in litt.*) Comments on the behaviour and ecology of Giant Jumping Rat (*Hypogeomys antimena*) at Kindry in western Madagascar. University of Tübingen (unpublished PhD research).

Sommer, S. (1997) Monogamy in *Hypogeomys antimena,* an endemic rodent of the deciduous dry forest in western Madagascar. *J. Zool.* (London) 241: 301-314.

Stephenson, P.J. (1995) Small mammal micro-habitat use in lowland rainforest of north east Madagascar. *Acta Theriologica* 40(4): 425-438.

Thomas, O. (1895) On a new species of *Eliurus. Annals & Magazine of Natural History,* series 6, 16: 164-165.

Thomas, O. (1908) A new species of the Mascarene genus *Eliurus. Annals & Magazine of Natural History,* series 8, 2: 453-454.

Veal, R.H. (1992) Preliminary notes on breeding, maintenance and social behaviour of the Malagasy giant jumping rat (*Hypogeomys antimena*) at Jersey Wildlife Preservation Trust. *Dodo* 28: 84-91.

Order Carnivora

Albignac, R. (1969) Notes éthologiques sur quelques carnivores Malgaches: le *Galidia elegans. La Terre et la Vie* 23: 202-215.

Albignac, R. (1969) Nuissance et élevage en captivité de jeunes *Cryptoprocta ferox,* viverrides malgaches. *Mammalia* 33: 93-97.

Albignac, R. (1970) Notes éthologiques sur quelques carnivores Malgaches: le *Fossa fossa. La Terre et la Vie* 24: 383-394.

Albignac, R. (1970) Notes éthologiques sur quelques carnivores Malgaches: le *Cryptoprocta ferox. La Terre et la Vie* 24: 395-402.

Albignac, R. (1971) Notes éthologiques sur quelques carnivores Malgaches: le *Mungotictis lineata. La Terre et la Vie* 25: 328-343.

Albignac, R. (1971) Une nouvelle sous-espèce de *Galidia elegans: G. e. occidentalis* (Viverridae de Madagascar). Mise au point de la répartition géographique de l'espèce. *Mammalia* 35: 307-310.

Albignac, R. (1972) The Carnivora of Madagascar. In Battistini, R. and Richard-Vindard, G. (eds.) *Biogeography and Ecology of Madagascar,* pp. 667-682. Dr W. Junk, The Hague.

Albignac, R. (1973) *Faune de Madagascar* vol. 36 Mammifères carnivores. Paris, O.R.S.T.O.M. C.N.R.S.

Albignac, R. (1974) Observations éco-éthologiques sur le genre *Eupleres,* viverride de Madagascar. *La Terre et la Vie* 28: 321-351.

Albignac, R (1976). L'écologie de *Mungotictis decemlineata* dans les forêt decidués de l'ouest de Madagascar. *La Terre et la Vie* 30: 347-376.

Albignac, R. (1984) the carnivores. In Jolly, A., Oberle, P. and Albignac, R. (eds.) *Key Environments – Madagascar,* pp. 167-181. Pergamon Press, Oxford.

Barden, T.L., Evans, M.I., Raxworthy, C.J., Razafimahimodison, J.C. and Wilson, A. (1991) The mammals of Ambatovaky Special Reserve. In Thompson, P.M. and Evans, M.I. (eds.) *A Survey of Ambatovaky Special Reserve, Madagascar,* pp. 19-20. Madagascar Environmental Research Group.

Carlsson, A. (1902) Über die Stellung von *Eupleres goudotii. Zool. Jahrb., Abt. Syst.* 16: 217-236.

Carlsson, A. (1911) Über *Cryptoprocta ferox. Zool. Jahrb., Abt. Syst.* 30: 419-470.

Coetzee, C.G. (1977) The carnivores. In Meester, J. and Setzer, H.W. *The Mammals of Africa: an identification manual.* Smithsonian Inst. Press, Washington, D.C.

Doyère, (1835) Notice sur un mammifère de Madagascar formant le type d'un nouveau genre de la famille des carnaciers insectivores de Monsieur Cuvier. *Ann. Sci. Nat.* 4(2): 270-283.

Duckworth, J.W. and Rakotondraparany, F. (1990) The mammals of Marojejy. In Safford, R. J. and Duckworth, J.W. (eds.) A Wildlife Survey of Marojejy Nature Reserve, Madagascar, pp.54-60. *Int. Council Bird Preserv. Study Report No.* 40.

Ewer, R.F. (1973) *The Carnivores.* Cornell Uni. Press, Ithaca, N.Y.

Garbutt, N. (1994) Two together: Fossas look a lot more special. *BBC Wildlife Magazine* 12(5): 11.

Goodman, S.M. (1996) A subfossil record of *Galidictis grandidieri* (Herpestidae: Galidiinae) from southwest Madagascar. *Mammalia* 60(1): 150-151.

Goodman, S.M. (1996) The carnivores of the Réserve Naturelle Intégrale d'Andringitra, Madagascar. *Fieldiana Zoology* 85: 289-292.

Goodman, S.M, Langrand, O. and Rasolonandrasana, B.P.N. (in press) Food Habits of *Cryptoprocta ferox* in the High Mountain Zone of the Andringita Massif, Madagascar. *Mammalia.*

Hawkins, A.F.A. (in litt.) *Eupleres goudotii* in western Malagasy deciduous forest. *Small Carnivore Conservation* 11: 20.

Hawkins, C. (in litt.) Comments on the behaviour and ecology of the Fosa (*Cryptoprocta ferox*) at Kirindy in western Madagascar. University of Aberdeen (unpublished PhD research).

Kohncke, M. and Leonhardt, K. (1986) *Cryptoprocta ferox. Mammalian Species* 254.

Larkin, P. and Roberts, M. (1979) Reproduction in the ring-tailed mongoose (*Galidia elegans*) at the National Zoological Park, Washington, D.C. *Int. Zoo Yearbook* 19: 189-193.

MacDonald, D. (1992) *The Velvet Claw: A Natural History of the Carnivores.* BBC Books, London.

Milne-Edwards, A. and Grandidier, A. (1867) Observations anatomiques sur quelques mammifères de Madagascar I. Le *Cryptoprocta ferox. Ann. Sci. Nat., Zool.,* 7: 314-338.

Nicoll, M.E. (in litt.) Observations of endemic Malagasy carnivores in the Ankarana Reserve in northern Madagascar. Unpublished.

Nowak, R.M. (1991) *Walker's Mammals of the World* (5th ed.). Johns Hopkins Uni. Press.

Perschke, M. (1996) Mongooses in the Tsimbazaza Zoo

and Ranomafana National Park, Madagascar. *Small Carnivore Conservation: Newsletter and Journal of the IUCN/SSC Mustelid, Viverrid & Procyonid Specialist Group No.14*: 1.

Pocock, R.I. (1915) On the species of the Mascarene Viverrid *Galidictis* with the description of a new genus and a note on *Galidia elegans. Ann. Sci. Nat. Hist.* 16: 113-124.

Pocock, R.I. (1915) On some external characters of the genus *Linsang,* with notes upon the genera *Poiana* and *Eupleres. Ann. Mag. Nat. Hist.* 16: 341-351.

Pocock, R.I. (1915) On some external characters of *Galidia, Galidictis* and related genera. *Ann. Mag. Nat. Hist.* 16: 351-356.

Pocock, R.I. (1915) The name of the species described by Gray *Galidictis vittatus. Ann. Mag. Nat. Hist.* 16: 505-506.

Pocock, R.I. (1916) On some external characters of *Cryptoprocta ferox. Ann. Mag. Nat. Hist.* 17: 413-425.

Rasoloarison, R.M., Rasolonandrasana, B.P.N., Ganzhorn, J.U. and Goodman, S.M. (1995). Predation on vertebrates in the Kirindy Forest, western Madagascar. *Ecotropica* 1: 59-65.

Raxworthy, C.J. and Rakotondraparany, F. (1988) Mammals Report. In Quansah, N. (ed.) *Manongarivo Special Reserve, Madagascar 1987/88 Expedition Report,* pp. 121-131. Madagascar Environmental Research Group.

Schreiber, A., Wirth, R., Riffel, M. and van Rompaey, H. (1989) *Weasels, Civets, Mongooses and their Relatives. An Action Plan for the Conservation of Mustelids and Viverrids.* IUCN, Gland, Switzerland.

Veron, G. (1995) La position systématique de *Cryptoprocta ferox* (Carnivora). Analyse cladistique des caractères morphologiques de carnivores Aeluroidea actuels et fossiles. *Mammalia* 59(4): 551-582.

Wozencraft, W.C. (1986) A new species of striped mongoose from Madagascar. *J. Mammal.* 67: 561-571.

Wozencraft, W.C. (1987) Emendation of a species name. *J. Mammal.* 68:198.

Wozencraft, W.C. (1989) The phylogeny of recent Carnivora. In Gittleman, J.L. (ed.) *Carnivore Behaviour, Ecology and Evolution,* pp. 495-535. Chapman and Hall, London.

Wozencraft, W.C. (1989) The classification of recent Carnivora. In Gittleman, J.L. (ed.) *Carnivore*

Behaviour, Ecology and Evolution, pp. 569-593. Chapman and Hall, London.

Wozencraft, W.C. (1990) Alive and well in Tsimanampetsotsa. *Natural History* 12/90: 28-30.

Wozencraft, W.C. (1993) Order Carnivora. In Wilson, D.E. and Reeder, D.H. (eds.) *Mammal Species of the World: a taxonomic and geographic reference* (2nd ed.), pp. 279-348. Smithsonian Inst. Press. Washington, D.C.

Order Primates

Family Cheirogaleidae

Andrianarivo, A.J. (1981) Étude comparée de l'organisation sociale chez *Microcebus coquereli*. Establissement d'Enseignement Supérieur de Science, Université de Madagascar.

Albignac, R., Justin, and Meier, B. (1991) Study of the first behaviour of *Allocebus trichotis* Gunther 1875 (hairy-eared dwarf lemurs): prosimian lemur rediscovered in the north west of Madagascar (Biosphere Reserve of Mananara-Nord). In: Ehara, A., Kimura, T., Takenaka, O. and Iwamoto, M. (eds.) *Primatology Today*. Elsevier Science, Amsterdam.

Baum, D.A. (1995) The comparative pollination and floral biology of baobabs (*Adansonia*: Bombacaceae). *Ann. Missouri Botanical Garden* 82: 322-348.

Baum, D.A. (1996) The ecology and conservation of the baobabs of Madagascar. In Ganzhorn, J.U. and Sorg, J.-P. (eds.) Ecology and Economy of a Tropical Dry Forest in Madagascar, pp. 311-327. *Primate Report*, Special Issue, 46-1(June 1996).

Buesching, C.D. and Zimmermann, E. (1995) Multimodal oestrous advertisement in grey mouse lemurs, *Microcebus murinus*. In the Abstracts, *International Conference on the Biology and Conservation of Prosimians*, North of England Zoological Soc., 13-16th Sept. 1995.

Charles-Dominique, P. and Petter, J.-J. (1980) Ecology and social life of *Phaner furcifer*. In Charles-Dominique, P., Cooper, H.M., Hladik, A., Hladik, C.M., Pagès, E., Pariente, G.F., Petter-Rousseaux, A., Petter, J.-J. and Schilling, A. (eds.) *Nocturnal Malagasy Primates: Ecology, Physiology and Behaviour*, pp. 75-96. Academic Press, N.Y.

Corbin, G.D. and Schmid, J. (1995) Insect secretions determine habitat use pattern by a female Lesser Mouse Lemur (*Microcebus murinus*). *Amer. J. Primatol.* 37: 317-324.

Duckworth, J.W. and Rakotondraparany, F. (1990) The mammals of Marojejy. In Safford, R. J. and Duckworth, J.W. (eds.) A Wildlife Survey of Marojejy Nature Reserve, Madagascar, pp.54-60. *Int. Council Bird Preserv. Study Report No. 40.*

Duckworth, J.W., Evans, M.I., Hawkins, A.F.A., Safford, R.J. and Wilkinson, R.J. (1995) The lemurs of Marojejy Strict Nature Reserve, Madagascar: a status overview with notes on ecology and threats. *Int. J. Primatol.* 16: 545-559.

Fietz, J. (1995) Distribution pattern and mating system in *Microcebus murinus*, J.F. Miller, 1777. In the Abstracts, *International Conference on the Biology and Conservation of Prosimians*. North of England Zoological Soc., 13-16th Sept. 1995.

Fietz, J. (1997) Mating and social system of the Lesser Mouse Lemur (*Microcebus murinus*, Cheirogaleidae, J.F. Miller, 1777) in the dry deciduous forests of western Madagascar. *Primate Report* 47: 95-96.

Fietz, J. (in litt.) Comments and observations on torpor and dormancy in the Fat-tailed Dwarf Lemur (*Cheirogaleus medius*) at Kirindy in western Madagascar. University of Tübingen (unpublished PhD research).

Foerg, R. (1982) Reproduction in *Cheirogaleus medius*. *Folia Primatologica* 39: 49-62.

Ganzhorn, J.U. (1988) Food partitioning among Malagasy primates. *Oecologia* (Berlin) 75: 436-450.

Ganzhorn, J.U. (1989) Niche separation in seven lemur species. *Oecologia* 79: 279-286.

Ganzhorn, J.U. (1992) Leaf chemistry and the biomass of folivorous primates in tropical forests. *Oecologia* (Berlin) 91: 540-547.

Ganzhorn, J.U. (1994) Les lémuriens. In Goodman, S.M. and Langrand, O. (eds.) *Inventaire Biologique Forêt de Zombitse, Recherches pour le Developpement, Série Science Biologiques*, pp. 70-72. No. Spécial 1994. Centre d'Information et de Documentation Scientifique et Technique, Antananarivo, Madagascar.

Ganzhorn, J.U. and Kappeler, P.M. (1996) Lemurs of the Kirindy Forest. In: Ganzhorn, J.U. and Sorg, J.-P. (eds.), Ecology and Economy of a Tropical Dry Forest in Madagascar, pp. 257-274. *Primate Report*, Special Issue, 46-1(June 1996).

Garbutt, N. (1998) Brief observations of Hairy-eared Dwarf Lemur (*Allocebus trichotis*) in Analamazaotra Special Reserve, eastern Madagascar (unpublished).

Goodman, S.M. and Langrand, O. (1993) The food habits of the Barn Owl *Tyto alba* and the Madagascar Long-eared Owl *Asio madagascariensis* on Madagascar: adaptations to a changing environment. *Proceedings VIII Pan-African Ornithological Congress.* Pp. 147-154.

Goodman, S.M., Langrand, O. and Raxworthy, C.J. (1993) The food habits of the Madagascar Long-eared Owl, *Asio madagascariensis*, at two habitats in southern Madagascar. *Ostrich* 64: 79-85.

Goodman, S.M., Langrand, O. and Raxworthy, C.J. (1993) The food habits of the Barn Owl, *Tyto alba*, at three sites on Madagascar. *Ostrich* 64: 160-171.

Goodman, S.M., O'Connor, S. and Langrand, O. (1993) A review of predation on lemurs: implications for the evolution of social behaviour in small, nocturnal primates. In Kappeler, P.M. and Ganzhorn, J.U. (eds.) *Lemur Social Systems and their Ecological Basis*, pp. 51-66. Plenum Press, London & N.Y.

Groves, C.P. and Eaglen, R.H. (1988) Systematics of the Lemuridae (Primates, Strepsirhini). *J. Human Evol.* 17: 513-538.

Groves, C.P. and Tattersall, I. (1991) Geographical variation in the fork-marked lemur *Phaner furcifer* (Primates, Cheirogaleidae). *Folia Primatologica* 56: 39-49.

Harcourt, C.S. (1987) Brief trap/re-trap study of the brown mouse lemur (*Microcebus rufus*). *Folia Primatologica* 49: 209-211.

Harste, L. (in litt.) Comments on reproduction in Brown Mouse Lemurs (*Microcebus rufus*). University of Liverpool (unpublished PhD research).

Hawkins, A.F.A., Chapman, P., Ganzhorn, J.U., Bloxam, Q.M.C., Barlow, S.C. and Tonge, S.J. (1990) Vertebrate conservation in Ankarana Special Reserve, northern Madagascar. *Biol. Conserv.* 54: 83-110.

Hawkins, A.F.A., Durbin, J. and Reid, D. (in press) The primates of the Baly Bay area, north-western Madagascar. *Folia Primatologica*.

Hladik, C.M. (1979) Diet and ecology of prosimians. In Doyle, G.A. and Martin, R.D. (eds.) *The Study of Prosimian Behaviour*, pp. 307-357. Academic Press, London & N.Y.

Hladik, C.M., Charles-Dominique, P. and Petter, J.-J. (1980) Feeding strategies of five nocturnal prosimians in the dry forest of the west coast of Madagascar. In Charles-Dominique, P., Cooper, H.M., Hladik, A., Hladik, C.M., Pagès, E., Pariente, G.F., Petter-Rousseaux, A., Petter, J.-J. and Schilling, A. (eds.) *Nocturnal Malagasy Primates: Ecology, Physiology and Behaviour*, pp. 41-73. Academic Press, N.Y.

Jolly, A., Albignac, R. and Petter, J.-J. (1984) The lemurs. In: Jolly, A., Oberle, P. and Albignac, R. (eds.) *Key Environments: Madagascar*, pp. 183-202. Pergamon Press, Oxford, U.K.

Kappeler, P.M. (1990) The evolution of sexual dimorphism in prosimian primates. *Amer. J. Primatol.* 21: 201-214.

Kappeler, P.M. (1991) Patterns of sexual dimorphism in body weight among prosimian primates. *Amer. J. Primatol.* 57: 132-146.

Kappeler, P.M. (1995) Scramble competition polygyny and the social organisation of *Mirza coquereli*. In the Abstracts, *International Conference on the Biology and Conservation of Prosimians*. North of England Zoological Soc., 13-16th Sept. 1995.

Kappeler, P.M. (in press) Intrasexual selection and testis size in strepsirhine primates. *Behavioural Ecology*.

Kappeler, P.M. (in litt.) Comments on possible revisions to the Taxonomy of genus *Microcebus*. Unpublished.

Kappeler, P.M. (in litt.) Comments on male competion and polygyny in Coquerel's Dwarf Lemur (*Mirza coquereli*). Unpublished.

Martin, R.D. (1972) A preliminary field study of the lesser mouse lemur (*Microcebus murinus* J.F. Miller, 1777). *Zeitschrift fur Tierpsychologie*, Supplement, 9: 43-89.

Martin, R.D. (1973) A review of the behaviour and ecology of the lesser mouse lemur (*Microcebus murinus* J.F. Miller, 1777). In Michael, R.P. and Crook, J.H. (eds.) *Comparative Ecology and Behaviour of Primates*, pp. 1-68. Academic Press, London.

McCormick, S.A. (1981) Oxygen consumption and torpor in the fat-tailed dwarf lemur (*Cheirogaleus medius*): rethinking prosimian metabolism. *Comp. Biochem. Physiol.* 68A: 605-610.

Meier, B. and Albignac, R. (1989) Hairy-eared dwarf lemur (*Allocebus trichotis*) rediscovered. *Primate Conservation* 10. 30.

Meier, B. and Albignac, R. (1991) Rediscovery of *Allocebus trichotis* in north east Madagascar. *Folia Primatologica* 56: 57-63.

Nicoll, M.E. (in litt.) The occurance of Fat-tailed Dwarf Lemurs (*Cheirogaleus medius*) and Greater Dwarf Lemurs (*Cheirogaleus major*) in forests near Daraina. Unpublished.

Nilsson, L.A., Rabakonandrianina, E., Petterson, B. and Grunmeier, R. (1993) Lemur pollination in the Malagasy rainforest: Liana *Strongylodon craveniae* (Leguminosae). *Evolutionary Trends in Plants* 7: 49-56.

Ortmann, S., Schmid, J., Ganzhorn, J.U. and Heldmaier, G. (1996) Body temperature and torpor in a Malagasy small primate, the mouse lemur. In Geiser, F., Hulbert, A.J. and Nicol, S.C. (eds.) Adaptations to the Cold. *Proceedings, 10th International Hibernation Symposium*, pp.55-61. Univ. New England Press, Armidale.

Pagès, E. (1978) Home range, behaviour and tactile communication in a nocturnal Malagasy lemur, *Microcebus coquereli*. In: Chivers, D.A. and Joysey, K.A. (eds.), *Recent Advances in Primatology 3*, pp. 171-177. Academic Press, London.

Pagès, E. (1980) Ethoecology of *Microcebus coquereli* during the dry season. In Charles-Dominique, P., Cooper, H.M., Hladik, A., Hladik, C.M., Pagès, E., Pariente, G.F., Petter-Rousseaux, A., Petter, J.-J. and Schilling, A. (eds.), *Nocturnal Malagasy Primates: Ecology, Physiology and Behaviour*, pp. 97-116. Academic Press, N.Y.

Perret, M. (1992) Environmental and social determinants of sexual function in the male lesser mouse lemur (*Microcebus murinus*). *Folia Primatologica* 59: 1-25.

Petter, J.-J. (1978) Ecological and physiological adaptations of five sympatric nocturnal lemurs to seasonal variation in food production. In Chivers, D.J. and Herbert, J. (eds.) *Recent Advances in Primatology 1: Behaviour*, pp. 211-223. Academic Press, London.

Petter, J.-J. (1978) Contribution à l'étude du *Cheirogaleus medius* dans la forêt de Morondava. In Rakotovao, L., Barre, V. and Sayer, J. (eds.) *L'Equilibre des Ecosystèmes Forestiers à Madagascar: Actes d'un Séminaire International*, pp. 57-60. IUCN, Gland, Switzerland.

Petter, J.-J., Schilling, A. and Pariente, G. (1975) Observations on the behaviour and ecology of *Phaner furcifer*. In Tattersall, I. and Sussman, R.W. (eds.) *Lemur Biology* pp. 209-218. Plenum Press, London & N.Y.

Petter-Rousseaux, A. (1980) Seasonal activity rhythms, reproduction and body weight variations in five sympatric nocturnal prosimians, in simulated light and climatic conditions. In Charles-Dominique, P., Cooper, H.M., Hladik, A., Hladik, C.M., Pagès, E., Pariente, G.F., Petter-Rousseaux, A., Petter, J.-J. and Schilling, A. (eds.), *Nocturnal Malagasy Primates: Ecology, Physiology and Behaviour*, pp. 137-152. Academic Press, N.Y.

Rakotoarison, N. (1995) First sighting and capture of the hairy-eared dwarf lemur (*Allocebus trichotis*) in the Strict Nature Reserve of Zahamena. Unpublished report to Conservation International, May 1995.

Rakotoarison, N., Zimmermann, H. and Zimmermann, E. (1996) Hairy-eared dwarf lemur (*Allocebus trichotis*) discovered in a highland rain forest of eastern Madagascar. In Lourenco, W.R. (ed.) *Biogéographie de Madagascar*, pp. 275-282. Editions de l'ORSTOM, Paris.

Rasoloarison, R.M., Rasolonandrasana, B.P.N., Ganzhorn, J.U. and Goodman, S.M. (1995) Predation on vertebrates in the Kirindy Forest, western Madagascar. *Ecotropica* 1: 59-65.

Raxworthy, C.J. and Rakotondraparany, F. (1988) Mammals Report. In Quansah, N. (ed.) *Manongarivo Special Reserve (Madagascar), 1987/88 Expedition Report*. Madagascar Environmental Research Group, London, U.K.

Rumpler, Y., Warter, S., Hauwy, M., Meier, B., Peyrieras, A., Albignac, R., Petter, J.-J. and Dutrillaux, B. (1995) Cytogenetic study of *Allocebus trichotis*, a Malagasy prosimian. *Amer. J. Primatol.* 36: 239-244.

Schmid, J. (1995) Daily torpor in mouse lemurs (*Microcebus* spp.): metabolic rate and body temperature. In the Abstracts, *International Conference on the Biology and Conservation of Prosimians*. North of England Zoological Soc., 13-16th Sept. 1995.

Schmid, J. (1996) Oxygen consumption and torpor in mouse lemurs (*Microcebus murinus* and *M. myoxinus*): preliminary results of a study in western Madagascar. In Geiser, F., Hulbert, A.J. and Nicol, S.C. (eds.) *Adaptations to the Cold. Proceedings, 10th International Hibernation Symposium*, pp.47-54. Univ. New England Press, Armidale.

Schmid, J. (*in litt.*) Comments on fat reserves and aestivation in Grey Mouse Lemurs (*Microcebus murinus*). Unpublished.

Schmid, J. and Kappeler, P.M. (1994) Sympatric mouse lemurs (*Microcebus* spp.) in western Madagascar. *Folia Primatologica* 63: 162-170.

Schmid, J. and Smolker, R. (in press) Lemurs in the Réserve Special d'Anjanaharibe-Sud. *Fieldiana Zoology*.

Stanger, K., Coffman, B. and Izard, M. (1995) Reproduction in Coquerel's dwarf lemur (*Mirza coquereli*). *Amer. J. Primatol.* 36: 223-237.

Sterling, E.J. and Ramaroson, M.G. (1996) Rapid assessment of the primate fauna of the eastern slopes of the Réserve Naturelle Intégrale d'Andringitra, Madagascar. *Fieldiana Zoology* 85: 293-305.

Sterling, E.J. and Rakotoarison, N. (in press) Rapid assessment of primate species richness and density on the Masoala Peninsula, eastern Madagascar. In Crompton, R.H., Feistner, A.T.C. and Harcourt, C. (eds.) Proceedings International Conference on the Biology and Conservation of Prosimians 1995. *Folia Primatologica*.

Thalmann, U. and Rakotoarison, N. (1994) Distribution of lemurs in central western Madagascar, with a regional distribution hypothesis. *Folia Primatologica* 63: 156-161.

van Schaik, C.P. and Kappeler, P.M. (1993) Life history, activity period and lemur social systems. In Kappeler, P.M. and Ganzhorn, J.U. (eds.) *Lemur Social Systems and their Ecological Basis*, pp. 241-260. Plenum Press, London & N.Y.

Wright, P.C. and Martin, L.B. (1995) Predation, pollination and torpor in two nocturnal prosimians, *Cheirogaleus major* and *Microcebus rufus*, in the rainforests of Madagascar. In Alterman, L., Doyle, G.A. and Izard, K. (eds.), *Creatures of the Dark: the Nocturnal Prosimians*, pp. 45-60. Plenum Press, London & N.Y.

Yoder, A. (1996) Pilot study to determine the status of *Allocebus trichotis* in Madagascar. *Lemur News* 2: 14-15.

Yoder, A. (1996) The use of phylogeny for reconstructing lemuriform biogeography. In Lourenco, W.R. (ed.) *Biogéographie de Madagascar*, pp. 245-258. Editions de l'ORSTOM, Paris.

Zimmermann, E. (1995) Loud calls in nocturnal prosimians: structure, evolution and ontogeny. In Zimmermann, E., Newman, J.D. and Jürgens, U. (eds.) *Current Topics in Primate Vocal Communication*, pp. 47-72. Plenum Press, London & N.Y.

Zimmermann, E. (1995) Acoustic communication in nocturnal prosimians. In Alterman, L., Doyle, G.A. and Izard, K. (eds.) *Creatures of the Dark: the Nocturnal Prosimians*, pp. 311-330. Plenum Press, London & N.Y.

Zimmermann, E. (*in litt.*) observations on the behaviour of the Golden-brown Mouse Lemur (*Microcebus ravelobensis*) at Ampijoroa in north west Madagascar. Unpublished.

Zimmermann, E., Cepok, S., Rakotoarison, N., Zietemann, V. and Radespiel, U. (1998) Sympatric mouse lemurs in north west Madagascar: a new rufous mouse lemur species (*Microcebus ravelobensis*). *Folia Primatologica* 69: 106-114.

Family Megaladapidae
Subfamily Lepilemurinae

Albignac, R. (1981) Lemurine social and territorial organisation in a north western Malagasy forest (restricted area of Ampijoroa). In Chiarelli, A.B. and Corruccini, R.S. (eds.) *Primate Behaviour and Sociobiology*, pp. 25-29. Springer Verlag, Berlin.

Andrews, J. (*in litt.*) Utilisation of nest boxes by Grey-backed Sportive Lemurs (*Lepilemur dorsalis*) on Nosy Be, north west Madagascar. Unpublished.

Charles-Dominique, P. and Hladik, C.M. (1971) Le *Lepilemur* du sud de Madagascar: écologie, alimentation et vie sociale. *La Terre et la Vie* 25: 3-66.

Dagosto, M. (1995) Seasonal changes in the positional behaviour of Malagasy lemurs. *Int. J. Primatol.* 16: 807-833.

Duckworth, J.W. and Rakotondraparany, F. (1990) The Mammals of Marojejy. In: Safford, R.J. and Duckworth, J.W. (eds.) *A Wildlife Survey of Marojejy Nature Reserve, Madagascar. Int. Council Bird Preserv., Study Report* No. 40, pp. 54-60.

Duckworth, J.W., Evans, M.I., Hawkins, A.F.A., Safford, R.J. and Wilkinson, R.J. (1995) The lemurs of Marojejy Strict Nature Reserve, Madagascar: a status overview with notes on ecology and threats. *Int. J. Primatol.* 16: 545-559.

Fowler, S.V., Chapman, P., Checkley, D., Hurd, S., McHale, M., Ramangason, G.S., Randriamasy, J.-E., Stewart, P., Walters, R. and Wilson, J.M. (1989) Survey and management proposals for a tropical deciduous forest reserve at Ankarana in northern Madagascar. *Biol. Conserv.* 47: 297-313.

Ganzhorn, J.U. (1988) Food partitioning among Malagasy primates. *Oecologia* (Berlin) 75: 436-450.

Ganzhorn, J.U. (1989) Niche separation in seven lemur species. *Oecologia* 79: 279-286.

Ganzhorn, J.U. (1992) Leaf chemistry and the biomass of folivorous primates in tropical forests. *Oecologia* (Berlin) 91: 540-547.

Ganzhorn, J.U. (1993) Flexibility and constraints of *Lepilemur* ecology. In Kappeler, P.M. and Ganzhorn, J.U. (eds.) *Lemur Social Systems and their Ecological Basis*, pp. 153-165. Plenum Press, London & N.Y.

Ganzhorn, J.U. (1994) Les lémuriens. In Goodman, S.M. and Langrand, O. (eds.) *Inventaire Biologique Forêt de Zombitse, Recherches pour le Developpement, Série Science Biologiques*, pp. 70-72. No.Spécial 1994. Centre d'Information et de Documentation Scientifique et Technique, Antananarivo, Madagascar.

Ganzhorn, J.U. and Kappeler, P.M. (1996) Lemurs of the Kirindy Forest. In Ganzhorn, J.U. and Sorg, J.-P. (eds.), Ecology and Economy of a Tropical Dry Forest in Madagascar, pp. 257-274. *Primate Report*, Special Issue, 46-1(June 1996).

Goodman, S.M., Langrand, O. and Raxworthy, C.J. (1993) The food habits of the Madagascar Long-eared Owl, *Asio madagascariensis*, at two habitats in southern Madagascar. *Ostrich* 64: 79- 85.

Goodman, S.M., Langrand, O. and Raxworthy, C.J. (1993) The food habits of the Barn Owl, *Tyto alba*, at three sites on Madagascar. *Ostrich* 64: 160-171.

Goodman, S.M., O'Connor, S. and Langrand, O. (1993) A review of predation on lemurs: implications for the evolution of social behaviour in small, nocturnal primates. In Kappeler, P.M. and Ganzhorn, J.U. (eds.) *Lemur Social Systems and their Ecological Basis*, pp. 51-66. Plenum Press, London & N.Y.

Hawkins, A.F.A., Chapman, P., Ganzhorn, J.U., Bloxam, Q.M.C., Barlow, S.C. and Tonge, S.J. (1990) Vertebrate conservation in Ankarana Special Reserve, northern Madagascar. *Biol. Conserv.* 54: 83-110.

Hawkins, A.F.A., Durbin, J. and Reid, D. (in press) The primates of the Baly Bay area, north-western Madagascar. *Folia Primatologica*.

Hladik, C.M. (1979) Diet and ecology of prosimians. In Doyle, G.A. and Martin, R.D. (eds.) *The Study of Prosimian Behaviour*, pp. 307-357. Academic Press, London & N.Y.

Hladik, C.M. and Charles-Dominique, P. (1974) The behaviour and ecology of the sportive lemur (*Lepilemur mustelinus*) in relation to its dietary peculiarities. In Martin, R.D., Doyle, G.A. and Walker, A.C. (eds.) *Prosimian Biology*, pp. 23-37. Duckworth, London.

Hladik, C.M., Charles-Dominique, P. and Petter, J.-J. (1980) Feeding strategies of five nocturnal prosimians in the dry forest of the west coast of Madagascar. In Charles-Dominique, P., Cooper, H.M., Hladik, A., Hladik, C.M., Pagès, E., Pariente, G.F., Petter-Rousseaux, A., Petter, J.-J. and Schilling, A. (eds.), *Nocturnal Malagasy Primates: Ecology,*

Physiology and Behaviour, pp. 41-73. Academic Press, N.Y.

Ishak, B., Warter, S., Dutrillaux, B. and Rumpler, Y. (1992) Chromosomal rearrangements and speciation of sportive lemurs (*Lepilemur* species). *Folia Primatologica* 58: 121-130.

Nash, L.T. (1995) Seasonal changes in time budgets and diet of *Lepilemur leucopus* from south western Madagascar. In the Abstracts: *International Conference on the Biology and Conservation of Prosimians*. North of England Zoological Soc., 13-16th Sept. 1995.

Nash, L.T. (in press) Vertical clingers and sleepers: seasonal influences on the activity and substrate use of *Lepilemur leucopus* at Beza Mahafaly Special Reserve, Madagascar. In Crompton, R. H., Feistner, A.T.C and Harcourt, C. (eds.) Proceedings International Conference on the Biology and Conservation of Prosimians 1995. *Folia Primatologica*.

Nash, L.T. (in litt.) Comments on inactivity and foraging behaviour in White-footed Sportive Lemurs (*Lepilemur leucopus*). Unpublished.

O'Connor, S., Pidgeon, M. and Randria, Z. (1986) Lemur conservation program for the Andohahela Reserve, Madagascar. *Primate Conservation* 7: 48-52.

Petter, J.-J., Albignac, R. and Rumpler, Y. (1977) *Mammifères: lémuriens. Faune de Madagascar* No. 44. ORSTOM-CNRS, Paris.

Petter, J.-J. and Petter-Rousseaux, A. (1979) Classification of the prosimians. In Doyle, G.A. and Martin, R.D. (eds.) *The Study of Prosimian Behaviour*, pp. 1-44. Academic Press, London.

Petter-Rousseaux, A. (1980) Seasonal activity rhythms, reproduction and body weight variations in five sympatric nocturnal prosimians, in simulated light and climatic conditions. In Charles-Dominique, P., Cooper, H.M., Hladik, A., Hladik, C.M., Pagès, E., Pariente, G.F., Petter Rousseaux, A., Petter, J. J. and Schilling, A. (eds.) *Nocturnal Malagasy Primates: Ecology, Physiology and Behaviour*, pp. 137-152. Academic Press, N.Y.

Rakotoarison, N., Mutschler, T. and Thalmann, U. (1993) Lemurs in Bemaraha (World Heritage Landscape, Western Madagascar). *Oryx* 27: 35-40.

Rasoloarison, R.M., Rasolonandrasana, B.P.N., Ganzhorn, J.U. and Goodman, S.M. (1995). Predation on vertebrates in the Kirindy forest, western Madagascar. *Ecotropica* 1: 59-65.

Ratsirarson, J., Anderson, J., Warter, S. and Rumpler, Y. (1987) Notes on the distribution of *Lepilemur septentrionalis* and *L. mustelinus* in northern Madagascar. *Primates* 28: 119-122.

Ratsirarson, J. and Rumpler, Y. (1988) Contribution à l'étude comparée de l'éco-éthologie de deux espèces de lémuriens, *Lepilemur mustelinus* (I. Geoffroy, 1850) and *Lepilemur septentrionalis* (Rumpler and Albignac, 1975). In Rakotovao, L., Barre, V. and Sayer, J. (eds.) *L'Equilibre des Ecosystèmes Forestiers à Madagascar: Actes d'un Séminaire International*, pp. 100-102. IUCN, Gland, Switzerland.

Raxworthy, C.J. (1986) The lemurs of Zahamena Reserve. *Primate Conservation* 7: 46-48.

Raxworthy, C.J. and Rakotondraparany, F. (1988) Mammals Report. In Quansah, N. (ed.) *Manongarivo Special Reserve (Madagascar), 1987/88 Expedition Report*. Madagascar Environmental Research Group, London, U.K.

Rumpler, Y. and Albignac, R. (1975) Intraspecific chromosome variability in a lemur from the north of Madagascar: *Lepilemur septentrionalis*, species nova. *Amer. J. Physical Anthropol.* 42: 425-429.

Russell, R.J. (1980) The environmental physiology and ecology of *Lepilemur ruficaudatus* (=*L. leucopus*) in arid southern Madagascar. *Amer. J. Physical Anthropol.* 52: 273-274.

Schmid, J. and Ganzhorn, J.U. (1996) Resting metabolic rates of *Lepilemur ruficaudatus*. *Amer. J. Primatol.* 38: 169-174.

Schmid, J. and Smolker, R. (in press) Lemurs in the Réserve Special d'Anjanaharibe-Sud. *Fieldiana Zoology*.

Sterling, E.J. and Ramaroson, M.G. (1996) Rapid Assessment of the primate fauna of the eastern slopes of the Réserve Naturelle Intégrale d'Andringitra, Madagascar. *Fieldiana Zoology*, 85. 293-305.

Sussman, R.W. and Richard, A.F. (1986) Lemur conservation in Madagascar: the status of lemurs in the south. *Primate Conservation* 7: 85-92.

Tattersall, I. and Schwartz, J.H. (1991) Phylogeny and nomenclature in the *Lemur* group of Malagasy Strepsirhine primates. *Anthropological Papers of the Amer. Mus. Nat. Hist.* 69: 1-18.

Thalmann, U. and Rakotoarison, N. (1994) Distribution of lemurs in central western Madagascar, with a regional distribution hypothesis. *Folia Primatologica* 63: 156-161.

Tomiuk, J., Bachmann, L., Leipoldt, M., Ganzhorn, J.U., Ries, R., Weis, M. and Loeschcke, V. (in press) Genetic diversity of *Lepilemur mustelinus ruficaudatus*, a nocturnal lemur of Madagascar. *Conserv. Biol.*

Warren, R.D. (1997) Habitat use and support preference of two free-ranging saltatory lemurs, *Lepilemur edwardsi* and *Avahi occidentalis*. *J. Zool.* (London), 241: 325-341.

Warren, R.D. (in litt.) Comments on the behaviour and ecology of Milne-Edwards's Sportive Lemur (*Lepilemur edwardsi*) at Ampijoroa in north west Madagascar. University of Liverpool (unpublished PhD research).

Warren, R.D. and Crompton, R.H. (1996) Lazy leapers: energetics, phylogenetic inertia and the locomotor differentiation of the Malagasy primates. In Lourenco, W.R. (ed.) *Biogéographie de Madagascar*, pp. 259-266. Editions de l'ORSTOM, Paris.

Warren, R.D. and Crompton, R.H. (in press) A comparative study of the ranging behaviour, activity rhythms and sociality of *Lepilemur edwardsi* and *Avahi occidentalis*, at Ampijoroa, Madagascar. *J. Zool.* (London).

Warren, R.D. and Crompton, R.H. (in press) Lazy leapers: locomotor behaviour and ecology of *Lepilemur edwardsi* and *Avahi occidentalis*. In: Crompton, R. H., Feistner, A.T.C and Harcourt, C. (eds.) Proceedings International Conference on the Biology and Conservation of Prosimians 1995. *Folia Primatologica*.

Warren, R.D. and Crompton, R.H. (in press) Diet, body size and the energy costs of locomotion in saltatory primates. *Amer. J. Physical Anthropol.*

Wilson, J.M., Stewart, P.D. and Fowler, S.V. (1988) Ankarana — a rediscovered nature reserve in northern Madagascar. *Oryx* 22: 163-171.

Family Lemuridae

Subfamily Hapalemurinae

Curtis, D.J, Zaramody, A. and Rabetsimialona, O.D. (1995) Sighting of the western gentle lemur *Hapalemur griseus occidentalis* in north-west Madagascar. *Oryx* 29: 215-217.

Elisabete, A.M. and Palka, S. (1994) Feeding behaviour and activity patterns of two Malagasy bamboo lemurs, *Hapalemur simus* and *Hapalemur griseus*, in captivity. *Folia Primatologica* 63: 44- 49.

Feistner, A.T.C. and Rakotoarinosy, M. (1993) Conservation of the gentle lemur *Hapalemur griseus alaotrensis* at Lac Alaotra, Madagascar: local knowledge. *Dodo* 29: 54-65.

Fowler, S.V., Chapman, P., Checkley, D., Hurd, S., McHale, M., Ramangason, G.S., Randriamasy, J.-E., Stewart, P., Walters, R. and Wilson, J.M. (1989) Survey and management proposals for a tropical deciduous forest reserve at Ankarana in northern Madagascar. *Biol. Conserv.* 47: 297-313.

Ganzhorn, J.U. (1989) Niche separation in seven lemur species. *Oecologia* 79: 279-286.

Glander, K.E., Wright, P.C., Seigler, D.S. and Randrianasolo, B. (1989) Consumption of cyanogenic bamboo by a newly discovered species of bamboo lemur. *Amer. J. Primatol.* 19: 119-124.

Glander, K.E., Wright, P.C., Daniels, P.S. and Merenlender, A.M. (1992) Morphometrics and testicle size of rainforest lemur species from south eastern Madagascar. *J. Human Evol.* 22: 1-17.

Godfrey, L. and Vuillaume-Randriamanantena, M.

(1986) *Hapalemur simus*: endangered lemur once widespread. *Primate Conservation* 7: 92-96.

Gray, J.E. (1870) Notes on *Hapalemur simus*, a new species lately living in the Gardens of the Society. *Proc. Zool. Soc.* (London) 40: 828-831.

Groves, C.P. and Eaglen, R.H. (1988) Systematics of the Lemuridae (Primates, Strepsirhini). *J. Human Evol.* 17: 513-538.

Hawkins, A.F.A., Chapman, P., Ganzhorn, J.U., Bloxam, Q.M.C., Barlow, S.C. and Tonge, S.J. (1990) Vertebrate conservation in Ankarana Special Reserve, northern Madagascar. *Biol. Conserv.* 54: 83-110.

Hawkins, A.F.A., Durbin, J. and Reid, D. (in press) The primates of the Baly Bay area, north-western Madagascar. *Folia Primatologica*.

Kappeler, P.M. (1991) Patterns of sexual dimorphism in body weight among prosimian primates. *Folia Primatologica* 57: 132-146.

Meier, B. (1987) Preliminary report of a field study on *Lemur rubriventer* and *Hapalemur simus* (nov. subspecies) in Ranomafana-Ifanadiana 312 Faritany Fianarantsoa, Madagascar, July 1986- January 1987. Unpublished report to the Ministry of Scientific Research, Antananarivo, Madagascar.

Meier, B. and Rumpler, Y. (1987) Preliminary survey of *Hapalemur simus* and of a new species of *Hapalemur* in eastern Betsileo, Madagascar. *Primate Conservation* 8: 40-43.

Meier, B., Albignac, R., Peyrieras, A., Rumpler, Y. and Wright, P.C. (1987) A new species of *Hapalemur* (Primates) from south east Madagascar. *Folia Primatologica* 48: 211-215.

Morris, P. (in .litt.) Comments on vocalisations in Golden Bamboo Lemurs (*Hapalemur aureus*) at Ranomafana National Park, south east Madagascar. Unpublished.

Morris, P. (in .litt.) Comments on group size, maternal behaviour and locomotion in Lac Alaotra Reed Lemurs (*Hapalemur griseus alaotrensis*). University of Zürich (unpublished PhD research).

Mutschler, T., Nievergelt, C. and Feistner, A.T.C. (1994) Biology and conservation of *Hapalemur griseus alaotrensis*. Unpublished report, Jersey Wildlife Preservation Trust, Jersey, U.K.

Mutschler, T. and Feistner, A.T.C. (1995) Conservation status and distribution of the Alaotran gentle lemur *Hapalemur griseus alaotrensis*. *Oryx* 29: 267-274.

Petter, J.-J. and Peyrieras, A. (1975) Preliminary notes on the behaviour and ecology of *Hapalemur griseus*. In Tattersall, I. and Sussman, R.W. (eds.) *Lemur Biology*, pp. 281-286. Plenum Press, London and N.Y.

Petter, J.-J. and Andriatsarafara, S. (1987) Conservation status and distribution of lemurs in the west and north west of Madagascar. *Primate Conservation* 7: 169-171.

Pollock, J. (1986) A note on the ecology and behaviour of *Hapalemur griseus*. *Primate Conservation* 7: 97-101.

Rakotoarison, N., Mutschler, T. and Thalmann, U. (1993) Lemurs in Bemaraha (World Heritage Landscape, Western Madagascar). Oryx 27: 35-40.

Raxworthy, C.J. (1986) The lemurs of Zahamena Reserve. Primate Conservation 7: 46-48.

Raxworthy, C.J. and Rakotondraparany, F. (1988) Mammals Report. In Quansah, N. (ed.) Manongarivo Special Reserve (Madagascar), 1987/88 Expedition Report. Madagascar Environmental Research Group, London, U.K.

Schmid, J. and Smolker, R. (in press) Lemurs in the Réserve Special d'Anjanaharibe-Sud. Fieldiana Zoology.

Sterling, E.J. and Ramaroson, M.G. (1996) Rapid assessment of the primate fauna of the eastern slopes of the Réserve Naturelle Intégrale d'Andringitra, Madagascar. Fieldiana Zoology 85: 293-305.

Tattersall, I. (1987) Cathemeral activity in primates: a definition. Folia Primatologica 49: 200.

Thalmann, U. and Rakotoarison, N. (1994) Distribution of lemurs in central western Madagascar, with a regional distribution hypothesis. Folia Primatologica, 63: 156-161.

Vuillaume-Randriamanantena, M., Godfrey, L. and Sutherland, M. (1985) Revision of Hapalemur (Prohapalemur) gallieni (Standing, 1905). Folia Primatologica 45: 89-116.

Warter, S., Randrianasolo, G., Dutrillaux, B. and Rumpler, Y. (1987) Cytogenetic study of a new subspecies of Hapalemur griseus. Folia Primatologica 48: 50-55.

Wright, P.C. (1986) Diet, ranging behaviour and activity pattern of the gentle lemur (Hapalemur griseus) in Madagascar. Amer. J. Physical Anthropol. 69: 283.

Wright, P.C. (1989) Comparative ecology of three sympatric bamboo lemurs in Madagascar. Amer. J. Physical Anthropol. 78: 327.

Wright, P.C., Daniels, P.S., Meyers, D.M., Overdorff, D.J. and Rabesoa, J. (1987) A census and study of Hapalemur and Propithecus in south eastern Madagascar. Primate Conservation 8: 84-87.

Family Lemuridae

Subfamily Lemurinae

Albignac, R. (1981) Lemurine social and territorial organisation in a north western Malagasy forest (restricted area of Ampijoroa). In Chiarelli, A.B. and Corruccini, R.S. (eds.) Primate Behaviour and Sociobiology, pp. 25-29. Springer Verlag, Berlin.

Amato, G. and Wyner, Y. (in litt.) Comments of the systematics of the genus Varecia. Unpublished.

Andrews, J. (1990) A preliminary survey of Black Lemurs (Eulemur macaco) in north west Madagascar: the final report of the Black Lemur Survey 1988. Unpublished RGS Study Report.

Andrews, J. (in litt.) Comments on the behaviour and ecology of the Black Lemur (Eulemur macaco macaco) on Nosy Be, north west Madagascar. Unpublished.

Andrews, J. and Birkinshaw, C. (1995) A comparison between the day-time and night-time feeding ecology of the black lemur, Eulemur macaco macaco, in Lokobe forest, Madagascar. In the Abstracts: International Conference on the Biology and Conservation of Prosimians. North of England Zoological Soc., 13-16th Sept. 1995.

Andrews, J. and Birkinshaw, C. (in press) A comparison between the day-time and night-time activity and feeding height of the black lemur, Eulemur macaco macaco (Primates: Lemuridae) in Lokobe Forest, Madagascar. In Crompton, R. H., Feistner, A.T.C. and Harcourt, C. (eds.), Proceedings of the International Conference on the Biology and Conservation of Prosimians 1995. Folia Primatologica.

Andriatsarafara, R. (1988) Étude ecoéthologique de deux lémuriens sympatriques de la forêt sèche caducifoliée d'Ampijoroa (Lemur fulvus fulvus, Lemur mongoz). Doctorat de Troisième Cycle, Université de Madagascar, Laboratoire de Zoologie (Biologie Générale).

Arbelot-Tracqui, V. (1983) Étude ethoécologique de deux primates prosimiens: Lemur coronatus Gray et Lemur fulvus sanfordi Archbold: contribution à l'etude des mécanismes d'isolement reproductif intervenant dans la spéciation. Unpublished PhD thesis. University of Rennes, France.

Balko, E.A. (1992) A survey of black and white ruffed lemurs (Varecia variegata variegata) inhabiting five separate forest communities within the eastern rainforests of Madagascar. Unpublished report to The World Conservation Monitoring Centre/IUCN, Cambridge, U.K.

Balko, E.A. (1996) Foraging ecology of Varecia variegata variegata at Ranomafana National Park, Madagascar. Amer. J. Physical Anthropol. supplement 22, p.64.

Balko, E.A. (1997) A behaviourally plastic response to forest composition and habitat disturbance by Varecia variegata variegata in Ranomafana National Park, Madagascar. Unpublished PhD dissertation. State Univ. New York, College of Environmental Science and Forestry, Syracuse, New York.

Balko, E.A. (in litt.) Comments on group composition and dynamics in the Black-and-white Ruffed Lemur (Varecia variegata variegata) at Ranomafana National Park in south east Madagascar. Unpublished.

Balko, E.A., Chambers, R., Wright, P. and Underwood, B. (1995) The relationship of logging disturbance to forest composition and to population density and distribution of black and white ruffed lemur (Varecia variegata variegata) in Ranomafana National Park, Madagascar. In Patterson, B.D., Goodman, S.M. and Sedlock, J.L. (eds.) Environmental Change in Madagascar, pp. 36-37. Field Museum of Natural History, Chicago.

Birkel, R. (1987) International Studbook for the Black Lemur (Eulemur macaco Linnaeus 1766). St. Louis Zoo, St. Louis, Missouri.

Bogart, M.H., Cooper, R.W. and Benirschke, K. (1977) Reproductive Studies of Black and Ruffed Lemurs, Lemur macaco macaco and Lemur variegatus ssp. Int. Zoo Yearbook 17: 177-182.

Boskoff, K.J. (1977) Aspects of reproduction in ruffed lemurs (Lemur variegatus). Folia Primatologica 28: 241-250.

Budnitz, N. (1978) Feeding behaviour of Lemur catta in different habitats. In Bateson, P.P.G. and Klopfer, P.H. (eds.) Perspectives in Ethology 3, pp. 85-108. Plenum Press, London & N.Y.

Budnitz, N. and Dainis, K. (1975) Lemur catta: ecology and behaviour. In Tattersall, I. and Sussman, R.W. (eds.) Lemur Biology, pp. 219-235. Plenum Press, London & N.Y.

Ceska, V., Hoffman, H.-U. and Winkelsträter, K.-H. (1992) Lemuren im Zoo. Verlag Paul Parey, Berlin.

Colquhoun, I.C. (1993) The socioecology of Eulemur macaco: a preliminary report. In Kappeler, P.M. and Ganzhorn, J.U. (eds.) Lemur Social Systems and their Ecological Basis, pp. 11-23. Plenum Press, London & N.Y.

Colquhoun, I.C. (1995) The dark night and the moon: observations on the relationship between black lemur cathemeral behaviour and the lunar cycle. In the Abstracts: International Conference on the Biology and Conservation of Prosimians. North of England Zoological Soc., 13-16th Sept. 1995.

Colquhoun, I.C. (in press) Cathemeral behaviour of Eulemur macaco macaco at Ambato Massif, Madagascar. In Crompton, R. H., Feistner, A.T.C. and Harcourt, C. (eds.), Proceedings of the International Conference on the Biology and Conservation of Prosimians 1995. Folia Primatologica.

Colquhoun, I.C. (in litt.) Comments on the behaviour and ecology of the Black Lemur (Eulemur macaco macaco) at Ambato Massif, north west Madagascar. Unpublished.

Constable, I.D., Mittermeier, R.A., Pollock, J.I., Ratsirarson, J. and Simons, H. (1985) Sightings of aye-ayes and red ruffed lemurs on Nosy Mangabe and the Masoala Peninsula. Primate Conservation. 5: 59-62.

Curtis, D.J. (1997) The Mongoose Lemur (Eulemur mongoz): A Study in Behaviour and Ecology. Unpublished Ph.D. Thesis. Anthropological Institute, University of Zurich.

Curtis, D.J. (in litt.) Comments on the behaviour and ecology of Mongoose Lemurs (Eulemur mongez) in north west Madagascar. Unpublished.

Curtis, D.J. and Zaramody, A. (1995) Le comportement et l'écologie du Gidro (Eulemur mongoz). Unpublished report.

Dague, C. and Petter, J.-J. (1988) Observations sur le Lemur rubriventer dans son milieu naturel. In Rakotavao, L., Barre, V. and Sayer, J. (eds.), L'Equilibre des Ecosystèmes Forestiers à Madagascar: Actes d'un Séminaire International. IUCN, Gland, Switzerland.

Daniels, P. (1991) A first look at the Zahamena Reserve. Tropicus (Conservation International) 5: 8-9.

Duckworth, J.W. and Rakotondraparany, F. (1990) The Mammals of Marojejy. In: Safford, R.J. and Duckworth, J.W. (eds.) A Wildlife Survey of Marojejy Nature Reserve, Madagascar. Int. Council Bird Preserv., Study Report No. 40, pp. 54-60.

Duckworth, J.W., Evans, M.I., Hawkins, A.F.A., Safford, R.J. and Wilkinson, R.J. (1995) The lemurs of Marojejy Strict Nature Reserve, Madagascar: a status overview with notes on ecology and threats. Int. J. Primatol. 16: 545-559.

Engqvist, A. and Richard, A. (1991) Diet as a possible determinant of cathemeral activity patterns in primates. Folia Primatologica, 57: 169-172.

Evans, M.I., Thompson, P.M. and Wilson, A. (1993-1994) A survey of the lemurs of Ambatovaky Special Reserve, Madagascar. Primate Conservation 14-15: 13-31.

Foerg, R. (1982) Reproductive behaviour in Varecia variegata. Folia Primatologica 38: 108-121.

Fowler, S.V., Chapman, P., Checkley, D., Hurd, S., McHale, M., Ramangason, G.S., Randriamasy, J.-E., Stewart, P., Walters, R. and Wilson, J.M. (1989) Survey and management proposals for a tropical deciduous forest reserve at Ankarana in northern Madagascar. Biological Conservation 47: 297-313.

Freed, B.Z. (1995) The ecology of crowned lemurs and Sanford's lemurs in Montagne d'Ambre, Madagascar. In the Abstracts: International Conference on the Biology and Conservation of Prosimians. North of England Zoological Soc., 13-16th Sept. 1995.

Ganzhorn, J.U. (1985) Utilisation of eucalyptus and pine plantations by brown lemurs in the eastern rainforests of Madagascar. Primate Conservation 6: 34-35.

Ganzhorn, J.U. (1987) A possible role of plantations for primate conservation in Madagascar. Amer. J. Primatol. 12: 205-215.

Ganzhorn, J.U. (1988) Food partitioning among Malagasy primates. Oecologia (Berlin) 75: 436-450.

Ganzhorn, J.U. (1989) Niche separation in seven lemur species. Oecologia 79: 279-286.

Ganzhorn, J.U. (1992) Leaf chemistry and the biomass of folivorous primates in tropical forests. Oecologia (Berlin) 91: 540-547.

Ganzhorn, J.U. (1995) Low level forest disturbance effects on primary production, leaf chemistry and lemur populations. Ecology 76: 2084-2096.

Ganzhorn, J.U. (1995) Cyclones over Madagascar: fate or fortune? Ambio 24: 124-125.

Ganzhorn J.U. (in press) Diversity and processes maintaining diversity in lemur communities. In Crompton, R. H., Feistner, A.T.C and Harcourt, C. (eds.) Proceedings of the International Conference on the Biology and Conservation of Prosimians 1995. Folia Primatologica.

Ganzhorn, J.U. and Kappeler, P.M. (1996) Lemurs of the Kirindy Forest. In Ganzhorn, J.U. and Sorg, J.-P. (eds.), Ecology and Economy of a Tropical Dry Forest in Madagascar, pp. 257-274. Primate Report, Special Issue, 46-1(June 1996).

Ganzhorn, J.U., Malcomber, S., Andrianantoanina, O. and Goodman, S.M. (in press) Habitat characteristics and lemur species richness in Madagascar. Biotropica.

Goodman, S.M. (1994) The enigma of anti-predator behaviour in lemurs: evidence of a large extinct eagle on Madagascar. Int. J. Primatol. 15: 129-134.

Goodman, S.M., O'Connor, S. and Langrand, O. (1993) A review of predation on lemurs: implications for the evolution of social behaviour in small, nocturnal primates. In Kappeler, P.M. and Ganzhorn, J.U. (eds.) Lemur Social Systems and their Ecological Basis, pp. 51-66. Plenum Press, London & N.Y.

Goodman, S.M. and Langrand, O. (1996) A high mountain population of the ring tailed lemur, Lemur catta on the Andringitra Massif, Madagascar. Oryx 30: 259-268.

Glander, K.E., Wright, P.C., Daniels, P.S. and Merenlender, A.M. (1992) Morphometrics and testicle size of rainforest lemur species from south eastern Madagascar. J. Human Evol. 22: 1-17.

Green, G.M.G. and Sussman, R.W. (1990) Deforestation history of the eastern rainforests of Madagascar from satellite images. Science 248: 212-215.

Groves, C.P. and Eaglen, R.H. (1988) Systematics of the Lemuridae (Primates, Strepsirhini). J. Human Evol. 17: 513-538.

Halleux, D. (in litt.) Reported sightings of Red Ruffed Lemurs (Varecia variegata rubra) south west of Andapa. Unpublished.

Hamilton, A., Tattersall, I., Sussman, R.W. and Buettner-Janusch, J. (1980) Chromosomes of Lemuriformes, VI. Comparative karyology of Lemur fulvus: a G-banded karyotype of Lemur fulvus mayottensis Schlegel, 1866. Int. J. Primatol. 1: 81-93.

Harrington, J.E. (1975) Field observations of social behaviour of Lemur fulvus fulvus E. Geoffroy 1812. In Tattersall, I. and Sussman, R.W. (eds.) Lemur Biology, pp. 259-279. Plenum Press, London & N.Y.

Harrington, J.E. (1978) Diurnal behaviour of Lemur mongoz at Ampijoroa, Madagascar. Folia Primatologica 29: 291-302.

Hawkins, A.F.A., Chapman, P., Ganzhorn, J.U., Bloxam, Q.M.C., Barlow, S.C. and Tonge, S.J. (1990) Vertebrate conservation in Ankarana Special Reserve, northern Madagascar. Biol. Conserv. 54: 83-110.

Hladik, C.M. (1979) Diet and ecology of prosimians. In Doyle, G.A. and Martin, R.D. (eds.) The Study of Prosimian Behaviour, pp. 307-357. Academic Press, London & N.Y.

Howarth, C.J., Wilson, J.M., Adamson, A.P., Wilson, M.E. and Boase, M.J. (1986) Population ecology of the ring tailed lemur, Lemur catta, and the white sifaka, Propithecus verreauxi verreauxi, at Berenty, Madagascar. Folia Primatologica 47: 39-48.

Iwano, T. (1989) Some observations of two kinds of Lemuridae (Varecia variegata variegata and Lemur fulvus albifrons) in the reserve of Nosy Mangabe. Primates 30: 241-248.

Izard, K. (1995) Comparative reproduction among subspecies of Eulemur fulvus. In the Abstracts: International Conference on the Biology and Conservation of Prosimians. North of England Zoological Soc., 13-16th Sept. 1995.

Jenkins, P.D. and Albrecht, G. (1991) Sexual dimorphism and sex ratios in Madagascar Prosimians.

Amer. J. Primatol. 24: 1-14.

Jolly, A. (1966) Lemur Behaviour. University of Chicago Press, Chicago.

Jolly, A. (1972) Troop continuity and troop spacing in Propithecus verreauxi and Lemur catta at Berenty (Madagascar). Folia Primatologica 17: 335-362.

Jolly, A., Oliver, W.L.R. and O'Connor, S.M. (1982) Population and troop ranges of Lemur catta and Lemur fulvus at Berenty, Madagascar: 1980 census. Folia Primatologica 39: 115-123.

Jolly, A., Rasamimanana, H.R., Kinnaird, M.F., O'Brien, T.G., Crowley, H.M., Harcourt, C.S., Gardner, S. and Davidson, J.M. (1993) Territoriality in Lemur catta groups during the birth season at Berenty, Madagascar. In Kappeler, P.M. and Ganzhorn, J.U. (eds.) Lemur Social Systems and their Ecological Basis, pp. 85-109. Plenum Press, London & N Y

Jones, K.C. (1983) Inter-troop transfer of Lemur catta males at Berenty, Madagascar. Folia Primatologica 40: 145-160.

Kappeler, P.M. (1987) Reproduction in the crowned lemur (Lemur coronatus) in captivity. Amer. J. Primatol. 12: 497-503.

Kappeler, P.M. (1991) Patterns of sexual dimorphism in body weight among prosimian primates. Folia Primatologica, 57: 132-146.

Kappeler, P.M. (1993) Sexual selection and lemur social systems. In Kappeler, P.M. and Ganzhorn, J.U. (eds.) Lemur Social Systems and their Ecological Basis, pp. 223-240. Plenum Press, London & N.Y.

Klopfer, P.H. and Boskoff, K.J. (1979) Maternal behaviour in prosimians. In Doyle, G.A. and Martin, R.D. (eds.) The Study of Prosimian Behaviour, pp.123-156. Academic Press, London & N.Y.

Klopfer, P.H. and Dugard, J. (1976) Patterns of maternal care in lemurs: III: Lemur variegatus. Zeitschrift für Tierpsychologie 48: 87-99.

Koenders, L., Rumpler, Y. and Brun, B. (1985) Notes on the recently rediscovered Sclater's lemur (Lemur macaco flavifrons). Primate Conservation 6: 35.

Koenders, L., Rumpler, Y., Ratsirarson, J. and Peyrieras, A. (1985) Lemur macaco flavifrons (Gray, 1867): a rediscovered subspecies of primate. Folia Primatologica 44: 210-215.

Kress, W.J., Schatz, G.E., Adrianifihanana, M., Morland, H.S. and Love, S.H. (1994) Pollination of Ravenala madagascariensis by lemurs in Madagascar: evidence for an archaic coevolutionary system? Amer. J. Botany 81: 542-551.

Lernould, J.-M. (1996) A joint Franco-German-Malagasy conservation programme for Sclater's lemur. Int. Zoo News 43: 289-293.

Lindsay, N.B.D. and Simons, H.J. (1986) Notes on Varecia in the northern limits of its range. Dodo 23: 19-24.

Marsh, C.W., Johns, A.D. and Ayres, J.M. (1987) Effects of habitat disturbance on rain forest primates. In Marsh, C.W. and Mittermeier, R.A. (eds.) Primate Conservation in the Tropical Rain Forest, pp. 83-107. Alan R. Liss, N.Y.

Meier, B. (1987) Preliminary report of a field study on Lemur rubriventer and Hapalemur simus (nov. subspecies) in Ranomafana-Ifanadiana 312 Faritany Fianarantsoa, Madagascar, July 1986- January 1987. Unpublished report to the Ministry of Scientific Research, Antananarivo, Madagascar.

Meyers, D. (1988) Behaviorial ecology of Lemur fulvus rufus in rain forest in Madagascar. Amer. J. Physical Anthropol. 75: 250.

Meyers, D., Rabarivola, C. and Rumpler, Y. (1989) Distribution and conservation of Sclater's lemur: implications of a morphological cline. Primate Conservation 10: 78-82.

Mittermeier, R.A. (1988) Primate diversity and the tropical forest: case studies from Brazil and Madagascar and the importance of megadiversity countries. In Wilson, E.O. and Peters, F.M. (eds.) Biodiversity, pp. 145-154. National Academy Press, Washington DC.

Mittermeier, R.A., Rakotovao, L.H., Randrianasolo, V.,

Sterling, E.J. and Devitre, D. (1987) Priorités en Matière de Conservation des Espèces à Madagascar. Occasional Papers of the IUCN/SSC, No.2, Gland, Switzerland.

Morland, H.S. (1989) Infant survival and parental care in ruffed lemurs (Varecia variegata) in the wild. Amer. J. Primatol. 18: 157.

Morland, H.S. (1990) Parental behaviour and infant development in ruffed lemurs (Varecia variegata) in a northeast Madagascar rain forest. Amer. J. Primatol. 20: 253-265.

Morland, H.S. (1991) Preliminary report on the social organisation of ruffed lemurs (Varecia variegata variegata) in a northeast Madagascar rain forest. Folia Primatologica 56: 157-161.

Morland, H.S. (1993) Seasonal behavioural variation and its relation to thermoregulation in ruffed lemurs. In Kappeler, P.M. and Ganzhorn, J.U. (eds.) Lemur Social Systems and their Ecological Basis, pp. 193-203. Plenum Press, London & N.Y.

Nilsson, L.A., Rabakonandrianina, E., Petterson, B. and Grunmeier, R. (1993) Lemur pollination in the Malagasy rainforest: Liana Strongylodon craveniae (Leguminosae). Evolutionary Trends in Plants 7: 49-56.

O'Connor, S., Pidgeon, M. and Randria, Z. (1986) Conservation program for the Andohahela Reserve, Madagascar. Primate Conservation 7: 48-52.

Oda, R. (1996) Predation on a chameleon by a ring-tailed lemur in the Berenty Reserve, Madagascar. Folia Primatologica 67: 40-43.

Overdorff, D.J. (1988) Preliminary report on the activity cycle and diet of the red-bellied lemur (Lemur rubriventer) in Madagascar. Amer. J. Primatol. 16: 143-153.

Overdorff, D.J. (1990) Flower predation and nectarivory in Lemur fulvus rufus and Lemur rubriventer. Amer. J. Physical Anthropol. 81: 276.

Overdorff, D.J. (1992) Differential patterns in flower feeding by Eulemur fulvus rufus and Eulemur rubriventer in Madagascar. Amer. J. Primatol. 28: 191-196.

Overdorff, D.J. (1993) Ecological and reproductive correlates to range use in Red-Bellied Lemurs (Eulemur rubriventer) and Rufous Lemurs (Eulemur fulvus rufus). In Kappeler, P.M. and Ganzhorn, J.U. (eds.) Lemur Social Systems and their Ecological Basis, pp. 167-178. Plenum Press, London & N.Y.

Pastorini, J. (in litt.) Weights of Mongoose Lemurs (Eulemur mongoz) caught in the wild. Unpublished.

Pereira, M.E., Klepper, A. and Simons, E.L. (1987) Tactics of care for young infants by forest living ruffed lemurs (Varecia variegata variegata): ground nests, parking and biparental care. Amer. J. Primatol. 13: 129-144.

Pereira, M.E. Seeligson, M.L. and Macedonia, J.M. (1988) The behavioural repertoire of the black and white ruffed lemur, Varecia variegata variegata (Primates: Lemuridae). Folia Primatologica 51: 1-32.

Petter, J.-J. and Andriatsarafara, S.(1987) Conservation status and distribution of lemurs in the west and north west of Madagascar. Primate Conservation 7: 169-171.

Pollock, J.I. (1979) Spatial distribution and ranging behaviour in lemurs. In Doyle, G.A. and Martin, R.D. (eds.) The Study of Prosimian Behaviour, pp. 359-409. Academic Press, London & New York.

Rabarivola, C., Meyers, D. and Rumpler, Y. (1991) Distribution and morphological characteristics of intermediate forms between the black lemur (Eulemur macaco macaco) and Sclater's lemur (E. m. flavifrons). Primates 32: 269-273.

Rabarivola, C., Scheffrahn, W. and Rumpler, Y. (1996) Population genetics of Eulemur macaco macaco (Primates: Lemuridae) on the islands of Nosy Be and Nosy Komba and the peninsula of Ambato (Madagascar). Primates 37: 215-225.

Ralisoamalala, R.C. (1996) Role de Eulemur fulvus rufus (Audebert, 1899) et de Propithecus verreauxi verreauxi (A. Grandidier, 1867) dans la dissemination des graines. In Ganzhorn, J.U. and Sorg, J.-P. (eds.), Ecology and Economy of a Tropical Dry Forest in

Madagascar, pp. 285-293. *Primate Report*, Special Issue, 46-1(June 1996).

Ramaroson, M.G. (*in litt.*) Possible sightings of Black-and-white Ruffed lemurs (*Varecia variegata variegata*) towards the north of the Marojejy Massif in north east Madagascar. Unpublished.

Rasoloarison, R.M., Rasolonandrasana, B.P.N., Ganzhorn, J.U. and Goodman, S.M. (1995). Predation on vertebrates in the Kirindy forest, western Madagascar. *Ecotropica* 1: 59-65.

Raxworthy, C.J. (1986) The lemurs of Zahamena Reserve. *Primate Conservation* 7: 46-48.

Raxworthy, C.J. and Rakotondraparany, F. (1988) Mammals Report. In Quansah, N. (ed.) *Manongarivo Special Reserve (Madagascar), 1987/88 Expedition Report*. Madagascar Environmental Research Group, London, U.K.

Richard, A.F. (1987) Malagasy prosimians: female dominance. In Smuts, B.B., Cheny, D.L., Seyfarth, R.M., Wrangham, R.W. and Struhsaker, T.T. (eds.) *Primate Societies*, pp. 25-33. University of Chicago Press, Chicago.

Rigamonti, M.M. (1993) Home range and diet in red ruffed lemurs (*Varecia variegata rubra*) on the Masoala Peninsula, Madagascar. In Kappeler, P.M. and Ganzhorn, J.U. (eds.) *Lemur Social Systems and their Ecological Basis*, pp. 25-39. Plenum Press, London & N.Y.

Rigamonti, M.M. (1996) Red Ruffed Lemur (*Varecia variegata rubra*): A rare species from the Masoala rain forests. *Lemur News* 2:9-11.

Rohner, U. (1988) Observations des lémuriens diurnes sur le parcours phénologique du C.F.P.F. *Fiche technique 14.* CFPF, Morondava.

Rumpler, Y. (1975) The significance of chromosomal studies in the systematics of the Malagasy lemurs. In Tattersall, I. and Sussman, R.W. (eds.), *Lemur Biology*, pp. 25-40. Plenum Press, London & N.Y.

Safford, R.J. and Duckworth, J.W. (1990) A Wildlife Survey of Marojejy Nature Reserve, Madagascar. *Int. Council Bird Preserv., Study Report* No. 40.

Sauther, M.L. (1989) Anti-predator behaviour in troops of free-ranging *Lemur catta* at Beza-Mahafaly Special Reserve, Madagascar. *Int. J. Primatol.* 10: 595-606.

Sauther, M.L. (1991) Reproductive behaviour of free-ranging *Lemur catta* at Beza-Mahafaly Special Reserve, Madagascar. *Amer. J. Physical Anthropol.* 84: 463-478.

Sauther, M.L. (1993) Resource competition in wild populations of ring tailed lemurs (*Lemur catta*): implications for female dominance. In Kappeler, P.M. and Ganzhorn, J.U. (eds.) *Lemur Social Systems and their Ecological Basis*, pp. 135-152. Plenum Press, London & N.Y.

Sauther, M.L. (1995) Meeting the stresses of reproduction: reproductive and ecological synchrony in free-ranging ring-tailed lemurs, *Lemur catta*. In the Abstracts: *International Conference on the Biology and Conservation of Prosimians.* North of England Zoological Soc., 13-16th Sept. 1995.

Sauther, M.L. and Sussman, R.W. (1993) A new interpretation of the social organisation and mating system of the ring-tailed lemur (*Lemur catta*). In Kappeler, P.M. and Ganzhorn, J.U. (eds.) *Lemur Social Systems and their Ecological Basis*, pp. 111-121. Plenum Press, London & N.Y.

Scharfe, F. and Schlund, W. (1996) Seed removal by lemurs in a dry deciduous forest of western Madagascar. In Ganzhorn, J.U. and Sorg, J.-P. (eds.)

Ecology and Economy of a Tropical Dry Forest in Madagascar, pp. 295-304. *Primate Report*, Special Issue, 46-1(June 1996).

Schmid, J. and Smolker, R. (in press) Lemurs in the Réserve Special d'Anjanaharibe-Sud. *Fieldiana Zoology.*

Simons, E.L. and Rumpler, Y. (1988) *Eulemur*: a new generic name for species of *Lemur* other than *Lemur catta. C.R. Acad. Science*, Paris, Ser. 3, 307: 547-551.

Simons, H.J. and Lindsay, N.B.D. (1987) Survey work on ruffed lemurs (*Varecia variegata*) and other primates in the north eastern rain forests of Madagascar. *Primate Conservation* 8: 88-91.

Stephenson, P.J., Rakotoarison, N. and Randriamahazo, H. (1993-1994) Conservation in Ambohitantely Special Reserve, Madagascar. *Primate Conservation* 14-15: 22-24.

Sterling, E.J. and Ramaroson, M G. (1996) Rapid assessment of the primate fauna of the eastern slopes of the Réserve Naturelle Intégrale d'Andringitra, Madagascar. *Fieldiana Zoology* 85: 293-305.

Sussman, R.W. (1974) Ecological distinctions in sympatric species of lemur. In Martin, R.D., Doyle, G.A. and Walker, A.C. (eds.) *Prosimian Biology*, pp. 75-108. Duckworth, London.

Sussman, R.W. (1975) A preliminary study of the behaviour and ecology of *Lemur fulvus rufus* Audebert 1800. In: Tattersall, I. and Sussman, R.W. (eds.), *Lemur Biology*, pp. 237-258. Plenum Press, London & N.Y.

Sussman, R.W. (1977) Distribution of Malagasy lemurs. Part 2: *Lemur catta* and *Lemur fulvus* in southern and western Madagascar. *Annals, N.Y. Academy Science* 293: 170-183.

Sussman, R.W. (1977a) Socialisation, social structure and ecology of two sympatric species of lemur. In Chevalier-Skolnikoff, S. and Poirer, F. (eds.) *Primate Bio-Social Development*, pp. 515- 528. Garland, N.Y.

Sussman, R.W. (1989) Demography of *Lemur catta* in southern Madagascar. *Amer. J. Physical Anthropol.* 78: 312.

Sussman, R.W. (1991) Demography and social organisation of free-ranging *Lemur catta* in Beza Mahafaly Special Reserve. *Amer. J. Physical Anthropol.*, 84: 43-58.

Sussman, R.W. and Tattersall, I. (1976) Cycles of activity, group composition and diet of *Lemur mongoz* Linnaeus 1766 in Madagascar. *Folia Primatologica* 26: 270-283.

Sussman, R.W. and Raven, P.H. (1978) Pollination by lemurs and marsupials: an archaic coevolutionary system. *Science* 200: 731-736.

Sussman, R.W. and Richard, A.F. (1986) Lemur conservation in Madagascar: the status of lemurs in the south. *Primate Conservation* 7: 85-92.

Tattersall, I. (1976) Notes on the status of *Lemur macaco* and *Lemur fulvus* (Primates, Lemuriformes). *Anthropological Papers of the Amer. Mus. Nat. Hist.* 53: 257-261.

Tattersall, I. (1976) Group structure and activity rhythm in *Lemur mongoz* (Primates, Lemuriformes) on Anjouan and Moheli Islands, Comoro Archipelago. *Anthropological Papers of the Amer. Mus. Nat. Hist.* 53: 369-380.

Tattersall, I. (1977) Distribution of the Malagasy lemurs, Part 1: the lemurs of northern Madagascar. *Annals, N.Y. Academy Science* 293: 160-169.

Tattersall, I. (1977) The lemurs of the Comoro Islands. *Oryx* 13: 445-448.

Tattersall, I. (1977) Behavioural variation in *Lemur mongoz* (= *L.m.mongoz*). In Chivers, D.J. and Joysey, K.A. (eds.), *Recent Advances in Primatology*, Vol. 3, pp. 127-132. Academic Press, London.

Tattersall, I. (1987) Cathemeral activity in primates: a definition. *Folia Primatologica* 49: 200.

Tattersall, I. (1989) The Mayotte lemur: cause for alarm. *Primate Conservation* 10: 26-27.

Tattersall, I. and Schwartz, J.H. (1991) Phylogeny and nomenclature in the *Lemur* group of Malagasy Strepsirhine primates. *Anthropological Papers of the Amer. Mus. Nat. Hist.* 69: 1-18.

Tattersall, I. and Sussman, R.W. (1975) Observations on the ecology and behaviour of the mongoose lemur, *Lemur mongoz mongoz* Linnaeus (Primates, Lemuriformes) at Ampijoroa, Madagascar. *Anthropological Papers of the Amer. Mus. Nat. Hist.* 52: 195-216.

van Schaik, C.P. and Kappeler, P.M. (1993) Life history, activity period and lemur social systems. In: Kappeler, P.M. and Ganzhorn, J.U. (eds.) *Lemur Social Systems and their Ecological Basis*, pp. 241-260. Plenum Press, London & N.Y.

Vasey, N. (1995) Human resource use and habitat availability for red ruffed lemurs (*Varecia variegata rubra*) in the Anaovandrano river watershed, Masoala Peninsula, Madagascar. In Patterson, B.D., Goodman, S.M. and Sedlock, J.L. (eds.) *Environmental Change in Madagascar*, pp. 37-38. Field Museum of Natural History, Chicago.

Vasey, N. (1995) Ranging behaviour, community size and community composition of red ruffed lemurs, *Varecia variegata rubra*, at Andranobe, Masoala Peninsula, Madagascar. In the Abstracts: *International Conference on the Biology and Conservation of Prosimians.* North of England Zoological Soc., 13-16th Sept. 1995.

Vasey, N. (1996) Clinging to life: *Varecia variegata rubra* and the Masoala coastal forests. *Lemur News*, 2: 7-9.

Vick, E.G. and Pereira, M.E. (1989) Episodic targeting aggression and the histories of *Lemur* social groups. *Behaviour, Ecology and Sociobiology* 25: 3-12.

White, F.J. (1989) Diet, ranging behaviour and social organisation of the black and white ruffed lemur, *Varecia variegata variegata*, in south eastern Madagascar. *Amer. J. Physical Anthropol.* 78: 323.

White, F.J., Burton, A., Buchholz, S. and Glander, K.E. (1989) Social organisation, social cohesion and group size of wild and captive black and white ruffed lemurs. *Amer. J. Primatol.* 18: 170.

White, F.J., Overdorff, D.J., Balko, E.A. and Wright, P.C. (1995) The distribution of ruffed lemurs (*Varecia variegata variegata*) in Ranomafana National Park, Madagascar. *Folia Primatologica* 64: 124-131.

Wilson, J.M. (1987) The crocodile caves of Ankarana, Madagascar. *Oryx* 21: 43-47.

Wilson, J.M., Stewart, P.D. and Fowler, S.V. (1988) Ankarana – a rediscovered nature reserve in northern Madagascar. *Oryx* 22: 163-171.

Wilson, J.M., Stewart, P.D., Ramangason, G.-S., Denning, A.M. and Hutchings, M.S. (1989) Ecology and conservation of the crowned lemur, *Lemur coronatus*, at Ankarana, northern Madagascar, with notes on Sanford's lemur, other sympatric and sub-fossil lemurs. *Folia Primatologica* 52: 1-26.

Family Indriidae

Carrai, V. and Lunardini, A. (1996) Activity patterns and home range use of two groups of *Propithecus v. verreauxi* in the Kirindy Forest. In Ganzhorn, J.U. and Sorg, J.-P. (eds.), Ecology and Economy of a Tropical Dry Forest in Madagascar, pp. 275-284. *Primate Report*, Special Issue, 46-1(June 1996).

Curtis, D.J. (*in litt.*) Comments on population estimates

of Decken's Sifaka (*Propithecus verreauxi deckeni*) in north west Madagascar. Unpublished.

Curtis, D.J., Velo, A., Raheliarisoa, E.-O., Zaramody, A. and Müller, P. (1998) Surveys on *Propithecus verreauxi deckeni*, a melanistic variant, and *P. v. coronatus* in north west Madagascar. *Oryx* 32 (2): 157-164.

Duckworth, J.W. and Rakotondraparany, F. (1990) The Mammals of Marojejy. In Safford, R.J. and Duckworth, J.W. (eds.) A Wildlife Survey of Marojejy Nature Reserve, Madagascar. *Int. Council Bird Preserv., Study Report* No. 40, pp. 54-60.

Duckworth, J.W., Evans, M.I., Hawkins, A.F.A., Safford, R.J. and Wilkinson, R.J. (1995) The lemurs of

Marojejy Strict Nature Reserve, Madagascar: a status overview with notes on ecology and threats. *Int. J. Primatol.* 16: 545-559.

Evans, M.I., Thompson, P.M. and Wilson, A. (1993-1994) A survey of the lemurs of Ambatovaky Special Reserve, Madagascar. *Primate Conservation* 14-15: 13-31.

Fowler, S.V., Chapman, P., Checkley, D., Hurd, S., McHale, M., Ramangason, G.S., Randriamasy, J.-E., Stewart, P., Walters, R. and Wilson, J.M. (1989) Survey and management proposals for a tropical deciduous forest reserve at Ankarana in northern Madagascar. *Biological Conservation* 47: 297-313.

Ganzhorn, J.U. (1988) Food partitioning among Malagasy primates. *Oecologia* (Berlin) 75: 436-450.

Ganzhorn, J.U. (1989) Niche separation in seven lemur species. *Oecologia* 79: 279-286.

Ganzhorn, J.U., Abraham, J.P. and Razanahoera-Rakotomalala, M. (1985) Some aspects of the natural history and food selection of *Avahi laniger*. *Primates* 26: 452-463.

Ganzhorn, J.U. and Kappeler, P.M. (1996) Lemurs of the Kirindy Forest. In Ganzhorn, J.U. and Sorg, J.-P. (eds.), Ecology and Economy of a Tropical Dry Forest in Madagascar, pp. 257-274. *Primate Report*, Special Issue, 46-1(June 1996).

Glander, K.E. and Powzyk, J.A. (1995) Morphometrics of wild *Indri indri* and *Propithecus diadema diadema*. In the Abstracts: *International Conference on the Biology and Conservation of Prosimians*. North of England Zoological Soc., 13-16th Sept. 1995.

Goodman, S.M., O'Connor, S. and Langrand, O. (1993) A review of predation on lemurs: implications for the evolution of social behaviour in small, nocturnal primates. In Kappeler, P.M. and Ganzhorn, J.U. (eds.) *Lemur Social Systems and their Ecological Basis*, pp. 51-66. Plenum Press, London & N.Y.

Groves, C.P. and Eaglen, R.H. (1988) Systematics of the Lemuridae (Primates, Strepsirhini). *J. Human Evol.* 17: 513-538.

Harcourt, C. (1988) *Avahi laniger*: a study in inactivity. *Primate Eye* 35: 9.

Harcourt, C. (1991) Diet and behaviour of a nocturnal lemur, *Avahi laniger*, in the wild. *J. Zool.* (London) 223: 667-674.

Hawkins, A.F.A., Chapman, P., Ganzhorn, J.U., Bloxam, Q.M.C., Barlow, S.C. and Tonge, S.J. (1990) Vertebrate conservation in Ankarana Special Reserve, northern Madagascar. *Biological Conservation* 54: 83-110.

Hawkins, A.F.A., Durbin, J. and Reid, D. (in press) The primates of the Baly Bay area, north-western Madagascar. *Folia Primatologica*.

Hemingway, C.A. (1995) Feeding and reproductive strategies of the Milne-Edwards' sifaka, *Propithecus diadema edwardsi*. Ph.D. dissertation. D.U.P.C., North Carolina, U.S.A.

Jolly, A. (1972) Troop continuity and troop spacing in *Propithecus verreauxi* and *Lemur catta* at Berenty (Madagascar). *Folia Primatologica* 17: 335-362.

Jolly, A., Gustafson, H., Oliver, W.L.R. and O'Connor, S.M. (1982) *Propithecus verreauxi* population and ranging at Berenty, Madagascar, 1975-1980. *Folia Primatologica* 39: 124-144.

Jungers, W.L., Godfrey, L.R., Simons, E.L. and Chatrath, P.S. (1995) Subfossil *Indri* from the Ankarana Massif of northern Madagascar. *Amer. J. Physical Anthropol.* 97: 357-366.

Mertl-Millhollen, A.S. (1979) Olfactory demarcation of territorial boundaries by a primate – *Propithecus verreauxi*. *Folia Primatologica* 32: 35-42.

Meyers, D.M. and Ratsirarson, J. (1989) Distribution and conservation of two endangered sifakas in northern Madagascar. *Primate Conservation* 10: 81-86.

Meyers, D.M. (1993) Conservation status of the golden-crowned sifaka, *Propithecus tattersalli*. *Lemur News* 1(1): 6-8.

Meyers, D.M. (1996) Update on the endangered sifaka of the north. *Lemur News* 2:13-14.

Meyers, D.M. and Wright, P.C. (1993) Resource tracking: food availability and *Propithecus* seasonal reproduction. In Kappeler, P.M. and Ganzhorn, J.U. (eds.) *Lemur Social Systems and their Ecological Basis*, pp. 179-192. Plenum Press, London & N.Y.

Mutschler, T. and Thalmann, U. (1990) Sightings of *Avahi* (woolly lemur) in western Madagascar. *Primate Conservation* 11: 9-11.

Müller, P. (1997) Ökologie und Ernährungsstrategie des Kronensifakas (*Propethecus verrauxi coronatus*). University of Zürich (Diploma thesis).

Müller, P. (1997) Comments on the behaviour and ecology of the Crowned Sifaka (*Propithecus verreauxi coronatus*) in north west Madagascar. University of Zürich (unpublished research).

Oliver, W.L.R. and O'Connor, S.M. (1980) Circadian distribution of *Indri indri* group vocalisations: a short sampling period at two study sites near Perinet, eastern Madagascar. *Dodo* 17: 19-27.

Pastorini, J. (in litt.) Weights of Crowned Sifakas (*Propithrcus verreauxi coronatus*) caught in the wild. Unpublished.

Pollock, J.I. (1977) The ecology and sociology of feeding in *Indri indri*. In Clutton-Brock, T.H. (ed.) *Primate Ecology: Studies of Feeding and Ranging Behaviour in Lemurs, Monkeys and Apes*, pp. 37-69. Academic Press, London.

Pollock, J.I. (1979) Female dominance in *Indri indri*. *Folia Primatologica* 31: 143-164.

Pollock, J.I. (1986) The song of the indris (*Indri indri*, Primates, Lemuroidea): natural history form and function. *Int. J. Primatol.* 7: 225-267.

Powzyk, J. (in litt.) Comments on the behaviour and ecology of two sympatric Indriids – the Diademed Sifaka (*Propithecus diadema diadema*) and the Indri (*Indri indri*) – in Mantadia National Park, central eastern Madagascar. Duke University Primate Centre, North Carolina (unpublished PhD research).

Ralisoamalala, R.C. (1996) Role de *Eulemur fulvus rufus* (Audebert, 1899) et de *Propithecus verreauxi verreauxi* (A. Grandidier, 1867) dans la dissemination des graines. In Ganzhorn, J.U. and Sorg, J.-P. (eds.) Ecology and Economy of a Tropical Dry Forest in Madagascar, pp. 285-293. *Primate Report*, Special Issue, 46-1(June 1996).

Rakotoarison, N., Mutschler, T. and Thalmann, U. (1993) Lemurs in Bemaraha (World Heritage Landscape, Western Madagascar). *Oryx* 27: 35-40.

Rasoloarison, R.M., Rasolonandrasana, B.P.N., Ganzhorn, J.U. and Goodman, S.M. (1995) Predation on vertebrates in the Kirindy forest, western Madagascar. *Ecotropica* 1: 59-65.

Raxworthy, C.J. (1986) The lemurs of Zahamena Reserve. *Primate Conservation* 7: 46-48.

Raxworthy, C.J. and Stephenson, P.J. (1988) Lemur observations in the lowland rainforests of Anandrivola, Madagascar. *Primate Conservation* 8: 118-120.

Richard, A.F. (1974) Patterns of mating in *Propithecus verreauxi verreauxi*. In Martin, R.D., Doyle, G.A. and Walker, A.C. (eds.) *Prosimian Biology*, pp. 49-74. Duckworth, London.

Richard, A.F. (1974) Intra-specific variation in the social organisation and ecology of *Propithecus verreauxi*. *Folia Primatologica* 22: 178-207.

Richard, A.F. (1976) Preliminary observations on the birth and development of *Propithecus verreauxi* to the age of six months. *Primates* 17: 357-366.

Richard, A.F. (1977) The feeding behaviour of *Propithecus verreauxi*. In Clutton-Brock, T. (ed.) *Primate Ecology: Studies of Feeding and Ranging Behaviour in Lemurs, Monkeys and Apes*, pp. 71-96. Academic Press, London.

Richard, A.F. (1978) *Behavioural variation: case study of a Malagasy lemur*. Bucknell University Press, Lewisburg (PA).

Richard, A.F. (1978) Variability in the feeding behaviour of a Malagasy prosimian, *Propithecus verreauxi*: Lemuriformes. In Montgomery, G.G. (ed.) *The Ecology of Arboreal Folivores*, pp. 519-533. Smithsonian

Inst. Press, Washington, D.C.

Richard, A.F. (1985) Social boundaries in a Malagasy prosimian, the sifaka (*Propithecus verreauxi*). *Int. J. Primatol.* 6: 553-568.

Richard, A.F. (1992) Aggressive competition between males, female controlled polygyny and sexual monomorphism in a Malagasy primate, *Propithecus verreauxi*. *J. Human Evol.* 22: 395-406.

Richard, A.F. (1993) Dispersal by *Propithecus verreauxi* at Beza Mahafaly, Madagascar. *Amer. J. Primatol.* 30: 1-20.

Richard, A.F. and Nicoll, M.E. (1987) Female social dominance and basal metabolism in a Malagasy primate, *Propithecus verreauxi*. *Amer. J. Primatol.* 12: 309-314.

Richard, A.F., Rakotomanga, P. and Schwartz, M. (1991) Demography of *Propithecus verreauxi* at Beza Mahafaly: sex ratio, survival and fertility, 1984-88. *Amer. J. Physical Anthropol.* 84: 307-322.

Scharfe, F. and Schlund, W. (1996) Seed removal by lemurs in a dry deciduous forest of western Madagascar. In Ganzhorn, J.U. and Sorg, J.-P. (eds.) Ecology and Economy of a Tropical Dry Forest in Madagascar, pp. 295-304. *Primate Report*, Special Issue, 46-1(June 1996).

Schmid, J. and Smolker, R. (in press) Lemurs in the Réserve Special d'Anjanaharibe-Sud. *Fieldiana Zoology*.

Simons, E.L. (1988) A new species of *Propithecus* (Primates) from north east Madagascar. *Folia Primatologica* 50: 143-151.

Sterling, E.J. and Ramaroson, M.G. (1996) Rapid assessment of the primate fauna of the eastern slopes of the Réserve Naturelle Intégrale d'Andringitra, Madagascar. *Fieldiana Zoology*, 85: 293-305.

Sussman, R.W. and Richard, A.F. (1986) Lemur conservation in Madagascar: the status of lemurs in the south. *Primate Conservation* 7: 85-92.

Thalmann, U., Geissmann, T., Simona, A. and Mutschler, T. (1993) The Indris of Anjanaharibe-Sud, north east Madagascar. *Int. J. Primatol.*, 14: 357-381.

Thalmann, U. and Rakotoarison, N. (1994) Distribution of lemurs in central western Madagascar, with a regional distribution hypothesis. *Folia Primatologica* 63: 156-161.

Warren, R.D. (1997) Habitat use and support preference of two free ranging saltatory lemurs, *Lepilemur edwardsi* and *Avahi occidentalis*. *J. Zool.* (London) 241: 325-341.

Warren, R.D. (in litt.) Comments on the behaviour and ecology of the Western Avahi (*Avahi occidentalis*) at Ampijoroa in nortth west Madagascar. University of Liverpool (Unpublished PhD research).

Warren, R.D. and Crompton, R.H. (1996) Lazy leapers: energetics, phylogenetic inertia and the locomotor differentiation of the Malagasy primates. In: Lourenco, W.R. (ed.) *Biogéographie de Madagascar*, pp. 259-266. Editions de l'ORSTOM, Paris.

Warren, R.D. and Crompton, R.H. (in press) A comparative study of the ranging behaviour, activity rhythms and sociality of *Lepilemur edwardsi* and *Avahi occidentalis*, at Ampijoroa, Madagascar. *J. Zool.* (London).

Warren, R.D. and Crompton, R.H. (in press) Lazy leapers: locomotor behaviour and ecology of *Lepilemur edwardsi* and *Avahi occidentalis*. In Crompton, R.H., Feistner, A.T.C and Harcourt, C. (eds.) Proceedings of the International Conference on the Biology and Conservation of Prosimians 1995. *Folia Primatologica*.

Warren, R.D. and Crompton, R.H. (in press) Diet, body size and the energy costs of locomotion in saltatory primates. *Amer. J. Physical Anthropol.*

Wilson, J.M. (1987) The crocodile caves of Ankarana, Madagascar. *Oryx* 21: 43-47.

Wilson, J.M., Stewart, P.D. and Fowler, S.V. (1988) Ankarana – a rediscovered nature reserve in northern Madagascar. *Oryx* 22: 163-171.

Wright, P.C. (1987) Diet and ranging patterns of *Propithecus diadema edwardsi* in Madagascar. *Amer.*

J. Physical Anthropol. 72: 218.

Wright, P.C. (1988) Social behaviour of *Propithecus diadema edwardsi* in Madagascar. *Amer. J. Physical Anthropol.* 75: 289.

Wright, P.C., Daniels, P.S., Meyers, D.M., Overdorff, D.J. and Rabesoa, J. (1987) A census and study of *Hapalemur* and *Propithecus* in south eastern Madagascar. *Primate Conservation* 8: 84- 87.

Wright, P.C. (1995) Demography and life history of free-ranging *Propithecus diadema edwardsi* in Ranomafana National Park, Madagascar. *Int. J. Primatol.* 16: 835-854.

Family Daubentoniidae

Albignac, R. (1987) Status of the aye-aye in Madagascar. *Primate Conservation* 8: 44-45.

Ancrenaz, M., Lachman-Ancrenaz, I. and Mundy, N. (1994) Field observations of aye-ayes (*Daubentonia madagascariensis*) in Madagascar. *Folia Primatologica* 62: 22-36.

Constable, I.D., Mittermeier, R.A., Pollock, J.I., Ratsirarson, J. and Simons, H. (1985) Sightings of aye-ayes and red ruffed lemurs on Nosy Mangabe and the Masoala Peninsula. *Primate Conservation* 5: 59-62.

Duckworth, J.W. (1993) Feeding damage left in bamboos, probably by Aye-ayes (*Daubentonia madagascariensis*). *Int. J. Primatol.* 14: 927-931.

Duckworth, J.W. and Rakotondraparany, F. (1990) The Mammals of Marojejy. In: Safford, R.J. and Duckworth, J.W. (eds.) A Wildlife Survey of Marojejy Nature Reserve, Madagascar. *Int. Council Bird Preserv., Study Report* No. 40, pp. 54-60.

Duckworth, J.W., Evans, M.I., Hawkins, A.F.A., Safford, R.J. and Wilkinson, R.J. (1995) The lemurs of Marojejy Strict Nature Reserve, Madagascar: a status overview with notes on ecology and threats. *Int. J. Primatol.* 16: 545-559.

Erickson, C.J. (1991) Percussive foraging in the aye-aye (*Daubentonia madagascariensis*). *Animal Behaviour* 41: 793-801.

Erickson, C.J. (1995) Perspective on percussive foraging in the aye-aye (*Daubentonia madagascariensis*). In Alterman, L. Doyle, G.A. and Izard, K. (eds.) *Creatures of the Dark: the Nocturnal Prosimians*, pp. 251-259. Plenum Press, London & N.Y.

Feistner, A.T.C. and Sterling, E.L.(eds.)(1994) The aye-aye: Madagascar's most puzzling primate. *Folia Primatologica* 62 (1-3).

Feistner, A.T.C. and Sterling, E.L. (1995) Body mass and sexual dimorphism in the aye-aye. *Dodo* 31: 73-76.

Feister, A.T.C. and Taylor, T.D. (1995) Sexual cycles and mating behaviour of captive aye-ayes, *Daubentonia madagascariensis*. Poster presentation, *International Conference on the Biology and Conservation of Prosimians*. North of England Zoological Soc., 13-16th Sept. 1995.

Fowler, S.V., Chapman, P., Checkley, D., Hurd, S., McHale, M., Ramangason, G.S., Randriamasy, J.-E., Stewart, P., Walters, R. and Wilson, J.M. (1989) Survey and management proposals for a tropical deciduous forest reserve at Ankarana in northern Madagascar. *Biological Conservation* 47: 297-313.

Ganzhorn, J.U. (1986) The aye-aye (*Daubentonia madagascariensis*) found in the eastern rainforest of Madagascar. *Folia Primatologica* 46: 125-126.

Ganzhorn, J.U. and Rabesoa, J. (1986) Sightings of aye-ayes in the eastern rainforests of Madagascar. *Primate Conservation* 7: 45.

Ganzhorn, J.U. and Kappeler, P.M. (1996) Lemurs of the Kirindy Forest. In Ganzhorn, J.U. and Sorg, J.-P. (eds.), Ecology and Economy of a Tropical Dry Forest in Madagascar, pp. 257-274. *Primate Report*, Special Issue, 46-1(June 1996).

Glander, K.E. (1994) Morphometrics and growth in captive aye-ayes (*Daubentonia madagascariensis*). *Folia Primatologica* 62: 108-114.

Goodman, S.M. and Sterling, E.J. (1996) The utilisation of *Canarium* (Burseraceae) seeds by Vertebrates in the Réserve Naturelle Intégrale d'Andringitra, Madagascar. *Fieldiana Zoology* 85: 83-89.

Hawkins, A.F.A., Chapman, P., Ganzhorn, J.U., Bloxam, Q.M.C., Barlow, S.C. and Tonge, S.J. (1990) Vertebrate conservation in Ankarana Special Reserve, northern Madagascar. *Biological Conservation* 54: 83-110.

Iwano, T. and Iwakawa, C. (1988) Feeding behaviour of the aye-aye (*Daubentonia madagascariensis*) on nuts of ramy (*Canarium madagascariensis*). *Folia Primatologica* 50: 136-142.

Petter, J.-J. (1977) The aye-aye. In Prince Rainier and Bourne, G.H. (eds.) *Primate Conservation*, pp. 37-57. Academic Press, N.Y.

Petter, J.-J. and Peyrieras, A. (1970) Nouvelle contribution a l'étude d'un lémurien malgache, le aye-aye (*Daubentonia madagascariensis* E.Geoffroy). *Mammalia* 34: 167-193.

Petter, J.-J. and Andriatsarafara, F. (1987) Conservation status and distribution of lemurs in the west and north west of Madagascar. *Primate Conservation* 7: 169-171.

Pollock, J.I., Constable, I.D., Mittermeier, R.A., Ratsirason, J. and Simons, H. (1985) A note on the diet and feeding behaviour of the aye-aye, *Daubentonia madagascariensis*. *Int. J. Primatol.* 6: 435-447.

Raxworthy, C.J. and Rakotondraparany, F. (1988) Mammals Report. In Quansah, N. (ed.) *Manongarivo Special Reserve (Madagascar), 1987/88 Expedition Report.* Madagascar Environmental Research Group, London, U.K.

Schmid, J. and Smolker, R. (in press) Lemurs in the Réserve Special d'Anjanaharibe-Sud. *Fieldiana Zoology*.

Simons, E.L. (1993) Discovery of the western aye-aye. *Lemur News* 1(1): 6.

Simons, E.L. (1994) The giant aye-aye, *Daubentonia robusta*. *Folia Primatologica* 62: 14-2.

Simons, E.L. (1995) History, anatomy, subfossil record and management of *Daubentonia madagascariensis*. In Alterman, L. Doyle, G.A. and Izard, K. (eds.) *Creatures of the Dark: the Nocturnal Prosimians*, pp.133-140. Plenum Press, London & N.Y.

Sterling, E.J. (1992) Timing of reproduction in aye-ayes (*Daubentonia madagascariensis*) in Madagascar. *Amer. J. Primatol.* 27: 59-60.

Sterling, E.J. (1993) Behavioural ecology of the aye-aye (*Daubentonia madagascariensis*) on Nosy Mangabe. Ph.D. thesis, Yale University, New Haven, Connecticut, U.S.A.

Sterling, E.J. (1993) Patterns of range use and social organisation in aye-ayes (*Daubentonia madagascariensis*) on Nosy Mangabe. In Kappeler, P.M. and Ganzhorn, J.U. (eds.) *Lemur Social Systems and their Ecological Basis*, pp. 1-10. Plenum Press, London & N.Y.

Sterling, E.J. (1994) Aye-ayes: specialists on structurally defended resources. *Folia Primatologica* 62: 142-154.

Sterling, E.J. (1994) Taxonomy and distribution of *Daubentonia*: a historical perspective. *Folia Primatologica* 62: 8-13.

Sterling, E.J., Dierenfeld, E.S., Ashbourne, C.J. and Feistner, A.T.C. (1994) Dietary intake, food consumption and nutrient intake in wild and captive populations of *Daubentonia madagascariensis*. *Folia Primatologica* 62: 115-124.

Sterling, E.J. and Richard, A.F. (1995) Social organisation in the aye-aye (*Daubentonia madagascariensis*) and the perceived distinctiveness of nocturnal primates. In Alterman, L. Doyle, G.A. and Izard, K. (eds.) *Creatures of the Dark: the Nocturnal Prosimians*, pp. 439-451. Plenum Press, London & N.Y.

Sterling, E.J. and Ramaroson, M.G. (1996) Rapid assessment of the primate fauna of the eastern slopes of the Réserve Naturelle Intégrale d'Andringitra, Madagascar. *Fieldiana Zoology* 85: 293-305.

Non-Endemic Mammals

Estes, R.D. (1991) *The Behaviour Guide to African Mammals*. Russell Friedman Books, RSA.

Ganzhorn, J.U., Sommer, S., Abraham, J.-P., Ade, M., Raharivololona, B.M., Rakotovao, E.R., Rakotondrasoa, C. and Randriamarosoa, R. (1996) Mammals of the Kirindy Forest with special emphasis on *Hypogeomys antimena* and the effects of logging on the small mammal fauna. In Ganzhorn, J.U. and Sorg, J.-P. (eds.) Ecology and Economy of a Tropical Dry Forest in Madagascar, pp. 251-255. *Primate Report*, Special Issue, 46-1(June 1996).

Goodman, S.M. (1995) *Rattus* on Madagascar and the dilemma of protecting the endemic rodent fauna. *Conservation Biology* 9(2): 450-453.

Grubb, P. (1993) Taxonomy and description of the Afrotropical suids, *Phacochoerus, Hylochoerus* and *Potamochoerus*. In Oliver, W.L.R. (ed.) *Pigs, Peccaries and Hippos: Status Survey and Conservation Action Plan*, section 4.1, pp. 66-75. IUCN/SSC Action Plan. IUCN, Cambridge, U.K. and Gland, Switzerland.

Hasler, M.J., Hasler, J.F. and Nalbandov, A.V. (1977) Comparative breeding biology of musk shrews (*Suncus murinus*) from Guam and Madagascar. *J. Mammal.* 58: 285-290.

Hutterer, R. and Tranier, M. (1990) The immigration of the Asian house shrew (*Suncus murinus*) into Africa and Madagascar. In Peters and Hutterer, R. (eds.) *Vertebrates in the Tropics*, pp. 309-320. Museum A. Koenig, Bonn.

Nowak, R.M. (1991). *Walker's Mammals of the World* (5th ed.). Johns Hopkins Uni. Press.

Paulian, R. (1984) Introduction to the mammals. In Jolly, A., Oberle, P. and Albignac, R. (eds.) *Key Environments – Madagascar*, pp. 151-154. Pergamon Press, Oxford, U.K.

Rasoloarison, R.M., Rasolonandrasana, B.P.N., Ganzhorn, J.U. and Goodman, S.M. (1995). Predation on vertebrates in the Kirindy Forest, western Madagascar. *Ecotropica* 1: 59-65.

Vercammen, P., Seydack, A.H.W. and Oliver, W.L.R. (1993) Bush pigs (*Potamochoerus porcus* and *P. larvatus*). In Oliver, W.L.R. (ed.) *Pigs, Peccaries and Hippos: Status Survey and Conservation Action Plan*, section 4.4, pp. 93-101. IUCN/SSC Action Plan. IUCN, Cambridge, U.K. and Gland, Switzerland.

Extinct Mammals

Burney, D.A. and MacPhee, R.D.E. (1988) Mysterious island: what killed Madagascar's large native animals? *Natural History* 97: 46-55.

Dewar, R.E. (1984) Recent extinctions in Madagascar: the loss of the subfossil fauna. In: Martin, P.S. and Klein, R.G. (eds.) *Quaternary extinctions: a prehistoric revolution*, pp. 574-593. Uni. Ariz. Press.

Dewar. R.E. (1997) Were people responsible for the extinction of Madagascar's subfossils, and how will we ever know? In Goodman, S.M. and Patterson, B.D. (eds.) *Natural Change and Human Impact in Madagascar*, pp. 364-377. Smithsonian Inst. Press, Washington, D.C.

Godfrey, L.R., Simons, E.L., Chatrath, P.S. and Rakotosamimanana, B. (1990) A new fossil lemur (*Babakotia*, Primates) from northern Madagascar. *Comptes Rendus de l'Académie des Science*, Paris (série 2), 310: 81-87.

Godfrey, L.R., Sutherland, M.R., Petto, A.J. and Boy, D.S. (1990) Size, space and adaptation in some subfossil lemurs from Madagascar. *Amer. J. Physical Anthropol.* 81: 45-66.

Godfrey, L.R., Wilson, J.M., Simons, E.L., Stewart, P.D. and Vuillaume-Randriamanantena, M. (1996) Ankarana: window to Madagascar's past. *Lemur News* 2:16-17.

Godfrey, L.R., Jungers, W.L., Reed, K.E., Simons, E.L. and Chatrath, P.S. (1997) Subfossil lemurs: inferences about past and present primate communities in Madagascar. In Goodman, S.M. and Patterson, B.D. (eds.) *Natural Change and Human Impact in Madagascar*, pp. 218-256. Smithsonian Inst. Press, Washington, D.C.

Godfrey, L.R., Jungers, W.L., Wright, P.C. and Jernvall, J. (in press) Dental development in giant lemurs: implications for their evolution and ecology. *Folia Primatologica*.

Godfrey, L.R., Jungers, W.L., Wunderlich, R.E. and Richmond, B.G. (in press) Reappraisal of the postcranium of *Hadropithecus* (Primates, Indroidea). *Amer. J. Physical Anthropol.*

Goodman, S.M. and Rakotondravony, D. (1996) The Holocene distribution of *Hypogeomys* (Rodentia: Muridae: Nesomyinae) on Madagascar. In Lourenco, W.R. (ed.) *Biogéographie de Madagascar*, pp. 283-293. Editions de l'ORSTOM, Paris.

Jungers, W.L., Godfrey, L.R., Simons, E.L., Chatrath, P.S. and Rakotosamimanana, B. (1991) Phylogenetic and functional affinities of *Babakotia radofilai*, a new fossil lemur from Madagascar. *Proc. Nat. Acad. Sci.*, U.S.A. 88: 9082-9086.

Jungers, W.L., Simons, E.L. and Godfrey, L.R. (1994) Phalangeal curvature and locomotor adaptations in subfossil lemurs. *Amer. J. Physical Anthropol.* Supplement 18: 117-118.

Krause, D.W. (1994) Late Cretaceous mammals. *Nature* 368: 298.

Lamberton, C. (1946) Contribution à la connaissance de la faune subfossile de Madagascar. Note XV: Le *Plesiorycteropus madagascariensis* Filhol. *Bull. Acad. Malgache* 25 (1942-43): 25-53.

MacPhee, R.D.E. (1986) Environment, extinction and Holocene vertebrate localities in southern Madagascar. *National Geographic Research* 2: 441-455.

MacPhee, R.D.E. (1994) Morphology, adaptations and relationships of *Plesiorycteropus*, and a diagnosis of a new order of eutherian mammals. *Bull. Amer. Mus. Nat. Hist.* 220.

MacPhee, R.D.E. and Raholimavo, E.M. (1988) Modified subfossil aye-aye incisors from southwestern Madagascar: species allocation and paleoecological significance. *Folia Primatologica* 51: 126-142.

MacPhee, R.D.E. and Burney, D.A. (1991) Dating of modified femora of extinct dwarf *Hippopotamus* from southern Madagascar: implications for constraining human colonisation and vertebrate extinction events. *J. Archaeological Sci.* 18: 695-706.

MacPhee, R.D.E., Burney, D.A. and Wells, N.A. (1985) Early Holocene chronology and environment of Ampasambazimba, a Malagasy subfossil lemur site. *Int. J. Primatol.* 6: 463-489.

Patterson, B. (1975) The fossil aardvarks (Mammalia: Tubulidentata). *Bull. Mus. Comp. Zool. Harv. Univ.* 147: 185-237.

Ravololonarivo, G. (1990) Contribution à l'étude de la colonne vertébrale du genre *Pachylemur* (Lamberton 1946): anatomie et analyse cladistique. Doctorat 3ème Cycle. Université d'Antananarivo, Madagascar.

Ravosa, J.M. (1992) Allometry and heterochrony in extant and extinct Malagasy primates. *J. Human Evol.* 23: 197-217.

Simons, E.L. (1994) The giant aye-aye, *Daubentonia robusta*. *Folia Primatologica* 62: 14-2.

Simons, E.L. (1997) Lemurs: old and new. In Goodman, S.M. and Patterson, B.D. (eds.) *Natural Change and Human Impact in Madagascar*, pp. 142-166. Smithsonian Inst. Press, Washington, D.C.

Simons, E.L., Godfrey, L.R., Vuillaume-Randriamanantena, M., Chatrath, P.S. and Gagnon, M. (1990) Discovery of new giant subfossil lemurs in the Ankarana Mountains of northern Madagascar. *J. Human Evol.* 19: 311-319.

Simons, E.L., Godfrey, L.R., Jungers, W.L., Chatrath, P.S. and Rakotosamimanana, B. (1992) A new giant subfossil lemur, *Babakotia*, and the evolution of the sloth lemurs. *Folia Primatologica* 58: 197-203.

Simons, E.L., Burney, D.A., Chatrath, P.S., Godfrey, L.R., Jungers, W.L. and Rakotosamimanana, B. (1995) AMS 14C dates for extinct lemurs from caves in the Ankarana Massif, northern Madagascar. *Quaternary Research*, 43: 249-254.

Simons, E.L., Godfrey, L.R., Jungers, W.L., Chatrath, P.S. and Ravaoarisoa, J. (1995) A new species of *Mesopropithecus* (Primates, Palaeopropithecidae) from northern Madagascar. *Int. J. Primatol.* 16: 653-682.

Vuillaume-Randriamanantena, M., Godfrey, L.R., Jungers, W.L. and Simons, E.L. (1992) Morphology, taxonomy and distribution of *Megaladapis* – giant subfossil lemur from Madagascar. *Compes Rendus de l'Académie des Sciences*, Paris (série 2), 315: 1835-1842.

Wunderlich, R.E., Simons, E.L. and Jungers, W.L. (1996) New pedal remains of *Megaladapis* and their functional significance. *Amer. J. Physical Anthropol.* 100: 115-139.

INDEX

Numbers in plain text refer to the first page of the relevant systematic entry. Numbers in **bold** type refer to pages with photographs or illustrations of the species concerned.